ALSO AVAILABLE

The West Point History of the Civil War

THE
WEST POINT
HISTORY
OF
WORLD WAR II

VOLUME 1

THE UNITED STATES MILITARY ACADEMY

EDITORS: CLIFFORD J. ROGERS, TY SEIDULE, AND STEVE R. WADDELL

SIMON & SCHUSTER

NEW YORK   LONDON   TORONTO   SYDNEY   NEW DELHI

Simon & Schuster
1230 Avenue of the Americas
New York, NY 10020

First Simon & Schuster hardcover edition November 2015

SIMON & SCHUSTER and colophon are registered trademarks of Simon & Schuster, Inc.

For information about special discounts for bulk purchases, please contact Simon & Schuster Special Sales
at 1-866-506-1949 or business@simonandschuster.com.

The Simon & Schuster Speakers Bureau can bring authors to your live event. For more information or to book an event,
contact the Simon & Schuster Speakers Bureau at 1-866-248-3049 or visit our website at www.simonspeakers.com.

Manufactured in the United States of America

10   9   8   7   6   5   4   3   2   1

Library of Congress Cataloging-in-Publication Data is available.

ISBN 978-1-4767-8273-7
ISBN 978-1-4767-8274-4 (ebook)

Acknowledgments   VII

1 THE ROAD TO WAR
   BY STEVE R. WADDELL   1

2 GERMAN YEARS OF VICTORY
   BY ROBERT M. CITINO   47

3 BRITAIN STANDS ALONE
   BY RICHARD J. OVERY   95

4 THE GERMANS TURN EAST:
   OPERATION BARBAROSSA AND THE BEGINNINGS
   OF THE FINAL SOLUTION
   BY GEOFFREY P. MEGARGEE   137

5 JAPAN STRIKES:
   FROM PEARL HARBOR TO MIDWAY
   BY EDWARD J. DREA   179

6 PEOPLE AND ECONOMIES AT WAR
   BY RICHARD J. OVERY   233

   CONCLUSION:
   THE WAR AT MIDPOINT
   BY CLIFFORD J. ROGERS   281

   Notes   291
   Image Credits   317
   Index   327

To the West Point graduates who led American soldiers and airmen to victory in World War II

T he *West Point History of World War II, Volume 1* comprises five chapters of *The West Point History of Warfare* and adds a new introductory chapter and conclusion to make the volume self-standing. *The West Point History of Warfare* is a seventy-chapter enhanced e-book survey of military history from ancient times through the present day, originally designed to be used by cadets in the core History of the Military Art course at West Point. George S. Patton Jr. and Dwight Eisenhower took "MilArt," as it is called, but they could never have imagined such a book or its animated maps and interactive widgets. Because we created the two projects simultaneously, we owe a debt of gratitude to all of those who have contributed to making *The West Point History of Warfare* truly groundbreaking at West Point and beyond. In particular, we want to highlight those who have helped make *The West Point History of World War II, Volume 1* the exceptional book it is.

The West Point History of World War II, Volume 1 is a product of an extraordinary public-private partnership between the Department of History at West Point and Rowan Technology Solutions. We took the best aspects of government service and paired them with the best aspects of an agile education technology start-up. The result is the book you see before you.

This project required a visionary who believed that cadets at West Point deserved the best education possible and that providing the best education required employing the latest technology. Mr. Vincent Viola not only provided the money to put together this formidable project but also realized that a bunch of historians—both in uniform and out—had no business managing a massive, high-technology endeavor. He started a company called Rowan Technology Solutions to create this book. Vinnie named the company for the famed Lieutenant Rowan from the Elbert Hubbard pamphlet *A Message to Garcia*. In 1898 President William McKinley gave Andrew Rowan, an 1881 West Point graduate, a message to deliver to the Cuban leader Calixto García. With no idea of García's exact location and no explicit instructions on how to accomplish his mission, Rowan left Washington. After a short stop in Jamaica, Rowan met García in the Oriente Mountains and delivered McKinley's message. Since then, army officers have known that "taking a message to García" is shorthand for taking initiative.

The team at Rowan lives up to his redoubtable legacy of initiative. Vinnie gave the project to his West Point classmate Anthony Manganiello to execute. Tony, as the Rowan Chief Executive Officer, gave the team focus: create the best possible product for cadets and make sure, above all, that it improves cadets' understanding of military history. Tony needed someone who could help him execute a project of immense complexity that had to straddle the divide between the army and business. We are so lucky that Tim Strabbing, Rowan President, has led this project from the beginning. Tim was the driving force in making sure the book was ready, on schedule, to teach cadets. His leadership, intellect, and energy infuse every aspect of this project. Ryan Sparks, the Chief Operating Officer, gave the team a creative vision to grow a "project" into a business. Rucker Culpepper, Rowan's Chief Revenue Officer, has worked indefatigably to make sure the world knows about our *West Point History of Warfare*. Two interns ably assisted him: Alex Kuvshinoff, who created a marketing strategy, and Connor Cuccinelli, who handled sales.

Managing a project that requires the integration of business, the army, philanthropy, and academe is a difficult task. Finishing that project on time without compromising standards is extraordinary. Colleen McCanna managed to do both while also providing a much-needed boost to the production team. Our dedicated team of designers and cartographers routinely worked long hours, evenings, and weekends to complete this project. They brought an impressive array of dedication and talent to their work. This book is beautiful, informative, and innovative because of the extraordinary work of our cartographers—Jeremy Goldsmith, Michael Bricknell, and Morgan Jarocki—and our graphic designers Axelle Zemouli, Terry O'Toole, Nicholas Lituczy, Lulu Zhang, Michael Milazzo, and Dan Vassalo. Chase Stone drew the soldiers that help bring the book to life.

The words needed as much care as the maps and graphics, and required editors and copy editors who had the same sense of mission and dedication. We have the best. Grace Rebesco led with style the editing team that polished the text in the main body, captions, footnotes, maps, and interactives. She had a superb and tireless team: assistant editor Jackie Parziale and copy editors Matthew Manganiello and Christy Cefalu. Danielle Viola contributed above and beyond her role as general counsel, helping to secure rights and permissions as well as skillfully helping the team navigate a myriad of challenges along the way.

Adding interactive content for the enhanced e-book version posed its own set of challenges and required world-class technologists in support. Rowan's lead technologist, Ross Harrison, created and maintains the superb digital tools that make *The West Point History of Warfare* unlike any other book ever made. Ross is the proud son of a distinguished West Point graduate—his father was a colonel who served in Afghanistan. Back-end developer Mathieu Lue worked diligently with Ross to perfect these tools.

Our senior adviser, General (Ret.) John Abizaid provided us with sage counsel at the most crucial moments and fixed problems we knew about and headed off other issues before we even knew there was a problem. Brigadier General (Ret.) Lance Betros and Colonel (Ret.) Mat Moten led the Department of History as the project was conceived and launched, and gave it their wholehearted support. Second World War historian Colonel (Ret.) Kevin Farrell, then chief of the Military History Division, also served as one of the project's volume editors (including for the WWII chapters) until his retirement. John W. Hall, the Ambrose-Hesseltine chair in military history at the University of Wisconsin, a consulting editor for the whole *West Point History of Warfare* project, read and provided valuable feedback on all the chapters.

The West Point History of World War II, Volume 1 is, of course, a history book, and we had the finest historians working on it. For each chapter we picked the best possible historian: someone who combined excellent writing ability with deep expertise about the chapter's particular topic. Thankfully, each agreed to write for us. Drs. Robert Citino, Richard Overy, Geoffrey Megargee, and Edward Drea provided us with invigorating text reflecting the very latest scholarship. We also needed crack historians to help us design the maps, select the images, and provide guidance for cartographers and designers. Rowan's associate editors, Keith Altavilla, Colin Colbourn, and

Matthew Muehlbauer, delivered time and again. They are now experts in digital humanities. Drs. John Stapleton and Samuel Watson and Colonel Gail Yoshitani, volume editors for other sections of *The West Point History of Warfare*, made crucial contributions to the overall design, structure, and pedagogical underpinnings of the work.

Unlike most authors and publishers, we had access to the incredible collections in the West Point Museum. Thanks to Director David Reel, Mike McAfee, Les Jensen, Marlana Cook, and Paul Ackermann. Likewise the West Point Library's Special Collections and Archives has provided us with invaluable assistance. Thanks to Director Suzanne Christoff, Casey Madrick, Susan Lintelmann, Elaine McConnell, and Alicia Mauldin-Ware.

We tested *The West Point History of Warfare* with 2,400 cadets and 45 instructors over the course of two years. With feedback from cadets and instructors, we found what worked and what did not. Lieutenant Colonel Jason Musteen, chief of the Military History Division at West Point, ably led the faculty who taught the course over the last two years. Majors Rick Anderson and Chuck Bies served as the course directors for the History of the Military Art, leading a group of disparate historians to embrace a new text on the new medium of a tablet. Major Greg Jenemann oversaw our vigorous assessment process to make sure we benefited from the input of faculty members who were teaching from the textbook. For the WWII chapters, the assessment team was led by Prof. John Stapleton and included Majors Chuck Bies, Nate Jennings, Dave Musick, Stu Peebles, Rocky Rhodes, and John Zdeb. Major Dave Musick took point on a variety of technology-related issues. These "iron majors" proved their mettle on this project. Every Department of History faculty member who taught using the text assisted in making the course a success. Professor Sam Watson deserves special mention for his extensive comments on the draft versions. In the Department of History, we had an impressive support team for the entire project. Ms. Deb Monks, Lieutenant Colonel Ray Hrinko, Mr. Rich Stephenson, Ms. Melissa Mills, Ms. Yvette O'Neal, and Ms. Loretta Woody helped make this project go smoothly. We also want to thank the 2,400 cadets who used the text and helped us improve it. They had no choice—the army is an obedience-based organization, after all—but they really did give us great feedback.

We were able to execute this mammoth million-word, thousand-map project only because of the support of several members of USMA's senior staff. We were lucky to work with dedicated and competent administrators who were also innovative. West Point's chief information officer, Colonel Ron Dodge, completely changed the IT landscape at West Point to ensure we could teach the text on tablets in classrooms, connected to a network. This feat took time as well as determination; the course would not have taken the shape it has without Colonel Dodge. While the technological challenges were tough, the legal challenges also proved daunting. We could not have completed this project without Lori Doughty in the Staff Judge Advocate's office. She is a superb, innovative, and creative lawyer. Thanks also to Laura Heller for her fine work.

Our friends at Apple have supported us from the beginning of this project. Apple exec Adrian Perica (USMA, 1994) gave us early support and continues to help us. Kelly Gillis provided crucial help in deploying iTunes U internally at West Point and externally through our open digital courses. Our liaison at Apple, Deirdre Espinoza, helped us negotiate that huge company.

We are grateful to have had such an excellent team at Simon & Schuster, and give special thanks to Bob Bender, our editor. Coalescing so much content into a beautiful and cohesive print product was no small task. Associate editor Johanna Li's adept guidance was invaluable at every stage. Ruth Lee-Mui, the book's designer, worked closely with the Rowan team to ensure striking visual impact. Jonathan Cox provided valuable feedback on the manuscript, and Jonathan Evans led the copyediting effort. Hilda Koparanian skillfully supervised production.

Our agent at the William Morris Endeavor agency, Eric Lupfer, was, literally, born for this job. He made his earthly debut in Keller Army Community Hospital at West Point when his father, Tim, was teaching history at West Point. He has ably led us through the publishing industry.

Finally, Cliff, Ty, and Steve would like to thank the *West Point History of Warfare* widows: our wives, Shelley Reid, Shari Seidule, and Sharon Waddell. We spent nearly every evening and nearly every weekend for the past three years on this project and we have many more months to go. Their love and patience made this book possible.

The West Point History
of
World War II

VOLUME 1

MASTER LEGEND

⊙ Capital City

● Major City

● Minor City

• Town or Village

◈ Major Concentration Camp

• Sub-Camp

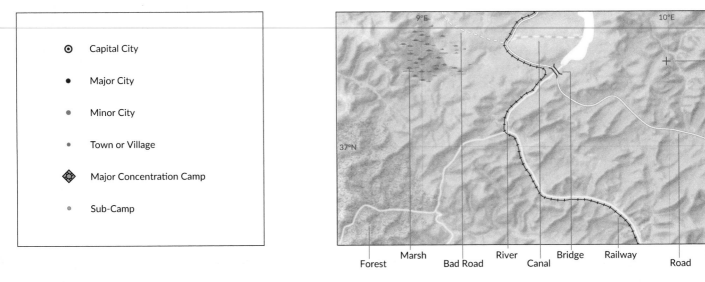

Forest Marsh Bad Road River Canal Bridge Railway Road Peak

BASE MAP

MILITARY FEATURES

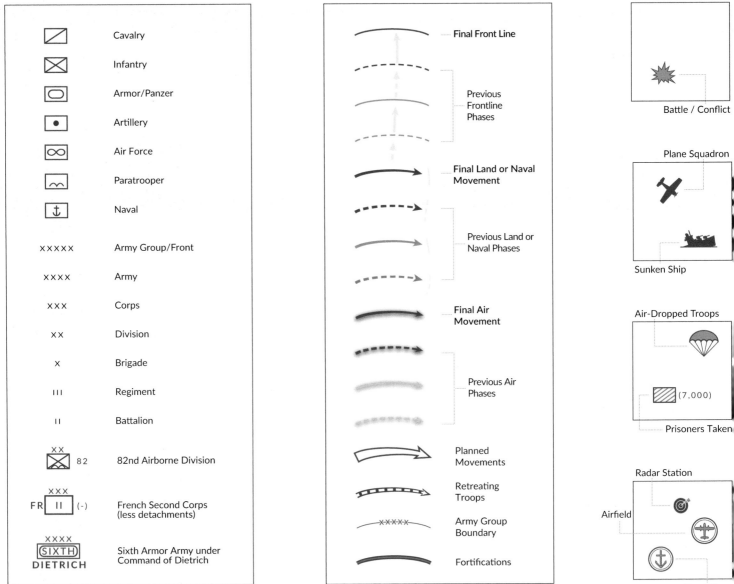

▱ Cavalry

⊠ Infantry

▭ Armor/Panzer

⊡ Artillery

∞ Air Force

⌢ Paratrooper

⚓ Naval

XXXXX Army Group/Front

XXXX Army

XXX Corps

XX Division

X Brigade

III Regiment

II Battalion

⊠ 82 82nd Airborne Division

FR II (-) French Second Corps (less detachments)

SIXTH DIETRICH Sixth Armor Army under Command of Dietrich

Final Front Line

Previous Frontline Phases

Final Land or Naval Movement

Previous Land or Naval Phases

Final Air Movement

Previous Air Phases

Planned Movements

Retreating Troops

Army Group Boundary

Fortifications

Battle / Conflict

Plane Squadron

Sunken Ship

Air-Dropped Troops

(7,000) Prisoners Taken

Radar Station

Airfield

Naval Base

The Toll of World War I

When the guns fell silent on the Western Front on November 11, 1918, the participants hoped that the end of the war would mark the beginning of a long period of peace. Victor and vanquished alike looked to mourn their dead, clear their rubble and rebuild from the destruction, and find meaning in all that had occurred. Approximately thirteen million people had been killed and over eighteen million wounded.[1] Over the course of the war, military dead averaged 6,000 per day. The financial toll totaled over $330 billion in direct and indirect costs—the equivalent of over $5 trillion today.[2]

Soldiers and civilians alike knew they had experienced something horrific, and they sought to make their sacrifices meaningful. Some sought to punish the defeated with harsh terms; others sought to prevent future war by disarming the vanquished and pushing for disarmament of the victors; others sought peace through cooperation and negotiations; while others sought to retreat into isolation. Yet hope that the terms of the Treaty of Versailles and subsequent disarmament efforts would lead to lasting peace gradually gave way to fear in the 1920s and 1930s as the Bolsheviks prevailed in Russia, raising the specter of the spread of Communist revolution, and a growing global economic crisis created vast numbers of unemployed, hungry, and fearful people. Totalitarian leaders emerged throughout Europe, determined to reverse the unsatisfactory terms of the Versailles settlement, to extend their countries' territories, and to enhance their own international prestige. Just twenty years after the Treaty of Versailles officially ended the Great War—"the war to end all wars"—the world would find itself marching into battle once again, now for a Second World War.

Peace Imagined: The Treaty of Versailles

Not long after the armistice of November 11, 1918, the representatives of the victorious Allies, led by France, Great Britain, Italy, and the United States, met in Paris to determine the peace terms. Russia, which had agreed to a separate peace with Germany in March 1918 and was in the midst of a civil war, was not invited. The victors saw themselves as committed to peace, but many were worried that Germany would try again. So the treaty was designed to punish the Germans enough to teach them a lesson, while simultaneously weakening them enough that if the lesson didn't take, they would not be able to instigate another global catastrophe.

The European allies also wanted reparations to help them recover from the devastating economic losses of the war. They decided that imposing heavy war indemnities on Germany would not only be just but also expedient, contributing to all three of the strategic components of the Versailles treaty: starving the German government of funds that might otherwise be spent on rearmament, transferring money to the European allies to allow them to rebuild, and setting the precedent

1
_____

THE ROAD TO WAR

STEVE R. WADDELL

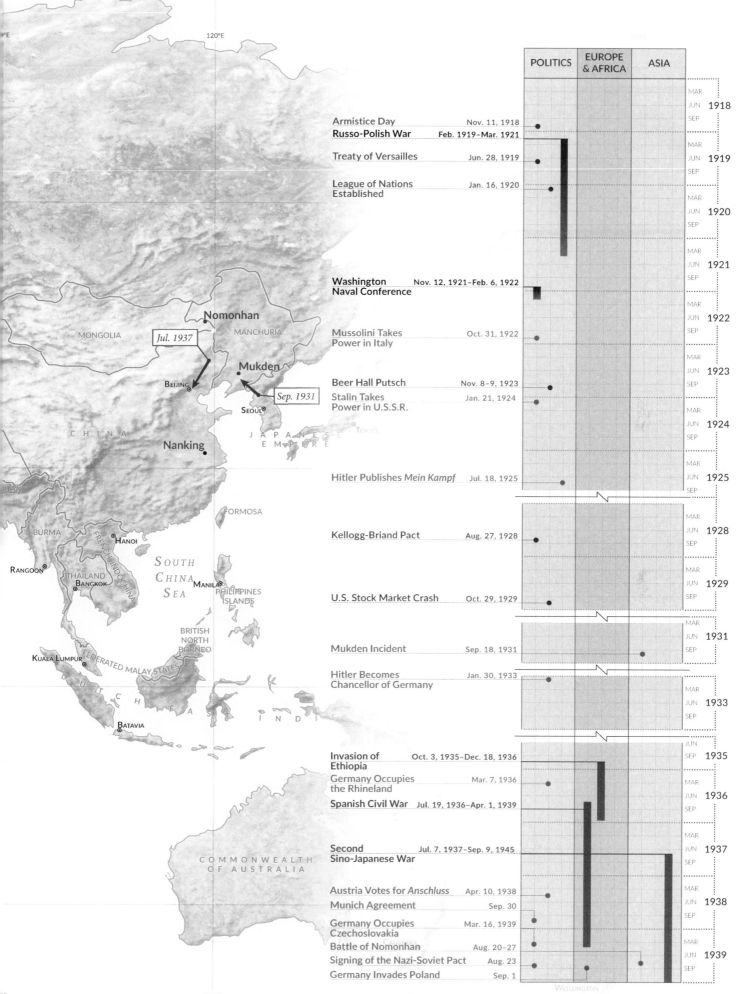

	POLITICS	EUROPE & AFRICA	ASIA	
				1918

Armistice Day — Nov. 11, 1918
Russo-Polish War — Feb. 1919–Mar. 1921

Treaty of Versailles — Jun. 28, 1919

League of Nations Established — Jan. 16, 1920

Washington Naval Conference — Nov. 12, 1921–Feb. 6, 1922

Mussolini Takes Power in Italy — Oct. 31, 1922

Beer Hall Putsch — Nov. 8–9, 1923
Stalin Takes Power in U.S.S.R. — Jan. 21, 1924

Hitler Publishes *Mein Kampf* — Jul. 18, 1925

Kellogg-Briand Pact — Aug. 27, 1928

U.S. Stock Market Crash — Oct. 29, 1929

Mukden Incident — Sep. 18, 1931

Hitler Becomes Chancellor of Germany — Jan. 30, 1933

Invasion of Ethiopia — Oct. 3, 1935–Dec. 18, 1936
Germany Occupies the Rhineland — Mar. 7, 1936
Spanish Civil War — Jul. 19, 1936–Apr. 1, 1939

Second Sino-Japanese War — Jul. 7, 1937–Sep. 9, 1945

Austria Votes for *Anschluss* — Apr. 10, 1938
Munich Agreement — Sep. 30
Germany Occupies Czechoslovakia — Mar. 16, 1939
Battle of Nomonhan — Aug. 20–27
Signing of the Nazi-Soviet Pact — Aug. 23
Germany Invades Poland — Sep. 1

Map labels: 120°E, MONGOLIA, MANCHURIA, Nomonhan, *Jul. 1937*, Mukden, *Sep. 1931*, Beijing, Seoul, Tokyo, JAPANESE EMPIRE, CHINA, Nanking, FORMOSA, BURMA, Hanoi, Rangoon, THAILAND, Bangkok, FRENCH INDOCHINA, SOUTH CHINA SEA, Manila, PHILIPPINES ISLANDS, BRITISH NORTH BORNEO, Kuala Lumpur, FEDERATED MALAY STATES, DUTCH EAST INDIES, Batavia, COMMONWEALTH OF AUSTRALIA, Wellington

30°W   15°W   0°   15°E   30°E   45°E

REYKJAVÍK
ICELAND

60°N

FINLAND

HELSINKI

NORWAY
OSLO
ESTONIA
U.S.S.R.
STOCKHOLM
SWEDEN
BALTIC SEA
MOSCOW
LATVIA

ATLANTIC
OCEAN

LITHUANIA
Memel *Nemunas*
WHITE
RUSSIA

NORTH SEA
COPENHAGEN
DENMARK
EAST PRUSSIA
Danzig

IRELAND
Elbe
BERLIN
WARSAW

UNITED
KINGDOM
AMSTERDAM
NETHER-
LANDS
GERMANY
POLAND
UKRA
LONDON
BELGIUM
BRUSSELS
Oder
Vistula
Rhine
SAAR
PRAGUE
LUX.
CZECHOSLOVAKIA

PARIS
Seine
VIENNA
BUDAPEST
Tisza
ROMANIA

Loire
45°N
FRANCE
BERNE
SWITZERLAND
AUSTRIA
HUNGARY
BUCHAREST

Rhône
Po
Savva
Danube
B

BAY OF BISCAY
BELGRADE
YUGOSLAVIA
BULGARIA
SOFIA

Douro
SPAIN
ITALY
TIRANA
PORTUGAL
Ebro
ROME
ALBANIA
TUR
LISBON
MADRID
Tagus
Guadiana
GREECE
Guadalquivir
ATHENS

M E D I T E R R A N E A N   S E A

30°N

<u>LEGEND</u>
Territory Ceded By Germany
Territory Formerly Part of
the Austro-Hungarian Empire
Territory Ceded By the
Soviet Union
Territory Ceded By Bulgaria

*Europe in 1933 and Territorial Changes
Resulting from World War I and the
Treaty of Versailles*

0   125   250 Miles

15°E

0°

that aggressors would be punished enough to make them regret their aggressions. The return of the provinces of Alsace and Lorraine to France, a principal war aim of the Allies from the start, also helped accomplish the same ends, as did Germany's surrender of substantial lands in the east to the new independent states of Poland and Czechoslovakia.

The dismantling of the multiethnic empires of the Central Powers (including parts of the now-defunct Russian Empire, which had collapsed under the pressure of the war and been succeeded by the troublesomely revolutionary Union of Soviet Socialist Republics) served the same geostrategic logic of both weakening and punishing. But this decision also addressed a separate theme of the overall plan to ensure that the Great War would indeed serve as a "war to end all wars." The diplomats recognized that a major reason for the outbreak of the war had been the tension between the Austro-Hungarian monarchy's desire to sustain the empire and the forces of ethnic nationalism, as individual regions tried to break free. Giving Hungarians, Czechs and Slovaks, Poles, Latvians, Lithuanians, Estonians, and southern Slavs each their own state would reduce the tinder that had helped ignite the great conflagration in 1914.

The idea of national self-determination had been one of President Woodrow Wilson's Fourteen Points, an idealistic statement of American war aims announced in January 1918. Two others that were particularly significant for shaping the postwar world were the pursuit of international disarmament and the creation of a League of Nations. Nearly everyone believed that arms merchants and arms races (particularly the Anglo-German naval competition) had contributed to the start of the World War, and that the Old World traditions of secret and mainly bilateral diplomacy had exacerbated the problem. The British political scientist and philosopher Goldsworthy Lowes Dickinson, the first prominent advocate for the creation of the League of Nations, argued that the probability of another Great War would decrease "in proportion as the issues of foreign policy should be known to and controlled by public opinion."[3] In the new international order envisioned by the postwar statesmen, each nation would have to operate more openly and cooperatively. Each would be strong enough to defend itself and to contribute to collective resistance to aggressors, but no single nation would be strong enough to try to impose its will on other nations by violence. The League would help sustain that situation, creating a forum in which the global community could resolve disputes before they got out of hand and prevent the sort of misunderstandings and false expectations that, for example, had led the Germans to think they could invade Belgium and attack France without drawing Great Britain into the war.

◀ EUROPE AFTER THE TREATY OF VERSAILLES, 1919–29

The collapse of the multinational Austro-Hungarian and Russian Empires at the end of World War I led to the formation of more ethnically unified countries in Eastern Europe as part of the Versailles settlement. But the principle of national self-determination was applied somewhat inconsistently, and this was a root of future trouble.

INHERENT FLAWS IN THE SYSTEM

Most survivors of the Great War held out hope that the provisions of the Treaty of Versailles would lead to lasting peace. But confidence in the peace began to erode almost immediately, as the second- and third-order effects of the treaty's provisions became apparent. The "war guilt" clause, which required Germany to assume responsibility for the war and resulting damages, and the indemnities, seemed unjust to most Germans, leaving them angered over the terms of peace rather than regretful for provoking war.

In redrawing the map of Eastern Europe, the victors allowed geostrategic considerations to trump their own rhetoric of national self-determination. In particular, they separated substantial areas with majority German populations (by language and ethnicity) from Germany itself, and instead, integrated them into Czechoslovakia, Lithuania, and Poland. The newly created state of Czechoslovakia included the Sudetenland, a large area occupied by German-speaking people. The "Polish Corridor" that gave the new state of Poland access to the sea had more Polish than German inhabitants, but that was not true of the key port of Danzig, which nonetheless was separated from Germany to become a "Free City." Austria, which had been part of the "Germany" region for centuries before the creation of the German Empire in 1871, was now made into its own independent state rather than being joined (or allowed to join) with Germany.

The victors hoped that the new states in Eastern Europe, Poland in particular,

would replace Russia as a British and French ally in the East. But the newly independent nations were relatively small and were poised to squabble over disputed borders. They could not replace Russia as an ally and deterrent to German expansionism.

The League of Nations established itself in Geneva, Switzerland, in 1920 and went to work advocating for disarmament, collective security, and the peaceful settlement of disputes between nations. Unfortunately, the Assembly required unanimous agreement, and even when agreement was reached, the League lacked any means of enforcing its decisions. As violations of the League charter occurred, the body could do little more than issue condemnations. And eventually the worst offenders, Japan (in 1933), Germany (1933), Italy (1937), and the Soviet Union (1939), either formally left or were expelled from the League of Nations to pursue their national objectives without concern for what the League's members might think.

The vote of the U.S. Senate to block America's accession to the League in 1919 both reflected and worsened the weaknesses of the new structure. The Great War had awakened the world to the immense latent strength of the United States. It had a larger population than France and Britain combined, and possessed a larger industrial manufacturing sector than all the other six Great Powers (Germany, the United Kingdom, France, the Soviet Union, Italy, and Japan) put together.[4] The League's charter committed its members to assist one another in resisting aggression. If the United States had joined them, the major nations most committed to sustaining the Versailles structure and keeping the peace, France and Britain, would have been

▲ BRITAIN'S LOST GENERATION
The First World War had cost the British Empire about 1 million dead and 2 million wounded soldiers. The leaders of the United Kingdom were naturally reluctant to even contemplate the possibility of another Continental war.

overwhelmingly stronger than those countries that were most unhappy with the Versailles treaty and most inclined to militarism: Germany, the Soviet Union, Italy, and Japan. But without the United States, the nations committed to defending the status quo lacked the imposing superiority of resources that would have increased the likelihood of deterring the aggressive actions that culminated in the outbreak of World War II.

The Treaty of Versailles might have ended the Great War, but it fell far short of bringing peace and prosperity, law and order, and happiness and contentment to all. Most Germans felt they were being blamed unjustly for the Great War. The Italian people were resentful of the British and French for not granting Italy its "fair share" of rewards for the more than a million military and civilian lives it lost fighting for Allied victory. Japan, which had made a small but not entirely trivial contribution as an ally of Britain, was granted the German colonies in the Far East north of the equator and the German concession in Shandong, China. But its leaders felt slighted by the delegates' refusal to accept the principle of racial equality, and Japan began to shift toward more nationalistic policies, determined to expand and gain recognition as a major power. Many Americans were disillusioned by the peace terms. They had fought in the cause of a war to end all wars and a "war to make the world safe for democracy," but the seeming triumph at Versailles of the victors' national interests over idealistic principles and generosity to the defeated increasingly made those ideas seem like mere propaganda. Americans grew more and more determined to avoid future overseas entanglements.

Despite the flaws in the treaty, Britain and France—ravaged by the war though they were—were much stronger in 1920 than the even more devastated Germany. Even without the backing of the United States, the Western democracies still had their colonies: France had gained Alsace-Lorraine, with its valuable resources, population, and industry; and it was not constrained by the treaty terms, whereas the Germans were limited to a very small military. If Britain and France had possessed the political will to do so, they could have enforced the treaty and kept Germany militarily weak. But they did not. Too many people questioned whether the immense cost of the war had been worth the sacrifice. Had the cause been just? Was the decimation of an entire generation, the "Lost Generation," worth the price? Were pacifism and isolationism the answer? The system created at the end of the Great War to preserve the peace faced many challenges, and only time would tell if it would succeed.

GERMANY OPPRESSED BY THE TREATY OF VERSAILLES ▶

The Treaty of Versailles following World War I was immensely unpopular in Germany. Here we see the hand of a finely dressed man representing England and France—and by extension, capitalism—holding down the poor farmers of Germany. Depictions such as this helped fuel the success of the National Socialist Party headed by Adolf Hitler.

The ambitious American naval buildup undertaken by President Wilson during the Great War endangered Britain's status as the premier naval power and threatened to trigger a very costly naval race. The American determination to maintain a large "two-ocean navy" and the British tradition of maintaining the world's largest fleet—as large as the combined strength of the second- and third-ranked navies in the world—were in conflict. Ships were increasingly expensive, and the major naval powers found themselves hard pressed to justify spending more money on their navies. With the end of the war, the citizens of the United States and Britain were eager to see government expenditures and national debt reduced. It made sense to limit naval construction, especially since the world's naval powers had all been allies during the war.

President Warren G. Harding took the first step toward arms control by calling the Washington Naval Conference in November 1921. The resulting Washington Naval Treaties—the Four-, Five-, and Nine-Power Treaties—dealt with security issues. With the Four-Power Treaty, the United States, Great Britain, Japan, and France agreed to maintain the status quo in the Pacific.[5] The Nine-Power Treaty, signed by the same four and the Republic of China, Portugal, Belgium, Italy, and the Netherlands, affirmed the sovereignty of China and the open-door policy. The open-door policy advocated by the United States was intended to ensure that all the major powers had access to Chinese trade, not just those that had gotten there first. The Five-Power Treaty, signed by the United States, Great Britain, Japan, France, and Italy, limited naval tonnage for ten years and ended the naval building race. The treaty established a ratio of 5:5:3:1.75:1.75, with the British and United States limited to 525,000 tons of capital ships (battleships, battle cruisers, and aircraft carriers) each, Japan to 315,000 tons, and France and Italy to 175,000 tons each. In addition to total tonnage, the treaty limited the tonnage and maximum gun size of individual ship types. The treaty also prohibited the fortification of bases in the Pacific. The Washington Naval Treaty led to the scrapping of seventy existing or planned capital ships: thirty U.S., twenty-three British, and seventeen Japanese. Further limits were discussed at the Geneva Naval Conference of 1927, and agreed to at the London Naval Conferences of 1930 and 1935, which succeeded in placing limits on cruisers, destroyers, and submarines.[6] The agreements represented a major arms control success and limited global naval forces until Japan withdrew from the agreement in 1936, and the major powers again began major naval construction programs.

THE WASHINGTON DISARMAMENT CONFERENCE ▶

The 1921 Washington Conference represented a major success for the global disarmament movement. In a postwar world of tighter finances and strong antiwar feeling, the world's navies agreed on a variety of building restrictions.

BENITO MUSSOLINI
July 29, 1883–April 28, 1945
Prime Minister of Italy

Mussolini was a leading Socialist journalist until 1914. During World War I, he abandoned pacifism, anti-imperialism, and the class struggle, and embraced Italian nationalism and expansionism. Mussolini was wounded in the trenches, and after the war led other disgruntled veterans in founding a new "fascist" movement. Combining electoral success with street violence, Mussolini became prime minister in 1922. He exploited his personal popularity to eviscerate democratic institutions and centralize military, economic, judicial, and education functions into a police state. Mussolini embraced war as a means of building a warrior race, restoring the lost glories of the Roman empire and sidelining domestic opposition to his dictatorship. Thus, in addition to supporting General Francisco Franco in the Spanish Civil War of 1936 to 1939, he invaded Ethiopia in 1935 and Albania four years later. Mussolini disdained Hitler and objected to a premature European war, but their superficially common interests led to an ostensibly defensive "Pact of Steel" between Italy and Germany in May 1939. Hitler's aggressive example goaded Mussolini to further—and less successful—military operations in British East Africa, Egypt, Greece, and France in 1940. Defeat in North Africa undermined Fascist Party support for "the Leader" (*Il Duce*), who was dismissed from his offices and arrested by King Victor Emmanuel III on July 25, 1943. After he was rescued from detention by German commandos, Mussolini established a puppet government in northern Italy. When he attempted to flee at the war's end, he was captured and shot by Italian partisans. Although his party was outlawed in Italy after the war, Mussolini's political legacy lives on in some elements of modern Italian nationalism.

Efforts to control defense spending and limit the possibility of another war extended beyond navies and Pacific concerns. In 1928 the General Treaty for Renunciation of War as an Instrument of National Policy, also known as the Kellogg-Briand Pact, was signed in Paris. Led by U.S. Secretary of State Frank B. Kellogg and French Foreign Minister Aristide Briand, sixty-two nations eventually agreed to the pact. The treaty called for nations to agree that war would no longer be used to settle "disputes or conflicts of whatever nature or of whatever origin they may be, which may arise among them."[7] The agreement, however, proved to be unenforceable, and signatories began violating it by launching military operations without declaring war. (The treaty nonetheless remains legally in effect today.) Peace efforts continued in 1932, when over sixty nations met in Geneva to discuss further arms reductions.

The creation of the League of Nations, agreements such as the Kellogg-Briand Pact, and gatherings of nations to discuss arms control such as the Washington and Geneva Conferences gave people some peace of mind that war was, if not a thing of the past, at least not going to happen anytime soon. In 1919 the British government, confident that war was a distant threat, established the "Ten-Year Rule," which stated that defense estimates would be based on the assumption that there would be no war in the next ten years. The rule remained in effect until 1932. That peace of mind, however, waned as a global economic crisis and the rise of totalitarian states with leaders determined to achieve their objectives by any means necessary made war much more likely.

Fascist ideology called for action: for Italy to achieve Great Power status through an aggressive nationalist foreign policy. Despite Mussolini's major rearmament program for the Italian military, his dreams of an empire far exceeded the capabilities of the Italian economy. The modern aircraft, ships, and vehicles produced in the late 1920s and early 1930s were soon obsolete, as Italy could not afford to keep up with advances in military technology. They did, however, suffice to add Abyssinia (Ethiopia) and Albania to Italy's colonial empire in the 1930s.

Italy did lead the world in the creation of an independent air force in 1923. Giulio Douhet, an internationally recognized airpower theorist, promoted the concept of "strategic bombing" as the solution to the stalemate of the First World War. Douhet argued that civilian populations faced with the death and destruction of bombardment from the air (using incendiaries and poison gas) would demand peace. Mussolini found enough resources to build up his air force to an imposing strength of over 1,700 aircraft. Italian planes played a major role in the conquest of Abyssinia and performed fairly creditably in the Spanish Civil War. But the Fascists, who emphasized the prestige that Italy gained by deploying a large air force, shortchanged its logistical infrastructure and spent substantial resources keeping obsolete planes in the air. Only about half the Italian aircraft were considered "modern" even by the Italians, and fewer than two hundred really were. As the Second World War later showed, it would take very large fleets of bombers far more powerful than Italy's planes to truly devastate enemy cities. The 1936 Fiat BR.20 Cicogna ("Stork") bomber, for example, had only a quarter the bomb load and less than one-tenth the production run of the 1942 British Avro Lancaster. Moreover, civilian populations proved far more resilient under air attack than Douhet expected. During the interwar years, however, the concept of strategic bombing did gain traction in Great Britain and the United States among air force officers and airpower enthusiasts.

The focus of the Regia Aeronautica (the Italian air force) on independent strategic bombing capabilities meant that the potential of airplanes to support land and naval operations was relatively neglected. By 1938 to 1940, more money was going to the air force than to the navy. This, and the costs of operations in Africa, Spain, and Albania, left the army short of funds for modernization and training. The navy fared better in that respect. With 6 battleships, 19 cruisers, 59 destroyers, 67 torpedo boats, and 116 submarines, the Regia Marina constituted a formidable force in the Mediterranean. But it too was hindered by the air force officers' focus on strategic bombing, which led them to oppose—and effectively block—the navy's desire to build aircraft carriers and a strong force of torpedo bombers.

By the time Italy entered the Second World War on June 10, 1940, Mussolini's Fascist regime had built up the armed forces to a level that on paper qualified the nation for the Great Power status Il Duce craved, though only barely. But experience would soon demonstrate that neither the Italian military nor the economy supporting it was really ready for the demands of modern war.

PEACE THREATENED: THE GLOBAL ECONOMY, THE RISE OF FASCISM, JAPANESE MILITARISM, AND THE SOVIET UNION

The system for preventing major wars appeared to be working in the 1920s, but there were growing threats to the peace. The Weimar Republic, which was named after the city where its new assembly met and had replaced the imperial government in 1919, was printing money to make reparations payments. This caused hyperinflation in Germany in the early 1920s, which in turn contributed to the German population's increasing resentment of the strict terms of the Treaty of Versailles. The United States was able to help stabilize the European economy for a time. Through the Dawes Plan, the United States loaned money to Germany so that it could pay its reparations to Britain and France, which then allowed the latter to pay their wartime debts to the United States. But the rise of the United States as the leader in international trade disrupted global cash flows, and it made Europe increasingly dependent upon the health of the U.S. economy. The arrangement worked only until 1929, when the Great Crash of the stock market in the United States plunged the world into a severe global depression.

As a newly minted second lieutenant, Tominaga Shōzō took command of a platoon fighting in China in 1941. As a test of their readiness for command, Shōzō and the twenty-one other just-arrived lieutenants were each ordered to behead a Chinese prisoner of war.

I was fourth. When my turn came, the only thought I had was "Don't do anything unseemly!" I didn't want to disgrace myself. I bowed to the regimental commander and stepped forward... One thin, worn-out prisoner was at the edge of the pit, blindfolded. I unsheathed my sword, a gift from my brother-in-law, wet it down as the lieutenant had demonstrated, and stood behind the man. The prisoner didn't move. He kept his head lowered. Perhaps he was resigned to his fate. I was tense, thinking I couldn't afford to fail. I took a deep breath and recovered my composure. I steadied myself, holding the sword at a point above my right shoulder, and swung down with one breath. The head flew away and the body tumbled down, spouting blood. The air reeked from all that blood. I washed blood off the blade, then wiped it with the paper provided. Fat stuck to it and wouldn't come off. I noticed, when I sheathed it, that my sword was slightly bent... At that moment, I felt something change inside me. I don't know how to put it, but I gained strength somewhere in my gut.[8]

In the aftermath, people under economic strain, out of work, and hungry proved very susceptible to political radicalization.

Although Italy was a member of the victorious Entente powers, increasing unemployment, the fear of Socialism, and an increasing distrust in the Italian government created the conditions for dramatic change in that country. Benito Mussolini and his Fascist Party took advantage of the chaos and confusion. They promised work, food, order, and national greatness, all while crushing their political opposition in the streets. Fascist candidates were elected around the country, and in 1922 Mussolini took control of Italy. He set out to make it a great power and to make the Mediterranean Sea a Roman lake. Spurred by the militaristic and machine-oriented outlook of the Fascists, he began a large-scale program of military modernization, building tanks, planes, and warships at a rate disproportionate with Italy's relatively small economy. His dreams of an empire eventually led to Italian expansion in East Africa in 1935 and the Balkans in 1939.

While the world grappled with the global economic crisis, it moved ever closer to another Great War. On September 18, 1931, following the Mukden Incident, in which the Japanese Army staged an attack on the railroad near Mukden in northeastern China and blamed the Chinese, the Japanese Army invaded the Chinese province of Manchuria, and occupied it over the course of the next year. Although the Japanese civilian government had not approved the move into Manchuria, it was unable to stop the military. The militarization of Japan took another step forward. The League of Nations condemned the Japanese invasion as a violation of the League's charter. Following further League efforts to stop the Japanese shelling of Shanghai the next year, the Japanese responded by walking out of the League of Nations. The Japanese military continued to solidify its hold on Japan, increasingly determined to accomplish its foreign policy objectives regardless of world opinion.

At the war's end in 1918, Imperial Russia had collapsed, and the Reds (Bolsheviks) were waging a bloody civil war against the White (anti-Communist) forces. The Reds won, but their victory in the civil war did not translate into a national victory against

SOVIET TUPOLEV ▲
TB-3 BOMBER

An advanced design when it entered service in 1930, the all-metal TB-3 four-engine heavy bomber was obsolete by 1939. Nonetheless, it was used heavily by the Soviets during World War II, especially in 1941—a reflection of the serious technological deficit faced by the U.S.S.R. in the first phase of the war.

Poland in the Russo-Polish War of 1919–21. The Bolsheviks' defeat in that conflict seemed to confirm the notion in the West that Russia posed little threat to peace. But at the same time, it taught Soviet leaders Vladimir Lenin and then Joseph Stalin that the new Soviet Union had to modernize to defend itself and to regain lost Russian territory. After Lenin's death in 1924, Stalin took over and set out to forcibly modernize the Soviet Union. Recognizing that a lack of manufacturing capacity had contributed greatly to the collapse of Russia during the First World War, he set out to convert the Soviet Union from a predominately agricultural economy to a predominately industrial economy. The forced collectivization of agriculture and industrialization led to the death and imprisonment of millions in the 1920s and 1930s but did generate extraordinary economic growth. For instance, Russian pig iron production rose from a half million tons in 1918 to five million tons in 1930 and fifteen million tons (more than Britain, France, and Italy combined) in 1940.[9] The emergence of the Soviet Union as a major industrial power heightened the fear of Communism and Socialism in the West, especially during an economic crisis with large numbers of unemployed workers seeking better options. The fear of Bolshevism increased as the Soviet Union grew more powerful and increasingly became the subject of political discussions around the world in the 1920s and 1930s.

LONG LIVE THE RED ARMY ▶

Soviet doctrine relied on large quantities of troops and material. Stalin hoped that the size of his military would deter a German attack, but Hitler expected the Red Army to be a weak adversary despite its imposing number of divisions.

ДА ЗДРАВСТВУЕТ КРАСНАЯ АРМИЯ—
ВООРУЖЕННЫЙ ОТРЯД ПРОЛЕТАРСКОЙ РЕВОЛЮЦИИ!

After World War I, many German veterans joined Freikorps paramilitary organizations. The Freikorps helped suppress left-wing and Communist uprisings in Germany. Many early Nazi Party members came from the Freikorps.

THE RISE OF HITLER

In the years directly following World War I, the German people were increasingly concerned about employment and food, as well as the growing Bolshevik menace in the East. Lacking a strong democratic tradition, and fearful of chaos and disorder, the German people proved willing to support right-wing parties promising order in the streets. Adolf Hitler and his National Socialist followers tried to take advantage of the situation with an attempted coup d'etat in 1923. His failure and imprisonment for nine months, in which time he wrote his book *Mein Kampf*, only strengthened his resolve. Nonetheless, the Nazi Party was in decline from 1925 to 1928, with its representation in the Reichstag, the German parliament, falling from thirty-two to twelve seats. The 1930 election, however, marked an extraordinary revival for the National Socialists, who gained 18 percent of the popular vote and no fewer than 107 Reichstag seats. In 1932 those figures rose to 37 percent and 230 seats. The next year, Hitler gained the chancellorship. The fundamental cause of the Nazis' startling rise to power—and so to a substantial degree the fundamental cause of the Versailles settlement's failure and the outbreak of World War II—was the crash of the stock market

Germany found itself with the skeleton of a military after the Treaty of Versailles. Limited to 100,000 men and prohibited from having offensive weapons, the German military leadership could do little in the 1920s other than study the First World War and plan for the time when it could rebuild the Reich's military forces. Army Chief of Staff Hans von Seeckt set about preserving the German Army, and kept only the highest-quality officers and soldiers in uniform.

The rise of Adolf Hitler and his assumption of power in 1933 with the support of the military led to the rebirth of the German Army, Navy, and Air Force. The Nazis undertook a massive rearmament program that enabled the armed forces to expand and simultaneously to reequip with modern weapons and equipment.

German military doctrine in the interwar years, like French doctrine, was the product of an intense effort to study the history of the Great War. The German offensives of March–April 1918 had demonstrated that concentrated attacking forces, relentlessly penetrating deep into enemy rear areas, could break the tactical deadlock of trench warfare. The task of the German General Staff was to construct an army that could build on the successful tactics of 1918 to find a war-winning formula. Innovative officers like Heinz Guderian and Erich von Manstein pushed for an emphasis on armored forces using the internal combustion engine to advance at a pace so far unseen in warfare. The new armored forces would be backed by motorized support elements and by a modern air force that specialized in the operational and tactical support of the ground forces, rather than in strategic bombing. The challenge for the German General Staff was how much to gamble on these new armored forces. Germany had the resources to motorize only a small fraction of its rapidly expanding army. The resulting debate among the senior military leaders over the composition of German forces and the role to be played by armored and motorized forces ultimately led to a conception of modern mobile operations that after 1939 became known around the world as Blitzkrieg, or "lightning war."

Despite the development of a few expensive motorized and tank-based Panzer divisions, about 85 percent of the German Army in 1939 was little changed from the army of 1918. The vast majority of the troops still marched or rode a train to the front, marched while on campaign, and were supplied by railroads and horse-drawn wagons. But, like their predecessors of the First World War, Hitler's regular infantry divisions marched hard, fought hard, and benefited from aggressive, well-educated leaders.

in the United States in October 1929 and the ensuing global economic crisis that extended through the 1930s.[10]

As chancellor, Hitler immediately began consolidating power and soon established firm control of Germany. The Nazi Party stressed jobs, food relief, and the restoration of German national greatness. Hitler soon renounced the Treaty of Versailles, ending Germany's payments of reparations and permitting him to redirect those funds to a military buildup. He then withdrew from the League of Nations and announced the rearmament of Germany. The world paused and took notice, but the international community lacked the public support and military capability to respond with anything other than verbal condemnations. Many around the world had become disillusioned by the cost of the Great War and were determined not to be drawn into an unnecessary war; others recognized that their nations were too unprepared for war to contemplate military action in the mid-1930s. Adolf Hitler and the Nazis might talk about German national greatness, the Western statesmen thought, but surely they were in no hurry to repeat the universal tragedy of the Great War.

The Treaty of Versailles prohibited the German military from operating west of the Rhine River, but on March 7, 1936, German troops marched into the demilitarized Rhineland, the portion of Germany located west of the Rhine River, with bands playing and were welcomed by the local population as liberators. Hitler had ordered his troops to withdraw to avoid an armed confrontation if the French military acted to halt their advance. However, the French and British governments were unprepared and unwilling to respond. There was very little public support in the democracies for starting a war to keep German soldiers out of German territory.

While there were voices warning of the dangers of Adolf Hitler and the Nazi regime, they remained in the minority. Most in the West chose to focus on domestic issues such as the Great Depression, and argued for isolationism. The outbreak of civil war in Spain on July 17, 1936, further distracted Europe's diplomats from the potential risks of German rearmament. The nationalist forces of General Francisco Franco fought to overthrow the elected republican government of Spain. Germany and Italy supported Franco, and the Soviet Union supported the republican forces. The British, French, and American governments, and the League of Nations, attempted to avoid being drawn into the conflict. The Western nations made it illegal for their nationals to fight in Spain, and the United States reaffirmed its Neutrality Act of the year before. The Neutrality Act prohibited trade with belligerents, thus removing the economic incentive to join one side or the other in the conflict; it was intended to prevent the United States from repeating the "error" of getting involved in the First World War.

Hitler used the Spanish Civil War to test military equipment and train elements of his military forces. Germany rearmed, rebuilt, and—without the knowledge of most German citizens—prepared for war. For the average German, the Nazi regime appeared to be delivering what it had promised: jobs, bread, law and order, and a restoration of pride to the German nation. The worst aspects of the Treaty of Versailles were being overthrown, and Germany was on a path once more to national greatness.

The son of a German general, Seeckt was a broadly educated and well-traveled professional soldier. During World War I, he served first as a staff officer on the Eastern Front, and then served as chief of staff of the Ottoman Army. His advice to the Turks reflected his later attitude toward Weimar Germany; he supported the aspirations of the "Young Turks" to create a modern—and therefore militarily efficient—Turkish state and evidenced few qualms about the Armenian Genocide, in which the Ottoman Empire, citing national security concerns, undertook a brutal campaign to exterminate the Armenian people.

After the armistice, Seeckt commanded German forces fighting an anti-Communist rearguard campaign as they withdrew from Russia. Seeckt was effectively chief of staff in 1919, became army commander in 1920, and did much to shape the future of the German Army. He was politically and socially conservative, and strove to preserve the army's independence from political authority.

He loathed the Versailles treaty and, because he believed war to be a vital human activity, worked to reestablish German military strength. Although Seeckt's program has earned him the title of "Father of the Blitzkrieg," he had to work within the limits of contemporary technological capabilities and strategic possibilities, and therefore focused on perfecting the army's intellectual capabilities and technical skills rather than on instilling a specific operational vision.

Seeckt's contempt for the Weimar government led to his dismissal, whereupon he entered right-wing politics. He supported Hitler briefly, and traveled to China in 1932 as a military advisor to Chiang Kai-shek's army. There, as in Turkey and Germany, Seeckt sought to synergize military efficiency and nationalist politics; his methods contributed to Nationalist Chinese victories in 1935. Seeckt later became disillusioned with Hitler. He died in Germany in 1936.

JOHANNES FRIEDRICH HANS VON SEECKT
April 22, 1866–December 27, 1936
Lieutenant General

Hitler, however, was determined to reunite the German-speaking peoples under one flag and to seize Eastern European lands as *Lebensraum*, living space, for an expanding German population. And he was fully prepared to start a war to get what he wanted.

While Hitler continued solidifying his control of Germany and rearming at an accelerating rate, the Japanese moved to invade China proper. On July 7, 1937, following a manufactured incident at the Marco Polo Bridge in Beijing, Japan launched a major invasion of China. Japanese forces rapidly seized the country's coastal areas, taking Shanghai and Nanking. The mass atrocities committed by the Japanese forces at Nanking, known as the Rape of Nanking, led to international condemnations. In December 1937 the Japanese bombing of the U.S.S. *Panay*, an American gunboat on the Yangtze River near Nanking, created a temporary crisis in U.S.-Japanese relations, but Japan paid an indemnity, and little ultimately came of it. The British and the French were increasingly occupied by the rise of Nazi Germany, and the U.S. Congress and the American people were determined to avoid war if at all possible—so support for China was limited largely to criticisms of Japanese actions. The Chinese would have to accept what aid they could find and fight the Japanese on their own.

In 1938 Hitler took his next steps toward war. To unite Austria with Germany, he supported the formation and growth of an Austrian Nazi Party and called for the Austrian government to unite the German-speaking peoples. To counter the rising German pressure, Austrian chancellor Kurt Schuschnigg called for an election on the

On April 26, 1937, the Luftwaffe launched a terror-bombing raid on the Spanish town of Guernica; it is considered the first such raid on a civilian population inside Europe. Pablo Picasso's famous painting depicts the attack's devastation and horror in stark colors.

issue of *Anschluss*, or union, with Germany on March 21. Not prepared to risk losing the election, Hitler ordered his forces into Austria on March 12. The Austrian people welcomed the German troops and voted overwhelmingly, albeit in a less than totally fair election, for *Anschluss* on April 10, 1938. The rest of the world looked on with growing concern but was powerless to stop the unification of Germany and Austria. The crisis did convince a growing number of people outside Germany that Adolf Hitler represented a threat to peace. Others held on to the belief that Hitler would in the end be reasonable: after all, occupying Austria could be seen as a step toward reuniting Europe's German-speaking territories, thus a step toward restructuring Europe around ethno-linguistic nation-states that the Treaty of Versailles and Wilson's Fourteen Points had supported.

Adolf Hitler made his next move in September 1938. Following a lengthy propaganda campaign to the German people, the Czechs, and the people of Europe to justify his upcoming move into the Sudetenland, he ordered the Army High Command to prepare for the invasion of Czechoslovakia—or, more specifically, its borderland Sudetenland region with its large German-speaking population. The high command feared that such an invasion would compel France and Britain to act, as they both had mutual defense treaties with the Czechs. But their fears proved unwarranted as the British and French, realizing their military organizations were not prepared for war, sought a negotiated settlement to the crisis. Adolf Hitler for Germany, Prime Minister Neville Chamberlain for Great Britain, Edouard Daladier for France, and Benito Mussolini for Italy met in Munich to settle the Sudetenland crisis. The resulting agreement, signed on September 30, 1938, put the Czechs in the position of having to fight alone or cede the Sudetenland to Germany. Abandoned by their Western allies, they had little choice but to accept the loss of the border region—and with it the mountain barrier that had given the country some degree of strategic security.

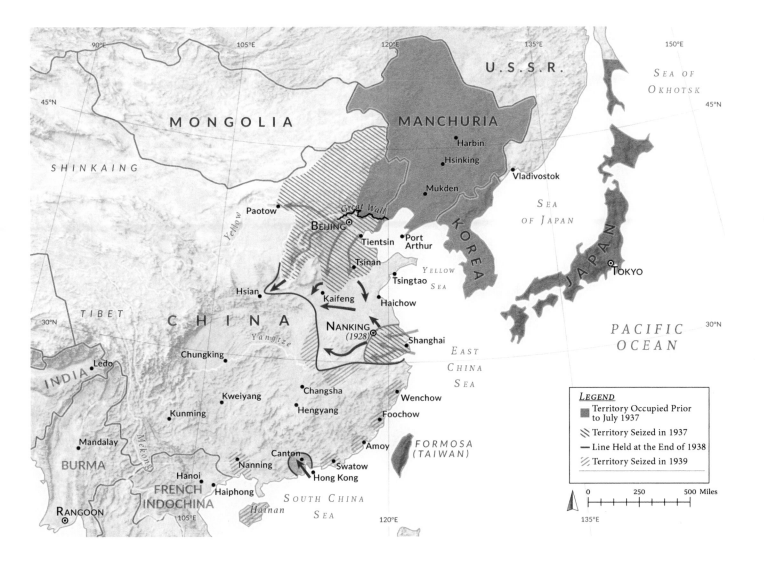

SECOND SINO-JAPANESE WAR, 1937-39

Japan's militaristic government sought to build a great overseas empire by conquest. By 1940, nearly a decade of warfare had brought much of China under Japanese control—but Chinese resistance continued.

Chamberlain returned home proclaiming that the agreement meant "peace in our time." But many skeptics in Britain and France opposed the deal. The Munich Agreement later became the symbol of appeasement—of giving in to Hitler to maintain the peace even though Hitler could not be trusted. The reality Chamberlain faced, though, was that Great Britain was not prepared to go to war. Both the British and the French needed time to rearm. And though the Munich Agreement hinged on Hitler's claim of having no more territorial ambitions, the British and French leadership did not bet everything on Hitler's word. Both countries redoubled their rearmament efforts and reconfirmed their defense agreement with Poland. If Chamberlain proved correct about achieving a peaceful solution, then the cost would have been worth it. If he proved wrong, then the British needed the time to prepare for a full-on war.

By 1939, the future was becoming clearer, and war looked increasingly likely. Hitler didn't wait long before breaking his word. In March 1939 he violated his pledge not to seek further territorial expansion by marching his forces into the remainder of Czechoslovakia. It was now abundantly clear that he could not be trusted to maintain the peace, and with his latest move, the world turned its attention to Poland.

Tens of thousands (or, by some estimates, hundreds of thousands) of Chinese civilians were killed or raped after the Japanese Army entered the walled city of Nanking, the capital of the Republic of China, in 1937.

Most believed that Poland would be different from the Rhineland, Austria, the Sudetenland, and Czechoslovakia. The country had a respectable army with forty divisions, and it had defeated the Russians in the Russo-Polish War of 1919–21. The British and French governments reaffirmed their support for the Poles on March 31, 1939, after Hitler occupied the Czech territories of Bohemia and Moravia and turned Slovakia into a German client state. The leaders of the Western democracies, at least in public, expressed confidence that with their help Poland could deter Hitler from starting another Great War. Though the nation was no match for Germany by itself, it was strong enough to stop German armies and fight long enough for French and British forces to come to its aid. Now the line had been drawn. It could still be hoped that Hitler would not cross it.

FIRST TO FIGHT ▶

During the interwar years, American sympathy for Chinese victims of Japanese aggression was real, but it did not extend to military support. After 1941, the United States considered China as one of its principal allies in the Second World War and recognized that the Chinese had been fighting the Axis longer than any other people.

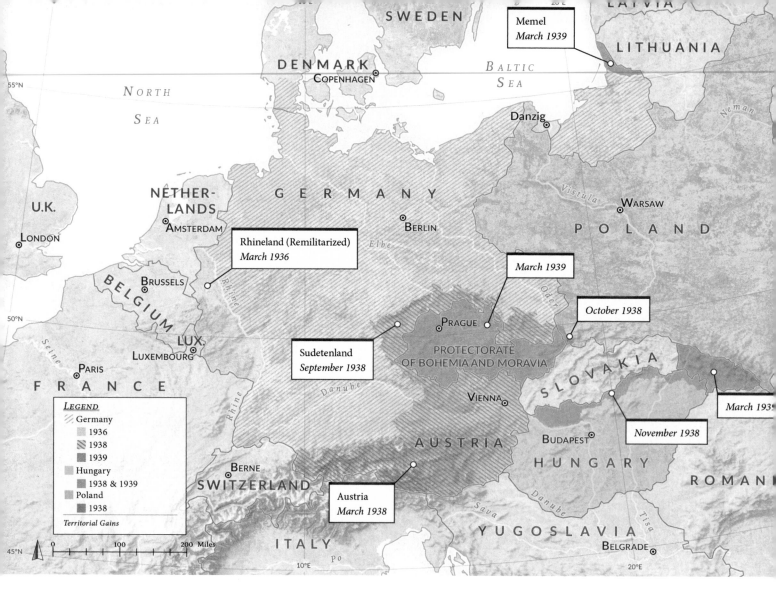

In March 1936 Hitler sent troops into the Rhineland, which was supposed to remain demilitarized, according to the Treaty of Versailles. Over the next three years, he dispatched armed forces to occupy territories beyond Germany's borders. None of these acts was contested. Britain and France even condoned the partitioning of Czechoslovakia in 1938–39, which resulted in the transfer of territory to Hitler's ally Hungary, as well as to Poland and Germany.

PREPARING FOR WAR

GERMAN EXPANSION

As it became clear over the course of the 1930s that the effort to eliminate war as a means of settling political disputes had failed, all the Great Powers devoted more thought and effort to preparing for war. The buildup began as the bellicose and nationalistic leadership of Germany, Italy, and Japan prepared their nations for what would likely be a titanic struggle with Britain and France (and their large overseas empires and dominions). In response, the Western democracies began to rebuild their armed forces, though not quickly enough to eliminate the three- to four-year advantage that the more militaristic countries had gained. Each national government—for different reasons, reflecting different lessons drawn from the experience of World War I—viewed the future with some degree of confidence.[11]

Even as Prime Minister Neville Chamberlain (center, holding paper) celebrated an apparent end to German aggression, British rearmament escalated in case the policy of appeasement failed.

Hitler's armed forces had the edge in doctrine, training, armored formations, and airpower (especially dive-bombers for close air support). As his Nazi ideology required, he also counted on what he believed to be the racial superiority of the German people over their anticipated adversaries. Believing that Germany had lost the First World War only because of the massive material advantages of an alliance that included Russia, Britain, France, and later the United States, he was reassured by the fact that this time around the Soviet Union would be supplying Germany with resources rather than fighting it and that Italy would now be a German ally rather than an enemy. He also believed that in the Great War, Germany had received a stab in the back from Jews and Communists who had undermined morale on the home front. This time he was confident that his party would be able to enforce national unity behind him as "Führer" (leader).[12]

Italy's leaders had no intention of fighting head-on against the truly powerful European nations. Instead, they aimed to take advantage of any opportunities for expansion that might arise. Mussolini and the Fascists had modernized the Italian

'Remember . . . One More Lollypop, and Then You All Go Home!'

AN INSATIABLE APPETITE ▲

In 1938 there was still some reason to hope that Hitler could be appeased by the annexations of Austria and the Sudetenland. By August 1941, when Theodor Geisel (better known as Dr. Seuss) penned this cartoon, it had become increasingly clear that the German leader would not be satisfied by anything less than world domination.

military in the early to mid-1930s at great expense, but by 1939, the major powers had already passed them by in terms of military technology and war-fighting ability. Having made very large military expenditures relative to the size of Italy's economy, and having succeeded in the conquests of Ethiopia in 1936 and Albania in 1939, the Italian government expected to fight victoriously against second-rate European powers such as Greece and Yugoslavia. And if favorable conditions permitted, it also planned to advance into Africa against the colonial armies of Britain and France.

The Japanese hoped that the only strong nations among its potential adversaries—

ITALIAN FASCES, CA. 1930s ▶

The word "Fascism" is derived from the fasces, a symbol of power in classical Rome. Fascism in Italy generated popular support not only through the promise of a better future but also by an evocation of the nation's glorious past.

"SUPERBATTLESHIP" *YAMATO* ▲

Still expecting naval battles to be decided by big guns, Japan focused its interwar energies on the construction of "superbattleships." The *Yamato*, laid down in 1937 and commissioned in 1941, remains the largest, most powerfully armed battleship ever constructed.

the United States, Britain, and the Soviet Union—would be too concerned by the rising threat in Germany, or by their own versions of isolationism, to intervene against Japan in China or elsewhere in Asia. But if it came to war, the Japanese, like the Germans, believed firmly in their racial superiority.[13] Moreover, Japan's sailors were highly skilled, and the modernization of the Japanese economy had progressed to the point where its battleships, aircraft carriers, and fighter planes were as good as anyone's, while its torpedoes—important weapons in a potential naval war against the United States—were a quantum leap ahead of everyone else's. Japanese torpedoes carried larger warheads, were faster in the water, and were much more reliable than American torpedoes. Besides, the targets of Japan's ambitions were all within relatively easy reach of its homeland, and very far away indeed from America or Great Britain.

Thus, in different ways, the three Axis powers all expected that this new war would be fundamentally different from the last: Germany would have an easier task and emerge victorious; Japan and Italy would be more aggressive and seize what they wanted during the fighting, rather than trusting their partners to share the spoils after victory had been won.

Britain and France, by contrast, hoped that the strategic logic of a Second World

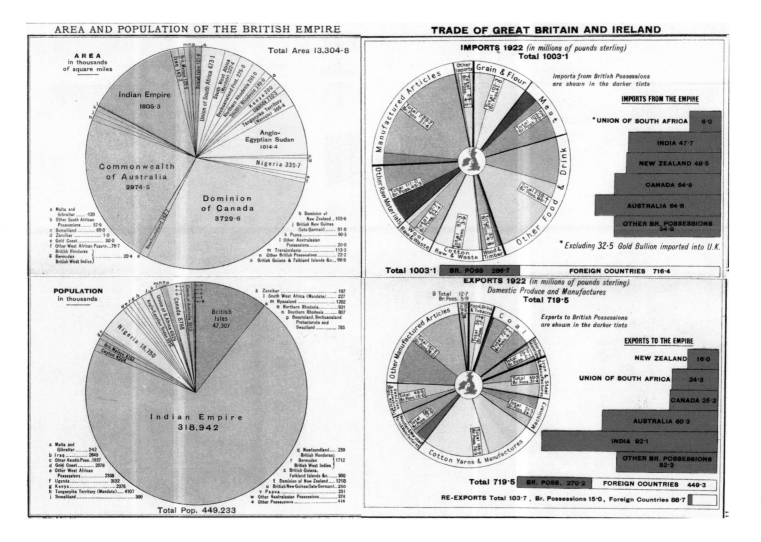

▲ THE BRITISH EMPIRE

The British Empire dwarfed the mother country in terms of area and population. The global responsibilities of the United Kingdom were a problem in peacetime, but the Empire was also a great source of potential strength.

War would be basically similar to that of the Great War: together they would halt the initial German thrust, and then mobilize their populations and economies fully in order to fight a "total war," in which their access to the world's resources would eventually enable them to triumph. Both countries had extensive empires, and they were confident that the United States could be expected to help—at the very least economically, even if isolationist sentiment prevented an actual military alliance. Moreover, both France and Britain had, so they thought, learned military lessons from the last war that would enable them to win without paying quite the horrendous price they had suffered in the war of 1914–18.

France had invested immense resources in the creation of the Maginot Line fortifications, all along the frontier with Germany: this time it would not give up its key industrial and resource-rich areas at the start of the fighting, and so would not have to expend rivers of blood simply trying to push the invaders off French soil. To fight the forthcoming battles, the French Army studied 1918 and prepared for "Directed Battle," fielding an army with more tanks and artillery than the Germans, and supported by a modern air force.[14]

The British, too, intended to avoid any offensives on the ground like the costly battles of the Somme or Passchendaele. They expected to benefit from the French

Japan came out of World War I on the victorious side and made significant territorial gains by seizing German colonies in the Far East. The country believed it was an emerging major power and deserved to be treated as such. As the government came increasingly under the control of militaristic nationalists, the goal of acquiring the natural resources needed to sustain Great Power status became the overriding national priority. In 1931 Japan seized Manchuria and turned it into the puppet state of Manchukuo. In 1937 Japanese forces invaded China proper and began seizing as much territory as they could. While Manchuria and China provided the Japanese with many needed resources, one of the most important remained beyond their grasp: oil. The only major oil fields within reach of Japan were in the Netherlands East Indies.

The Japanese Army in the 1930s was largely a force structured around light infantry and light artillery, capable of rapid movement. Japanese industry proved unable to produce sufficient steel to simultaneously support a major naval buildup and also supply the heavy artillery, tanks, and trucks that would have permitted a German-style armored force. The army suffered from serious logistical difficulties and thus did without adequate supplies much of the time. A soldier with a bayonet, guided by the traditional martial ethos of Bushido, the way of the samurai, was expected to prevail over better-equipped but decadent Western troops.

Unlike the Japanese Army, the navy had superior equipment as well as excellent doctrine and personnel. The ships of the Japanese Navy were well built, fast, and heavily armed. Though they lacked some crew amenities that American sailors would have missed, it did not seem to hinder their effectiveness. The Japanese sailors were professional seamen who spent much of their time at sea and excelled at navigation, gunnery, night fighting, and the use of the Type 93 torpedo, the best of the war. Although the battleship admirals ran the navy, the Japanese invested heavily in aircraft carriers, aircraft, and trained pilots. Japanese ships and aircraft were designed for Pacific operations with long operational ranges. Recognizing that any attempt to seize territory in the Pacific required the movement of troops from the sea to the land, the Japanese did put some emphasis on amphibious operations. They were very proficient at moving troops by sea and getting them ashore at undefended beaches.

The Japanese military understood that victory had to come quickly; that Japan lacked the resources for a lengthy war. It would count on the quality of the army and navy; the fighting spirit of their soldiers, sailors, and airmen; and the spiritual weakness of their opponents.

THE MAGINOT LINE ▶

Rather than being a continuous "Great Wall of France," the Maginot Line (named for the French minister of war who conceived it) was composed of a series of fighting positions along the frontiers. It was the strongest and most elaborate system of border defenses ever constructed.

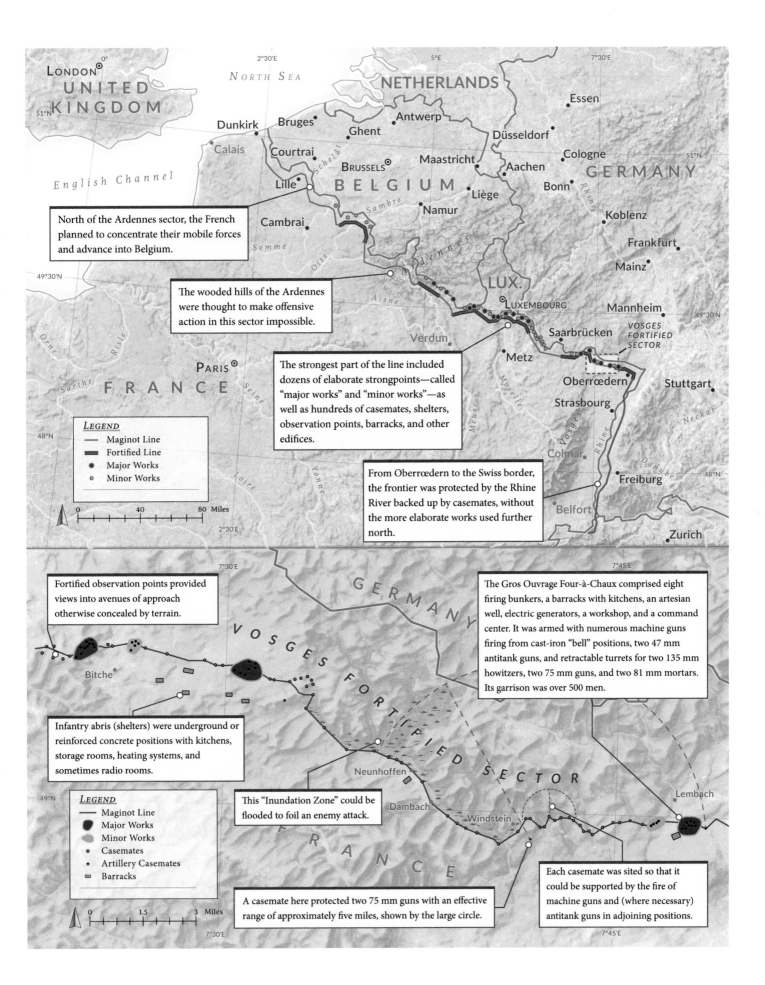

North of the Ardennes sector, the French planned to concentrate their mobile forces and advance into Belgium.

The wooded hills of the Ardennes were thought to make offensive action in this sector impossible.

The strongest part of the line included dozens of elaborate strongpoints—called "major works" and "minor works"—as well as hundreds of casemates, shelters, observation points, barracks, and other edifices.

From Oberrœdern to the Swiss border, the frontier was protected by the Rhine River backed up by casemates, without the more elaborate works used further north.

LEGEND
— Maginot Line
▬ Fortified Line
● Major Works
○ Minor Works

0   40   80 Miles

Fortified observation points provided views into avenues of approach otherwise concealed by terrain.

The Gros Ouvrage Four-à-Chaux comprised eight firing bunkers, a barracks with kitchens, an artesian well, electric generators, a workshop, and a command center. It was armed with numerous machine guns firing from cast-iron "bell" positions, two 47 mm antitank guns, and retractable turrets for two 135 mm howitzers, two 75 mm guns, and two 81 mm mortars. Its garrison was over 500 men.

Infantry abris (shelters) were underground or reinforced concrete positions with kitchens, storage rooms, heating systems, and sometimes radio rooms.

This "Inundation Zone" could be flooded to foil an enemy attack.

A casemate here protected two 75 mm guns with an effective range of approximately five miles, shown by the large circle.

Each casemate was sited so that it could be supported by the fire of machine guns and (where necessary) antitank guns in adjoining positions.

LEGEND
— Maginot Line
● Major Works
◗ Minor Works
• Casemates
▪ Artillery Casemates
▬ Barracks

0   1.5   3 Miles

CHAR B1 BATTLE TANK, 1940 ▲

The heavily armed and armored B1 had the advantage over contemporary German Panzers in tank-to-tank fighting. But its slow speed and short range limited its value in a war of maneuver. Note the large size of the B1 compared with the German Panzer II visible on the left.

investment in defensive fortifications and to be able to provide the offensive punch necessary for ultimate victory, especially in the air. They could rely on their navy to control the seas and the Royal Air Force, with its new fighter aircraft and radar air-defense system, to control the air. The British also believed that the tactics and technologies, particularly sonar, that they had developed during World War I had rendered ineffective the German U-boats (submarines), which had caused so much damage during that earlier war—at one point threatening Britain with starvation.[15]

The Americans, with an ocean off each shore, could afford to be isolationists and severely limit defense spending. The U.S. Army and Navy did what they could with their limited resources. The army spent its limited research-and-development funds on dealing with modern threats and maximizing its firepower. The Army Air Corps developed the B-17 heavy bomber to support its concept of strategic bombing: the idea that large aircraft with strong defensive armaments could level enemy cities from the air and force an enemy to make peace. Beginning with the Naval Acts of 1936 and 1938 and culminating with the Two-Ocean Navy Act in 1940, the U.S. Navy began a major expansion. The ships that would win the war in the Pacific in 1945 had their origins in 1938.

The lack of troops and money for training did not prevent American military

leaders during the interwar years from studying the lessons of the Great War and wartime mobilization. Support for the army training schools—the Command and General Staff School, the Army War College, and the Army Industrial College—remained strong. In 1933 the army was placed in charge of the Civilian Conservation Corps, a New Deal jobs program that trained thousands of reserve officers how to run company-sized units and gave more than three million Americans experience living in a military environment while undertaking conservation projects all around the country.[16] With the outbreak of the war in Europe in 1939, American defense preparations increased steadily. By the time the Japanese attacked Pearl Harbor on December 7, 1941, the U.S. military was better prepared for battle than it had ever been at the outset of a war in its national history.

The British, French, and Americans all hoped to avoid another Great War, and planned to fight mainly on the defensive if war did come: the great strength of the defenders seemed to many to be the obvious lesson of the First World War—though they recognized that 1918 had shown that aggressive tactics and operational plans, supported by artillery, tanks, and aircraft, had made decisive victories possible.

▲ 25 MM ANTITANK GUN

By May 1940, the French Army deployed some six thousand Hotchkiss 25 mm antitank light cannon, each capable of firing fifteen high-velocity solid-shot armor-piercing rounds per minute. These were expected to halt attacking German armor as effectively as machine guns stopped infantry.

◀ THE MAGINOT LINE
(ISOMETRIC VIEW POINT 1)

French engineers built a sophisticated series of underground defenses from Switzerland to Luxembourg. The purpose of the Maginot Line was to protect France's eastern frontier and channel German operations into Belgium.

◀ THE MAGINOT LINE
(SECTIONAL VIEW POINT 2)

Foreign observers generally agreed that the Maginot Line forts were, in British general Alan Brooke's words, "an astonishing engineering feat." They tended to emphasize the electric railways and elevators used for moving ammunition; the elaborate communications systems; and the barracks, kitchens, hospital rooms, and other facilities that made one of the major works "like a huge battleship" sunk into the earth. Captain Laurence Twomey of the British Royal Artillery, however, was more impressed with the skill with which the positions he saw had been laid out and prepared to deliver precisely directed fire against any enemy advance. As he wrote in his diary:

> The Maginot Line is a perfect example of the A B C of defence laid out in a system of mutually supporting posts with cross fire—no post firing to its immediate front but firing across the fronts of the posts on either flank . . .
>
> In the afternoon we had a conducted tour of the Hackenberg Fort in the Maginot Line. This is the largest fort in the whole line . . . Actually, there are other forts with a greater number of guns but there are a lot of Infantry and machine guns in the Hackenberg. It has 16 guns of 75 mm and 60 mm and two cupolas mounting a pair of 80 mm How[itzers] each. The fort cost as much as the Battleship *Queen Elizabeth*. The B.B.C. and every journalist in the world have tried to describe the Maginot Forts, and I can't hope to improve on their efforts. The things which fascinated me most were the mechanisms of the cupolas, the way rate of fire can be speeded up when in a fixed emplacement so that one gun equals almost two, the arrangement for machine guns with all round traverse to be traversed at night with an adjustment to elevate and depress them in conformity with the slopes of the ground, the arrangements for antitank gun shooting over open sights with photographic panoramas with ranges marked on them, and above all the system of mutual support of the forts and a perfectly worked out fire plan which of course we did not see in entirety—it would take a week to grasp.
>
> There are twelve kilometres of tunnel in the Hackenberg, we did not walk all that but we were all quite tired when we got home and felt well exercised.[17]

However much sense that made, the Western powers' decision to adopt a strategy that focused on repelling rather than conducting attacks left them with very limited options for responding to the early expansionary actions of Germany, Italy, and Japan.

The Soviet Union devoted the bulk of its new industrial output to building the Red Army into the largest army in the world in the 1930s, with more aircraft, tanks, and guns than the other major powers combined. Much of the equipment was soon obsolete or unserviceable, but the images coming out of the Soviet Union highlighted the growing Soviet power. Under the leadership of officers such as Marshal Mikhail Tukhachevsky, the Red Army developed a doctrine of Deep Battle that utilized mechanized forces supported by aircraft to carry the offense deep into the enemy rear areas, encircling enemy forces, and maintaining the initiative.[18] Unfortunately for the Soviet Union, Stalin's purges of the officer corps in the late 1930s greatly weakened his nation's military power. Recognizing the growing threat of Nazi Germany, the Soviet dictator sought time to improve Soviet defenses in order to prepare for a war with Germany that he feared was coming.[19]

Poland would prove less sturdy than the British and French had hoped. In 1939, German forces surrounded Poland on three sides: in East Prussia to the north, Germany proper to the west, and in the former Czechoslovakia to the south. To the east, the Soviet Union also remained a threat. Geography did little to aid the Poles' defense, and they were determined to defend all their territory, since much of their industry was located in border areas. The Polish military had forty divisions,

France emerged from the Great War victorious, with the largest army in Europe. The French military studied that last war and believed that quick victories were no longer possible. The key to victory in the future would be to fight a long, defensive war in which France preserved its strength and manpower while Germany wore itself out conducting costly offensives, ultimately falling to the strength of French mobilization and Allied support from Great Britain and the United States.

The emphasis on defense took the form of a modern underground defensive system running from the Swiss border to Belgium. Named after the war minister who conceived the plan, the Maginot Line turned the trench system of World War I into the most modern defensive positions in existence. Around a hundred underground strongpoints (*ouvrages*), with room for a hundred to a thousand men each, and several hundred smaller dug-in bunkers (casemates) were sited to provide a continuous wall of fire from antitank guns and machine guns. Each protected firing position could be supported by fire from neighboring posts. To back up these defenses, the army counted on its doctrine of Directed Battle, which brought together the lessons learned in 1916–18. Where offensive action was necessary, infantry forces supported by maximum firepower from artillery and tanks were to conduct carefully planned and executed advances. When the breakthrough took place, the French mechanized units would exploit the breach and defeat the retreating enemy. Many French military leaders were confident that the Maginot Line, combined with the doctrine of Directed Battle, would either deter any German offensive or defeat an attack if one did come.

Some officers, including Charles de Gaulle, called for a greater emphasis on mechanization and the creation of armored forces. These officers found themselves opposed by senior military leaders unwilling to stray too far from the war-winning doctrine of 1918, and a government more willing to pay for a defense line than to create a force best suited for the offense. France built slow but well-armed and heavily armored tanks to support the infantry in directed battles, and light tanks and motor vehicles to assume the role of light cavalry forces, capable of exploiting successful penetrations of the enemy line. In addition to limiting development of independent armored forces, the focus on the lessons of 1918 led the French Air Force to de-emphasize direct tactical support of ground troops.

The French Army in 1939 was large, modern, and comparable with the German Army in quantity of men, divisions, tanks, and guns. While Germany outnumbered France in modern aircraft, that advantage ceased to exist when the British Royal Air Force was included in the calculation. The French Army of the interwar period was an internationally respected military force, and it seemed ready to counter the growing German threat and preserve the peace in Europe.

B. H. Liddell Hart was one of the twentieth century's most prolific and controversial military theorists. As a journalist, author, and advisor to politicians, he shaped British military thought, public policy, and popular opinion. Liddell Hart served three brief tours on the Western Front during the First World War; and was wounded and gassed on the Somme. The gas weakened his heart, which forced him to retire from the army. Liddell Hart was sickened by the futility of trench warfare, and argued that history had demonstrated that rapid victory was achievable only by an "indirect approach." Borrowing from the work of J. F. C. Fuller, a British Army officer and military theorist, he called for tank forces designed to paralyze rather than destroy enemy armies. He also advocated gas warfare and the bombing of civilians in cities as forms of "indirect approach." Over time, Liddell Hart came to doubt that such methods could achieve the proper objective of warfare: a prosperous and stable peace. Seeing only mutual destruction in continental fighting and strategic bombing, Liddell Hart advocated bomber deterrence and insisted that the historic "British way of war" avoided ground fighting in Europe. He called for a policy of "limited liability" in supporting Britain's continental allies and objected to conscription; these positions resonated with politicians in the 1930s. After the Nazi-Soviet Non-Aggression Pact of 1939, Liddell Hart rejected futile efforts to assist France and instead supported a defensive strategy and possible accommodation with Germany. His reputation revived after the war when he claimed credit for inventing the armor doctrines used by the German armed forces (Wehrmacht) and the Israeli Defense Forces. Liddell Hart was knighted in 1966 in acknowledgment of his contributions to the British Army.

a thousand armored vehicles, and four hundred modern aircraft, but had avoided fully mobilizing to avoid provoking the Germans. The Polish position, extremely difficult at best, became largely untenable when Soviet foreign minister Vyacheslav Molotov and German foreign minister Joachim von Ribbentrop signed the Nazi-Soviet Non-Aggression Pact on August 23, with its secret provision for Germany and the Soviet Union to divide Poland. The alliance between the two countries was a surprise to the powers of the West, but it made strategic sense for both parties: the Germans needed to avoid a two-front war, and the Soviet Union needed more time to prepare for war.

On September 1, 1939, the German armies rolled across the border into Poland. The British and French made one last attempt to avoid war, giving Hitler until eleven o'clock on the morning of September 3 to withdraw from Poland. Receiving no reply from Germany, Britain declared war on Germany on September 3. Despite the Great Powers' best efforts in the aftermath of World War I, the world was at war once again.

After the Great War, Britain faced the challenge of maintaining its empire while controlling defense costs. The Ten-Year Rule, begun in 1919, stipulated that budgets would be prepared based on the assumption that the British would not fight in a major European war in the next ten years. The rule, which justified greatly reduced defense spending, was renewed each year until 1932. But the Japanese invasion of Manchuria in 1931, Adolf Hitler's assumption of power in Germany in 1933, and Mussolini's invasion of Ethiopia in 1935 led the British to begin reassessing their defense requirements. The question was: What allocation of resources would best prepare the nation for war?

The Royal Navy remained convinced that command of the seas was Britain's principal strategic necessity, and that the battleship was the primary warship. The British did start constructing aircraft carriers, but the United States and Japan had more and better ones. Submarine and antisubmarine warfare lagged due to overconfidence in ASDIC (the first sonar device, named after the Anti-Submarine Detection Investigation Committee).

The Royal Air Force expected that attacking bombers would always get through and, if they flew in sufficient numbers, would break the will of the enemy population, thereby ending any future war. But Parliament had little desire to pay for the cost of such a force. The threat that enemy bombers would be able to reach Britain, however, did prove convincing enough that air defenses began receiving more funding. The British acquired millions of gas masks and 1.5 million prefabricated bomb shelters for civil defense, along with searchlights, antiaircraft guns, and barrage balloons. Two great fighter aircraft, the Hurricane and the Spitfire, and the Chain Home radar early-warning system (all deployed from 1936 to 1940) would prove crucial to Britain's survival when war finally came.

The British army was faced with very low budgets and the task of policing an empire. Doctrinal debates, led by theorists such as J. F. C. Fuller and B. H. Liddell Hart, remained largely academic, with little money available to test concepts. Both Fuller and Liddell Hart advocated the use of mechanized forces to penetrate enemy lines and strike their command-and-control systems to paralyze the enemy forces. The army did create a tank regiment in 1931 to conduct some tests. The armored-forces advocates would remain disappointed, but the British Army did lead in the procurement of trucks. When war finally broke out in 1939, the British Army was fully motorized—which was possible only because the army was so small.

The British military in September 1939 included a small professional army, motorized, with extensive colonial commitments. The navy remained focused on capital ships with limited capabilities for antisubmarine or amphibious warfare. The air force was focused on strategic bombing and air defense. In 1939, as in 1914, Great Britain was not fully prepared to fight a world war.

Except for the U.S. Navy, which was arguably the most powerful in the world throughout the interwar period, the American military after World War I reverted to a very small peacetime force. The U.S. Army soon had only 125,000 troops and a very limited budget, which also had to pay for the planes of the Army Air Service, even as it grew to become the Army Air Corps in 1926. Rising isolationism and the Great Depression meant that money for new technology remained tight for both the army and the navy.

Doctrinal development in the United States remained more intellectual than real during this period. A key lesson learned in World War I was that mobilization and logistics were critical to victory. Officers at the Army War College and the Army Industrial College studied the issues of mobilization and logistics and laid the groundwork for the success in those areas during the Second World War. The Americans might have lacked sufficient money and equipment for actual field tests and maneuvers, but a great deal of intellectual work was carried out in the classroom, as the future wartime leaders addressed issues they felt would be important in the next war.

A good portion of what money was available was spent wisely. The War Department developed the 3-inch antiaircraft gun to deal with enemy airpower, and the M1 Garand semiautomatic rifle to maximize the firepower of American infantrymen. It also motorized the army. Aviators pushed for an independent air force focused on strategic bombing. When Congress showed little interest in strategic offense, they repackaged the B-17 as a coastal-defense bomber and gained approval to begin construction of the heavy bomber that later became the symbol of the American strategic bombing effort. The army ground forces also took advantage of America's strong industrial base, replacing horses with trucks as the foundation of the supply system. Advocates of mechanized warfare, however, had little success in pushing the development of expensive armored forces. The navy developed aircraft carriers and experimented with carrier operations, testing the concept by launching simulated raids on the Panama Canal and Pearl Harbor. The U.S. Marine Corps expanded on its notion of amphibious operations and developed new landing craft, culminating with the LVT (revolutionary landing vehicle, tracked) in 1941.

The U.S. military in September 1939 was deceptively weak when viewed by Germany and Japan. Indeed, the Army had only 189,839 officers and enlisted soldiers, and it was thought that it would take the Americans a long time to prepare for war. What the Axis leaders failed to appreciate was that a great deal of the groundwork for wartime mobilization had been laid during the interwar years. The Naval Expansion Act of 1938 authorized a 20 percent expansion of the U.S. Navy, and the all-important design work for the ships that would win World War II was well under way by the time Hitler invaded Poland. Production of the B-17 bomber was already under way. The U.S. Army remained small in 1939, but the military potential of the United States was growing steadily as overseas threats increased.

Following Russia's withdrawal from the Great War, the Bolsheviks and the newly formed Red Army fought a lengthy civil war over great distances against anti-Communist forces to gain power. The new Soviet Union, surrounded by enemies, understood the necessity of having a strong military. As Joseph Stalin rose to power, he began to modernize the Soviet Union through the forced collectivization of agriculture and forced industrialization of the economy. The Red Army leadership demonstrated the ability to learn during the Russian Civil War, and it sought to build on that experience in the years that followed.

By the mid-1930s, the Red Army was the world's largest, with the largest fleets of tanks and aircraft. To guide the use of this massive force, Soviet military leaders developed a military doctrine known as Deep Battle, which focused on operations rather than tactics. Deep Battle involved the use of mechanized forces supported by artillery and air support to penetrate enemy defenses, followed by second and third echelons to reinforce success and to maintain forward momentum over great distances. Chief of Staff Mikhail Tukhachevsky pushed for the formation of combined-arms tank and mechanized corps to conduct these deep operations. The Red Army was well on its way to becoming a leader in mechanized warfare theory when Stalin, always fearful of losing power, chose to purge his army leadership. The execution and imprisonment of thousands of senior officers in the army stifled innovation and personal initiative. General Tukhachevsky became one of the highest-ranking victims in 1937. His execution and replacement with the loyal but less innovative Kliment E. Voroshilov led to the breaking up of the new tank and mechanized corps. The Deep Battle concept contained all the elements of what would become the German Blitzkrieg. What the Red Army lacked to make the doctrine successful in the late 1930s was an officer corps with the knowledge and confidence to execute the doctrine on the battlefield, and the structures necessary for the maintenance and support of units organized to undertake such operations.

Although the Red Army in 1939 was largely an unknown quantity, with questions about the quality of its officers, soldiers, equipment, and doctrine, it could not be ignored. What the Soviet military needed was time to recover from the negative effects of Stalin's purges. Hitler needed freedom of action in the East. The resulting Nazi-Soviet Non-Aggression Pact in August 1939 benefited both parties.

U.S. ARMY RIFLEMAN, 1938 ▶

Relying on the Navy and two expansive oceans for security, the United States kept the interwar Army small, with an average strength of 147,000 active duty soldiers and 400,000 reserves from 1922 to 1939. Especially after the Great Depression, the military budget was tight, but nonetheless the American infantryman of the late interwar period was adequately trained and fairly well equipped. Nearly every item of his kit was an improvement relative to World War I gear, and his M1 Garand rifle was by far the best issued in any army of the time.

M1917A1 Helmet

At the end of World War I, the U.S. stock of M1917 trench helmets numbered in the millions. Instead of discarding the old helmet, the army modified it in 1934 with a new "head pad assembly," which consisted of a frame with four leather flaps that laced together and a khaki cotton web chinstrap. The steel helmet was also painted with a new cork aggregate, which made the surface less reflective.

1926 Wool Service Coat

A new coat replaced the hated high-collar ("standup") style worn by doughboys in World War I. Rather than spend money on both a dress uniform and a field/combat uniform, army leaders tried to combine the two. Soldiers were issued a tie that they could add for more formal occasions and discard for field maneuvers.

Gas Mask in Carrier Bag

Gas was widely used in WWI, and the Army issued gas masks to soldiers from 1919 to 1941. The 1919 M1 had irreplaceable eye pieces and came in five sizes. In 1928, the M1A1 improved the design with removable eye pieces, which made repairs easier. The M1A2 from 1934 featured a universal facepiece that fit 95 percent of soldiers. In 1941, the army created the popular and effective M2 mask with a fully molded facepiece. Although gas was not used in WWII, the army produced 8 million M2 gas masks during the conflict.

Field Equipment

Most of the infantry equipment of the interwar army soldier, and even of the soldier in World War II, was leftover stock from World War I. That included the M1910 Infantry Equipment, which comprised a pack, poncho, blanket, shelter half, haversack, cartridge belt, entrenching tool, bayonet, scabbard, and first-aid pouch.

M1 Garand Rifle

The biggest change in the American soldier's equipment during the interwar period came with the introduction in 1936 of the .30-caliber M1 Garand rifle, which Patton called the "greatest battle implement ever devised." The M1 was the first standard issue semiautomatic military rifle in history. A heavy weight of nearly ten pounds made the Garand unpopular with interwar soldiers, but wartime GIs cherished the increased firepower that its high rate of fire provided.

Wool Service Trousers

The interwar U.S. Army eliminated the baggy jodhpur-style trousers in 1938 for everyone except for troops actually involved with horses. General George S. Patton Jr. famously ignored that regulation: as a cavalry officer, he wore the riding breeches throughout World War II.

Leggings

In 1938, the army created dismounted leggings, which eliminated the spiral canvas puttees that were hated by soldiers. The leggings were designed to keep mud and water from entering the boots and to provide ankle support. During World War II, airborne forces adopted higher boots and tossed their leggings. Paratroopers called non-airborne forces "legs," a shortened form of "leggings." By the end of World War II, all soldiers had eliminated the leggings, but the name "leg" for a non-airborne soldier remains part of the paratrooper's vocabulary.

▲ B-17 "FLYING FORTRESS"

The four-engine B-17 "Flying Fortress" represented the ambition of the U.S. Army Air Corps to win wars through strategic bombing alone. It was designed to fly high enough and fast enough to escape enemy fighters, and to be so well armed and durable that it could fight them off if necessary. In practice, though, B-17 formations flying in daylight suffered intolerable casualties unless accompanied by fighter escorts.

A professional officer from an impoverished noble family, Tukhachevsky joined the Bolsheviks for practical reasons rather than ideological affinity. He received his commission in 1914, was captured by the Germans in 1915, and escaped back to Russia in 1917. He was an effective commander against the White (anti-Communist) forces, and proved ruthless in his subjugation of the revolution's domestic enemies, but Tukhachevsky came into conflict with Stalin over blame for the failed Soviet attack on Warsaw in 1920.

In the 1920s, Tukhachevsky advocated for the professionalization and mechanization of the Red Army and achieved significant reforms. As chief of staff from 1925 to 1928, he pressed his theory of Deep Operations, which involved using mechanized forces and aircraft to strike into enemy rear areas, but Tukhachevsky suffered repeated political denunciations by jealous rivals.

He believed that Hitler would inevitably attack the Soviet Union, and argued that the Red Army should conduct a defense in depth. This angered Stalin, who insisted on an unrelentingly offensive-minded doctrine. In 1937 Stalin ordered Tukhachevsky's execution on trumped-up charges of conspiring with the Germans. His wife and sons were also shot, and his sister and daughter were exiled. Tukhachevsky's military ideas were vindicated during the war.

MIKHAIL TUKHACHEVSKY
February 16, 1893–June 12, 1937
Marshal of the Soviet Union

MILITARY EXPENDITURES, 1935–38 ▶

In the years leading up to WW2, the Western democracies lacked the political will to match the military spending of the Axis nations. They paid the price of unpreparedness in 1939–40.

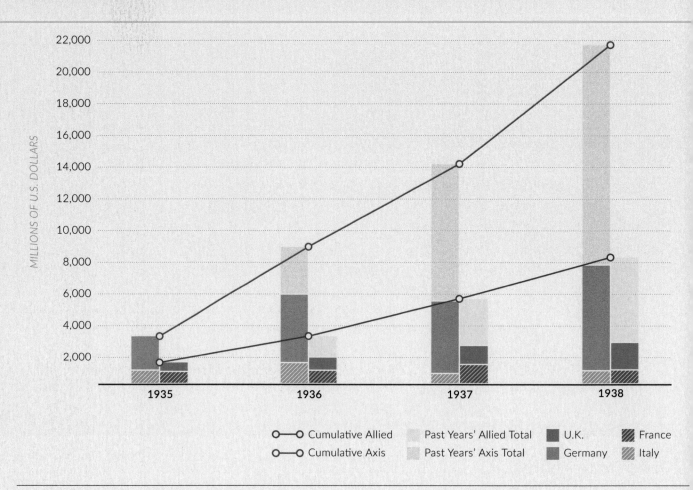

MILLIONS OF U.S. DOLLARS

22,000
20,000
18,000
16,000
14,000
12,000
10,000
8,000
6,000
4,000
2,000

1935   1936   1937   1938

○──○ Cumulative Allied   Past Years' Allied Total   U.K.   France
○──○ Cumulative Axis   Past Years' Axis Total   Germany Italy

MILITARY EXPENDITURE AS A PERCENTAGE OF NATIONAL EXPENDITURE

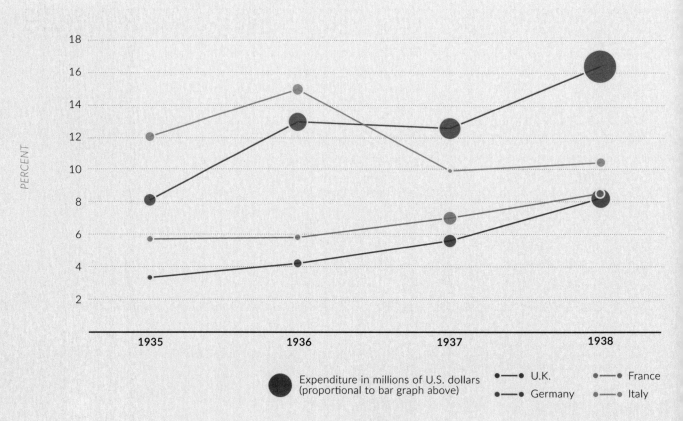

PERCENT

18
16
14
12
10
8
6
4
2

1935   1936   1937   1938

● Expenditure in millions of U.S. dollars   ●──● U.K.   ●──● France
  (proportional to bar graph above)   ●──● Germany ●──● Italy

INTRODUCTION

In 1939 Germany held a number of clear war-fighting advantages over its British, French, and Polish adversaries. Since this was a war of choice—a war that Adolf Hitler and the German high command had opted to fight rather than one they had thrust upon them—the Germans held the initiative at the start.[1] As in all German wars, the Reich sat in the "central position" in the midst of its enemies. Since Germany's adversaries were not about to take the offensive, the German armed forces could fight on one front at a time rather than both at once, at least for the time being. The armed forces had aggressive leadership at all levels, from the Führer on down to the platoon level, as well as young soldiers imbued with faith in their political leadership, however misguided and immoral we may find that leadership today. Compared with 1914, it was a rosy picture, especially thanks to the Nazi-Soviet Pact, which eliminated the possibility of a two-front war and recast the Soviet Union as an ally instead of an enemy.

Balancing those advantages, however, were a number of disadvantages. Germany was a Continental power, but Great Britain and France both possessed vast overseas empires, from which they could draw manpower and resources, and the ability to trade with neutral nations all over the world. Germany had no colonies, and once the war began, even its access to overseas commerce would be entirely cut by the Allied naval blockade. As one modern German historian has pointed out, what Germany really needed to beat Great Britain was a navy, but it hardly had one at all in 1939.[2] Consequently, even the relatively favorable strategic constellation of 1939 posed a difficult problem for Germany: although the country was hedging its bets by preparing for another long war, the Wehrmacht needed to win this war quickly. It needed to strike heavy blows against its opponents to bring them to the negotiating table early, or it would probably not win at all.

The Wehrmacht opened the conflict with a run of decisive victories that was unlike anything in living memory, overrunning first Poland, and then Denmark and Norway, and then Belgium, Holland, and France. With its highly mobile armored, or Panzer, formations operating as an insuperable spearhead, and with a powerful air force, or Luftwaffe, patrolling overhead, the German army ran over or around every defensive position thrown in its path for the first year of the war. These were quick campaigns with very low German casualties, and they gave the world a new word to add to its military vocabulary: *Blitzkrieg.*[3]

Purists might note that the Germans themselves hardly ever used this term, and they didn't use it at all in any precise doctrinal or theoretical sense. Moreover, Germany did not exactly have a Blitzkrieg army: it was composed mostly of straight-leg infantry divisions, and virtually all of its supplies were still brought forward on horse-drawn wagons. But the term "Blitzkrieg" itself is so omnipresent, so tightly fixed in our historical consciousness, that it hardly seems to matter. The dramatic German victories of 1939–40 shocked the world and ushered in a new era in military history: one of hard-hitting, rapid mechanized operations dominated by the omnipresent image of the tank. We are still living in the age of Blitzkrieg.

2

GERMAN YEAR OF VICTORY

ROBERT M. CITINO

30°W   15°W   0°   15°E   30°E   45°E   60°E

Narvik

NORWEGIAN SEA

ICELAND
REYKJAVÍK

Dec. 1939

FINLAND

NORWAY   SWEDEN

60°N

HELSINKI

Moscow

OSLO   STOCKHOLM

NORTH
SEA

TALLINN

ESTONIA

BALTIC
SEA

RIGA LATVIA

DENMARK COPENHAGEN

LITHUANIA

SOVIET
UNION

Apr. 1940

KAUNAS

IRELAND

NETHERLANDS
AMSTERDAM

BERLIN

Sep. 1939

Warsaw

UNITED KINGDOM

LONDON

GERMANY

Mechelen

Dunkirk BELGIUM
BRUSSELS   *May 1940*

Compiègne
PARIS   LUX. Luxembourg

PROTECTORATE OF
BOHEMIA AND MORAVIA

PRAGUE

SLOVAKIA

VIENNA

BUDAPEST

Jun. 1940

FRANCE   BERNE
SWITZERLAND

HUNGARY

ROMANIA

45°N

Vichy

BAY OF
BISCAY

*Vichy France established
July 1940*

BELGRADE

BUCHAREST

ITALY   YUGOSLAVIA

BULGARIA

SOFIA

PORTUGAL

MADRID

SPAIN

ROME

TIRANA

ALBANIA

GREECE

LISBON

ATHENS

MEDITERRANEAN

ITALY

ALGIERS   TUNIS

Mers-el-Kébir

SEA

30°N

TRIPOLI

0°   15°E

POLITICS	EUROPE	MEDITER-RANEAN

Nazi-Soviet Pact Signed — Aug. 23, 1939

Invasion of Poland — Sep. 1–Oct. 6
Britain and France Declare — Sep. 3
War on Germany

U.S.S.R. Invades Poland — Sep. 17

Germany and U.S.S.R. — Oct. 6
Divide and Annex Poland

Winter War — Nov. 30, 1939–Mar. 13, 1940
with Finland

Mechelen Incident — Jan. 10, 1940

Halder Issues New — Feb. 24
Orders for Case Yellow

Invasion of Scandinavia — Apr. 9–Jun. 10

Invasion of France — May 10–Jun. 25

Operation Dynamo, — May 27–Jun. 4
the Evacuation at Dunkirk

France Signs — Jun. 22
Armistice at Compiègne
Britain Destroys — Jul. 3
French Fleet at Mers-el-Kébir
Establishment of Vichy France — Jul. 10

JUL
AUG
SEP
OCT
NOV
DEC

1939

FEB
MAR
APR
MAY

1940

JUN
JUL
AUG

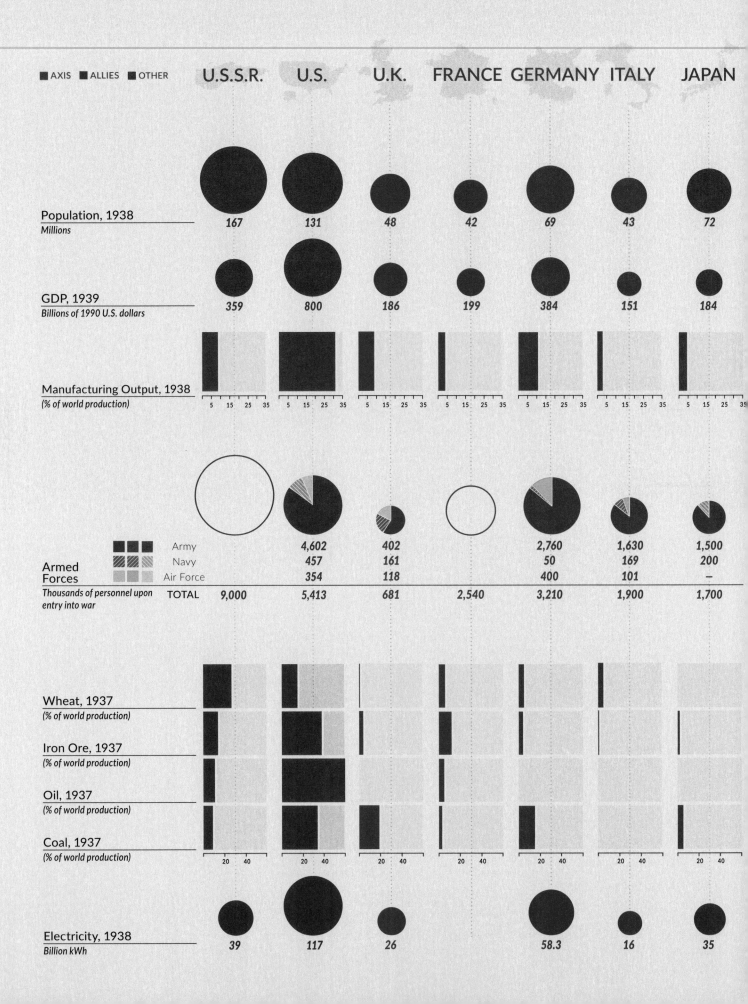

AXIS ALLIES OTHER

U.S.S.R. U.S. U.K. FRANCE GERMANY ITALY JAPAN

Population, 1938
Millions

U.S.S.R.	U.S.	U.K.	FRANCE	GERMANY	ITALY	JAPAN
167	131	48	42	69	43	72

GDP, 1939
Billions of 1990 U.S. dollars

U.S.S.R.	U.S.	U.K.	FRANCE	GERMANY	ITALY	JAPAN
359	800	186	199	384	151	184

Manufacturing Output, 1938
(% of world production)

Armed Forces

Army
Navy
Air Force

Thousands of personnel upon entry into war

	U.S.S.R.	U.S.	U.K.	FRANCE	GERMANY	ITALY	JAPAN
Army		4,602	402		2,760	1,630	1,500
Navy		457	161		50	169	200
Air Force		354	118		400	101	–
TOTAL	9,000	5,413	681	2,540	3,210	1,900	1,700

Wheat, 1937
(% of world production)

Iron Ore, 1937
(% of world production)

Oil, 1937
(% of world production)

Coal, 1937
(% of world production)

Electricity, 1938
Billion kWh

U.S.S.R.	U.S.	U.K.	FRANCE	GERMANY	ITALY	JAPAN
39	117	26		58.3	16	35

It is rare that one can trace the outbreak of a great conflict to one man. World War II in Europe, however, is inconceivable without Adolf Hitler.

Though born and raised in Austria-Hungary, he fled across the border to Germany when war broke out in 1914. Hitler served the entire war as a German enlisted soldier and was decorated twice for valor. The defeat of 1918 came as a shock to him and may have led to a short case of hysterical blindness. Like many returned German veterans, he had nothing but contempt for the comfortable verities of bourgeois life. He joined one of the dozens of small parties springing up in Germany and soon became its leader. The National Socialist German Workers' Party (NSDAP, or "Nazis") denounced democracy and Marxism as threats to Germany's existence, and linked both of them to Germany's small but influential Jewish community. Hitler's gift for public speaking, which featured theatrical gestures and a torrent of angry words, soon made him famous. The NSDAP rode economic troubles and popular discontent to power after the onset of the Great Depression in 1929. By 1932, it was the largest party in Germany by far.

After he became chancellor in January 1933, Hitler pursued an aggressive foreign policy designed to restore German power. He rearmed Germany in 1935, marched into the Rhineland in 1936, and forced the unification (*Anschluss*) with Austria in 1938. The Western powers seemed paralyzed. Their policy was appeasement: trying to meet Hitler's demands short of war. Not until 1939 did Britain and France draw a line in the sand by giving Poland a security guarantee. Hitler invaded Poland anyway, and general war broke out in September.

As a wartime commander in chief, Hitler presented a dual face. Certainly his intuition and interest in unconventional stratagems was effective in the 1940 campaign. His lack of interest in systematic planning, however, as well as his contempt for his military professionals, plagued the German war effort. His worst error was starting a war against a coalition with superior resources, a fact increasingly evident by 1942–43.

More than the war itself, Hitler may well be remembered for his attempted genocide of the Jews (the Holocaust), which killed at least six million people. No other historical crime has impacted the Western psyche as much as Hitler's. In that sense, he was the most infamous mass murderer of all time.

ADOLF HITLER
April 20, 1889–April 30, 1945

POLAND: THE OPENING ROUND

Case White, the code name for the invasion of Poland, would set the pattern for Germany's early victories.[4] The operational plan aimed to deliver an overwhelming blow from the outset, with air raids on Polish airfields in the opening minutes and massed Panzer assaults at multiple locations along the border. It also featured the typical German method of concentric operations: converging drives by widely separated forces; in this case, two individual army groups. The first, General Fedor von Bock's Army Group North, was split geographically between the Fourth Army in Pomerania and the Third Army in East Prussia, separated by a thin strip of Polish territory. The second, General Gerd von Rundstedt's Army Group South, included the Eighth and Tenth Armies in Silesia, and the Fourteenth Army spread between Silesia and occupied Slovakia. In its simplest terms, the plan called for the two army groups to smash through the Polish defensive positions along the border and catch the main body of

◄ THE BELLIGERENTS IN 1940

In the underlying sources of national strength, Germany and Italy had a clear though not immense advantage over Britain and France. The latter two, however, could hope to redress the balance by drawing on the huge resources of the United States—a neutral power, but friendly to them.

the Polish forces in a great pincer movement, with the main weight of the attack borne by Army Group South.

Facing the mass of the German army, the Poles had few good deployment options. The supreme commander of the Polish army, General Eduard Rydz-Smigly, chose a linear defense of the entire national border rather than adopting a defense in depth, in which most of his forces would concentrate well back from the frontier, ready to counterattack after the lines of the German offensive became clear. The latter strategy might have involved drawing his forces into a tight ring around the capital, Warsaw, or establishing a defensive position along the Narew, Vistula, and San Rivers in the East. Instead, Rydz-Smigly placed a thin crust of defenders spread out along the entire

GERMAN PLANS FOR THE INVASION OF POLAND, AUGUST 31, 1939 ▶

The two German pincers closing on Warsaw from north and south were intended to cut off and trap the Polish Pomorze and Poznań Armies in a giant "cauldron battle" (*Kesselschlacht*): an operational-level double envelopment.

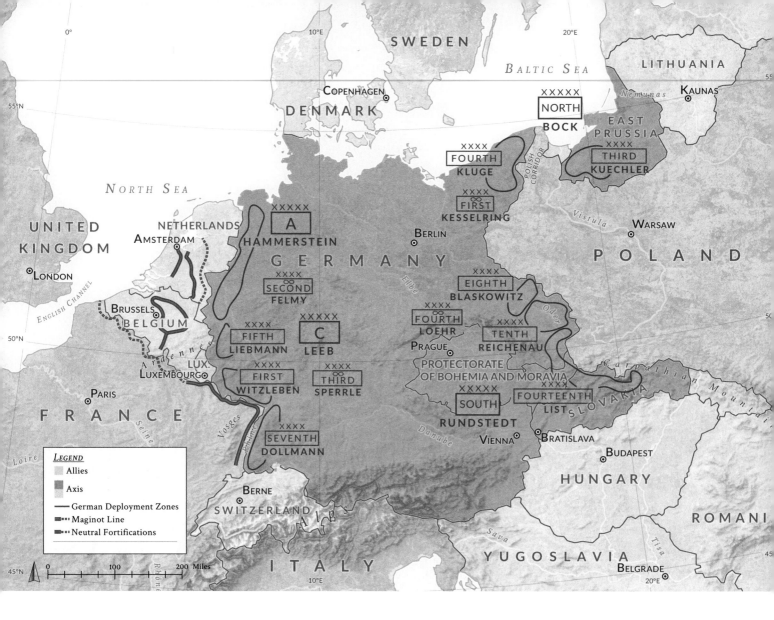

DEPLOYMENT AND ▲ ORGANIZATION OF THE WEHRMACHT, SEPTEMBER 1, 1939

Germany's central position faced Hitler with the risk of a two-front war. But it also gave the Wehrmacht the opportunity to operate on interior lines: holding one foe at bay with relatively small forces while concentrating the maximum strength to knock out the other.

870-mile-long border, with very few operational reserves. Indeed, so committed to defense of the national territory was he that he even stationed large forces in the district of Poznań, an extensive salient, or bulge, jutting west into German-held territory.

Analysts then and now have pointed out problems with the Polish deployment at the outset of the conflict, but such criticism is unfair. No government is ever likely to adopt a strategy that abandons a major portion of the national territory before a shot has even been fired. The Polish Army's "cordon defense" did indeed run the risk of penetration and exploitation at one or more points, but a strategy of making a stand around Warsaw or along the river lines in the East would have surrendered most of the country and turned Polish forces into a massed target for the superior German Luftwaffe.[5] Given the geographical situation, with the Germans poised to the south, west, and north, and the Soviets to the east, no Polish deployment was going to be ideal.

ORDER OF BATTLE FOR THE INVASION OF POLAND, SEPTEMBER 1, 1939 ▶

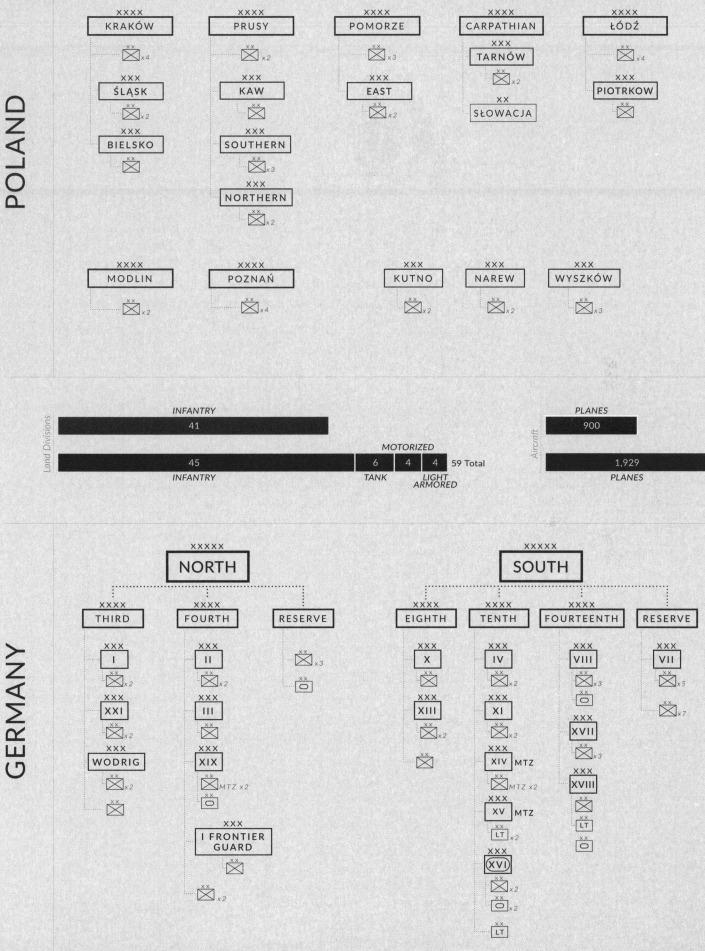

POLAND

KRAKÓW xxxx — ⊠ x4
ŚLĄSK xxx — ⊠ x2
BIELSKO xxx — ⊠

PRUSY xxxx — ⊠ x2
KAW xxx — ⊠
SOUTHERN xxx — ⊠ x3
NORTHERN xxx — ⊠ x2

POMORZE xxxx — ⊠ x3
EAST xxx — ⊠ x2

CARPATHIAN xxxx
TARNÓW xxx — ⊠ x2
SŁOWACJA xx

ŁÓDŹ xxxx — ⊠ x4
PIOTRKOW xxx — ⊠

MODLIN xxxx — ⊠ x2
POZNAŃ xxxx — ⊠ x4
KUTNO xxx — ⊠ x2
NAREW xxx — ⊠ x2
WYSZKÓW xxx — ⊠ x3

Land Divisions

INFANTRY			
41			

INFANTRY	TANK		LIGHT ARMORED
45	6	4	4 — 59 Total
	MOTORIZED		

Aircraft

| PLANES | 900 |
| PLANES | 1,929 |

GERMANY

NORTH (xxxxx)

THIRD xxxx
- **I** xxx — ⊠ x2
- **XXI** xxx — ⊠ x2
- **WODRIG** xxx — ⊠ x2 — ⊠

FOURTH xxxx
- **II** xxx — ⊠ x2
- **III** xxx — ⊠
- **XIX** xxx — ⊠ MTZ x2 — ○
- **I FRONTIER GUARD** xxx — ⊠ — ⊠ x2

RESERVE xxxx — ⊠ x3 — ○

SOUTH (xxxxx)

EIGHTH xxxx
- **X** xxx — ⊠
- **XIII** xxx — ⊠ x2 — ⊠

TENTH xxxx
- **IV** xxx — ⊠ x2
- **XI** xxx — ⊠ x2
- **XIV** MTZ xxx — ⊠ MTZ x2
- **XV** MTZ xxx — LT x2
- **XVI** xxx — ⊠ x2 — ○ x2 — LT

FOURTEENTH xxxx
- **VIII** xxx — ⊠ x3 — ○
- **XVII** xxx — ⊠ x3
- **XVIII** xxx — ⊠ — LT — ○

RESERVE xxxx
- **VII** xxx — ⊠ x5 — ⊠ x7

Gerd von Rundstedt was a German field marshal during World War II. His career is unique for the sheer number of major operations he conducted, if not for any particular military brilliance.

Rundstedt was a General Staff officer during World War I, and he remained in the German Army after 1918, commanding the 2nd Cavalry Division and then the 3rd Infantry Division. In World War II, he was in charge of major formations. He commanded Army Group South during the Polish campaign, Army Group A in the French campaign (in which he oversaw the great Panzer drive through the Ardennes Forest), and Army Group South in Operation Barbarossa. He was a sound military administrator who trusted his subordinates but never got carried away by any of them.

As for so many German officers, however, Barbarossa was his undoing. Tasked with conquering the Ukraine, Rundstedt faced large Soviet forces in prepared positions between the Pripet Marshes and the Carpathian Mountains, broke in late, and lagged behind Army Group Center. Though the great German encirclement at Kiev, which destroyed a vast Soviet force in the Ukraine in September 1941, brightened the picture momentarily, the field marshal ran into increasing Soviet opposition as he headed east. In November a massive Soviet counterattack near Rostov struck his extended columns, and he ordered a withdrawal. Hitler sacked him, and he was the first casualty of what became a purge of the German generals.

Rundstedt returned in 1944 as the supreme commander in the West. In that role, he argued with Field Marshal Erwin Rommel about the correct placement of the armored reserve against the Allied invasion of Europe in June, and he argued with Hitler about the feasibility of the Ardennes offensive in December. When that last German offensive, commonly known as the Battle of the Bulge, failed in March 1945, Hitler removed him from command.

Rundstedt has a fairly good reputation today as the "last Prussian"—an essentially honorable man. He did serve on the courts of honor that executed officers who had taken part in the July 1944 plot to kill Hitler. The trials were travesties, the accused without representation and the evidence supplied solely by the secret police (Gestapo). Rundstedt sincerely detested the Nazis, but his career demonstrated that service to the regime inevitably led to moral compromise.

Another hallmark of the German tradition—independent-minded and highly aggressive field commanders who liked to run things as they saw fit, without a great deal of central control—also influenced the planning process. From the start, General Bock had registered unhappiness with what he saw as a subsidiary role. His army group was split into two separate zones by the Polish Corridor, the narrow strip of land that had been given to the Poles by the Treaty of Versailles so that their country would have access to the sea. Bock's first task, therefore, would be to overrun the Corridor and establish overland communications between his two armies. Only then could he take part in the major operation: the drive into Poland proper and the destruction of the Polish Army. There were no such operational distractions in the South, which was why the original plan called for Rundstedt's Army Group South to be the operation's point of main effort, or *Schwerpunkt*.

Bock deemed his secondary role insulting, and had spent the summer peppering the high command of the army (Oberkommando des Heeres, or OKH) with plans to expand it.[6] After overrunning the Corridor, he wanted to ship his entire Fourth Army from Pomerania and across East Prussia, inserting it on the left of Third Army and sending it on a wide sweep to the east of Warsaw. If Polish forces tried to regroup in the interior of the country, he would then be in position to encircle them east of the capital. The chief of the OKH, General Walther von Brauchitsch, took a dim view of

In Army Group North's sector, Fourth Army, aided by XXI Corps, quickly seized control of the Polish Corridor. Third Army's other two corps pushed Modlin Army back toward the defensive line that shielded Warsaw from the north.

On September 10, Tenth Army's rapid drive toward Warsaw halted temporarily so that its armored units could swing west to help Eighth Army defeat the Poznań Army's counterattack on the Bzura. Meanwhile the "outer jaws" of the German invasion—Fourteenth Army in the south and a redeployed Fourth Army in the north—headed toward Lvov and Brest.

Poznań Army, with German forces threatening its rear from both north and south, hastily retreated behind the Warthe River.

Spearheaded by Hoepner's XVI Panzer Corps, Tenth Army punched through Polish defenses and crossed the Warthe River, making it impossible for Łódź Army to stabilize a defensive line.

LEGEND
Sep. 6–14
Sep. 1–5

0   50   100 Miles

▲ THE GERMAN INVASION OF POLAND, SEPTEMBER 1–14, 1939

The German operational design aimed at trapping and destroying as many Polish divisions as possible, rather than merely pushing them back toward Warsaw.

Ju87 "Stuka" Dive Bombers ▲
Once German fighter planes had attained air superiority over Poland, ground-attack aircraft, such as the Ju87 "Stuka" dive bomber (pictured here in 1943), were free to support German ground operations.

such a major redeployment in the midst of the fighting. He warned Bock that committing troops too far to the east of Warsaw could have serious repercussions in case of an attack by France and Britain in the west.[7] Eventually, however, he acquiesced, allowing Bock's army group full freedom of action.[8]

The campaign went as well as the Germans could have hoped. Army Group North crossed the border before dawn on September 1. There was some hard fighting here and there, but by the end of the day, the Germans had sealed off the southern end of the Corridor, trapping two Polish infantry divisions and a cavalry brigade. Polish attempts to break out came to naught, as German forces smashed all three formations in the course of the fighting and took 15,000 prisoners by day three.[9] The next day, the Fourth and Third Armies linked up to the east of the Corridor.

In the south, Rundstedt was swinging a far heavier bat: the mass of the German Army. It is always easy to detect the main effort of German operations in World War II: simply count the Panzer divisions. Army Group South contained four of the six divisions then in existence, along with three of the four "light divisions": mainly

Hans von Luck was a professional officer who had served as a lieutenant in the peacetime army under Guderian and Rommel. He led an armored reconnaissance company during the Polish campaign. This passage from the memoir he wrote late in life describes his experiences on the first day of World War II:

Where were the Polish troops?

We still had the feeling of being on maneuvers although we were 15 kilometers inside Poland. Vigilant reconnaissance patrols on motorcycles with sidecars tried to make headway through the thickly wooded terrain, to spy out the land. I had the armored cars follow and continued the advance.

Late on the evening of 1 September we came up against our first opposition. In front of us lay an open, rising tract of land, at the end of which was a village and a forest. Here the Poles had set up a line of resistance on a hill, and opened a heavy fire from machine guns and mortars. Shell splinters hissed through the trees. Branches broke off and fell on our heads. Our stomachs now felt distinctly uneasy. We had often practiced under combat conditions, of course, and had been able thereby to get used to the firing and the landing of artillery shells, as well as the sharp hammering of machine guns. But that had always been at a safe distance or from bunkers under cover.

Now we were directly exposed to enemy fire. We could find no cover, nor could we dig ourselves in, since we were supposed to attack. We formed up for the assault. Armored scout cars moved forward, as far and as well as the terrain allowed, so as to give us covering fire from the MG24s [machine guns].

Suddenly a round of machine-gun fire hit Private Uhl, not far from me. He was dead at once. He was the first casualty in my company, and many of my men saw it. Now we were all afraid. Which of us would be the next? This was no longer a maneuver; it was war.

"No. 1 and No. 2 platoons attack," I shouted. "No. 3 platoon in reserve, the heavy platoon to give fire-cover."

No one stirred. Everyone was afraid of being the next to die. Including me. Anyone who says he was never afraid in his first engagement is a liar.

It was up to me, the CO, to set the example. "Everyone follow me," I shouted, and rushed forward with my machine-pistol.

The training prevailed, and they all followed.[11]

---

mechanized infantry with a small number of tanks, intended for traditional cavalry duties such as flank security and reconnaissance.[10] Altogether, Rundstedt had three armies assembled at the Polish border: from left to right, the Eighth, Tenth, and Fourteenth. It was their task to destroy the mass of the Polish Army by a direct thrust northeast toward Warsaw. The Tenth Army in the center would form the spearhead, with no fewer than six mobile formations: two Panzer divisions, two light divisions, and two motorized infantry divisions, with most of the soldiers riding trucks. It was, by 1939 standards, an immense concentration of force.

It should not be surprising, then, that Rundstedt broke through almost everywhere. On the left, Eighth Army reached the Prosna River on the second day of operations, slashing through the defenses of the Polish Łódź Army. This was largely the work of well-drilled infantry; Eighth Army had no Panzer elements outside of the few tanks of the SS Leibstandarte Adolf Hitler (the Führer's personal SS bodyguard), at the time a motorized infantry regiment. On the right, the Fourteenth Army, including XXII Motorized Corps, broke into Poland from the Jablunka Pass in the west to Novy Targ in the east. However, it was the center of the army group that made the most progress. Here the Tenth Army blasted through the seam between the Łódź Army on its left and the Kraków Army on its right, reaching the Warthe River and crossing it in stride. The drive across the Warthe gave the Poles their first look at the full German mechanized

GERMAN BOMBER ▲
OVER POLAND

The close coordination of air and ground assets was essential to the Blitzkrieg. Here the nose gunner (who also served as navigator and bombardier) of an He111 bomber looks down on a Polish town. His aircraft has just accomplished its mission of destroying a bridge, thus hindering the efforts of the Polish ground forces to react to the German Army's invasion.

package: tank columns motoring at speed until they hit a roadblock, and then veering off road and bypassing the defenders on both flanks; heavy air attacks by Stuka dive-bombers, their screeching sirens adding a note of terror to the bombing run; and rapid advances by tank columns deep into the rear that suddenly materialized into blocking positions when the Poles tried to retreat.[12]

In concert with Fourteenth Army to its right, the advance of Tenth Army also had the benefit of working concentrically against the Kraków Army, which was tucked into the southwestern corner of Poland. Soon its remnants were attempting to re-treat into the interior, a task that in many places meant running a gauntlet of German armor that had already established itself behind its position. By September 6, Kraków itself had fallen to the invaders. The collapse of the Kraków Army in the south and the Pomorze (Pomeranian) Army on the far right side of the Corridor in the north meant disaster in turn for the two Polish armies between them: the Łódź Army, already hard pressed by the Eighth Army's attacks; and the Poznań Army, deployed deep in the sec-tion of the Polish border bulging out toward Germany. Facing only German border de-fense units, the latter was at the moment still largely untouched by enemy action, but it was already doomed: it was one hundred miles from the relative safety of Warsaw, with two complete German army groups now closing in on its only possible route of retreat.

On September 1, 1939, the German Army marched into Poland, leading to declarations of war by Great Britain and France, and starting the Second World War in Europe.

By week two, the Germans were in full throttle all across the front. The armored spearheads of the Tenth Army slashed across the southern Polish plain toward the capital, and the first German Panzer forces reached the outskirts of Warsaw by September 8. In the course of its headlong rush, the Tenth Army actually overran the Polish Prusy Army while it was still in the process of assembling. Polish troop trains arrived at the front to disgorge their occupants straight into Luftwaffe bombing runs, artillery bombardment, and tank attacks. Everywhere, the Poles suffered horrendous casualties. The few defending formations with an open retreat path to Warsaw were desperately trying to get there, but they were gradually coming apart under an unrelenting air attack. Polish command and control had broken down, and the only army still functioning as such was the isolated Poznań Army.

In fact, it was Poznań Army's belated attempt to retreat that would bring about the climax of the campaign. As it tried desperately to slither out of the jaws clamping down on it from both right and left, it contacted the northern (left) flank guard of the advancing German Eighth Army along the Bzura River west of Warsaw on September 9.[13] The 14th, 17th, and 25th Infantry Divisions, along with the Podolska and Wielkopolska Cavalry Brigades, hit the overextended German 24th and 30th Infantry Divisions strung out along the river. It was half counterattack, half formless melee: the Poles were in the midst of a hurried retreat, after all. Still, the initial thrust managed to achieve surprise and made good progress at first, capturing some 1,500 German prisoners from the panic-stricken 30th Division alone.

It certainly caused heartburn at German headquarters, but it was only a fleeting turn of events. The Poznań Army was trying to break out, but to where? It was isolated,

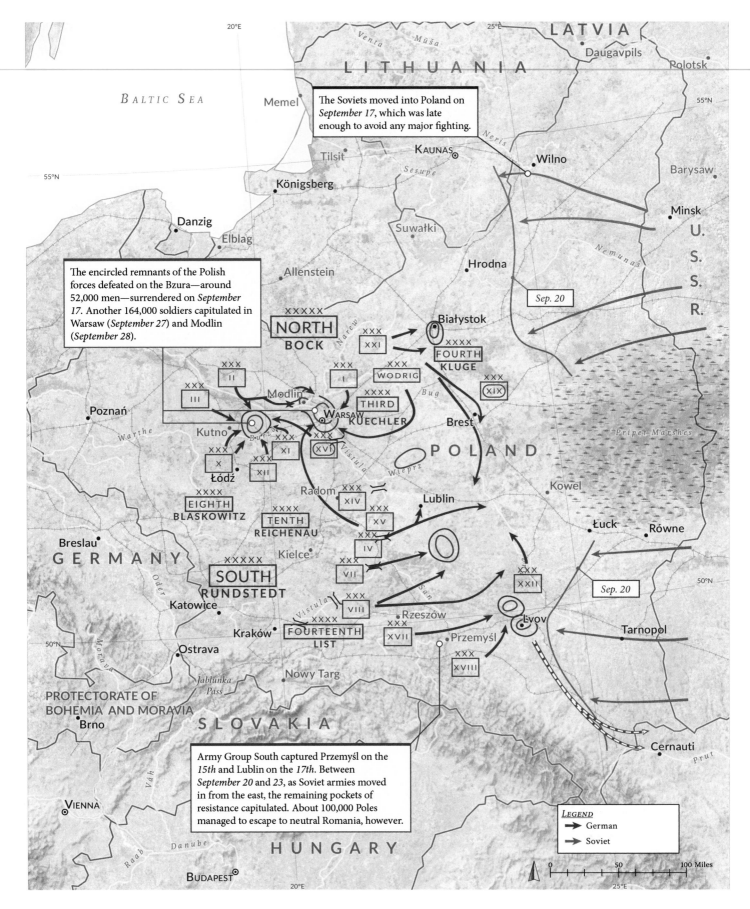

The Soviets moved into Poland on *September 17*, which was late enough to avoid any major fighting.

The encircled remnants of the Polish forces defeated on the Bzura—around 52,000 men—surrendered on *September 17*. Another 164,000 soldiers capitulated in Warsaw (*September 27*) and Modlin (*September 28*).

Army Group South captured Przemyśl on the *15th* and Lublin on the *17th*. Between *September 20* and *23*, as Soviet armies moved in from the east, the remaining pockets of resistance capitulated. About 100,000 Poles managed to escape to neutral Romania, however.

LEGEND
→ German
→ Soviet

0   50   100 Miles

▲ THE INVASIONS OF POLAND, SEPTEMBER 15–22, 1939

On September 17, 1939, Soviet forces invaded from the east. By month's end, all Polish resistance had ended.

German doctrine emphasized rapid maneuver leading to knockout victories long before the Panzer divisions were developed. Foot soldiers and horse-drawn artillery could not move as fast as tanks, but they did sustain remarkably high rates of movement.

without any hope of support or reinforcement from forces in the rest of the country. Within a day, German reinforcements were on the way to the Bzura, including the mass of the Tenth Army's armored units. Summoned away from the drive on Warsaw, they shifted their axis of advance 180 degrees in effortless fashion. Faced with concentric attacks from all four points of the compass, the mass of the Polish attackers was soon hemmed into a shrinking pocket on the Bzura, along with remnants of the Pomorze Army that had managed to escape the blows of Army Group North. They were in a hopeless operational situation, subjected to nonstop attack by the Luftwaffe and punished heavily by the German artillery. Over 100,000 men would surrender. At this point, the Tenth Army's armored divisions turned back around, shifting their axis of advance 180 degrees for the second time in a week, and hurried back toward Warsaw.[14] By September 19, the capital city was the only spot on the map still in Polish hands, and the Germans, in fact, would speak of an "Eighteen Days' Campaign."[15]

The final blow to Poland came from the east, when Soviet forces invaded Poland on September 17. Two Soviet army groups crossed the border against minimal opposition and overran the eastern half of the country with little fighting. As the spearheads of the two invading forces met, what was left of the Polish Army dissolved, although some 100,000 ragged survivors did manage to escape to neutral Romania.

The Germans had won this campaign in its opening days. By the end of week one, five out of the seven Polish armies in the initial order of battle had been mauled (Łódź,

Modlin), completely encircled (Poznań, Kraków), or both (Pomorze). As Army Group South and Army Group North drove in toward Warsaw, their concentric advance caught most of the Polish Army in a giant battle of encirclement—what Germans call the *Kesselschlacht* ("cauldron battle"). The Poles lost 65,000 men killed in action, along with 144,000 wounded, while German losses were just 11,000 and 30,000, respectively. The prisoner of war totals really tell the tale, however: the Germans captured the incredible figure of 587,000, with another 200,000 falling into Soviet hands.[16] Surrounded and under constant bombardment from the air, Warsaw fell on September 27. Refusing to negotiate or capitulate to Germany, the Polish government had already fled the country, first to Romania and eventually to Great Britain.

While the Polish campaign had proven once and for all that large-scale operations with mechanized forces were possible, there were the inevitable foul-ups, friendly fire incidents, and missed opportunities. The commander of the XIX Motorized Corps, General Heinz Guderian, was nearly killed in a German bombing raid early on, and air-ground cooperation had its share of problems throughout. The first German attempt to break into Warsaw, by the 4th Panzer Division on September 8, failed, with Polish antitank guns and artillery taking a heavy toll of German tanks in the streets of the suburbs. Finally, the Germans had ended the campaign with their logistics in disarray and their ground formations in serious need of new equipment and repairs after only a month of operations. It could well have been a cause for concern if events had forced the campaign to continue.

To their credit, German commanders recognized all these problems, and spent the winter of 1939–40 studying things that had gone wrong and attempting to rectify them.

While the Panzer divisions and the mass of the active army had fought well, the same could not be said of newly mobilized reserve divisions. They lacked march endurance, maneuvered clumsily, and often went to ground at the first sign of Polish fire. To remedy these deficiencies, they received particularly intensive training in the course of the winter, including a comprehensive program of war games, exercises, and open-field maneuvers. Another issue was that the light divisions had proven too heavy to function as nimble flank guards in the style of cavalry, and too light to stand up to sustained combat, so they were transformed into full-fledged Panzer divisions. Likewise, the Luftwaffe undertook a complete overhaul of its communications with the ground forces, placing greater emphasis on radio to reduce friendly fire losses.

Even as they rectified these problems, however, the German General Staff could also be satisfied that a great deal more had gone right in the course of the fighting. In contrast to virtually every campaign since the days of Napoléon I, German momentum did not flag but increased as the first week of the campaign passed. The Germans managed to pry open small tactical breaches in the Polish defenses in the first few days. With tanks and aircraft, infantry and artillery all cooperating efficiently, those tactical breaches soon widened into operational ones, large enough for entire divisions to pass through in narrow column formations. Thus, we see Army Group South taking four days to reduce the border defenses and then lunging 150 miles clear across central Poland in four more. Factors that had stalled offensives in previous wars—fortifications such as the ones at Modlin northwest of Warsaw—were now simply smothered by air

Many French soldiers were frustrated by their inability to take greater advantage of the respite offered by the phony war, as evidenced by this entry from the wartime diary of Captain D. Barlone, then serving in the 2nd North African Division.

> 5 February 1940. All our available vehicles are placed at the service of the Engineers, who are building a series of block-houses along the Belgian frontier. They are sited along an antitank ditch which, in its turn, is protected by a net-work of barbed wire and mine-fields right up to the very edge of this antitank ditch. Some of these fortifications have been constructed by civilian contractors who employ Italians, Belgians, Czechs. Furthermore, country-folk, inquisitive folk, and spies wander about continuously. No one makes any attempt to preserve any secrecy about our defences. The antitank ditches, whose earth sides are retained merely by light wattles, appear very unpretentious. A quarter of an hour's bombardment and the earth would crumble away and leave free passage, I fear, to any armoured vehicle, but they are a sufficient guarantee against a surprise attack . . . The most surprising thing is that when the main works are complete, they are neither armed nor guarded. Any one is free to enter, to sabotage anything and everything. When I diffidently make a remark to this effect to Captain Perrier of the General Staff, [he answers] me confidentially, "What are we to arm them with?"[18]

attack. The Stuka dive-bombers proved especially effective throughout the campaign. Massed into a "Close Battle Division" of 160 aircraft, they destroyed the Modlin position, cracking what would have been a tough nut indeed for ground forces alone.[17] Popular imagination throughout the world still viewed grinding battles of attrition like those of 1916–17 as the norm in warfare. Poland's defeat was no surprise, but the rapidity and completeness of the German victory were a shock: they seemed to herald a new era of warfare, and to demand a new word to describe it. From this point forward, the term "Blitzkrieg" was universally understood to mean the use of hard-driving armored spearheads in combination with unrelenting bombing from the air to knock out enemy resistance in a single decisive campaign.

PHONY WAR TO REAL WAR: THE INVASION OF SCANDINAVIA

Modern observers often puzzle over what happened after the fall of Poland: months of inaction on all fronts that extended into 1940. Americans called this period the "phony war," and the Germans, too, had a playful name for it, the *Sitzkrieg* ("Sit-down war," a play on "Blitzkrieg"). In fact, there was nothing particularly puzzling about it. The German high command was wrestling with what to do next, as it would repeatedly in this war. Hitler wanted an immediate attack in the West, but most of his generals were aghast at that prospect. Beating Poland was one thing; fighting Great Powers like France and Britain was guaranteed to be more difficult. For their part, the British and French were wedded to a strategy of 1914—slowly smothering the economy of the Reich—though it would now be executed by strategic bombing as well as naval blockade. It was a strategy designed to avoid risky offensives, and explains why there was no attack on the Western Front to support Poland.

Tromsø

XX
6
3,000
Narvik

Bodø

2 Battle Cruisers
10 Destroyers

NORWEGIAN SEA

2,000

1 Heavy Cruiser
4 Destroyers

ATLANTIC OCEAN

1,700

Luleå

GULF OF BOTHNIA

N O R W A Y

S W E D E N

F I N L A N D

Kemi

Trondheim
XX
5
4,000

60°N

2 Light Cruisers
Auxiliaries

XX
4
1,500

Lillehammer

XX
2
3,500

1st Norwegian Division retreated
across the border and was interned
in Sweden, *April 15.*

HELSINK

1,900
Bergen

XX
1
3,000

3rd Norwegian Division
surrendered *April 15.*

OSLO
Fornebu
Fort Oscarborg

3,000

TALLIN

ES

On *April 14,* German forces moved out of
Oslo to seize control of surrounding areas
and establish communications with the units
that had landed on the Norwegian coast.

Sola
Stavanger

XX
3
2,000

2,500

Kristiansand

2,000

RIG

*B A L T I C
S E A*

1 Pocket Battleship
1 Heavy Cruiser
1 Light Cruiser

LATVI

*UNITED
KINGDOM*

Edinburgh

1,100

NORTH SEA

Ålborg

COPENHAGEN

D E N M A R K

LITHUAN

KAU

2 Light Cruisers
Auxiliaries

Kiel
Travemünde
Lübeck

Rostock
Swinemünde

*ENGLISH
CHANNEL*

AMSTERDAM
NETHERLANDS

Elbe

Berlin

Oder

Vistula

50°N

LONDON

BRUSSELS
BELGIUM

G E R M A N Y

GENERAL

Rhine

F R A N C E

LUX.
LUXEMBOURG

PARIS

PRAGUE

PROTECTORATE OF

LEGEND
→ April 14–15
→ April 9–13

0   100

10°E

The German surprise attack on neutral Norway was extremely effective, but the Norwegians did not surrender without fighting back.

And so the two sides sat through the fall of 1939, through the New Year, and well into the spring. It was not until April that the phony war came to an end, as the Wehrmacht invaded Denmark and Norway. The purpose of this attack was twofold: Germany needed to secure its principal supply of iron ore, mined at Kiruna in neutral Sweden, transported by rail to the Norwegian port of Narvik, then shipped down the Norwegian coast to Germany. The commander of the German Navy, Admiral Erich Raeder, also saw the Norwegian coast, with its thousands of protected inlets and fjords, as a useful base for U-boat operations against Britain. The British, too, were casting their gaze at Norway, and, indeed, in late March, the first lord of the Admiralty, Winston Churchill, actually ordered plans drawn up to mine Norwegian waters and perhaps even to dispatch an occupation force to Norway, to prevent it from falling into Nazi hands.

As happened so often this early in the war, the Wehrmacht beat its enemies to the

SCANDINAVIA

◀ Blitzkrieg to the North, April 9–15, 1940

Exercise Weser (*Weserübung*) was a complex invasion of Denmark and Norway, encompassing multiple, coordinated attacks by German air, land, and naval forces beginning on April 9, 1940.

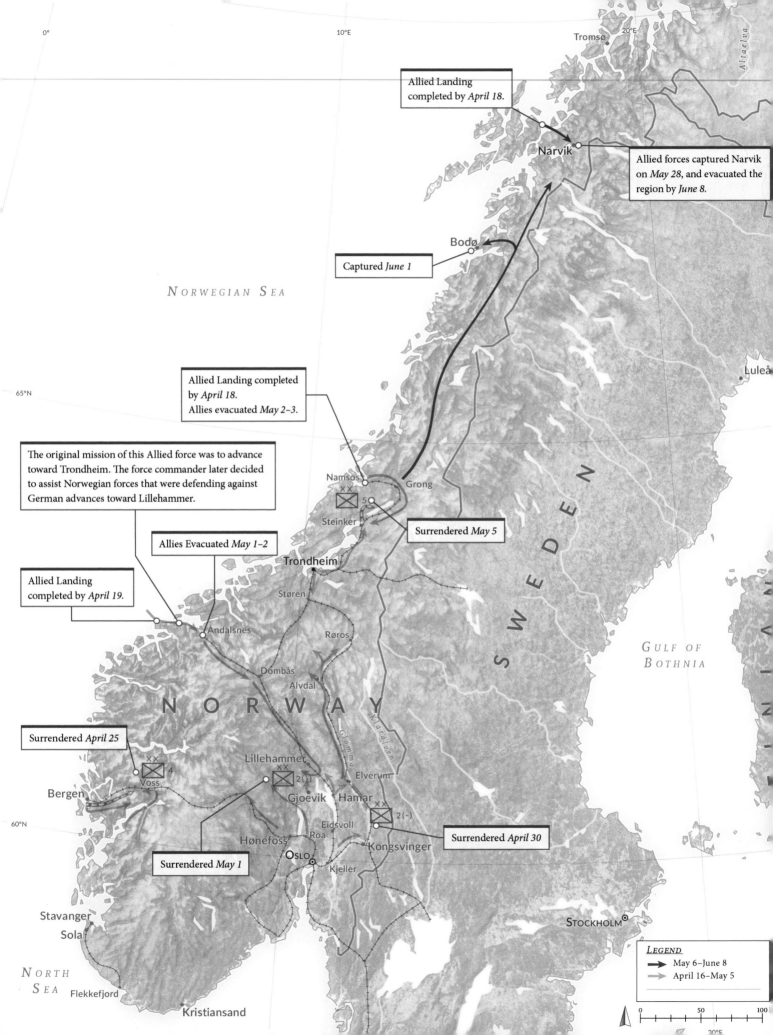

Allied Landing completed by *April 18.*

Allied forces captured Narvik on *May 28*, and evacuated the region by *June 8.*

Captured *June 1*

N O R W E G I A N   S E A

Allied Landing completed by *April 18.*
Allies evacuated *May 2–3.*

The original mission of this Allied force was to advance toward Trondheim. The force commander later decided to assist Norwegian forces that were defending against German advances toward Lillehammer.

Allies Evacuated *May 1–2*

Surrendered *May 5*

Allied Landing completed by *April 19.*

Surrendered *April 25*

Surrendered *April 30*

Surrendered *May 1*

S W E D E N

N O R W A Y

G U L F   O F   B O T H N I A

Tromsø

Narvik

Bodø

Grong

Namsos

Steinker

Trondheim

Støren

Røros

Andalsnes

Dombås

Alvdal

Elverum

Lillehammer

Gjoevik

Hamar

Voss

Bergen

Hønefoss

Roa

Eidsvoll

Kongsvinger

OSLO

Kjeller

Stavanger

Sola

Flekkefjord

Kristiansand

STOCKHOLM

Luleå

LEGEND
→ May 6–June 8
→ April 16–May 5

0   50   100

N O R T H
S E A

punch. On April 9, 1940, the Germans carried out *Weserübung*, or "Exercise Weser," which was code-named after the Weser River in Germany.[19] It was one of the most complex undertakings in military history up to that point. Well-coordinated landings struck Denmark on the first morning, including the first combat paratroop landing in military history.[20] It was a small group, just ninety men, whose mission was to secure the long bridge linking the Gedser ferry terminal to the Danish capital, Copenhagen. A perfect landing led to a bloodless capture of the bridge's small garrison. Meanwhile, other air landings took place at Aalborg, in the far north of the Jutland Peninsula, to capture the airfield there. Simultaneous naval landings along the Danish coast secured Esbjerg, Thyboron, Middelfart, Nyborg, and Gedser against light resistance. Finally, a land drive, conducted by two motorized brigades and an infantry division, swept up the Jutland Peninsula and by the end of the day had covered its entire length, linking up with the paratroopers and securing the whole country.[21] Five naval landings, two airborne drops, and a vigorous drive by land, characterized by tight coordination and split-second timing—even the lack of serious opposition by the Danes does not make this operation any less impressive. Most of the fighting was over by lunchtime: "The plan worked out in action like a precision watch," a German analysis concluded.[22]

The Germans had a harder time in the much larger Norway. That same morning saw five simultaneous seaborne landings, at Narvik, Trondheim, Bergen, Kristiansand-Arendal, and Egersund; a paratroop landing to seize the air base at Sola; and a combined air-sea landing at Oslo. German troops in the first wave numbered fewer than 9,000 men, but they made up for their small numbers by appearing seemingly everywhere all at once.[23] Since the dispersed nature of the landings placed a premium on rapidity and precision, warships rather than slower transport ships carried the first wave. As some of these ships could not carry sufficient fuel to reach their destinations, the navy pre-positioned tankers, disguised as merchant ships, at strategic points along the route. Likewise, an "export group," consisting again of disguised merchant vessels, was placed in various Norwegian ports before the invasion, carrying vital equipment and supplies for the landing forces.[24]

The landings were not without incident. A Norwegian plane spotted the German naval group coming into Kristiansand. Led by the cruiser *Karlsruhe*, the German group's mission was to dispatch a battalion in patrol boats to the shore to capture the two island forts guarding the entrance into Kristiansand Fjord. With the Norwegians now on alert, that became impossible. The commander of the *Karlsruhe*, in a pattern that would come to characterize this campaign, had to call in the Luftwaffe. A force of seven Heinkel medium bombers arrived, and when they were unable to get the job done, a larger force of sixteen managed to silence the guns on both forts, blowing one of the Norwegian ammunition dumps sky-high.[25]

There was also one genuine disaster for the Germans on that first day: the loss

◀ OPERATIONS IN NORWAY, APRIL 16–JUNE 8, 1940

After capturing Oslo and numerous points along the Norwegian coast, German forces advanced to secure the rest of the country. At about the same time, British and French troops began arriving by sea to help resist the invasion. Allied forces recaptured Narvik briefly in early June. But shortly thereafter, German successes in southern Norway and in France prompted British and French troops to evacuate.

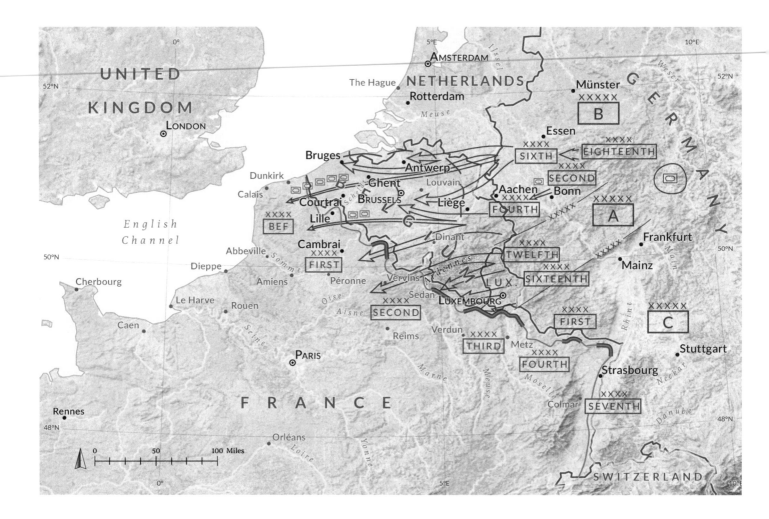

An early version of the OKH plan for the invasion of France looked rather like a replay of the 1914 Schlieffen Plan, with a strong German right wing overrunning Belgium while the center and left held their positions.

of the heavy cruiser *Blücher*.[26] Sailing into Oslo Fjord at a reckless twenty-five knots (twenty-nine miles per hour), with Nazi Party and Gestapo officials gathered on the fantail as a band played, the ship came under shell fire and torpedo fire from the Norwegian fortresses guarding the Dröbak Narrows. There were multiple torpedo hits on its hull, and then a gigantic explosion. *Blücher* rolled over and sank, with the loss of a thousand men. The *Blücher* was to have provided fire support for the drive on Oslo. German paratroopers heading toward Fornebu airfield near Oslo had to turn back, and it seemed that the crucial assault on the capital was in serious trouble. A second wave, of German transports intending to land at Fornebu airfield once the paratroopers had secured it, was also ordered back—but the commander of the transport wing landed at the unsecured airfield anyway. There was minimal resistance, since the Norwegian defenders had already retreated. The happiest men at Fornebu were the pilots of a flight of Me 110s who were nearly out of fuel and who were supposed to land at the airfield once it had been secured by airborne forces. They had watched the entire strange affair with amazement—one eye, no doubt, on their increasingly frightening fuel gauges.[27] Enough troops were able to land at Fornebu that by the evening of April 9, the German invaders had secured Oslo, along with all their other objectives. Luftwaffe units now staged forward, and were operating from Norwegian bases by the end of the day.

Norway was not secure yet, however. From Oslo, the Germans had to launch a land drive to relieve the posts they had occupied on Norway's west coast.[28] Norwegian

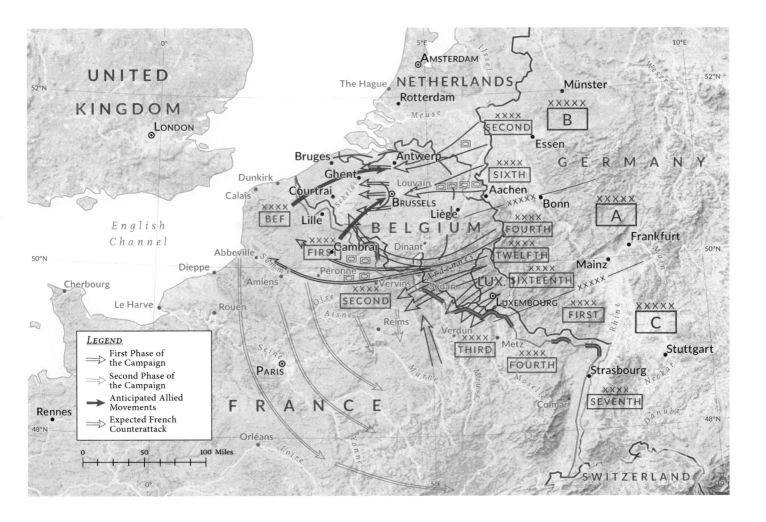

units in the interior blocked the coastal positions from overland supply, and once the German Navy had lost strategic surprise, the seas were firmly in the hands of Britain's Royal Navy. Relatively tiny German forces had to make a long slog up Norway's mountains and valleys against a game but outclassed Norwegian force. Whenever the Germans found themselves held up, however, they called upon air support that was well-nigh impossible to combat. With the Germans in total control of the air, the bewildered defenders never did form a cohesive resistance.

Unlike in Poland, the Allies did try to come to Norway's assistance. Within a week of the invasion, taking advantage of British staff work done in preparation for an invasion, they began landing forces north and south of Trondheim. On April 16 the British 146th Infantry Brigade and the French 5th Demi-Brigade of Chasseurs-Alpins landed at Namsos, 127 miles north of Trondheim.[29] Two days later, the British 148th Infantry Brigade landed at Andalsnes, about the same distance to the south of the city. Its mission was to advance on the key German position in central Norway and eliminate it.

In fact, the "Trondheim pincer" was a debacle. Command and control for the Allied landings was a nightmare, with each of the on-site commanders actually reporting back to London or Paris, due to the lack of a single unified command for the operation. Both the British and French contingents were seeing their first action, and it showed. They were lacking in antitank and antiaircraft batteries—both essential arms even by this early point in the war—and their general lack of serious military deportment seemed to

▲ THE EVOLUTION OF PLAN YELLOW: MANSTEIN'S PROPOSAL, OCTOBER 31, 1939

General Erich von Manstein, a brilliant operational planner, worried that the great wheel through Belgium would push back the French but not knock them out. He proposed shifting about half of the German armored forces to Army Group A and punching through the supposedly impassable Ardennes—thus trapping the advancing Allied forces in a "cauldron" and subjecting them to inevitable destruction.

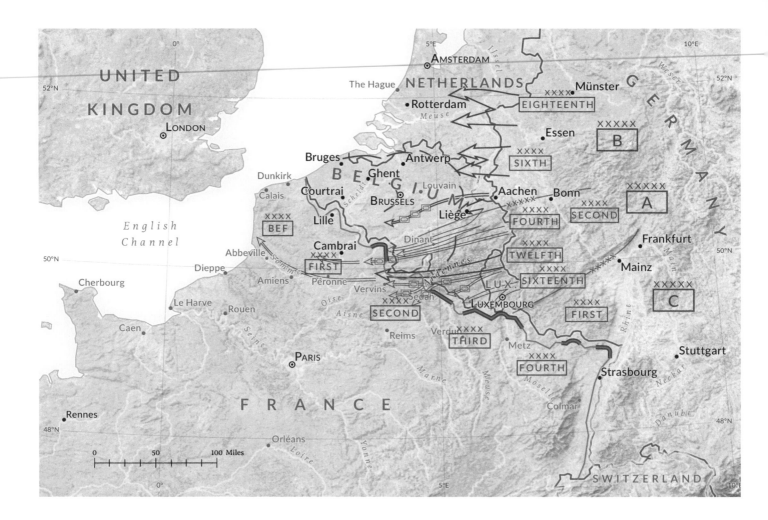

THE EVOLUTION OF PLAN ▲
YELLOW: THE FINAL PLAN,
FEBRUARY 24, 1940

Hitler liked Manstein's concept. General Gerd von Rundstedt and other senior officers, once they decided to support the basic idea, took it further and developed an operational plan that committed an even higher proportion of the German armored and mechanized divisions to the southern "sickle cut" toward the English Channel.

shock Norwegian forces, who by now had a week of heavy fighting under their belts.[30] The immediate threat to the Allies was the Luftwaffe, which barraged them with a constant and heavy air attack. Hitler gave his air force orders to destroy the port and rail facilities of the two Allied-held towns "without consideration for the civilian population," and this is essentially what it did.[31] The Allied force at Namsos, under General Adrian Carton de Wiart, did begin a desultory advance south toward Trondheim, but he made it only about halfway there, to Steinkjer. Under constant pounding from the air here, threatened by small parties of Germans to his west, and under harassing fire from German destroyers active in Trondheim Fjord, he halted and eventually fell back on Namsos. It was a harrowing march and countermarch for the Allies, dodging German Stukas without any antiaircraft guns to fend them off.[32] Failing to exert any real pressure on their operational objective of Trondheim, both forces soon reembarked and departed Norway altogether.

Far to the north, another landing fared much better. On April 15 the British 24th Guards Brigade landed on the island of Hinnöy, near Narvik. In combination with a devastating naval attack that sunk all ten German destroyers anchored there, the British assault threatened to drive the German 3rd Mountain Division, under General Eduard Dietl, from the town.[33] With Dietl's force operating well outside of the Luftwaffe's

ORDER OF BATTLE FOR THE BATTLE OF FRANCE, MAY 10, 1940 ▶

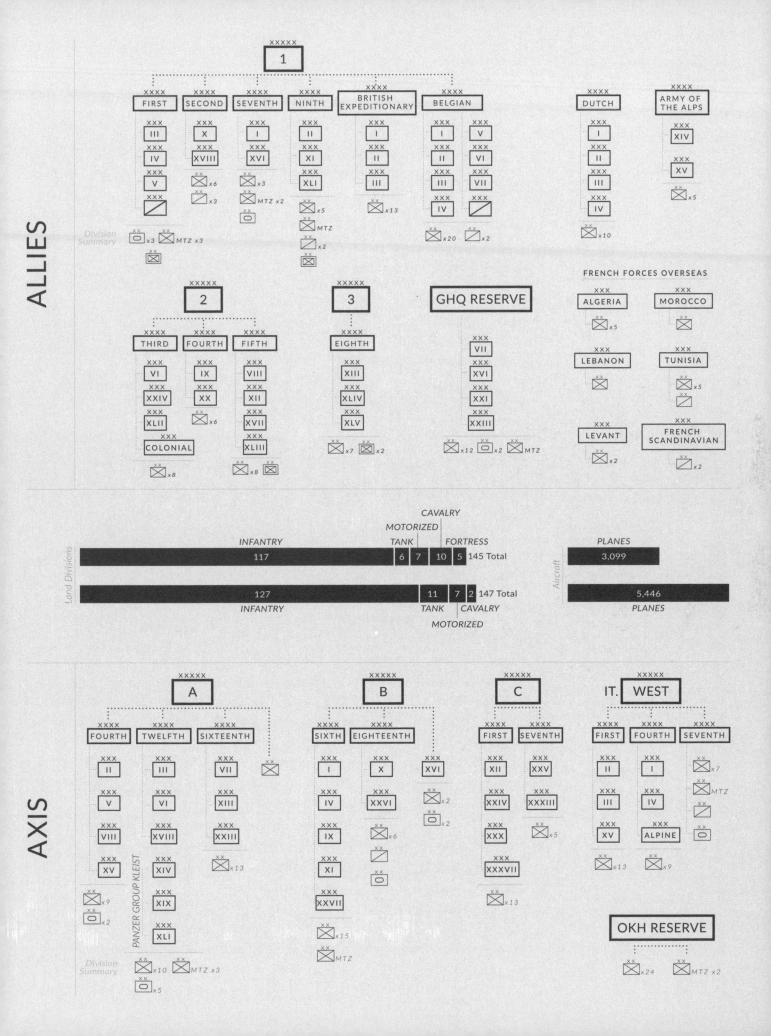

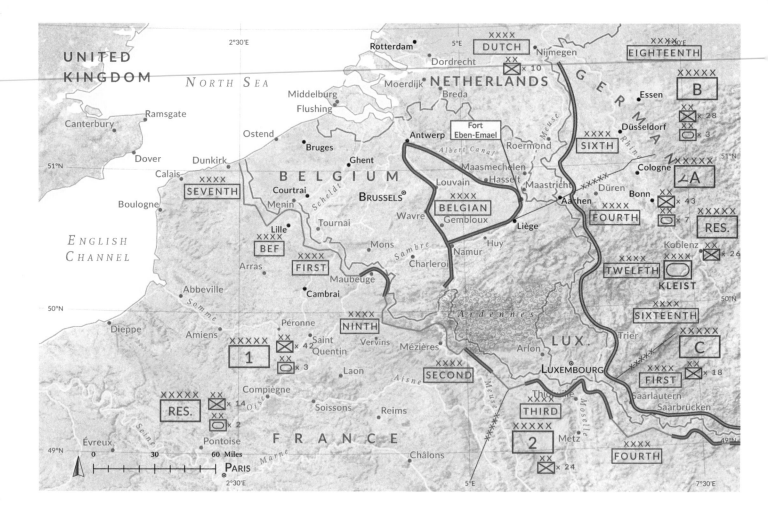

DEPLOYMENTS AND PLANS, ▲ MAY 1940

The French had about half their strength arrayed behind the Maginot Line and half poised to advance into Belgium. Including the British Expeditionary Force (BEF) and the General Headquarters (GHQ) reserves behind its front, the mobile force amounted to some sixty-five divisions. They would have to face German Army Groups A and B (seventy-one divisions) and practically all of the OKH reserves (twenty-six divisions).

air umbrella, the German art of war seemed much less artful. Two German divisions were pushing up from Trondheim toward Narvik to relieve Dietl's beleaguered force, but they were still some three hundred miles away, and the Allies were able to disrupt and delay their advance with small parties landed from the sea. The Allies, by now a robust force of British, French, Norwegian, and Polish troops, actually took Narvik on June 3. Dietl retreated to the mountains in a seemingly hopeless position, contemplating death or imprisonment for the duration of the war. Soon, however, the great German offensive against France and the Low Countries opened, and Narvik was suddenly very much a backwater to the Allies. They had taken Narvik, it turned out, simply to use it at as a port of embarkation for home.[34]

Exercise Weser required an exceptional degree of coordination among air, land, and sea units. Each service had to do its part, and each did. The amphibious component—both planning and execution—was quite impressive. This, of course, was not an area in which the Germans had any real experience or historical tradition. The loss of much of Germany's tiny surface fleet, particularly its destroyers in action around Narvik, was significant but also unavoidable. Army units had fought with their usual skill. Their mission had called for aggressive attacks without the usual panoply of tanks and modern equipment, but the German infantry proved its mettle, if anyone doubted it.

The real difference in Norway, however, was airpower. The X Fliegerkorps (Air Corps) was an omnipresent force in this campaign. It broke up Norwegian resistance

and fortified positions in the crucial first hours; it spearheaded the German land forces in their two-pronged drive from Oslo to Trondheim, a tough little campaign all its own; it kept the highly superior Allied naval forces at bay for much of the campaign; and, above all, after the Allies made seaborne landings, it convinced them that Norway was an inhospitable place in which to operate. The Luftwaffe's share of Exercise Weser was an effective example of what German air officers called the "operational air war."[35]

VICTORY IN THE WEST: CASE YELLOW

If one campaign defined the Wehrmacht's success in this era, it was the offensive in the West in May 1940, code-named Case Yellow.[36] It emerged out of a protracted planning process that stretched from the end of the Polish campaign until March 1940. The first iterations to emerge from the General Staff were quite similar to the war plan of 1914. The German Army deployed on Germany's western frontier facing Holland, Belgium, and France would deploy most of its strength on the right wing and

GERMAN GLIDER TROOPS ▲
German troops landed on top of the largely underground Eben Emael fortress using gliders like this DFS 230 (photographed during exercises in 1943). Then they used a secret weapon—shaped-charge explosives—to blast into the gun turrets.

carry out a wide wheel to the west and south. The main goal was to reach the coast of the Channel in order to seize bases and airfields from which to prosecute an air war against Britain, rather than any sort of decisive victory. Historians emphasize how dissatisfied Hitler was with the plan, but they rarely add that so were many German generals.[37]

The event that led the Germans to discard their original plan was a mishap in the air. A command aircraft carrying a staff officer misjudged its position and accidentally put down in Mechelen in neutral Belgium, and Belgian authorities managed to seize a number of documents in his possession before he could destroy them. While the documents were hardly a detailed instruction manual for the upcoming operation, they included enough information that the Germans now had to operate on the assumption that their plans had been compromised.[38]

The Mechelen incident thus led to a complete redesign of the offensive. Various new schemes had been bubbling up within the staff and field command, and one of them, drawn up by the brilliant and acerbic General Erich von Manstein, eventually caught Hitler's eye.[39] It was a gambling, go-for-broke plan, and while it offered the prospect of striking a decisive blow, the risks were equally great. Army Group B, under Bock, would invade Belgium and the Netherlands in order to attract the attention of the Allied forces in France, and perhaps lure them to the north. Once they had swallowed the bait, Army Group A, under Rundstedt, would carry out a massive Panzer

Though arguably technically superior to their German counterparts, French tanks like these SOMUA S-35s were not used as effectively.

thrust through the difficult terrain of the Ardennes Forest. With its dense old-growth forest, steep-banked rivers, and winding roads and trails, the Ardennes was the last place in the world anyone would think of as "tank country."

But that, of course, was precisely the point. The Panzers would likely meet little resistance in the forest, Manstein believed, since the French and Belgians considered it unsuitable for operations by armor. Having passed the Ardennes, the Panzers would have only a single river to cross, the Meuse, beyond which there would be nothing but open country all the way to the English Channel. In this manner, the Germans would get onto the rear of the Allied force operating to the north, and could then subject it to a crushing concentric attack and destroy it.[40]

On February 24, 1940, Army Chief of Staff General Franz Halder issued the new operational directives for the upcoming offensive.[41] Bock's Army Group B would contain two armies: the Eighteenth (General Georg von Küchler) would overrun the Netherlands; the Sixth (General Walter von Reichenau) would push into Belgium. Bock's main task was to serve a feint, but he had to be convincing. Thus, his command included a hefty sampling of the new mobile units: a number of paratrooper and glider units, including the 7th Flieger (Paratrooper) Division and 22nd Air-Landing Division; two complete Panzer corps, the XVI and the XXXIX; and a significant commitment of airpower.

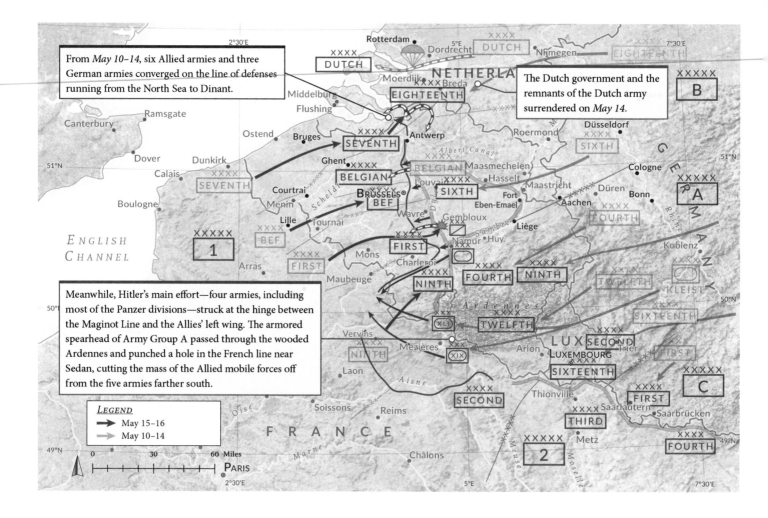

From *May 10–14*, six Allied armies and three German armies converged on the line of defenses running from the North Sea to Dinant.

The Dutch government and the remnants of the Dutch army surrendered on *May 14.*

Meanwhile, Hitler's main effort—four armies, including most of the Panzer divisions—struck at the hinge between the Maginot Line and the Allies' left wing. The armored spearhead of Army Group A passed through the wooded Ardennes and punched a hole in the French line near Sedan, cutting the mass of the Allied mobile forces off from the five armies farther south.

LEGEND
➡ May 15–16
➡ May 10–14

0   30   60 Miles

CASE YELLOW, ▲
MAY 10–16, 1940
The first week of the campaign went much as the Germans had planned it.

The *Schwerpunkt*, or point of main effort, lay in the south. Army Group A contained three armies: the Fourth (General Günther von Kluge), Twelfth (General Wilhelm von List), and Sixteenth (General Ernst Busch), plus a newly organized Panzer Group under General Ewald von Kleist containing seven of Germany's ten Panzer divisions organized into three Panzer corps. Since the Panzer Group would have to pass through the Ardennes and then launch its attack on an exceedingly narrow front, the plan echeloned it in some depth. The first echelon would consist of Guderian's XIX Corps, now upgraded from its 1939 designation of "motorized" to "Panzer"; the second, the XLI Panzer Corps under General Georg-Hans Reinhardt; and the third, the XIV Motorized Corps under General Gustav von Wietersheim. The I Flak (antiaircraft) Corps would advance between the XIX and the XLI Panzer Corps, providing protection from any Allied planes that might penetrate the Luftwaffe's air umbrella.[42] It was the mightiest mechanized force that the world had ever seen: 134,000 men, 41,000 vehicles, 1,250 tanks, and 362 reconnaissance vehicles.

The actual operation, opening on May 10, 1940, went more smoothly than expected. As the Germans intended, there were a series of shocks to the Allied commanders early in the fighting.[43] In the Netherlands, the Germans used both airborne (parachute) and air-landing (glider) troops—two complete divisions—to seize airfields, bridges over the numerous watercourses, and other strategic installations.[44] It was a remarkable success, but not all of these special operations went according to

▲ THE ARDENNES
Despite the narrow roads and the consequent traffic jams, Guderian got his Panzer corps through the forested hills of the Ardennes far more quickly than the French had thought possible.

plan. Although a number of bridges did fall to the landing forces (the Moerdijk causeway south of Rotterdam, for example), many of the direct jumps against the airfields proved disastrous. The attempt to seize the Ockenburg, Valkenburg, and Ypenburg airfields around the Hague collapsed in the face of larger-than-expected airfield garrisons and the failure of Luftwaffe raids to knock out Dutch antiaircraft batteries in the area. Disaster begot disaster when the German transports arrived with the air-landing troops, expecting to land at the captured fields. At Ypenburg, Dutch fire destroyed eleven of the first thirteen transport aircraft to arrive. It might be argued that the shock and panic caused by these landings made them worthwhile, in that they overwhelmed the Dutch command by confronting it with combat outside the very walls of its capital and throughout the four corners of the land from the conflict's very first moment, but their cost in highly trained specialist troops was high. In that sense, the German landings in the Netherlands set the tone for all future airborne operations, which are potentially lucrative but always laden with risk for the troops involved.

To the south, the Germans launched a more successful coup: a glider assault on the modern Belgian fortress of Eben Emael, at the junction of the Meuse and the Albert Canal.[45] The operation involved landing a force on top of the fort itself, knocking out its guns, then forcing the surrender of the troops inside. This too had its share of problems. The glider carrying the commander of the operation, Lieutenant Rudolf Witzig, was one of two that released prematurely. He had his pilot glide back over the Rhine, called the nearest Luftwaffe headquarters, and got himself another tow

CROSSING THE MEUSE ▲

The first German forces to cross the Meuse were infantrymen in rubber assault boats. They took heavy casualties, but once they had secured bridgeheads, German engineers could lay pontoon bridges and allow the tanks to reach the west bank of the river.

plane. Nevertheless, the main assault force landed successfully on target, and within ten minutes it had knocked out all of the guns and installations on the surface of the fort. It was an impressive debut for a new weapon, the shaped-charge explosive, which proved effective against the armored cupolas of the Belgian guns.[46] The tiny force—just seventy-eight men—did have some problems fighting and overcoming a Belgian garrison ten times its own size, although German morale rose considerably when a lone glider appeared over the fort, landed, and disgorged the fiery Lieutenant Witzig. He and his men managed to keep the garrison bottled up until German ground forces, elements of the 4th Panzer Division, arrived the next day.

The rest of Army Group B played its role to the hilt. The large Sixth Army (with five corps) entered the southern Netherlands with General Erich Hoepner's XVI Panzer Corps in the van. The plan called for a quick crossing of the "Maastricht appendage"—the narrow strip of Dutch territory separating Germany from Belgium—and then entry into the central Belgian plain west of the Meuse and Sambre Rivers. The Dutch, however, blew the Meuse bridges before the Germans could seize them, and Hoepner's Panzers spent a full day immobilized in Dutch territory. On May 11 they got moving again and the next day crashed into a large French mechanized force advancing from the south. This was part of the French Second Army: the Cavalry Corps of General René Prioux, containing the 2nd and 3rd Light Mechanized Divisions. In a clash of armor near Gembloux, Belgium, the French managed to hand the Germans a "hard

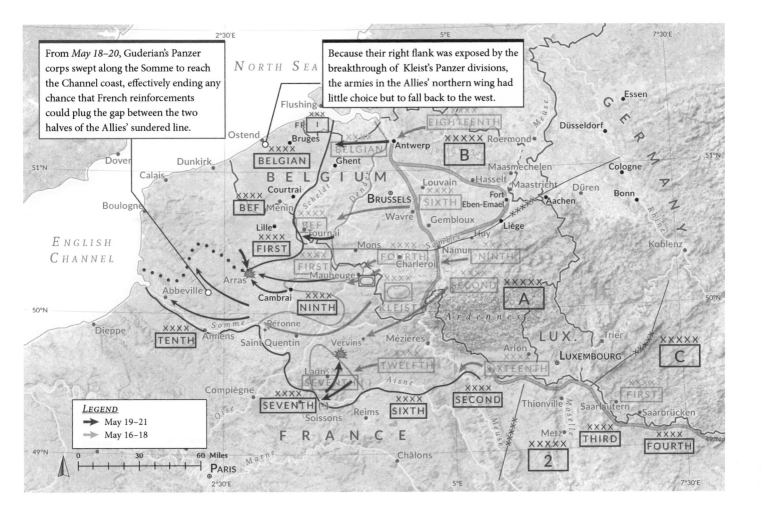

From *May 18–20*, Guderian's Panzer corps swept along the Somme to reach the Channel coast, effectively ending any chance that French reinforcements could plug the gap between the two halves of the Allies' sundered line.

Because their right flank was exposed by the breakthrough of Kleist's Panzer divisions, the armies in the Allies' northern wing had little choice but to fall back to the west.

LEGEND
→ May 19–21
→ May 16–18

and bitter day," in the words of Captain Ernst von Jungenfeld of the 35th Panzer Regiment, bringing them to a standstill in many spots. This should not surprise us, as the French tanks, especially the medium SOMUA S-35, were in most respects superior to their German counterparts.[47] Nevertheless, the skills of the veteran and better-trained German crews eventually began to tell against a French force that was tasting combat for the first time. After a concentrated German attack managed to penetrate the front of the 3rd Light Mechanized Division, Prioux had no choice but to order the Cavalry Corps to retire on May 14.

In fact, the French Cavalry Corps was at Gembloux not to seek decisive battle but merely to cover the major Allied operational maneuver of the campaign. The Allies were following "plan D," which called for the Anglo-French force to enter Belgium and take up a strong defensive position along the Dyle River.[48] Four complete armies were involved: from west to east, the French Seventh Army, the British Expeditionary Force, and the French First and Ninth. The advance was to proceed in tandem with a wheel to the right, so that by the time they had finished their advance, the Allies would be facing nearly due east, from Monthermé in the south to the Dutch border. In March the French had introduced the so-called Breda variant to the plan, with the Seventh Army on the left extending the line up to the city of Breda in the Netherlands, far to the north.[49] This "Dyle-Breda position," the Allies believed, would be an ideal place to meet the principal German thrust coming down on them from the north. As the

▲ CASE YELLOW, MAY 16–21, 1940

The rapid advance of the Panzer spearheads to the Channel coast exceeded German expectations and threw the Allied commanders completely off balance.

As Guderian pushed across the Meuse near Sedan on May 13, farther north at Dinant, the 7th Panzer Division was doing the same. The defenders were in some disorder, as the French 18th Infantry Division (which had just arrived, without antitank guns or artillery) replaced the retreating 1st Cavalry Division. Nonetheless, the river crossing, led by infantry in rubber boats, was a close-run thing. The story is told here by Major General Erwin Rommel, the German division commander:

> The situation when I arrived was none too pleasant. Our boats were being destroyed one after the other by the French flanking fire, and the crossing eventually came to a standstill. The enemy infantry were so well concealed that they were impossible to locate even after a long search through glasses . . . Minute by minute the enemy fire grew more unpleasant. From up river a damaged rubber boat came drifting down to us with a badly wounded man clinging to it, shouting and screaming for help—the poor fellow was near to drowning. But there was no help for him here, the enemy fire was too heavy . . .

Rommel checked a second crossing point, where the Germans had gotten a few troops across before their crossing equipment was "shot to pieces." Back at division headquarters, he arranged more tank and artillery support for the leading riflemen, and then returned to the river.

> The crossing had now come to a complete standstill, with the officers badly shaken by the casualties which their men had suffered. On the opposite bank we could see several men of the company which was already across, among them many wounded. Numerous damaged boats and rubber dinghies lay on the opposite bank . . . The tanks I had ordered to the crossing point soon arrived, to be followed shortly afterward by two field howitzers . . . All points . . . likely to hold enemy riflemen were now brought under fire, and soon the aimed fire of all weapons was pouring into rocks and buildings. Lieutenant Hanke knocked out a pill-box on the bridge ramp with several rounds. The tanks, with turrets traversed left, drove slowly north at fifty yards' spacing along the Meuse valley, closely watching the opposite slopes.
>
> Under cover of this fire, the crossing slowly got going again.[50]

Belgian and Dutch armies retreated, they would plug themselves into it as well, adding another twenty-seven divisions to the Allied order of battle—a key consideration to the final shape of the plan.

But, in fact, French operational plans played into German hands—just as they had in 1914 at the start of World War I. As Allied forces concentrated on the north, the German *Schwerpunkt*, an immense armored force aiming toward Sedan, France, had to contend only with the French Second Army. Its task was simply to function as a hinge for the Allied swing into Belgium, and it was essentially performing an economy-of-force operation.[51] It had low priority in manpower, equipment, and air support. Of its five divisions, two were overage reservists, one was a North African division configured for light infantry combat, and another was a lightly armed and poorly trained colonial unit from Senegal.

Once the two rival plans and deployments are understood, the unfolding of the actual campaign in the south is a simple story. The Panzers entered the Ardennes without incident—a long snake of tanks, trucks, and reconnaissance vehicles fifty miles long. A single sortie by French or British bombers could have wreaked havoc on it, but neither air force was interested in probing deeply into German rear areas. Rather, they were holding back for the slow, methodical war of attrition that the Allied high command was expecting. Instead of scrambling to avoid destruction, therefore, the most anxious moments for the Wehrmacht were the inevitable traffic jams. The Germans brushed aside weak Belgian resistance, little more than roadblocks and demolitions,

in the forest itself. Early in the evening of May 12—just day three of the operation—the head of the German snake emerged from the forest. It was Guderian's XIX Panzer Corps, heading toward Sedan. Rather than pause and stage a set-piece river crossing the next day, Guderian forced his way across the Meuse that evening on his own initiative. A handful of his infantry in rubber assault boats, as well as a few tanks and motorcycles, managed to establish a bridgehead on the far bank.[52]

The next day, the French Second Army defending along the Meuse took the kind of pounding that only Polish veterans could have understood. There were tanks—a huge mass of them stretching as far as the eye could see—along with heavy artillery concentrations, both 105 millimeter and 150 millimeter, and finally the ceaseless dive-bombing of the Stukas. Units of the French Second Army broke in panic even before

▲ **GERMAN TROOPS IN BELGIUM**

At the time and ever since, the popular image of the German Blitzkrieg has focused on the tanks and mechanized forces. But the Panzer and motorized divisions were only a small fraction of the German Army's strength, and the success of the Wehrmacht in 1939–40 owed much to the effectiveness of its infantry divisions.

The quintessential "Panzer leader," Heinz Guderian was an important theoretician of armored warfare in the 1930s, and one of Germany's key field commanders in wartime.

After serving in the German signals corps in World War I, he joined the 7th Motorized Transport Battalion in 1922. Under battalion commander Colonel Oswald Lutz, Guderian became an expert on the use of motorized transport in combat. He wrote doctrine and took part in large open-field maneuvers featuring tanks. When Hitler rearmed Germany, Guderian received command of one of the first three Panzer divisions (the 2nd). He also wrote a book, *Achtung—Panzer!* (1937), which expressed his views of armored warfare. The book, which is usually summed up in his phrase "*Klotzen, nicht kleckern*" ("Pound 'em, don't play around"), called for concentrating tanks at the decisive operational point rather than distributing them among the infantry.

During the war's early years, he went from success to success and became the public face of Blitzkrieg. He commanded a motorized corps in Poland, a Panzer corps in France, and one of Germany's four Panzergruppen (tank armies) in the campaign in the Soviet Union. His corps crossed the Meuse at Sedan in May 1940, the operational maneuver that doomed the French Army. In the Soviet Union, he sealed off one of the greatest encirclements of all time at Kiev in September 1941.

It was the end of his glory years. Guderian was sacked by Hitler after the disaster in front of Moscow in December 1941, and spent 1942 in retirement. He was brought back in 1943 and was inspector general of armored forces during the Kursk debacle. He became chief of the German General Staff in 1944 and presided over the Wehrmacht's final defeat.

Like his superior, Field Marshal Gerd von Rundstedt, Guderian served willingly on the courts of honor that executed fellow officers who had taken part in the plot to kill Hitler. Despite the merits of his great Panzer drives, Guderian's historical reputation will always remain linked with that of the regime, and the Führer, he served.

---

the Germans were over the river in force, and the same thing happened to the French Ninth Army at the two Meuse River crossings to the north: one at Monthermé, where Reinhardt's XLI Panzer Corps crossed; and one at Dinant, where the Ninth was hit by General Hermann Hoth's XV Panzer Corps, part of the Fourth Army. By the end of the day on May 13, the Germans had torn a great gash in the French line some fifty miles wide.[53]

It was not simply a tactical success of local importance, but an operational one that shaped the course of the whole following campaign. Over the next week, the three armies of Army Group A would pour through the gap. With the Panzers in the lead and the infantry force-marching until it dropped, the Germans slid across the rear of the huge Allied army in Belgium. This was a triumphal moment for the German commanders, all veterans of the previous war. Those very places in Flanders that had hung just tantalizingly out of reach in 1918 were falling in a rush: Arras, Amiens, Mont Kemmel. The reeling Allied command could do nothing for the moment to halt the onrushing armored divisions.

The Germans reached yet another milestone on May 20. Late in the day, the 2nd Panzer Division reached Abbeville at the mouth of the Somme River. This meant the destruction of the Allied army to the north: a million and a half men. It was the greatest *Kesselschlacht*, or battle of encirclement, in military history up to this point. During their drive across northern France, the Panzers had been nearly unmolested— though the French did manage a pair of counterattacks, led by the commander of the

BLITZKRIEG TACTICS

1 German air units seize control of the sky over the battlefield. Fighters, medium bombers, and dive-bombers attack airfields, bridges, known headquarters, communications facilities, rail yards, and supply dumps to disrupt the ability of the enemy to mobilize and to react to the German ground attack. Initial attacks target enemy assets immediately behind the front or up to a couple hundred miles behind the lines. Fighter aircraft engage and destroy any enemy aircraft on the ground and in the air. Reconnaissance aircraft seek out enemy troop movements and concentrations and report any that are found so the bombers can target these locations.

With a breakthrough accomplished the armored/motorized forces begin **2** driving through the initial enemy defenses and into the enemy's rear. When German reconnaissance detects enemy troop trains or reserve units on the move, German air assets attack these elements. The Panzer and motorized infantry divisions continue moving into the enemy rear, bypassing or engaging enemy reserves as necessary when encountered. The German infantry deals with isolated enemy forces and marches as quickly as possible to maintain contact with the enemy and to keep up with the mechanized forces as best as they can.

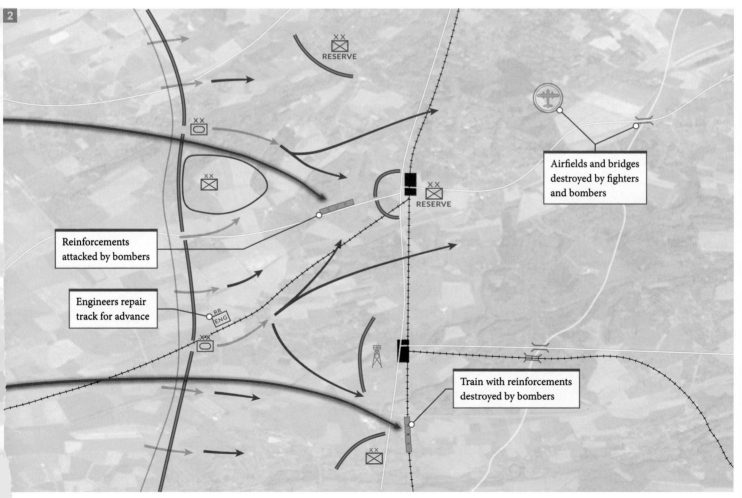

Reinforcements attacked by bombers

Engineers repair track for advance

Airfields and bridges destroyed by fighters and bombers

Train with reinforcements destroyed by bombers

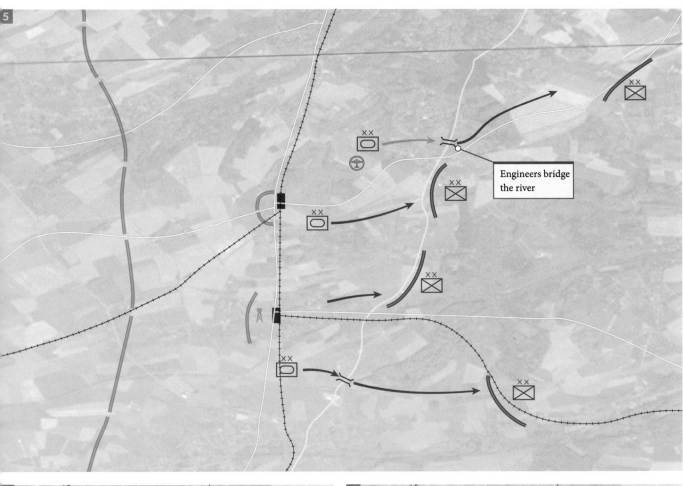

Engineers bridge
the river

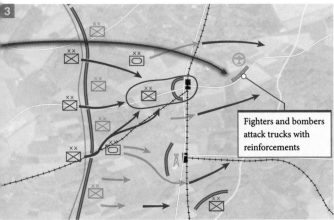

Fighters and bombers
attack trucks with
reinforcements

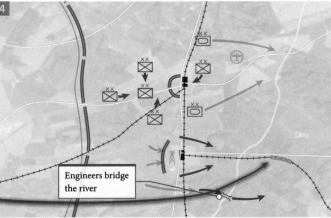

Engineers bridge
the river

German infantry units, in conjunction with [3]
mechanized forces, encircle enemy forces
when possible. The infantry takes responsibility for the encirclements as soon as possible
to free up the mechanized forces to continue
forward movement. German air assets continue to respond to enemy troop movements.

The enemy front is collapsing with a large force encircled. With the capture of the [4]
airfield, Luftwaffe troops move in to prepare the airfield for German use. Moving air
units forward ensures continued air support of the advance. The defenders continue their efforts to establish a line of defense that will hold, but continue to be hindered at every turn by German air assets and motorized formations. When German
mechanized forces run into an obstacle, their motorized engineers tackle the problem by clearing roadblocks and repairing bridges or constructing temporary ones.

[5] The German Panzer units with motorized engineers cross the river before the enemy forces can prepare a defense. The defenders
attempt to establish a new line but can't move fast enough because their transportation and communications have been disrupted. It
appears that another pocket is forming. The German movement is so quick that it is extremely difficult to coordinate a defense. Whereas
the defending forces could react more quickly than the offensive forces in World War I, the offensive forces have the advantage in the
early days of World War II. The result in the period of 1939–41 was a series of rapid defeats for those encountering Blitzkrieg for the
first time.

Blitzkrieg Tactics

Although the Germans themselves rarely used the term "Blitzkrieg," it has come to be the common term for the German way of war in the early years of World War II. It represents the successful combination of the internal combustion engine with leadership, doctrine, and modern equipment.

Blitzkrieg made the internal combustion engine the heart of warfare. The gasoline-powered motor gave the attacker the ability to move quickly with both armored vehicles and infantry. It made it possible for combined-arms forces to move at the same speed. It made effective air support possible.

The combination of trucks and armored vehicles—including tanks, armored cars, and armored personnel carriers—revolutionized the movement of armies. Artillery, engineer, signals, and logistics units could all move at the speed of trucks and motorcycles. The large-scale use of radio communications meant that attacking forces could report changing situations, seek assistance, and enable other units to adjust their plans and actions accordingly. Air support was a vital component of Blitzkrieg. The control of the sky meant that German units could move freely, while their opponents had to constantly look skyward, worried that they would be strafed or bombed, that the bridge or rails ahead would be destroyed, or that their communications would be disrupted by downed phone and telegraph lines or radio towers. Troops could now be delivered by air, landing behind the lines and further disrupting the defense. Blitzkrieg changed the pace of operations, the relationship between offense and defense. A key question was how long it would take for the other nations to adapt to mechanized warfare.

As significant as the development of mechanized warfare was in World War II, it is important to remember that the bulk of the German Army was not mechanized. The Wehrmacht accomplished its great breakthroughs and rapid victories with relatively few armored and motorized units.

The following describes the generalities of a Blitzkrieg attack rather than any particular event.

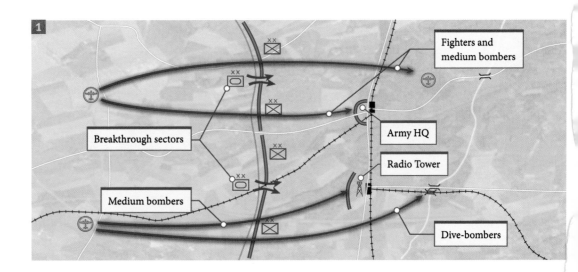

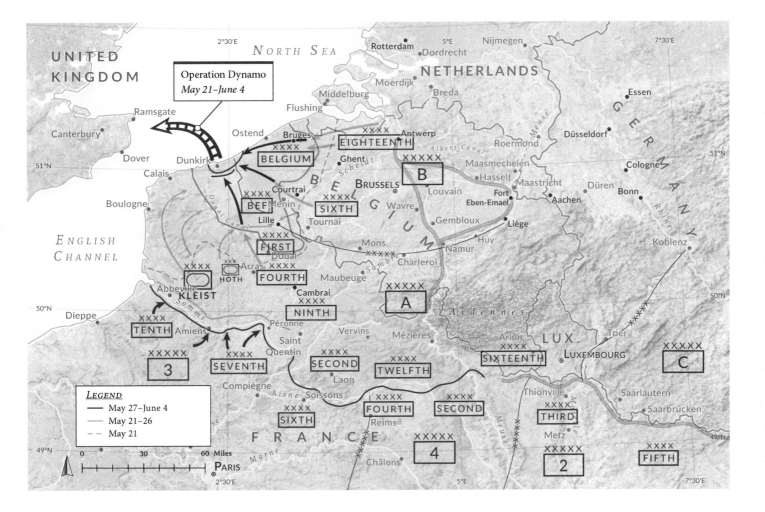

newly formed 4th Armored Division, General Charles de Gaulle. Neither his first attack at Montcornet (May 17), nor a second one at Crécy-sur-Serre (May 19) managed to halt German momentum. The same was true of the single British counterstroke of the campaign, near Arras on May 21.[54]

What all of these counterstrokes did achieve was to shake the confidence of the German high command, up to and including Hitler. The latest German situation maps showed an ominous picture: long, vulnerable armored spearheads strung out on the roads, completely out of contact with their follow-on infantry divisions. Orders actually went out to Guderian to halt and allow time for the infantry to catch up. Once they had consolidated a defensive position on his flanks, he could drive on. Anyone who has studied the centuries-long operational pattern of the German Army could not be surprised at Guderian's response. He ignored his orders and continued on, undertaking a "reconnaissance in force" that included—no surprise—his entire XIX Panzer Corps.[55] He reached the Channel, wheeled north, and kept on attacking, completing the encirclement of the Allied forces in Belgium. The time was coming when such independent action would no longer be tolerated in the Wehrmacht, but that time had not arrived yet.

By the end of May, the German offensive had hounded the Allies back to the last port still in their hands: Dunkirk, France. Here, Case Yellow would end on a disappointing note for the Germans. From May 27 to June 4, in a hectic, weeklong maneuver

▲ CASE YELLOW,
MAY 21–JUNE 4, 1940

After May 21, German commanders paused to consolidate their gains before turning to destroy Allied forces trapped against the English Channel. The British seized the opportunity and evacuated over 300,000 soldiers by sea before German troops overcame the last defenders at Dunkirk.

The Dunkirk evacuation could never have occurred were it not for a gritty rearguard action by the British infantry holding the perimeter around the port. Here Lieutenant Jimmy Langley (Coldstream Guards) and his commander, Major Angus McCorquodale, receive bad news from a captain from a neighboring unit:

He informed us that the Germans were massing for an attack on the bridgehead, that his men were exhausted, and that he proposed to withdraw while the going was good. Angus merely said, "I order you to stay put, and fight it out."

"You cannot do that. I have overriding orders from my colonel to withdraw when I think fit," came the reply.

Angus did not beat about the bush. "You see that big poplar tree on the road with the white milestone beside it? The moment you or any of your men go back beyond that tree, we will shoot you." The captain started to expostulate, but Angus cut him short. "Get back, or I will shoot you now, and send one of my officers to take command," and his hand moved toward his revolver. The captain departed without further words. "Get a rifle," Angus ordered me, picking up one that was lying nearby. When I returned with mine, he said: "Sights at 250. You will shoot to kill the moment he passes that tree. Are you clear?"

"Yes."

We had not long to wait before the captain appeared, followed by two men. They stood for a time by the tree, and then the captain walked on. Both our rifles went off simultaneously: he dropped out of sight, and the two men ran back.[56]

known as Operation Dynamo, the British managed to evacuate from the Continent most of the personnel of their expeditionary force: some 200,000 men, along with 140,000 French and Belgian troops. How it happened—or rather, how the Germans allowed it to happen—has generated much historical controversy. Most analysis begins with Hitler's decision to halt the Panzers at the Dunkirk perimeter, refusing to allow them to close in and crush the bridgehead, but it is wrong to focus on one man. By this point, many voices in the officer corps, both staff and field, were calling for a return to a more orthodox operational posture. That meant allowing the infantry and artillery to "close up" to the Panzer spearheads. Indeed, Rundstedt issued such an order on the evening of May 24, with the support of at least one of his subordinate commanders, Günther von Kluge of the Fourth Army. The point is that Hitler was not dictating to the generals at Dunkirk so much as he was adjudicating a dispute among them.[57]

Other factors were at work as well. As the Panzers bounded forward to the Channel, they were no longer operating under absolute air superiority, as British aircraft flying from bases in Britain could now intervene. At the same time, the British troops holding the Dunkirk perimeter fought bravely. Without having to endure a ceaseless pummeling from unopposed German dive-bombers, they gave a good accounting of themselves, holding back repeated German assaults on the Dunkirk perimeter. These forgotten soldiers too deserve credit for the success of Operation Dynamo.[58]

In the end, the German failure to seal the deal at Dunkirk was a classic example of what the great Prussian sage General Carl von Clausewitz called "friction." In all military campaigns, little things begin to go wrong and eventually add up to larger things. Focusing solely on the German "failure" at Dunkirk is a very narrow lens through which to view the overall operation, however. No less a figure than the new British prime minister, Winston Churchill, put it best when he warned his countrymen soon after Dunkirk that "wars are not won by evacuations."[59] Especially, we might add,

when the evacuation abandons all the army's tanks, vehicles, and heavy equipment. No military campaign is perfect, but in Case Yellow, the German armed forces came about as close as anyone has—through good planning, aggressiveness, and no small amount of luck.

No account of the victory in Case Yellow would be complete without some commentary on the French operational plan. Often criticized in simplistic terms as a hapless example of playing into enemy strength, it was actually based on sensible, rational principles. Based on their experience in the last war, the French were expecting a bloody and methodical clash of arms. Their supreme commander, General Maurice Gamelin, anticipated a campaign that would unfold systematically and slowly and eventually transform into a battle of attrition. His goal, therefore, was to absorb the initial German blow, maintain a cohesive operational line, and then ready his forces for the counterthrust when German momentum had flagged—just as the French Army had done successfully on the Marne in 1914. To that end, maintaining France's allies was crucial: hence Gamelin's decision to march up to the Dyle River in central Belgium and to dispatch his Seventh Army all the way up to Breda in the Netherlands. It is easy today to argue that the Netherlands barely mattered in 1940, but at the time, the Dutch Army included ten divisions—a major addition to French strength. Even Gamelin's most controversial decision—stationing weak forces at Sedan—made perfect sense. He had backstopped his less potent formations with a large amount of

▲ **OPERATION DYNAMO**

The British lost some 68,000 men during the Battle of France—about a quarter of the entire BEF. They would have lost nearly all of the rest had it not been for the remarkable success of Operation Dynamo, the evacuation from Dunkirk, thanks to which some 200,000 Britons and 140,000 French and Belgian soldiers escaped death or captivity.

Gamelin was a talented infantry officer, graduating first in his class at Saint-Cyr Military Academy and second from the French Staff College. He was known for his intelligence and culture, and published *A Philosophical Study of the Art of War* (1906) while a junior captain. The book impressed General (later Field Marshal) Joseph Joffre, on whose staff he served at the beginning of World War I. Gamelin's brilliance in that role earned him command of a brigade, a division, and then a corps, where he also shone. After the war, he served as a military advisor to Brazil and commanded French forces in Syria with notable success. Elevated over many older officers, he became chief of staff in 1931. The French Army did not have a peacetime commander in chief, but Gamelin was appointed to prepare the army he would command when war came. Gamelin's rapid rise owed much to political acumen learned from Joffre. Where many French generals despised their government, Gamelin embraced his constitutional duty and used his intelligence and tact to soothe the civil-military rifts that had been created by abrasive predecessors.

Although rivals attributed his professional rise to pandering to left-wing politicians, Gamelin moved shrewdly in a range of political circles and was widely admired in foreign armies as well. His political skill benefited the army in difficult times. He supported the security guarantee extended to Poland in 1939 and worked diligently to strengthen the Anglo-French coalition. The French plan to push forward to fight on the Dyle Line in Belgium, and the Breda variant that committed the French mobile reserve to a dash into the Netherlands, were his responsibility.

After the fall of France, Gamelin's republican politics and conservative military thinking—combined with the overwhelming scale of Germany's victory in 1940—made Gamelin a ready scapegoat for defeat. But his reputation has improved over time, as historians have looked dispassionately at his career and the 1940 campaign.

artillery, just the sort of thing that had worked in the later years of World War I. Times had changed since then, however. The pace of battle had definitely accelerated, and French doctrine did not anticipate it in the way that German doctrine did. Gamelin's strategy and operational design did not work in 1940, certainly, but that is a very different thing from saying that they made no sense at the time.

While the British had gone home after Dunkirk, the French campaign was not over yet. Remnants of the French Army managed to regroup along the line of the Somme and Aisne Rivers, and the Germans had to launch a second operation, Case Red, to defeat them. With the cream of the French Army encircled in Flanders to the north, the issue was never in doubt. The Germans now had 119 divisions in the front line and another 23 in reserve, facing a French force that amounted to no more than 50 divisions, many of them still tied up in the now-pointless task of garrisoning the Maginot Line—defending a position that the Germans never attacked frontally. Although there would be some tough fighting in the initial stages, the Germans quickly managed to pierce the French defenses and occupy Paris. The French were forced to sign an armistice, which they did on June 22, 1940, at Compiègne. They did so in the exact same spot, and in the exact same rail car—retrieved from a museum for the purpose—that Germany had signed the armistice of 1918. The terms were harsh,

CASE RED, JUNE 5–25, 1940 ▶

On June 5, German forces began a new campaign against a much-depleted French Army. They advanced deep into the country before fighting ceased on June 25.

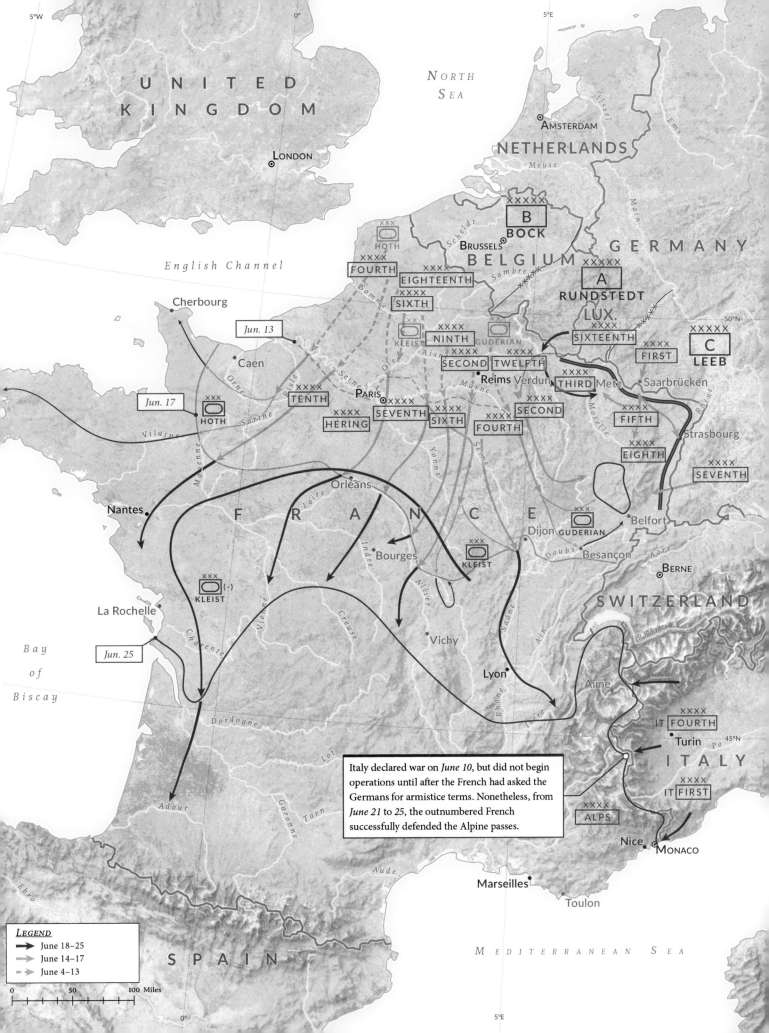

UNITED KINGDOM

NORTH SEA

London

English Channel

Cherbourg

Jun. 13

Caen

Jun. 17

Nantes

La Rochelle

Jun. 25

Bay of Biscay

F R A N C E

Orleans

Bourges

Vichy

Lyon

NETHERLANDS

Amsterdam

Meuse

BELGIUM

Brussels

GERMANY

XXXXX
B
BOCK

XXX
HOTH

XXXX
FOURTH

XXXX
EIGHTEENTH

XXXX
SIXTH

XXXX
NINTH

XXX
KLEIST

XXX
GUDERIAN

XXXXX
A
RUNDSTEDT

LUX.

XXXX
SIXTEENTH

XXXX
FIRST

XXXXX
C
LEEB

XXXX
SECOND

XXXX
TWELFTH

Reims   Verdun

XXXX
THIRD   Metz   Saarbrücken

XXXX
TENTH

Paris

XXXX
HERING

XXXX
SEVENTH

XXXX
SIXTH

XXXX
FOURTH

XXXX
SECOND

XXXX
FIFTH

XXXX
EIGHTH

Strasbourg

XXXX
SEVENTH

XXX
HOTH

Dijon

XXX
KLEIST

Besançon

Belfort

BERNE

SWITZERLAND

XXX
KLEIST (-)

XXX
KLEIST

Aime

IT FOURTH
XXXX

Turin

I T A L Y

IT FIRST
XXXX

ALPS
XXXX

Nice
Monaco

Marseilles

Toulon

MEDITERRANEAN SEA

SPAIN

Italy declared war on *June 10*, but did not begin operations until after the French had asked the Germans for armistice terms. Nonetheless, from *June 21* to *25*, the outnumbered French successfully defended the Alpine passes.

LEGEND
→ June 18–25
→ June 14–17
→ June 4–13

0   50   100 Miles

Marshal Philippe Pétain, the hero of Verdun during World War I, led the Vichy government, granting some legitimacy to the puppet state.

placing northern and western France under direct German occupation and erecting a French puppet regime in the south, with its capital at Vichy, while nearly two million French prisoners remained in German hands.

CONCLUSION

The first year of the war saw a series of decisive German victories, and the campaigns of this era continue to attract the attention of historians, military operators, and the general public. Certainly Germany's achievement was an impressive one. It had used modern weapons and tactics—armor, aircraft, and airborne attack—to good effect, marrying them to a traditionally aggressive way of war that stressed independent armies linking up far behind enemy lines to create gigantic battles of encirclement. Observers in the West might be able to explain away German victories in Poland, Denmark, or Norway. In all those cases, the opponents had been small or obsolete military forces. Case Yellow, however, in which the Wehrmacht dispatched the army of one Great Power and forced another into a humiliating evacuation from the Continent, compelled the entire world to realize the power of modern joint operations combining airpower with mechanized, combined-arms warfare. For that reason alone, these campaigns still reward careful study.[60]

There is no need to romanticize any of it, however. A lot had broken right for the Germans in these operations. They had won so easily in Poland at least partially because the Poles' two principal allies stood by passively and watched. They had overrun

German artillery participate in a victory parade through Paris, with Napoleon's Arc de Triomphe visible in the background. This photograph offers a valuable reminder that despite the prominent role of the Panzer forces in the 1940 Blitzkrieg, most German divisions still relied on feet and hooves for mobility.

Norway and Denmark due to the failure of the Royal Navy to detect and intercept the German invasion flotilla, as well as the extraordinarily clumsy nature of the Allied intervention on land. Perhaps the single most crucial factor in the triumph of Case Yellow was the Mechelen incident, which forced a last-minute switch in the German operational plan, to the Germans' great advantage. In 1939–40, in other words, circumstances had conspired to hand the Wehrmacht a perfect storm of opportunities, and to its credit, it had seized every one of them.

And yet, despite the victories, any analysis of these events is still justified in asking: What exactly had the Germans won in these operations? Their armies had been at war for nearly a year and had now reached the English Channel. As would soon become clear, neither Hitler nor the high command had much of an idea about how to proceed from this point on. Perhaps the best way to put it is this: the Wehrmacht now had to figure out a way to defeat Great Britain, an island that had not been invaded successfully since 1066 and that had not lost a war within living memory.

As Hitler and his aides peered across the English Channel in the summer of 1940, the fog of war must have seemed particularly thick. All the operational-level victories

of the first year, as impressive as they had been, had not transformed the basic German strategic conundrum: how to defeat Great Britain without a navy. Certainly, the conquest of Western Europe had given the Germans a more favorable balance of resources, as well as bases for submarines and aircraft that could strike hard blows against Britain, targeting both its cities and its seaborne commerce. Whether that would be enough to win the war was a question no one could answer yet.

◀ HITLER IN PARIS

Hitler stands in front of the Eiffel Tower in Paris on June 23, 1940, the day after the signing of the armistice with France. He had won decisive successes in the war's first year but would find his remaining adversary, Great Britain, a resolute and formidable foe.

INTRODUCTION

From July 1940 until the Axis invasion of the Soviet Union in June 1941, Britain and the British Empire stood alone in prosecuting the war against German and Italian aggression. Britain was the last barrier against complete Axis domination of Europe. The story of British survival, under threat of invasion and in the face of German attacks from the air in the Battle of Britain, lies at the heart of the narrative of the Second World War between 1940 and the summer of 1941. The Royal Air Force and the Royal Navy together kept the British war effort alive and frustrated the German hope for a cheap victory. In the Atlantic and the Mediterranean, British naval vessels and aircraft kept open vital supply lines and protected the Suez Canal; in the skies over Germany and Italy, the RAF made its first serious bombing raids. Above all, British survival meant that as the war expanded and the tide turned against the Axis, the Allies would have a base for the air, sea, and land offensives that eventually won the war.

NOT QUITE ALONE

The idea of a noble Britain embattled against the forces of Fascist evil helped rally the nation in the summer of 1940, and it has become embedded in popular memory of the wartime experience. On June 4, 1940, when it was clear that France was close to defeat, Winston Churchill, recently appointed prime minister, told the British people that the country would carry on fighting, "if necessary alone." To make clear Britain's strategic position to the enemy, Churchill added: "We shall never surrender." [1]

The reality in the summer of 1940 was never as stark as Churchill's defiant rhetoric suggested. Britain had been defeated on Continental Europe, but the United Kingdom was certainly not alone. In September 1939 Britain's so-called white dominions—Canada, Australia, New Zealand, and South Africa—as well as India had all declared war on Germany (and later, after Italy's declaration of war on June 10, 1940, on Italy too). The string of British colonies and protectorates around the world fell in automatically at Britain's side and provided large numbers to serve in local army units or as noncombatant labor. [2] The Irish state, which still had dominion status, remained neutral, but a stream of workers and goods continued to flow from Ireland to Britain. The United States, though formally neutral, was led by a president committed to upholding Britain's cause as the cause of the democratic West. Franklin Roosevelt had succeeded, against stern opposition from isolationist politicians, in allowing American arms to be sold to Britain for cash as a means of paying for the United States' own rearmament programs. Food and raw materials flowed to Britain as well but were denied to Germany by the British naval blockade. In addition, Britain was host to the exile governments of Belgium, the Netherlands, Norway, Poland, and Czechoslovakia, and thousands of servicemen and workers from all these states contributed to Britain's war effort. So too did a number of American airmen who came to Britain to fight in

3

BRITAIN STANDS ALONE

RICHARD J. OVERY

Major air assaults on
Britain begin *Aug. 1940*

Sinking of
the *Bismarck*

Vichy France
established
Jul. 1940

Apr. 1941

Nov. 1940

Oct. 1940

Mar. 1941

May 1941

Dec. 1940–Feb. 194

SWEDEN

NORTH
SEA

BALTIC
SEA

RIGA

KAUNAS

IRELAND

DUBLIN

UNITED

KINGDOM

LONDON

DENMARK

COPENHAGEN

AMSTERDAM

English Channel

BRUSSELS

BERLIN

WARSAW

GENERAL
GOVERNMENT

GERMANY

PRAGUE

Mönchengladbach

BOHEMIA

LUXEMBOURG

PARIS

SLOVAKIA

BRATISLAVA

BUDAPEST

ATLANTIC

OCEAN

Bay of
Biscay

FRANCE

BERN

Alps

HUNGARY

ROMANIA

BELGRADE

BUCHAREST

YUGOSLAVIA

BULGARIA

SOFIA

ITALY

CORSICA

ROME

TIRANA

GREECE

PORTUGAL

MADRID

SPAIN

ATHENS

LISBON

SARDINIA

Taranto

Strait of Gibraltar

M E D I T E R R A N E A N

SICILY

CRETE

SPANISH MOROCCO

ALGIERS

TUNIS

S E A

RABAT

TUNISIA

FRENCH

MOROCCO

Atlas Mountains

TRIPOLI

Tobruk

Ba

RIO
DE
ORO

A L G E R I A

L I B Y A

S a h a r a

SIERRA
LEONE

F R E N C H   W E S T   A F R I C A

F R E N C H

LIBERIA

GOLD

COAST

TOGO

N I G E R I A

E Q U A T O R I A L

A F R I C A

Map labels

50°E 60°E

COW

S O V I E T

U N I O N

C A S P I A N
S E A

Caucasus
Mountains

CK SEA

ANKARA

RKEY

IRAN

NICOSIA
YPRUS

SYRIA

IRAQ

Persian
Gulf

DAMASCUS

PALESTINE

AMMAN

TRANS-
JORDAN

JERUSALEM

Arabian

SAUDI ARABIA

Peninsula

GYPT

R E D S E A

YEMEN

Gulf of Ad

ERITREA

NGLO-

Jan. 1941

Amba Alagi

Berbera

YPTIAN

ETHIOPIA

Aug. 1940

UDAN

ADDIS ABABA

ITALIAN
SOMALILAND

30°E 40°E 50°E

Timeline

	EUROPE	MEDITER-RANEAN	POLITICS	
Churchill Becomes Prime Minister	May 10, 1940			MAY
RAF Bombs Mönchengladbach	May 11			
Operation Dynamo, the Evacuation at Dunkirk	May 27–Jun. 4			JUN
Churchill Announces "Battle of Britain"	Jun. 18			
France Signs Armistice at Compiègne	Jun. 22			JUL
Britain Destroys French Fleet at Mers-el-Kébir	Jul. 3			
Establishment of Vichy France	Jul. 10			
Special Operations Executive Founded	Jul. 22			AUG
Invasion of Somaliland	Aug. 3–19			1940
Battle of Britain	Aug. 13–Oct. 31			
Destroyers-for-Bases Deal	Sep. 2			SEP
First Heavy Bombing Raid on London	Sep. 7			
Graziani's Offensive	Sep. 13–16			
				OCT
Balkans Campaign	Oct. 28, 1940–Jun. 1, 1941			NOV
British Raid on Taranto	Nov. 11			
				DEC
Operation Compass	Dec. 8, 1940–Feb. 7, 1941			
Hitler Authorizes Operation Barbarossa	Dec. 18			
FDR Pledges "Arsenal of Democracy"	Dec. 29			
Invasion of Ethiopia	Jan. 19–May 19, 1941			
British Capture Tobruk	Jan. 22			FEB
Military Staff Conference (ABC-1)	Jan. 29–Mar. 24			
				MAR
British Troops Arrive in Greece	Mar. 7			1941
U.S. Passes "Lend-Lease" Bill	Mar. 11			
Rommel's Offensive	Mar. 24–Jun. 15			APR
Germany Invades Yugoslavia and Greece	Apr. 6			
				MAY
British Launch Operation Brevity	May 15			
German Invasion of Crete	May 20–31			
Sinking of the *Bismarck*	May 27			JUN
Operation Battleaxe	Jun. 15–17			

THE BRITISH COMMONWEALTH OF NATIONS

THE BRITISH COMMONWEALTH ▲ OF NATIONS

The British Commonwealth included both the so-called white dominions (Canada, Australia, New Zealand, and South Africa), which were sovereign countries, and also colonial possessions such as India and various African colonies, as well as many other territories not represented on this poster.

the air battles in the summer of 1940.[3] If Britain's own military and economic effort formed the centerpiece of resistance to the Axis states, the overall war effort was already international to a remarkable degree.

THE STRATEGIC POSSIBILITIES

The options facing Britain and its allies in the summer of 1940 were limited. The main fact was that Britain, even with its Commonwealth, empire, and allies, lacked the military means to defeat Germany and Italy. The most important strategic concerns were to avoid invasion and defeat at all costs, and to find some means, however modest, of bringing the war home to the Axis states. This involved politics as well as military means. The British government understood that help from the United States was essential not only in the long term but also in the immediate future. And Churchill made it a priority to try to win greater commitment from Washington. Antiwar sentiment in Congress limited what President Roosevelt could offer, but it was possible to increase the supply of armaments, including aircraft, as long as Britain paid for them in cash and transported them across the Atlantic. More important was the deal agreed upon in August 1940 to give Britain fifty older American destroyers in return for

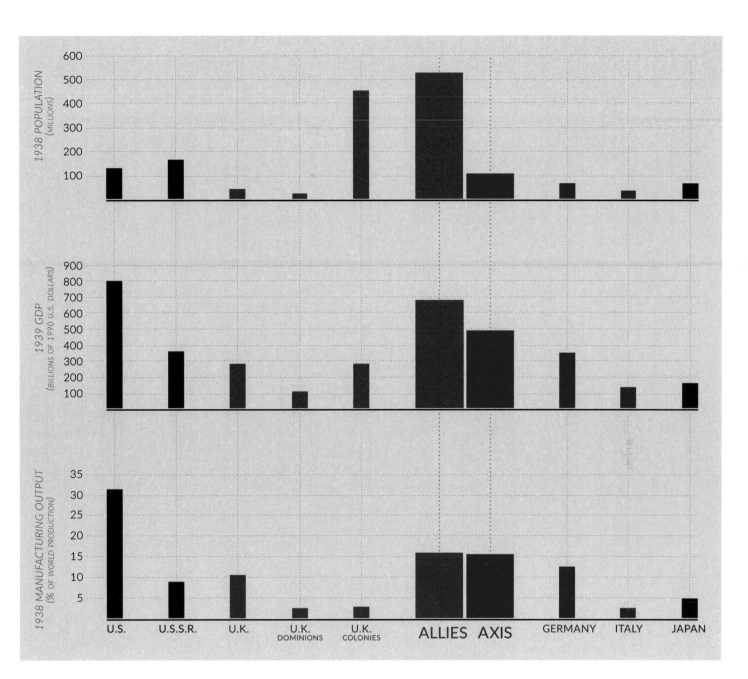

allowing the United States to build bases in British colonial possessions. Although the destroyers were of limited operational value, public opinion in Britain, and in Europe, greeted the exchange as evidence that America was committed to the British cause.[4]

Politics also played a part in Britain's decision to begin a program of political warfare in German-occupied Europe, aiming, in Churchill's phrase, "to set Europe ablaze." One principal means was propaganda—distributed chiefly through radio broadcasts and airborne leaflets—encouraging resistance from the occupied populations. Another was to engage in acts of subversion by agents of the Special Operations Executive (SOE), founded on July 22, 1940. Throughout the war, SOE operatives were infiltrated into Axis-occupied Europe to undertake sabotage and to help with the local Resistance movements.[5] The program was directed by the minister of economic warfare, Labour politician Hugh Dalton, who had already been put in charge

▲ THE BRITISH EMPIRE
AND THE AXIS

After the fall of France, it would have been difficult for the United Kingdom to carry on the struggle against the Axis if it had not been supported by its overseas colonies and dominions.

SIR WINSTON LEONARD SPENCER CHURCHILL
November 30, 1874–January 24, 1965

Winston Churchill was a politician, strategist, writer, orator, and historian. He won the Nobel Prize in Literature, helped lead Britain through both world wars, and was one of the greatest statesmen of the twentieth century.

The son of an aristocratic father and a wealthy American mother, Churchill graduated from the Royal Military College, Sandhurst, and joined the cavalry in 1894. He fought with distinction in the Second Anglo-Afghan War, at Omdurman, and in the Boer War.

Churchill was elected to Parliament in 1900 and became first lord of the Admiralty in 1911. Serving in that capacity until 1915, he pushed to modernize the Royal Navy, championing the use of airplanes and oil-powered battleships, and underwriting the development of the tank (called a "landship" so that the navy could fund it). His strategy for an amphibious thrust against Istanbul resulted in the Gallipoli debacle. After that failure, he left the government to command a battalion on the Western Front, then in 1917 returned to the cabinet as minister of munitions.

In the 1930s he stridently warned of the need for Britain to rearm to counter the rising threat of Germany. With the outbreak of World War II he again served as first lord of the Admiralty, then in May 1940 took office as prime minister. From that point through the end of the war, Churchill's brilliant mind, unbending resolution, and soaring oratory shaped and energized the British war effort.

He viewed modern war as fought with oil and steel, and made every effort to bring the United States into the fight, believing that America's vast resources would ensure an Allied victory in a long war. After the Japanese attack on Pearl Harbor, Churchill helped head off the premature 1943 cross-Channel invasion favored by the American Joint Chiefs of Staff, and pushed for aggressive Anglo-American movements into Eastern Europe (hoping to limit Soviet postwar dominance of the continent), but otherwise strove to minimize friction with U.S. military leaders. He was a strong supporter of strategic bombing, amphibious operations, the ULTRA decryption project, and any step that increased administrative or military efficiency.

Churchill was voted out of power in 1945, but served again as prime minister from 1951 to 1955. His efforts to oppose Communism and sustain Britain's global prominence led him to send troops to help defeat insurgencies in Kenya and Malaya.

of the economic blockade of Europe. In 1940 some twenty-six million leaflets were dropped on occupied territories, in 1941 a further twenty-eight million.[6] In 1941 a Political Warfare Executive was set up, directed jointly by the Ministry of Economic Warfare and the Information Ministry, working closely with the Foreign Office. Its purpose was to coordinate all the propaganda, intelligence, and subversive efforts to encourage the conquered peoples to play a part in their own liberation. It was designed to boost the morale of those who were occupied and to depress the morale of the occupiers. The impact of political propaganda on German opinion was negligible, but it did offer some evidence to the populations of the occupied states that Britain was still committed to the war against the Axis.[7]

Political warfare achieved very little in its early days. It was one part of a four-pronged strategy announced by the British Chiefs of Staff for challenging German power in Europe: blockade, propaganda, subversion, and bombing. Of these, bombing was the only one that involved direct military intervention against Germany and German-occupied territories. It is often suggested that bombing by the Royal Air Force began only in retaliation for German bombing during the "Blitz" bomber offensive in the winter of 1940–41. In reality, British bombing began on the night of May 11, 1940, with an attack

We Shall Never Surrender

On June 4, 1940, the day after the last remnants of the British Expeditionary Force were evacuated from Dunkirk, Winston Churchill addressed the House of Commons, and the nation, on the coming battle. The peroration of the address is one of Churchill's finest moments; it demonstrated his, and Britain's, resolve to win the war, whatever the cost. The last sentence of the speech reflects Churchill's confidence that the United States would eventually join the war against the Nazis.

I have, myself, full confidence that if all do their duty, if nothing is neglected, and if the best arrangements are made, as they are being made, we shall prove ourselves once again able to defend our Island home, to ride out the storm of war, and to outlive the menace of tyranny, if necessary for years, if necessary alone. At any rate, that is what we are going to try to do. That is the resolve of His Majesty's Government—every man of them. That is the will of Parliament and the nation. The British Empire and the French Republic, linked together in their cause and in their need, will defend to the death their native soil, aiding each other like good comrades to the utmost of their strength.

Even though large tracts of Europe and many old and famous States have fallen or may fall into the grip of the Gestapo and all the odious apparatus of Nazi rule, we shall not flag or fail. We shall go on to the end, we shall fight in France, we shall fight on the seas and oceans, we shall fight with growing confidence and growing strength in the air, we shall defend our Island, whatever the cost may be, we shall fight on the beaches, we shall fight on the landing grounds, we shall fight in the fields and in the streets, we shall fight in the hills; we shall never surrender, and even if, which I do not for a moment believe, this Island or a large part of it were subjugated and starving, then our Empire beyond the seas, armed and guarded by the British Fleet, would carry on the struggle, until, in God's good time, the New World, with all its power and might, steps forth to the rescue and the liberation of the old.[8]

on the western German town of Mönchengladbach. Bombing continued against German industrial targets almost without interruption throughout the summer months of 1940, totaling 103 nights of raiding between May and August.[9] At first, bombing was supposed to divert German aircraft away from the battle in France to the defense of the Reich, which it failed to do, but from June onward, it was designed in accordance with the Western Air Plans, drawn up in late 1939, to disrupt German oil supply and communications, and to bomb German industrial cities in the Ruhr industrial region.[10]

Churchill gave strong support to the bombing strategy. In July 1940 he told his friend William Maxwell Aitken, Lord Beaverbrook, then the minister of aircraft production, that the only means he could see for the defeat of Germany was "an absolutely devastating, exterminating attack by very heavy bombers."[11] Intelligence on the effects of the early bombing greatly exaggerated its achievements, since its wide inaccuracy was not yet evident, and prewar expectations about the potential of relatively few planes to destroy entire cities still prevailed.[12] This was also true of the early bombing of Italian targets, which began on the first night after Italy declared war and was expected to undermine Italian morale seriously. Although these hopes proved exaggerated, since the weight of bombs dropped on Italy was tiny, bombing did have the merit of demonstrating to the British home population that the British armed forces were actively doing *something* against the enemy.[13]

The military outlook for Britain was bleak in the summer of 1940, though not as desperate as accounts at the time, and many since, suggested. More than 400,000 British and French servicemen had managed to escape to Britain in June 1940, including

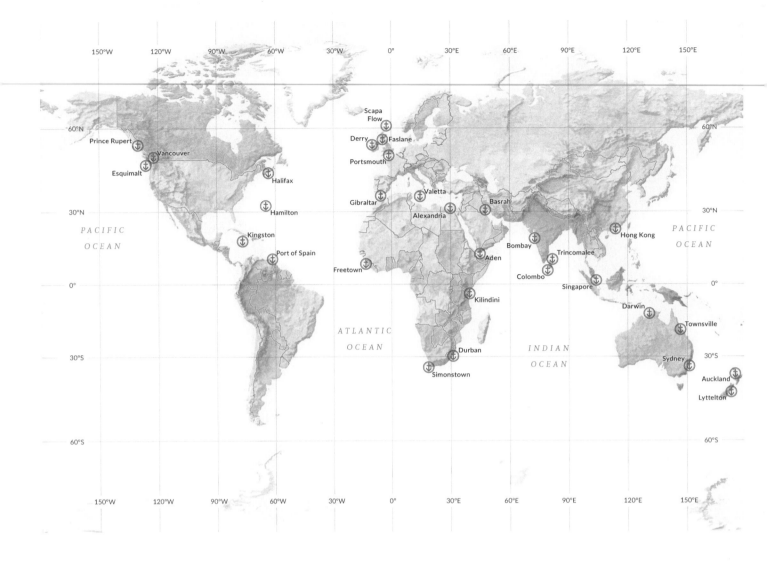

General Charles de Gaulle, who immediately set about creating new French armed forces from the scattered remnants of what became officially, in the summer of 1940, the Fighting French. But the army had left almost all its equipment behind in France, and the army units had to be slowly reorganized and reequipped in July and August 1940. Since the obvious threat was a German seaborne invasion, accompanied by paratroop operations, coastal defenses were reinforced and troops were posted where German landings were most likely. Although the British Army was not yet a match for the German Army in open combat, in prepared defensive positions against an army with no experience of large-scale amphibious operations, the British would have mounted a stiff resistance.

The Royal Navy also supplied a bulwark against the threat of invasion, although it was already evident that airpower was changing the nature of the war at sea. Once the Germans secured air and submarine bases along the northern and western coasts of France, they initiated a combined air-sea blockade directed at Britain's vital import/export trade. During the course of 1940, German aircraft (principally the converted airliner the Focke-Wulf 200 Condor) sank 580,000 tons of British and Commonwealth shipping, and in 1941 over a million tons: almost half the sinkings for the

North Atlantic theater.[14] It is questionable whether the bulk of the British home fleet, stationed in the far north of Scotland, could have successfully defended southern England against a seaborne invasion, given the threat posed by German aircraft stationed in northern France, the Low Countries, and Norway. In most other situations over the year that followed, British ships proved very vulnerable to determined dive-bomber and torpedo attacks where Axis aircraft could operate against them—principally in the Mediterranean but later in the Far East.[15]

In Britain and in Germany, it was soon realized that the possibility of a German invasion depended to a large extent on who could establish air superiority over southern England and for how long. British intelligence was unable to work out when German preparations would be completed, though air reconnaissance revealed the concentration of barges and small vessels along the French, Dutch, and Belgian coasts. Tidal analysis showed that there were relatively few days when an invasion force would enjoy the right conditions; even then, a cross-Channel operation in force would be feasible only if the Royal Air Force could be swept from the skies, to prevent it from attacking the transports and to allow the Luftwaffe to focus on keeping away the Royal Navy.

▲ **LEND-LEASE**
Dignitaries meet the first shipload of Lend-Lease food to arrive in England. In 1941 the actual provisions were perhaps less important than the boost to British morale provided by the increasingly active support offered by the United States.

▲ TORPEDO BOMBER

During the course of 1940, German aircraft sank 580,000 tons of British and Commonwealth shipping, and in 1941 over a million tons, accounting for almost half the sinkings for the North Atlantic theater.

THE BRITISH AIR-DEFENSE SYSTEM, SEPTEMBER 1939–SEPTEMBER 1940 ▶

Great Britain had developed a highly sophisticated air-defense system before the war began, and continued to improve it thereafter. This system employed both radar stations and ground observers to provide early warning of approaching enemy aircraft.

THE WEST POINT HISTORY OF WORLD WAR II

ATLANTIC
OCEAN

SHETLAND ISLANDS

°W   0°   0°

ORKNEY ISLANDS

THE DOWDING SYSTEM

Radar Stations → Filter Room | Fighter Command HQ → Group Headquarters

Observer Posts → Observer Corps HQ → Sector Airfield Controller

Direction Finder Stations

Satellite Airfields

Anti-Aircraft Batteries   Barrage Balloons   Fighter Aircraft

OUTER
HEBRIDES

INNER
SEAS

Grampian Mts.

SCOTLAND

NORTH
SEA

Edinburgh

Glasgow

GROUP 13

The British radar system used two
different technologies. The high-level
system could detect planes flying
above 1,500 feet out to the solid blue
line. Within the shaded area, the
low-level system could spot aircraft
at altitudes as low as 500 feet.

NORTHERN
IRELAND

Belfast

RELAND

IRISH
SEA

DUBLIN

UNITED

Hull

Liverpool

GROUP 12

Watnall

NETHERLANDS

AMSTERDAM

Fighters from Group 12 often
guarded the airfields of Group
11 while Group 11 pilots flew
to intercept German planes.

KINGDOM

ENGLAND

The Hague

Utrecht

Birmingham

Cambrian Mountains

Leicester

Coventry

Rotterdam

WALES

GROUP 10

Stanmore

Uxbridge

Canterburry

Antwerp

Ghent

Swansea

LONDON

Bruges

BRUSSELS

Cardiff

Bristol   Box

GROUP 11

Dunkirk

Courtrai

BELGIUM

Southampton

Calais

Lille

Portsmouth

Cambrai

Ardennes
50°N

Plymouth

English Channel

FRANCE

LEGEND

Low Cover (at 500 ft)
September 1939

High Cover (at 15,000 ft)
September 1940

NORMANDY

PARIS

0°

50   100 Miles

A civilian volunteer scans the skies over London for incoming aircraft. During 1940, some 50,000 women, men, and youths served as observers, normally standing duty for fifty-six or twenty-four hours per week.

In the last weeks of June and on through July, the Luftwaffe undertook a great many small exploratory raids, many at night, to probe the British defenses and to give their pilots experience, particularly for nighttime flights. But there were no large-scale German air attacks, while Bomber Command kept up its attacks on German targets and the areas where invasion vessels had been sighted. Churchill had alerted the British public to what he called "the Battle of Britain" in a speech on June 18, 1940, but the air contest that has been known by that name ever since did not begin fully until the second week of August.[16]

THE BATTLE OF BRITAIN

The one area of prewar preparation in which the British government had invested great amounts of money and effort was its defense against air attack. This had been

ORDER OF BATTLE FOR THE BATTLE OF BRITAIN, AUGUST 18, 1940 ▶

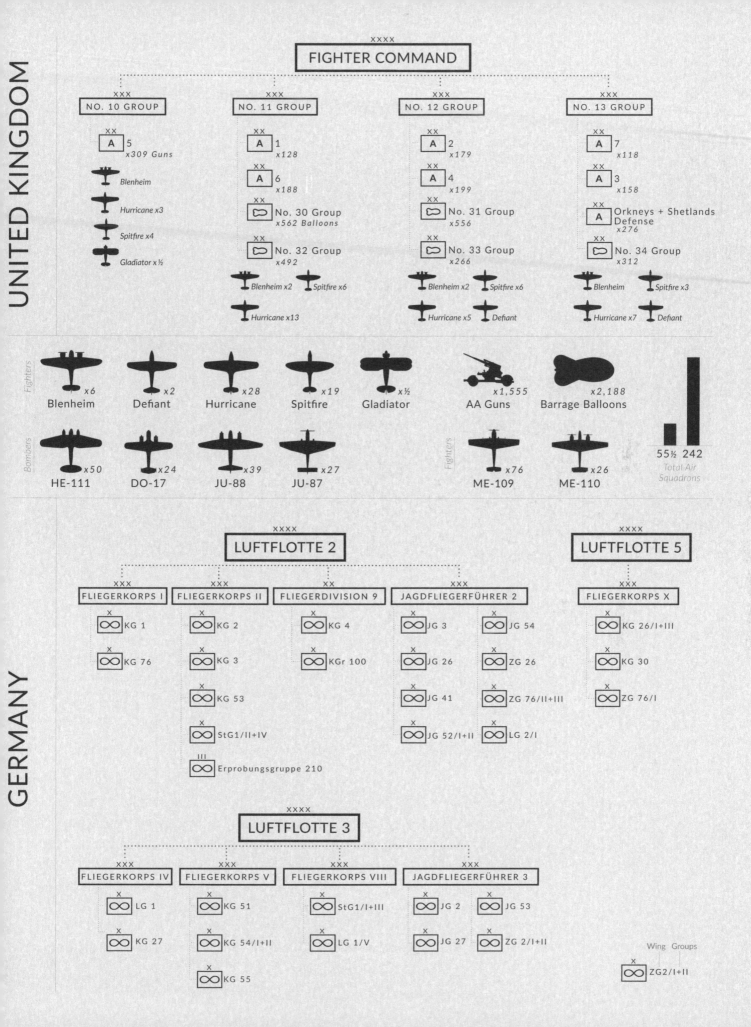

UNITED KINGDOM

FIGHTER COMMAND
××××

NO. 10 GROUP ×××
- A ×× 5 x309 Guns
- Blenheim
- Hurricane x3
- Spitfire x4
- Gladiator x ½

NO. 11 GROUP ×××
- A ×× 1 x128
- A ×× 6 x188
- No. 30 Group ×× x562 Balloons
- No. 32 Group ×× x492
  - Blenheim x2
  - Spitfire x6
  - Hurricane x13

NO. 12 GROUP ×××
- A ×× 2 x179
- A ×× 4 x199
- No. 31 Group ×× x556
- No. 33 Group ×× x266
  - Blenheim x2
  - Spitfire x6
  - Hurricane x5
  - Defiant

NO. 13 GROUP ×××
- A ×× 7 x118
- A ×× 3 x158
- Orkneys + Shetlands Defense A ×× x276
- No. 34 Group ×× x312
  - Blenheim
  - Spitfire x3
  - Hurricane x7
  - Defiant

Fighters
- Blenheim ×6
- Defiant ×2
- Hurricane ×28
- Spitfire ×19
- Gladiator ×½
- AA Guns ×1,555
- Barrage Balloons ×2,188

Bombers
- HE-111 ×50
- DO-17 ×24
- JU-88 ×39
- JU-87 ×27

Fighters
- ME-109 ×76
- ME-110 ×26

55½   242 *Total Air Squadrons*

GERMANY

LUFTFLOTTE 2
××××

FLIEGERKORPS I ×××
- ∞ × KG 1
- ∞ × KG 76

FLIEGERKORPS II ×××
- ∞ × KG 2
- ∞ × KG 3
- ∞ × KG 53
- ∞ × StG1/II+IV
- ∞ III Erprobungsgruppe 210

FLIEGERDIVISION 9 ××
- ∞ × KG 4
- ∞ × KGr 100

JAGDFLIEGERFÜHRER 2 ×××
- ∞ × JG 3
- ∞ × JG 26
- ∞ × JG 41
- ∞ × JG 52/I+II
- ∞ × JG 54
- ∞ × ZG 26
- ∞ × ZG 76/II+III
- ∞ × LG 2/I

LUFTFLOTTE 5
××××

FLIEGERKORPS X ×××
- ∞ × KG 26/I+III
- ∞ × KG 30
- ∞ × ZG 76/I

LUFTFLOTTE 3
××××

FLIEGERKORPS IV ×××
- ∞ × LG 1
- ∞ × KG 27

FLIEGERKORPS V ×××
- ∞ × KG 51
- ∞ × KG 54/I+II
- ∞ × KG 55

FLIEGERKORPS VIII ×××
- ∞ × StG1/I+III
- ∞ × LG 1/V

JAGDFLIEGERFÜHRER 3 ×××
- ∞ × JG 2
- ∞ × JG 27
- ∞ × JG 53
- ∞ × ZG 2/I+II

Wing Groups
- ∞ × ZG2/I+II

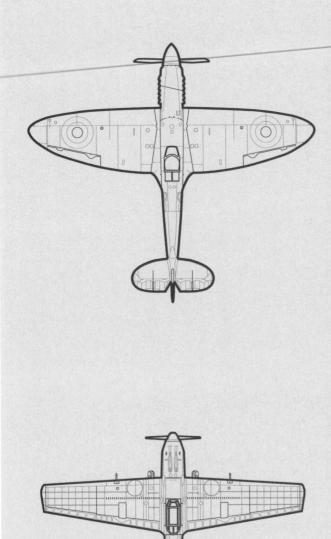

Supermarine Spitfire MK 1A

Entered Service	1938
Armament	Eight Browning .303 machine guns
Bombs	None
Engine	1,030 hp Rolls Royce Merlin III
Maximum Speed	362 mph
Maximum Range	395 miles
Rate of Climb	2,530 ft per minute
Ceiling	31,900 ft
Span	36 ft 10 in
Length	29 ft 11 in
Height	11 ft 5 in
Weight	4,810 lbs empty, 5,784 lbs loaded
Produced	20,351 (all variants)
Strengths	Tighter turning ability
Weaknesses	Fuel tank between the engine and cockpit could burn pilots if hit, .303 machine guns could not penetrate thicker areas of Bf 109E armor

Messerschmitt Bf 109E

Entered Service	1937
Armament	Two 20 mm cannons and two 7.9 mm machine guns
Bombs	Four 110 lb bombs or one 551 lb bomb
Engine	1,150 hp Daimler-Benz DB 601Aa inverted V
Maximum Speed	357 mph
Maximum Range	412 miles
Rate of Climb	3,100 ft per minute
Ceiling	36,000 ft
Span	32 ft 5 in
Length	28 ft 8 in
Height	8 ft 10 in
Weight	4,440 lbs empty, 5,520 lbs loaded
Produced	33,984 (all variants)
Strengths	Faster rate of climb, self-sealing fuel tanks, fuel-injected engine allowing negative-g maneuvers
Weaknesses	Accident-prone during takeoff and landing, somewhat less agile

BATTLE OF BRITAIN ▲ FIGHTER COMPARISON

Neither the Poles nor the French had a fighter plane equal to the German Bf 109. The British Supermarine Spitfire, however, matched the performance of the Messerschmitt. In fighter combat during the Battle of Britain, victory was determined by the skill of the pilots, tactics, luck, and numbers, not the capabilities of the planes.

viewed from at least 1936 as an urgent necessity in case the Luftwaffe launched a bomber offensive from the first day of the war. Extra finance had been made available to help build up RAF Fighter Command at the expense of the bombers. The Germans had no plans for such an offensive, but efforts to strengthen British air defenses—both Fighter Command and the network of antiaircraft and radar defenses—remained a priority during the months of the phony war and over the summer of 1940. The structure set up under the supervision of Fighter Command, led by Air Chief Marshal Sir Hugh Dowding, was the most sophisticated air-defense system then in existence.

The Dornier Do 17 "fast bomber," designed to outrun an enemy's defending fighters, enjoyed early successes during the invasions of Poland and France. In the Battle of Britain, however, the higher top speed of British fighters resulted in heavy casualties among Do 17 crews.

Fighter Command was divided into a number of territorial groups that covered the whole of the British Isles, though the most important were Eleven Group and Twelve Group, which were based south and north of London in the areas that the Germans were expected to attack most heavily. Each group was linked by telephone to all the air stations under its control, and each group headquarters connected with the Fighter Command headquarters at Stanmore, in north London.

This control structure meant that Dowding could deploy his fighters in the most efficient way rather than leaving operations to local initiative. But the whole system depended on up-to-the-minute information about incoming aircraft, so that fighters could get airborne (rather than be caught on the ground, an easy target for enemy bombers) in the short time it would now take the enemy to cross the Channel. Information was supplied by a chain of radar stations based on a science of "radio direction finding" developed in Britain beginning in 1935 and applied at once to air defense. They were not infallible, but by the summer of 1940, they could give sufficient advanced warning to allow the fighters and antiaircraft gunners to be ready.[17] The radar chain was enhanced by a Royal Observer Corps of trained men and women who reported directly to group headquarters the movement of enemy aircraft once they had crossed the coast. Without the exceptional advantage provided by a coordinated nationwide

Adolf Galland, commander of Luftwaffe Jagdgeschwader (Fighter Wing) 26, offers a German perspective on the aerial combats of the Battle of Britain:

Any encounter with British fighters called for maximum effort. One day on my way back from London I spotted a squadron of twelve Hurricanes north of Rochester. I attacked from 2,500 feet above them and behind, shooting like an arrow between the flights and from ramming distance fired on one of the aircraft in the rear of the line of the formation, tearing large pieces of metal out of the plane. At the last moment, I pulled my nose up and leaped over her, then flew right through the centre of the enemy's formation. It was not a pleasant sensation. Again I fired my cannon and machine gun into one of the Hurricanes from close range. Luckily, the British had had a similar or even bigger fright than I. No one attacked me. As I broke off, I saw two parachutes open below the broken formation.

It was not as simple as that with another Hurricane I shot down west of Dungeness. I had damaged her badly, and she was on fire and ought to have been a dead loss. Yet she did not crash but glided down in gentle curves. My flight companions and I attacked her three times without a final result. I flew close alongside the flying wreck, by now thoroughly riddled, with smoke belching from her. From a distance of a few yards I saw the dead pilot sitting in the shattered cockpit, while his aircraft spiraled slowly to the ground as though piloted by a ghostly hand.

I can only express the highest admiration for the British fighter pilots who, although technically at a disadvantage, fought bravely and indefatigably. They undoubtedly saved their country in this crucial hour.

The short range of the Me 109 became more and more of a disadvantage. During a single sortie of my wing, we lost twelve fighter planes, not by enemy action, but simply because after two hours' flying time, the bombers we were escorting had not yet reached the mainland on their return journey. Five of these fighters managed to make a pancake landing on the French shore with their last drop of fuel; seven of them landed in the "drink."[18]

structure of air defense, the Luftwaffe might well have succeeded in achieving air supremacy over southern Britain.

The British side enjoyed other advantages too. The new monoplane high-powered fighters—the Supermarine Spitfire and the Hawker Hurricane—were comparable with the German Messerschmitt Me 109. They were considerably superior to any of the other major German aircraft, particularly the Junkers Ju87 "Stuka" dive-bomber and the Heinkel He111 and Dornier Do 17 medium bombers that carried out much of the subsequent campaign.[19] German fighters, even from bases close to the Channel, had very limited combat time over England—generally little more than twenty minutes before they had to fly home to refuel—and at times this left bombers inadequately protected. In addition, British pilots who parachuted from damaged aircraft landed on British soil, whereas German crew members would be taken prisoner or land in the sea. Finally, British intelligence had the advantages of being able to read much low-level German radio traffic, and also (thanks to the early success in partially cracking the German Enigma codes in May 1940) access to high-level intelligence (known as Ultra) on German plans and dispositions.[20]

The battle for air superiority had neither a neat start nor a clear ending. Most British accounts of the Battle of Britain divide it into three distinct stages: a preliminary assault on the radar and communications chain; a sustained attack on the aircraft and base facilities of Fighter Command in southern England; and a final shift on September 7 to the attack on London and its port facilities. From the German point of view, the battle was supposed to follow a more seamless pattern, starting with an all-out

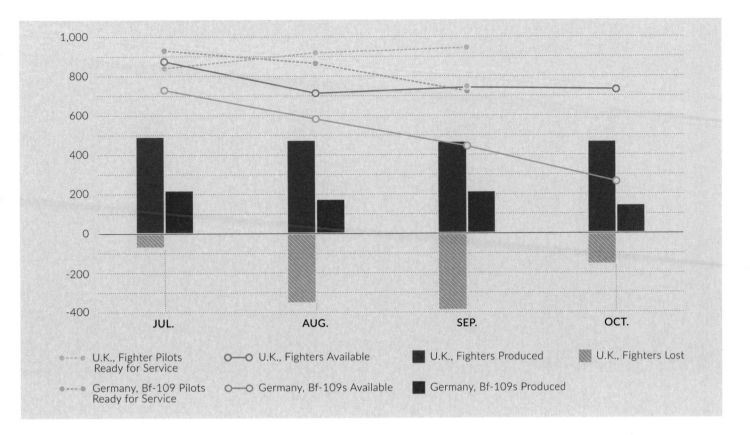

Chart legend:

- ●----● U.K., Fighter Pilots Ready for Service
- ○——○ U.K., Fighters Available
- ■ U.K., Fighters Produced
- ▨ U.K., Fighters Lost
- ●----● Germany, Bf-109 Pilots Ready for Service
- ○——○ Germany, Bf-109s Available
- ■ Germany, Bf-109s Produced

assault on Fighter Command and its organization; and then moving to an attack on military and war-economic targets across southern England; and finishing with a crushing blow against London as the prelude to the actual invasion, code-named Operation Sea Lion.[21] Regular night attacks, classed by the Germans as nuisance raids (*Störangriffe*), were also made during August to trigger the air-raid alarms and to inflict damage on utility services and war production.

The weather, however, prevented the initial all-out assault from happening when the German air command, under Reichsmarschall Hermann Göring, wanted it to start. Eagle Day, as it was called, had to be postponed from August 5 until August 13. On August 12 a concerted effort was made to destroy the radar network, but only two of the chain's stations were damaged, and auxiliary stations were available.[22] Then, on August 13, bad weather again intervened, and most aircraft were called back except for one group. The full assault began only on August 18, with destructive raids on a number of Fighter Command stations. Between August 12 and September 6, there were fifty-three raids on air bases, though only thirty-two of these were fighter stations. Damage was heavy at some bases, but effective dispersal of aircraft and personnel, and rapid repair of damaged runways, meant that only three stations were unavailable for operations, and then just briefly.[23] The commander of Fighter Command Eleven Group, Air Vice Marshal Keith Park, used his units sparingly but effectively, changing tactics to match the changes in German practice.[24]

In late August, believing that Fighter Command was close to collapse, German bombers turned their attention as planned to military-economic targets, principally

▲ THE BATTLE OF BRITAIN

Despite the large number of Hurricanes and Spitfires lost during the Battle of Britain, the United Kingdom sustained its air strength by producing equally large numbers of new planes and a sufficient number of new pilots. The same was not true of Germany.

SIR HUGH DOWDING
April 24, 1882–February 15, 1970
Air Chief Marshal

Hugh Dowding served in World War I first as an artillery officer, and then in the Royal Flying Corps, and ended the war with the rank of brigadier general. In 1936 he was appointed commander in chief of Fighter Command after having served as air member for supply and research in the British Air Ministry. He transformed the effectiveness of Fighter Command by introducing fast new monoplane fighters and setting up an integrated control and communications system based on radio, telephone, and a chain of radar and observation posts. He argued successfully against Churchill's plan to send more fighters to France in the battle there in May 1940. During the Battle of Britain, he dispersed RAF fighter forces across Britain, so that exhausted squadrons in the front line could be rotated out and fresh squadrons could take their place. The whole defensive system rested on a central control room at Fighter Command HQ, which gave orders to the different fighter groups in order to intercept incoming German aircraft. Dowding believed in using his fighters sparingly so that a number could intervene against each German incursion, and avoided a large-scale clash with the larger attacking force. The result was a campaign that forced high attrition levels on German aircraft and ensured that Fighter Command losses were not too high. In October 1940 he clashed with the Air Ministry over the failure of Fighter Command to prepare for night-fighter defense effectively, and in November he was replaced by Air Marshal Sholto Douglas. Dowding headed a delegation to the United States intended to secure more American aircraft, but his awkward, reserved personality hindered negotiations. He retired in July 1942.

ports and aircraft industry targets, and began to raid sites closer to the center of London. German intelligence assumed that the RAF had been almost eliminated by the attacks in mid-August, which explains the willingness to move away from attacks on airfields. The truth was entirely different, for on September 1 Fighter Command had over seven hundred operational fighters, no fewer than it had had at the start of the battle in early August, thanks to a high level of replacements from the factories and a steady flow of trained pilots. On September 7 the first heavy raids were carried out on the port of London. Although this has usually been viewed by historians of the battle as a result of Hitler's fury at the bombing of Berlin in late August, the final assault on London had always been part of the plan to support the invasion. The bombing of London was seen as the prelude to the cross-Channel operation, which was provisionally fixed for September 15.[25]

The change in German strategy compelled the RAF to adopt new tactics. The Germans were now attacking London by day with hundreds of bombers, supported by much of the German fighter force. Over the following week, the British Hurricane units (the majority of the fighters in Fighter Command squadrons) attacked the bombers, while the Spitfires engaged the German fighters. Losses escalated for both sides, but Fighter Command lost more heavily in the September air battles than it had in defense of the airfields.

The dramatic conclusion came a week after the start of heavy bombing attacks on London, on September 15. British intelligence had guessed correctly that this date was likely to be invasion day, given favorable tides and the imminence of bad autumn weather in the weeks that followed. On September 7 the code word *Cromwell* had been sent out to all military units to prepare them for imminent action. British troops were placed on standby, and the Royal Air Force's Bomber Command increased its raiding against the invasion ports. But since air superiority had evidently not been won, on

◀ LONDON'S NIGHT DEFENSE

Between September and December, most attacks were directed against London—the capital, largest port, and commercial center of the United Kingdom. Intricate networks of barrage balloons, searchlights, and antiaircraft guns were established to discourage the German attackers and to raise the morale of the beleaguered Londoners.

September 14 Hitler postponed the decision to invade—and on September 19 finally delayed it indefinitely. Instead, on September 15 (now celebrated as Battle of Britain Day), a force of two hundred bombers attacked London. A quarter of the planes were shot down or damaged, a rate of loss considerably higher than previous raids and insupportable for a bomber force already facing declining numbers. Daylight raids were suspended three days later, and night bombing became standard practice. In the nine days from September 7 to September 15, the Luftwaffe lost 298 aircraft—around one-fifth the number available, and a rate of attrition that the force could not sustain for more than a few weeks. The Luftwaffe then began a sustained bombing campaign directed principally at port cities, warehouses, shipping, and the aero-engine industry— partly as a contribution to the sea blockade of Britain, partly to prevent the revival of

The cables tethering barrage balloons to the ground made flying low through a protected area dangerous for enemy pilots.

British air strength and its deployment in other theaters, and partly to reduce the high daytime losses. The object was now to try to wear down Britain's war effort in the hope that this might force British surrender during the winter of 1940–41.[26]

The traditional history of the Battle of Britain has always emphasized how close to defeat the RAF came and, by extrapolation, how close England was to invasion and occupation. More recent studies have questioned just how narrow the margin was. The number of pilots and fighter aircraft available to Fighter Command was considerably greater than Churchill's famous description of "so few" would suggest, though the numbers on both sides were indeed small.[27] From June through September 1940, the British aircraft industry supplied 1,900 fighters, an increasing number of them the higher-performance Spitfires; German fighter production for the same four months was 775. Fighter Command had around 1,400 pilots available by the start of the battle, and thanks to an intensive training program, losses could be made good throughout the battle. Fighter Command had an average of 1,500 pilots on hand by the second half of September.[28] Against these numbers, the German single-engine fighter force had an average of 800 to 900 available for operations and a smaller scale of pilot training and replacement. The gap between the two sides was disguised by the fact that German pilots survived combat operations for longer thanks to their better training, thus reducing the need for regular replacement crews early in the battle. But they also suffered rising levels of flying fatigue as the air conflict continued, whereas British Fighter Command had the advantage of being able to ration the number of fighter sorties pilots were expected to undertake, in order to prevent insupportable levels of attrition and excessive flying fatigue. Park operated a rotating system of operational squadrons. When one squadron was worn out, it could be replaced by one from bases farther north or west, and then rested and returned to combat. During the battle, the RAF lost 915 aircraft; the Luftwaffe, 1,733.[29]

To maximize the conservation of crew and aircraft, the British air bases were decentralized with a system of subsidiary stores and satellite airfields, while the aircraft industry soon inaugurated a system of contract dispersal to reduce the threat from bomb damage. The balance of leadership is never easy to evaluate, but there is little doubt that in Dowding and Park the RAF possessed two commanders who combined shrewd tactical judgment, a proper attention to detail, and the capacity to outthink the enemy.[30] The Battle of Britain did not result in the decisive defeat of either air force, but it did ensure that Britain avoided German invasion, while demonstrating to the German side that it faced a powerful and resourceful enemy whose capacity to resist it had seriously underestimated.

THE BOMBING BLITZ

The change in German strategy to the bomber offensive threatened to be a more dangerous development for the British because there was no effective defense against the night bomber, and the bombing imposed heavy civilian casualties: more than 43,000 dead over the nine-month bomber offensive. For years, the British population had been subjected to a diet of scaremongering literature on the air threat.[31] The contemporary popular opinion was that domestic morale might well collapse under heavy raiding, and both political and military leaders assumed from the apparently indiscriminate nature of the bombing that the Luftwaffe was trying to undermine the home front and get the civilian population to pressure the Churchill government into abandoning the war. From German records, however, it is evident that the targets chosen fit a pattern of attacks on port cities, food stocks, and shipping as a contribution to the

EXPERIENCING THE BOMBING RAID

When war broke out, actress Barbara Nixon volunteered for service as an air-raid warden. In her postwar memoir, she describes experiencing her first bombing raid:

Suddenly, before I heard a sound, the shabby, ill-lit, five-storey building ahead of me swelled out like a child's balloon, or like a Walt Disney house having hiccups. I looked at it in astonishment, that bricks and mortar could stretch like rubber. At the point when it must burst, the glass fell out. It did not hurtle, it simply cracked and dropped out, allowing the straining building to deflate and return to normal. Almost instantaneously there was a crash and a double explosion in the street to my right. As the blast of air reached me I left my [bicycle] saddle and sailed through the air, heading for the area railings. The tin hat on my shoulder took the impact, and as I stood up I was mildly surprised to find that I was not hurt in the least. The corner buildings had diverted the full force of the blast; indeed, to judge by the number of idiotic thoughts that raced through my head, my progress to the railings might almost have been in "slow motion." I had not heard the whistle of the bombs coming down, only the explosion, and now the sound of an aeroplane's engine starting up. I thought, "So it's true—you don't hear the one that gets, or nearly gets, you."

For no reason except that one handbook had said so, I blew my whistle. An old lady appeared in her doorway and asked, "What was all that?" I told her it was a bomb, but she was stone-deaf and I had to abandon bawling for pantomime of a bomb exploding before she would agree to go to the surface shelter. After putting a dressing on some small cuts on a man's face, I turned back toward the site of the

damage. I did not know the locality, but, again, the handbook said that when an alert sounded, a warden away from his home area should report to the nearest Post. The damage was thirty yards away, but the corner building, which had diverted some of the blast from me, was still standing.

At four in the afternoon there would certainly be casualties. Now I would know whether I was going to be of any use as a warden or not, and I wanted to postpone the knowledge. I dared not run. I had to go warily, as if I were crossing a minefield with only a rough sketch of the position of the mines—only the danger-spots were in myself. I was not let down lightly. In the middle of the street lay the remains of a baby. It had been blown clean through a window, and had burst on striking the roadway. To my intense relief, pitiful and horrible as it was, I was not nauseated, and found a torn piece of curtain in which to wrap it . . .

The CD [civil defense] services arrived quickly. There was a large number of "white hats" [officers], but as far as one could see no one person took charge . . . I offered my services, and was thanked but given nothing to do, so busied myself finding blankets to cover the five or six mutilated bodies in the street. A small boy, aged about 13, had one leg torn off and was still conscious, though he gave no sign of any pain. In the garage a man was pinned under a capsized Thornycroft lorry, and most of the side wall and roof were piled on top of that. The Heavy Rescue Squad brought ropes, and heaved and tugged at the immense lorry. They got the man out, unconscious, but alive. He looked like a terra-cotta statue, his face, his teeth, his hair, were all a uniform brick colour.[32]

---

aero-naval blockade strategy approved by Hitler months beforehand, along with raids on the aircraft and aero-engine industries. Since London was by far the largest port and commercial center, most attacks between September and December were against London. In November Göring ordered a switch to targets in the British Midlands, and on the fourteenth and fifteenth of November, there was a heavy raid on Coventry and a series of heavy raids on Birmingham on November 19 and 20, and again on November 23 and 24. Over the whole campaign, around 85 percent of all incendiary and high-explosive bombs fell on port cities, including Liverpool, Plymouth, Bristol, Hull, Portsmouth, Southampton, and Cardiff.[33] The Luftwaffe did not attack entire industrial target systems, as the U.S. Eighth Air Force did later in the war with its attacks on the air industry, transportation, and chemicals, but focused on British docks, oil, and food stocks.[34]

The British government and armed forces relied on active and passive defenses

against night bombing. The night defenses consisted of antiaircraft guns, of which there were approximately 1,440 heavy and 950 light guns by early 1941, and a belt of searchlights and barrage balloons. Because the antiaircraft artillery had no radar guidance systems yet, the gunners relied on a barrage of fire from all available guns in the hope that they might hit something during a raid.[35] German records show that losses to antiaircraft fire were few: approximately 70 percent of bomber losses over the course of the Blitz resulted from accidents or bad weather.[36] The RAF had failed to anticipate the shift to night attacks, and in September 1940 there were almost no dedicated night fighters available fitted with equipment for detecting enemy bombers; nor were there pilots trained for nighttime operations. Squadrons of Bristol Blenheim light bombers were converted to the role of night fighters, but in the absence of radar guidance (called AI, or air interception), contact with enemy bombers was largely a matter of chance. Over a hundred British aircraft were airborne against the night raid on Coventry, but the German force lost only one plane, and that was due to accident. The British gradually installed radar guidance for antiaircraft guns and AI sets for night fighters during the late stages of the Blitz, but for most of the nine-month period of the bomber offensive—from September 1940 through May 1941—the equipment was not available yet. Only by the end of the campaign did loss rates for German bombers rise significantly, thanks to the new technology and the larger number of night-fighter squadrons. Ironically, British antiair defense became a serious threat only when the bombing was almost at an end, just before the Luftwaffe was transferred away from France to take part in the German invasion of the Soviet Union in June 1941.[37]

Civil defense was more thoroughly prepared for the bombing campaigns, but it still faced many challenges when bombing became a reality. The 1937 Air Raid Precautions Act made local authorities in Britain responsible for organizing a civil defense scheme

In this trenchant cartoon, Theodore Geisel (better known as Dr. Seuss) criticizes the morals of the Americans who wanted to keep the United States out of the war. The London Blitz generated sympathy for the British and increasing willingness to assist them, even at the risk of war.

... and the Wolf chewed up the children and spit out their bones ... But those were <u>Foreign</u> Children and it really didn't matter."

to minimize losses among the civilian population. By 1940, there was a network of air-raid shelters, auxiliary fire forces, air-raid wardens, emergency and rescue teams, antigas facilities, and first aid units in place.[38] The new structure was strained under the impact of heavy bombing, but in most cases it worked well enough to combat and contain the fires caused by bombing and to administer emergency aid and rescue. The shelter provision proved much less effective. For the sake of speed, many towns had built crude brick-and-concrete shelters aboveground on streets or sidewalks. They offered no protection from a direct or nearby hit, and many collapsed because of the poor quality of the materials. There were very few large purpose-built shelters deep underground. Instead, householders were encouraged to build an air-raid shelter in the basement or cellar, or to place a prefabricated Anderson shelter (designed by the engineer David Anderson) in the garden.

In poorer areas, houses had no gardens, and the buildings were flimsy. Here the

population relied on local improvised shelters under railway bridges, in caves and tunnels, or, in London, in the deeper Underground stations. Conditions in shelters improved over the course of the Blitz as a result of urgent government action, but the very high casualty rate among civilians was due partly to the poor level of preraid shelter provision.[39] The deficiencies in civil defense did not, however, provoke social unrest or political protest. City populations came to rely more on state help and looked to the authorities for assistance with welfare and rehabilitation. The response to heavy raiding outside London was to move out of the city to nearby countryside. The government was concerned that "trekking," as it was called, would undermine morale and affect industrial output, but it was soon found that those living outside the city could be organized with local billets and emergency housing, while workers continued to go back into the city during the day to keep industry and transport going.

The government propaganda in Britain during the Blitz played on the theme "Britain Can Take It," and there was an important sense that the shock brought by heavy bombing was an ordeal that British society ought to be able to overcome. The propaganda, in turn, engendered a widespread determination among the British public to show that the bombing could be endured. The slogan about "taking it" was soon dropped, however, in favor of the idea that Britain was "giving it" back. Throughout the period of the Blitz, RAF bombers also bombed German cities, dropping 50,000 tons of bombs in 1940 and 1941—not much smaller than the 58,000 tons the Luftwaffe loosed over Britain.[40] In October 1940, RAF crews were instructed to drop their bombs on any visible urban target, and in December the War Cabinet instructed Bomber Command to attack German cities indiscriminately in response to the bombing of

Coventry. In the early months of 1941, the Air Ministry made careful calculations, drawn from evidence of German bombing, about the effects of high-explosive bombs when compared with incendiaries. It was decided that a much larger load of incendiaries should be carried for use against the central residential areas where workers' housing was concentrated, because it was argued that killing workers and destroying their houses would affect war production much more than bombing a single factory. The problem for the RAF was the poor level of accuracy. Without a pathfinder system (using lead aircraft to mark the target clearly), and with no electronic or radar aids to

◀ GERMAN SUBMARINE
Unable to find success in the air, the Germans altered their tactics and switched to an underwater campaign against British commercial shipping in an attempt to starve the British into capitulation.

navigation, most bombs dropped somewhere other than the assigned target area, even when that target was a whole city center. In the summer of 1941, a report on bombing accuracy showed that only one in five aircraft got within *five miles* of the target.[41] The RAF responded to the evidence of poor accuracy and wasted effort by defining ever-larger target areas, but the effect was to disappoint those, like Churchill, who had assumed that bombing would achieve rapid results. Although there was wide support among sections of the British public for British bombing of Germany as the one way to get back at the enemy, Britain's military leaders remained skeptical that it would achieve anything decisive.

The work of the spotters was valuable only because of the phone communications system, which enabled their reports to reach Fighter Command in time to be of use.

ASSESSING THE BLITZ

The impact of the Blitz on British strategy has usually been described in terms of the effect on home morale. At the time and in many accounts since, it was assumed that morale remained firm enough not to affect Britain's continued bellicosity. But increasingly, historians have been critical of the so-called myth of the Blitz—the idea that the bombing strengthened rather than undermined the unity and determination to prevail of British society—citing evidence that alongside community solidarity could be found class discrimination, traditional racial and gender prejudices, and widespread crime. These factors may complicate the previously simplistic picture, but they did not of themselves prevent British society from enduring the ordeal of bombing.[42] The ability of the British to withstand the bombing also had important effects in Washington, not only in pushing many doubters away from isolation and toward the policy of offering more concrete assistance to Britain, but in affirming for the American government and public British determination to continue to oppose Hitler at all costs rather than reach a compromise agreement.[43]

The changing mood helped Roosevelt in his decision to try to drive through Congress a bill to supply "Lease-Lend" aid to Britain. In a well-known "fireside chat" radio broadcast in December 1940, Roosevelt promised that the United States would become "the arsenal of democracy." Lease-Lend was a plan to give Britain weapons, food, and resources at no charge on the assumption that Britain would repay the debt at some

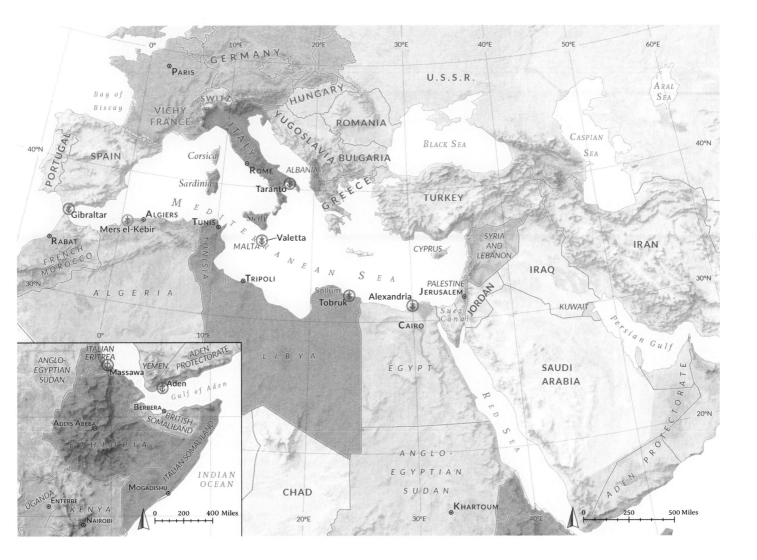

future date. The government in London watched the debate over the bill with anxiety, because by the winter of 1940–41, British financial resources abroad were nearing exhaustion.[44] After long arguments with Congress, Roosevelt finally succeeded in getting the Lend-Lease Act passed on March 11, 1941. The scheme was a critical factor in Britain's survival as a fighting power in 1941 and 1942, providing $6.7 billion of aid in the first two years—more than half of it military supplies of planes, vehicles, guns, and ammunition, but also substantial quantities of food, which made up 30 percent of Lend-Lease supplies in 1941. Britain also benefited from generous aid from Canada, which supplied over $4 billion in loans and aid during the war, as well as mobilizing 1.5 million men and producing 750,000 vehicles.[45] Britain was much less "alone" by the spring of 1941 than had been the case nine months before.

The Blitz had limited material effects on Britain, even if the human cost was exceptional at that stage of the war. Calculations made in the summer of 1941 by government agencies showed that Britain's economic output was reduced by only an estimated 5 percent by the bombing. German bombing of oil installations reduced British oil stocks by less than 1 percent. The deliberate targeting of flour mills and grain storage reduced stocks by only 5 percent. No railway line remained blocked for more than a few days.[46] Despite heavy bombing of docks and wharves, London and other ports

▲ ITALIAN, ENGLISH, AND FRENCH POSSESSIONS IN NORTH AFRICA AND THE MEDITERRANEAN

Naturally the war between Italy and the United Kingdom spilled over to the two nations' colonies in Africa. Control over North Africa, the Horn of Africa, and the adjacent waters was very important to Britain, because the Suez Canal provided the most efficient route between England and India.

nevertheless continued to function in an improvised way, with ships at anchor in the approaches to the port while a stream of smaller vessels unloaded the cargo.

The danger to Britain was much greater from the submarine. In March 1941 Churchill coined the phrase "the Battle of the Atlantic" in response to the rising rate of ship sinkings by submarines, which had orders to sink all Allied merchant ships on sight. Although merchant shipping sailed in convoy from the start of the war, there were always slower vessels or stragglers, or convoys with a limited naval escort, from which the German submarine "wolf packs," as they were known, could exact a high toll. British shipyards found it difficult to supply new shipping fast enough to compensate for the vessels that were sunk. Heavy losses threatened British supplies of food, raw materials, and oil. Domestic agriculture was rapidly expanded to provide more grain and vegetables from home sources, and food and raw material resources were stockpiled, but the battle against the submarines became a key military priority for the British Navy and the Royal Air Force. British and American ingenuity eventually produced technical, scientific, and tactical breakthroughs that would redress the balance—but until then, the losses to British shipping remained frighteningly high.[47]

The Blitz and the Battle of the Atlantic had greater effects on Britain's wider wartime strategy than they did on the home front because they compelled the armed forces to concentrate on the defense of mainland Britain and the transatlantic lifeline at the expense of other theaters of war. The German hope that it would keep Britain bottled up, preventing decisive intervention in the Mediterranean, was largely achieved. Britain did find its strategic options narrowed by the expense and effort of defending against the bombing and of repairing its effects. Civil defense absorbed almost two million full-time and part-time workers, and involved local army units in emergency work.

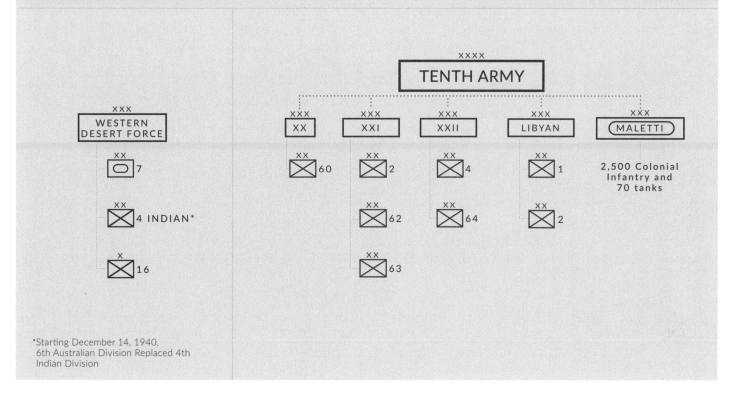

BRITISH COMMONWEALTH

ITALY

▲ ORDER OF BATTLE FOR
OPERATION COMPASS,
DECEMBER 8, 1940

Active defense was also costly. Few antiaircraft guns could be spared for use with the army in the Mediterranean or to station in the Far East against the threat from Japan. And while there were ninety-nine squadrons of Spitfires and Hurricanes in Britain by late 1941, very few were available for use elsewhere. In the Mediterranean, the Far East, and India, the RAF relied on American and British aircraft of considerably lower performance. The cost to the British war effort came not from the direct destruction of industry and resources but from the cost of defense itself.[48]

THE WAR IN THE MEDITERRANEAN:
THE BRITISH COMMONWEALTH AGAINST ITALY

The limitations that Britain faced over the period of bombing, from September 1940 to the summer of 1941, were evident in the Mediterranean theater, where U.K. forces struggled to contain the threat from the poorly equipped Italian armed forces, and then succumbed to German intervention in support of Italy in the Balkans, the Greek islands, and North Africa. The war with Italy was not entirely unexpected, but it forced Britain to fight in two separate theaters at a time when defense of the home islands was absorbing most of Britain's war effort. The Italian dictator, Benito Mussolini, took his country into war on June 10, 1940, despite advice from his generals that Italian forces were too weak. Mussolini did not want to be left behind in the rush for spoils following

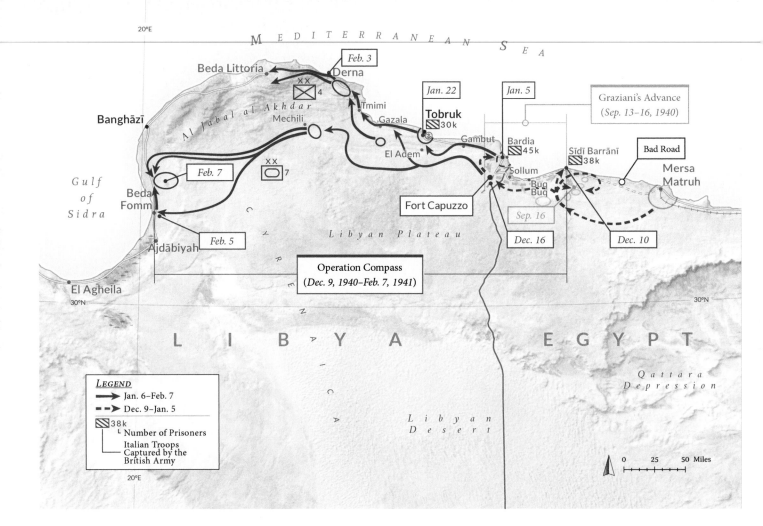

GRAZIANI'S ADVANCE AND ▲
OPERATION COMPASS,
SEPTEMBER 13–16, 1940

In September 1940, Italian forces pushed a short distance into Egypt. The following December, what began as a raid—Operation Compass—turned quickly into a pursuit, as British forces penetrated deep into Libya and captured about 130,000 prisoners.

Hitler's victory over France and Britain. He wanted to create a new "Roman Empire" across the Mediterranean and North Africa, and that meant fighting Britain.[49]

In August 1940 an Italian Army drove the British out of their protectorate in British Somaliland in East Africa. In September 1940 Marshal Rodolfo Graziani moved a large Italian Army out of the Italian colony of Libya across the Egyptian frontier. Egypt was a base for British forces in the Middle East, agreed by treaty with the Egyptian king. British Commonwealth forces were there to defend the Suez Canal, but more importantly, to protect the oil of Iran and Iraq, the seizure of which would have solved the serious oil shortages facing both Axis states. Fortunately for the limited air and ground forces available in Egypt, the Italian commander—who at that stage had overwhelming numerical superiority—halted on the frontier and waited to see what his enemy would do.

Over the following months, despite the Allied shortage of first-class equipment, the Italian position was reversed dramatically by British initiatives. In East Africa, a twin assault was undertaken by British Commonwealth forces based in Kenya and Sudan against the Italian Empire in Ethiopia and Somalia. From the north, in Sudan, a force of British, Indian, and African troops launched an offensive on January 19, 1941, against northern Ethiopia and by April had broken through to the Eritrean coast at

Wavell served in both the Boer War and World War I, losing his left eye at the Second Battle of Ypres. He ended the First World War as a staff officer in Egypt, supporting the British Empire's campaign in Palestine. He held a number of staff posts in the interwar period, and in July 1939 he was sent to Egypt as general officer commanding in chief of Middle East Command. In February 1940 his title was changed to commander in chief Middle East to reflect wider responsibilities in the region. He organized the campaign to drive the Italians out of Egypt and Libya that was launched in December 1940, and was on the point of annihilating Italian resistance when he was ordered to send forces to help the Greeks in their war against the Italians. His weakened forces in Africa recoiled before the new German Afrika Korps, and the Greek intervention ended with defeat and evacuation, first from Greece and then from Crete. Without sufficient reserves and with demands for forces in Iraq and Syria, his operation to drive Rommel back from the Egyptian frontier and to relieve Tobruk failed. Ironically, Rommel had read Wavell's book *Generals and Generalship* with approval. Churchill sacked Wavell in June 1941, and he went to India to serve as commander in chief there. In India, Wavell had to supervise further retreats in the face of Japanese aggression in Malaya (now Malaysia) and Burma (now Myanmar), though he stabilized the Indian-Burmese front by summer of 1942. In September 1943 he was relieved of command and became viceroy of India. He was a tough commander, expecting a lot from his men, and fully cognizant of the importance of supply and logistics for a successful campaign.

Massawa, routing the larger Italian force. From Kenya, the British commander, General Alan Cunningham, was able to exploit the fact that British cryptanalysts had broken the Italian secret communication codes, revealing Italian military movements. He led an assault by African and British Commonwealth forces through Somaliland and on into Ethiopia. The Allied force numbered no more than 77,000, supported by 100 South African air force planes, against an Italian force of more than 430,000 (200,000 of them African levies) and 244 aircraft, though these were mainly obsolete. The campaign opened on February 11 and achieved remarkable success. Italian forces fought with little commitment, were short of vehicles, and were cut off by British sea power from any chance of reinforcement or new supplies of munitions. Moreover, Italian forces were faced with a hostile Ethiopian population, which quickly sided with the approaching Allies when it could. On April 6 the Ethiopian capital of Addis Ababa was captured by the Allied forces, and on May 19 the Italian commander, the Duke of Aosta, surrendered. The Allies captured 420,000 enemy troops for the loss of just 3,100 casualties, the largest British catch of prisoners throughout the war.[50]

In the Mediterranean theater, it soon became clear that the Italian Navy, though superior in size to the Royal Navy's Mediterranean Fleet at Alexandria in Egypt, was cautious about engaging with the enemy. Perhaps it was inhibited by Britain's ruthless destruction on July 3 of the French fleet, which was stationed at Mers-el-Kébir on the Algerian coast. After France capitulated to Hitler in June, Churchill decided that Britain could not take the risk of these vessels falling under German control. When the French naval commander refused to join the Free French or to allow his ships to be peacefully neutralized, a British squadron opened fire, destroying the French battleship *Bretagne*, seriously damaging five other vessels, and killing 1,300 French servicemen.[51] The Italian Navy tried to avoid a similar fate, but on the evening of

ERWIN ROMMEL
November 15, 1891–October 14, 1944
Field Marshal

Field Marshal Erwin Rommel was the most famous and well-regarded German general during World War II (from a very, very short list).

As a young officer fighting in the Italian Alps during World War I with the elite Alpine Corps, he earned the Pour le Mérite, the German equivalent of the Medal of Honor. His war diaries, *Infantry Attacks*, were published during the interwar period and accelerated his fame, especially among officers in Great Britain and the United States. As World War II began, Rommel commanded Hitler's personal bodyguard battalion.

During the invasion of France, Rommel was at the head of the 7th Panzer Division. Leading from the front, he applied the tactics he learned in the Italian Alps to mechanized warfare, emphasizing rapid movement, surprise, and envelopment. In 1941 Rommel took command of the German forces dispatched to aid the reeling Italians in North Africa and won dramatic initial victories against the British. Weakened by logistical difficulties and facing improved British and American forces, Rommel was eventually defeated in Tunisia. After duty in Greece and Italy, Rommel, as an army group commander, organized German forces in preparation for the anticipated D-Day assault; he argued for a forward defense to throw the Allies back into the Channel.

From early 1944, Rommel secretly supported the overthrow of Hitler (though not his assassination) because he felt the war was being fought incorrectly. When this was discovered, Rommel took a cyanide capsule to spare his family and staff from Nazi execution squads. Hitler reported that Rommel's death was from combat wounds, and he was given a state funeral.

November 11, twenty-one Fairey Swordfish biplane torpedo bombers from the British carrier *Illustrious* raided the southern Italian naval base at Taranto. They inflicted heavy damage on three Italian battleships, and the weakened Italian fleet retreated to safer harbors, hoping to avoid a major engagement. Taranto was an important lesson, underlined by the next major engagement with the Italian fleet in the Battle of Cape Matapan, north of Crete. The major Italian battleship *Vittorio Veneto* led a squadron to intercept a British convoy, but because the Royal Navy could read Italian secret naval codes, the convoy was canceled and a large group of carriers and battleships assembled to meet the Italian squadron. An Italian cruiser and other smaller ships were sunk by combined air-naval action, and the *Vittorio Veneto* itself was hit by a torpedo launched from a Royal Navy aircraft, forcing it to limp away. The Italian Navy never ventured out to meet the British Navy in combat again. Instead, aircraft and submarines became the principal means of naval warfare for both sides.[52]

Italy's caution at sea was replicated in Graziani's stalled advance against Egypt, which gave the British Commonwealth forces time to build up supplies and men for a counteroffensive. The British Middle East commander in chief, General Archibald Wavell, ordered the commander in Egypt, Major General Richard O'Connor, to undertake a limited raid—code-named Operation Compass—against the Italian position in Egypt. Reinforced with the new Matilda tanks (which were useful only against the weaker Italians) and more aircraft, O'Connor's force of around 30,000 began a penetration of Italian lines on December 8, 1940. The 4th Indian Division infiltrated the insecure Italian front while the 7th Armoured Division circled round the Italian forces and attacked from the rear. The Italians panicked and broke; 38,000 of them surrendered as prisoners of war. O'Connor then increased the raid to a full-scale operation, and the Australian 6th Division and the 7th Armoured pursued the retreating

LIBYA

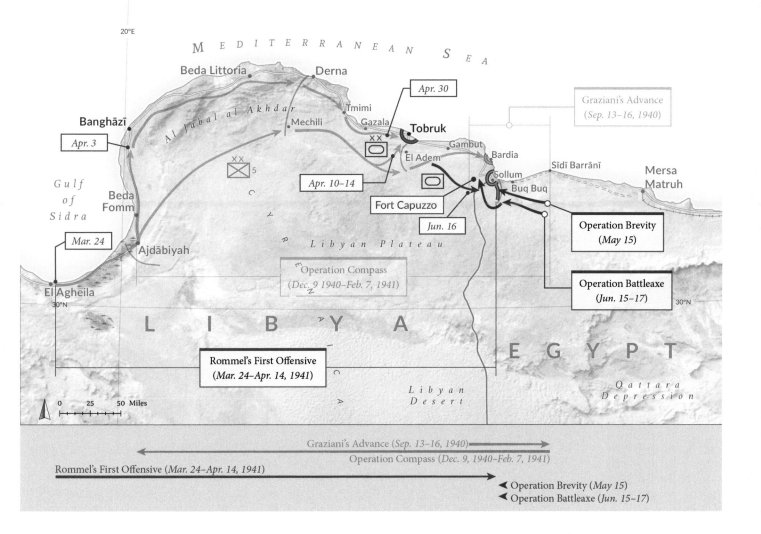

Italian army, capturing another 38,000 prisoners. The Libyan port of Bardia fell on January 4, and the port of Tobruk, the most important Italian supply base, surrendered on January 22. The British Commonwealth forces pushed on across Libya, finally reaching El Agheila on the coast of Cyrenaica with almost the entire Italian colony in their hands. The disparity in losses was once again extraordinary. For 2,000 British Commonwealth casualties, 130,000 Italians and Libyan levies were captured. Again Italy's compromised communications, poor armored equipment and air forces, and a lack of confidence among the rank and file all contributed to a costly and rapid collapse.[53]

THE GERMAN INTERVENTION IN THE MEDITERRANEAN

The situation in the Mediterranean theater was transformed by Mussolini's decision to launch a war against Greece on October 28, 1940. He was anxious to imitate German success by extending Italian territorial conquests into the Balkan Peninsula. It

▲ ROMMEL'S FIRST OFFENSIVE AND OPERATIONS BREVITY AND BATTLEAXE

A month and a half after Operation Compass ended, Axis forces under German general Erwin Rommel launched another offensive that drove the overextended British back into Egypt. It was a recurring pattern in North Africa: after a long push, an attacker faced difficult logistical problems and was very vulnerable to a counterattack. For this reason, combat in the region has been described often as a series of seesaw campaigns.

Operation Crusader

Bob Crisp was a South African cricket star who served during World War II in the British 3rd Royal Tank Regiment. This description of some of his experiences during the tenth day of fighting in Operation Crusader in 1941 is taken from *Brazen Chariots*, which is widely considered one of the best soldier's memoirs of the war.

The Honeys [American-made M3-Stuart light tanks] positively leapt over the top of the ridge and plunged down the steady incline to the Trigh... We were half-way down the slope and going like bats out of hell in the bright sunlight before the Jerries realised what was happening. Then the familiar pattern of alarm and confusion and panic-flight away from us at right angles to the road...

[W]ithin seconds the dust was full of the crisscross pattern of tracers drawing red lines through the yellow cloud and puncturing the fleeing dark shapes with deadly points. From the turret tops we let go with tommy-guns and revolvers, and every now and again the whip-crack of the 37-mm. interjected the staccato chatter of the Brownings [machine guns]. I could still see a Honey or two racing alongside, but what was happening beyond the narrow limits of vision I could only guess.

Suddenly, through the dust, I saw the flat plane of the ground disappear into space. I yelled like mad at the driver to halt. He had seen the danger only a fraction of a second after I had, and jerked back on the brakes even while I was shouting at him. The tracks locked fast and tore up sand, rock and scrub in a frantic tussle to stop the momentum of the tank. We skidded to a violent stop with the front sprockets hanging over a sharp drop that started the descent of a steep escarpment...

Suddenly there was a fearful bang... As I looked backwards I was already giving the order to the gunner to traverse the turret as fast as he bloody well could. In one flash I saw it all, and the fear leapt up in me. Not fifty yards away, a 50-mm. antitank gun pointed straight at the Honey, pointed straight between my eyes. Beyond it were other guns and then... the sight I had dreaded most—a number of motionless Honeys and the huddled figures of [our] black-bereted men crouched on the sand or stretched out in the agony of death.

It took less than a second for the whole scene and its awful meaning to register in my mind. I could see the German gunners slamming the next shell into the breach as the turret whirled. I yelled, "On. Machine gun. Fire." In the same moment I saw the puff of smoke from the antitank gun and felt and heard the strike on the armour-plating. Quickly I looked down into the turret. A foot or two below me the gunner was staring at his hand, over which a dark red stain was slowly spreading. Then he gave a scream and fell groveling on the floor. In the top right hand corner of the turret a jagged hole gaped, and through it, like some macabre peepshow, I could see the gun being reloaded...

I leaned down and pulled the trigger [of the Browning], and kept my finger there until the gun jammed... I suddenly saw the slim chance. If the tank would move at all, and we could drop over the edge of the escarpment, we would be out of sight of those blasted antitank guns. I said urgently into the mike: "Driver, advance. Over the edge. Quick!" [54]

proved a major miscalculation. Poorly equipped Italian forces pushed across the Albanian frontier into the mountainous areas of northern Greece only to be thrown back by determined Greek resistance. In late November the Greek Army began operations to push the Italians back into Albania, and by January, the Italian Army was facing defeat. If the British Commonwealth forces had had to deal only with Italy in the Mediterranean, then the North African campaign and the successful counteroffensive of the Greek Army would have resulted in complete victory in the theater in the spring of 1941. [55]

Hitler understood that the collapse of his Italian ally would have profound ramifications for the war he was planning to launch against the Soviet Union in the early summer of 1941. With some reluctance, he agreed to send a small German force southward to support his Axis ally. In November 1940 Air Corps X was sent to southern Italy and Sicily to reinforce Italian efforts to neutralize the British naval base on the

◀ BATTLE PLANNING, DECEMBER 9, 1940– FEBRUARY 7, 1941
British officers use a sand table to plan for battle near Tobruk. A determined defense kept the vital port out of Rommel's hands for 240 days, from April until November, when the garrison was relieved by Operation Crusader.

island colony of Malta. The goal was to make the Mediterranean, in Hitler's words, "the grave of the English fleet."[56] Around 350 aircraft arrived and soon imposed heavy losses on British shipping. Next, in February 1941 a small force of German armor under General Erwin Rommel arrived in Libya as the vanguard of what became known as the Afrika Korps.

Within weeks, he succeeded in reversing the situation against an overstretched British line. Italian armored divisions attacked along the coastal road while Rommel took his forces across the desert to cut off the British Commonwealth troops. By April 11, he had recaptured most of the territory that Italian forces had lost. Tobruk was under siege, and Axis forces were once again closing in on the Egyptian border. Rommel benefited from the use of the 88-millimeter antiaircraft gun as an effective tank killer and from the higher quality of German tanks compared with those of the British. He was also a master of the battle of maneuver, taking risks and surprising his enemy.[57] O'Connor was captured by an Axis patrol, unaware of how rapidly Rommel's forces could move. On May 15 in Operation Brevity and again on June 15 in Operation Battleaxe, Wavell tried to regain the initiative, but both operations failed to break the German-Italian front because of a lack of effective air support and the unsophisticated use of armor in frontal assaults against well-defended positions. By June 17, Rommel had pushed on to Sollum on the Egyptian frontier, where he dug in a new front line to prepare for the drive into Egypt.[58] Despite the presence of one million men in the Middle East and over seven hundred aircraft, British Commonwealth forces were not yet adept at the art of combined-arms fighting that the Germans had perfected in their conquests in 1939 and 1940. Wavell was relieved of command and replaced by General Claude Auchinleck.[59]

The intervention of the Germans was also the key factor in the failure of British efforts to reinforce the Greek armed forces against the Italian invasion. On February 23, 1941, the Greek government reached an agreement with the British to allow a Commonwealth expeditionary force, under New Zealand commander Major General Bernard Freyberg, to help repel the Italian Army. British forces had already occupied the Greek islands of Crete and Lemnos, and on March 7 Freyberg's unit, code-named W Force, arrived on the mainland. It managed to repel a major assault by twenty-eight Italian divisions on March 9. But Ultra intelligence warned the British Chiefs of Staff that the Germans were gathering in force in Bulgaria.

When German forces were finally unleashed on April 6 against Yugoslavia and Greece, the Greek and British Commonwealth forces could find no way of halting the rapid movement of German armor, motorized infantry, and air units. By April 23, the Greek commander in chief had surrendered, and British ships transported 50,000 Greek and Commonwealth forces to Egypt and the island of Crete. Cognizant of the major threat that the 35,000 British, Australian, New Zealand, and Greek troops on Crete constituted to Axis occupation of Greece, German forces mounted a paratroop assault on the island on May 20, 1941, led by General Kurt Student, inspector of airborne forces. Although W Force commander Freyberg had the advantage in troop numbers, he lacked aircraft, artillery, and communications equipment. German air superiority was telling not only against the battered ground forces, which finally abandoned Crete by May 31, but also against the Royal Navy vessels that tried to supply Crete and later carried out a brave evacuation under constant air attack. Three cruisers and six destroyers were sunk, and seventeen other vessels were damaged. Out of 3,700 Commonwealth dead, 2,000 were from the Royal Navy.[60]

By the time the Blitz ended in Britain, with the last major attacks in May 1941, British and Commonwealth forces in the Mediterranean had retreated almost everywhere. There was a danger that the whole region might be lost, since by then only Malta and Egypt remained between the Allies and complete defeat. The theater was important to the British partly because the Mediterranean could still be used as a sea artery between Britain and the Asian empire, but chiefly to prevent the Axis from controlling the oil of the Middle East and threatening India directly.

Losing the Mediterranean in 1941 would not have doomed Britain to losing the war. British vessels could, if necessary, take the long route around the Cape of Good Hope in South Africa to reach Asian and Middle Eastern destinations, and the crucial lifeline for Britain was across the Atlantic to the United States and Canada. Nevertheless, the weaknesses displayed in the fighting in North Africa, Greece, and Crete exposed how unready British forces were to conduct a modern ground war, using armor and aircraft together. Moreover, the failure to prevent heavy German bombing of mainland Britain and the evident weaknesses of the British strategic bombing campaign against Germany also showed that there were limitations in Britain's conduct of air warfare. Only in the sea war did British forces fight with advantage, shown not only at Taranto and Cape Matapan but also in the ability to keep open sea-lanes across the Atlantic and the Mediterranean despite determined Axis attack by aircraft and submarines.[61]

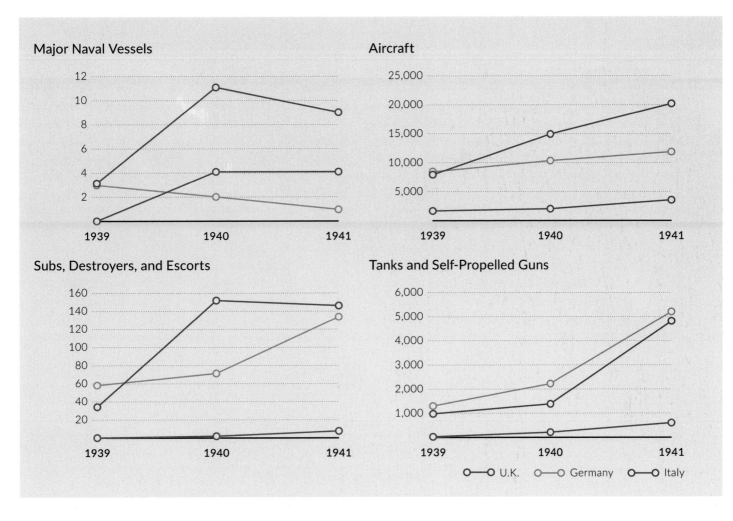

Major Naval Vessels

Aircraft

Subs, Destroyers, and Escorts

Tanks and Self-Propelled Guns

O—O U.K.   O—O Germany   O—O Italy

THE FACTORS BEHIND BRITISH SURVIVAL

The possibility for continued British resistance in 1940 and 1941 rested in many ways on nonmilitary factors. Since Britain was a democracy, great efforts were made by the Churchill government to ensure that political solidarity could be maintained. A coalition alliance between the Conservative and Labour Parties was an essential pre-condition for a united war effort.[62] Churchill, a Conservative, invited senior Labour leaders to join the Cabinet and War Cabinet, including Clement Attlee, Labour leader in the House of Commons and Churchill's deputy; Hugh Dalton; and Herbert Morrison, the former conscientious objector who became minister of "Home Security" in October 1940.[63] The political alliance ensured that there was no room to develop strong protest movements, and the few dissenters who emerged were watched closely and disciplined if necessary. Oswald Mosley, leader of the British Union of Fascists, was interned in June 1940; the Communist newspaper, the *Daily Worker*, was banned in January 1941. Communist opposition was weakened by the German-Soviet Pact, which caused many British Communists to abandon their support for the party, while popular hostility to Communism marginalized what remained of the movement until the onset of the invasion of the Soviet Union (the topic of the next chapter), when Communists suddenly became good patriots.

▲ WEAPONS PRODUCTION

Once geared up for war, British industry produced enough naval vessels to ensure that Britain continued to dominate the surface of the sea and to hold its own in the fight against the German U-boats. It simultaneously produced large numbers of tanks and enough aircraft to develop a growing lead over the Axis in the skies.

Ultra was the Allied designation for special intelligence obtained mainly by decrypting German radio messages that had been encoded with the Enigma cipher machine—though the term was also used sometimes to include intelligence derived from breaking other high-level German, Italian, and Japanese codes. The highest security classification in the British system before the war was "Most Secret," but once Enigma messages were deciphered, a new, even higher level was needed: "Ultra Secret." It was crucial that the Germans never learn that their codes had been broken.

The Enigma is an electromechanical rotor cipher machine that was thought to be unbreakable. However, brilliant Polish mathematicians, a spy, and a little luck opened the secrets of the encryption system. Weeks before World War II started, the Poles shared their work with the British and French. Building on that foundation, British code-breakers located at Bletchley Park, near London, read tens of thousands of German messages over the course of the war. The cryptanalysts' ability to decrypt the German communications was initially quite limited, and never complete. From February to December of 1942, for example, Bletchley Park could not decipher messages sent to German submarines, and British shipping losses rose dramatically. Nonetheless, Ultra did provide intelligence of immense value to Allied commanders in the Battle of the Atlantic, the Battle of Britain, the naval war in the Mediterranean, the air war over Germany, and ground operations in North Africa, Sicily, Italy, and France. Winston Churchill later told King George VI that it was thanks to Ultra that the Allies won the war.

The very existence of the Ultra program remained classified until 1974. With the publication of the Ultra secret, historians' understanding of how the Allies won World War II changed dramatically.

After political solidarity, the second factor was the economy. During World War I, economic staying power had become a critical factor in the prosecution of the war. Accordingly, in the late 1930s, plans were put in place to ensure that the government could operate a flexible macroeconomic management of the economy to avoid price inflation, financial crisis, and poor resource allocation. The conversion of industry to war production was carried out swiftly; by the third quarter of 1941, the rate of munitions production was more than triple the level at the end of 1939.[64] Britain out-produced Germany in most major classes of weapons between 1939 and 1941. Controls over levels of consumption, based on high taxes, rationing, and intensive propaganda about saving, meant that resources could be diverted to military use while maintaining a reasonable standard of living.[65] Most important was the allocation of manpower, which became the yardstick for the more general management of the economy. Two pieces of legislation, the National Service Act of September 3, 1939, and a second act signed on December 18, 1940, produced widespread compulsory mobilization of both men and women for all forms of war service. Even conscientious objectors, who by 1941 numbered more than 41,000, were directed to work in agriculture or civil defense. Work in air-raid precautions or the fire service suited many of the objectors because they could demonstrate that, even if they did not wish to kill their fellow man, they did not lack courage.[66] Management of labor resources meant that the British economy continued to produce at a high level while the armed forces expanded to record levels.

The third factor was the willingness of the government and armed forces to recruit science. Even before 1939, committees to supply scientific advice had been established. The relationship with the armed forces was not always easy, since commanders often disliked being told what to do by civilians, but under Churchill, who understood clearly that science could rapidly alter the nature of combat, scientists were given every opportunity to research and develop vanguard technologies. One of Churchill's closest advisors was the Oxford physicist Frederick Lindemann (later Lord Cherwell), and it was Lindemann who introduced Churchill to a young Oxford colleague, Reginald Victor Jones, whose work revealed in 1940 the nature of the German air force electronic navigation aids, or "beams," and an effective form of interference with them by jamming or distorting the radio signals on which the beams relied.[67]

The major breakthroughs were nevertheless slow to materialize. The proximity fuse, which allowed antiaircraft fire to destroy a higher proportion of bombers later in the war, and the cavity magnetron, which made possible shortwave centimetric radar, contributed to the military effort only from 1943 on. The most notorious scientific development was pioneered by the so-called Maud (Military Application of Uranium Detonation) Committee in 1940, which concluded that it would indeed be possible to produce an atomic bomb, and to do so during the war. The fate of the atomic project illustrates both the strengths and the limitations of the British position. Scientists were encouraged to explore military applications at the cutting edge of science, but Britain often lacked the resources to exploit what was discovered. In June 1942 the Maud Committee handed over its findings to the United States, where the Manhattan Project went on to produce a usable atomic bomb, though not in time for the war in

Europe.[68] The greatest success during 1940 and 1941 came with the cracking of the secret codes generated by the German Enigma enciphering machine by the British and Polish cryptographers at Bletchley Park. The codes could not all be read, and those that could be read could not be deciphered all the time, but the intelligence information derived from the radio intercepts, known as Ultra, supplied the British war effort with a precious window onto German operational intentions.

CONCLUSION

Britain found itself in a curious strategic position in 1941. It was unable to project military power effectively against its enemies, but it was also difficult to defeat thanks to its naval and air strength around the British Isles. Political and economic links with North America were vital to British survival, but with the United States still neutral and the U-boats making the ocean crossing perilous, the transatlantic flow of resources was not sufficient to allow much buildup of offensive capacity. The contribution of fighting forces from the Commonwealth and Empire made it possible to halt the Axis thrust toward the Suez, but a lack of adequate air support, inferior tanks, and insufficient antiaircraft artillery and antitank weaponry left numerically superior British forces unable to knock out Rommel's Afrika Korps. In the air too the RAF had performed very well in defeating the Germans' efforts to win air superiority over the Channel and to bomb Britain into submission—but with ineffective navigational aids and limited numbers of planes, Bomber Command had not yet shown much capacity to bring the war home to Germany.

Nonmilitary factors were also crucial to Britain's survival. Churchill's popular leadership and the establishment of a political consensus on wartime policy prevented internal fractures that could have led to defeat. Sound policies enabled the country to mobilize the economy extensively for war without either forcing too many sacrifices on the home population or preventing military recruitment sufficient for defensive purposes. But if all this meant Britain could avoid defeat, none of it offered any real prospect of victory.

British leaders therefore pinned their hopes for ultimate success on the prospect of gaining powerful allies: the Soviet Union, the United States, or hopefully both. And by the middle of 1941, Ultra decrypts of German secret messages made it clear that one of those hopes would soon be realized, as Hitler was preparing to attack Russia. A major German effort in the East would allow Britain the time it needed to develop more effective armed forces and a booming war economy. British armies could regroup and prepare for the day when, perhaps with the assistance of the United States, they could reenter the European Continent.

INTRODUCTION

On June 22, 1941, Adolf Hitler launched the Wehrmacht against the Soviet Union. This was a battle of two totalitarian states, two competing nations, and two rival ideologies, each of which sought to explain history and to shape it. For the Soviets, class struggle was history's defining principle; they expected, and worked to promote, the eventual fall of capitalism. In the short term, however, they faced an existential threat. Germany's governing ideology, National Socialism, found its explanation and its justification in the concept of race, and the Germans set out to conquer the territories and peoples of Eastern Europe upon the basis of their own proclaimed superiority. Their approach to this war would combine hubris with a level of brutality that would outdo even Joseph Stalin's. Ultimately, that approach would bring on their downfall, but only after taking the Soviet Union to the edge of destruction.

The importance of Germany's invasion of the Soviet Union is difficult to overstate. It opened up a front that would decide the Second World War in Europe. For all the efforts of the Western Allies, this was where Germany lost its war. The scale of the fighting is almost beyond comprehension. More people fought, and more died, on the Eastern Front than on all the war's other fronts combined.[1] Nearly 75 percent of German combat fatalities, almost four million men, fell there. As for the Soviets, their losses are literally incalculable, but the best estimates put them in the range of nine million military and fifteen million to twenty million civilian deaths.[2] Millions of those deaths occurred because of deliberate German policies, including the beginnings of the so-called Final Solution of the Jewish Question. Moreover, the war laid waste to a huge swath of the Soviet Union, as well as the lands to its west, as far as central Germany. This conflict came as close to true "total war" as the world has seen, and its repercussions, though difficult to quantify, linger to the present day.[3]

We can learn a great deal from studying the Great Patriotic War, as the Russians still call World War II. The interactions of policy, strategy, and operations stand out clearly. Additionally, there is a stark moral element. Neither the Nazi nor the Soviet regime is praiseworthy on moral grounds.[4] But only one of them launched an unprovoked war to conquer and colonize the other's territory and kill or enslave the people who lived there, and the German military played a central role in every aspect of that effort.[5] This chapter will examine the two sides' planning and preparations, and the course of the campaign and its associated crimes, up to the spring of 1942.

STRATEGY

Germany's unexpectedly quick victory over France in June 1940 presented both the Nazis and the Soviets with new opportunities, risks, and challenges. On the Soviet side, Stalin had hoped that Germany and the West would exhaust each other in a long war, thus guaranteeing the Soviet Union's security and perhaps giving him the chance

4

THE GERMANS
TURN EAST:
OPERATION
BARBAROSSA
AND THE
BEGINNINGS
OF THE FINAL
SOLUTION

GEOFFREY P. MEGARGEE

NORWEGIAN
SEA

0° 10°E 20°E 30°E 40°E

NORWAY

SWEDEN

FINLAND

60°N

OSLO

Gulf of Bothnia

HELSINKI

STOCKHOLM

Gulf of Finland

Leningrad

Vologda

TALLINN

ESTONIA

U. S. S. R.

DENMARK

Novgorod

Yaroslav

The shaded areas represent the
land occupied by Axis forces
between *June 25, 1941* and
December 5, 1941.

Pskov

Dec. 1941

Operation T
Sept.–Dec. 1

BALTIC

LATVIA

RIGA

COPENHAGEN

SEA

LITHUANIA

Mosco

Kiel

Vyaz'ma

Rostock

Königsberg

Kovno

Vitebsk

Kaluga

Tula

Danzig

Hamburg

Vilna

Smolensk

Stettin

Wannsee BERLIN

Hrodna

Minsk

Mogilev

Bryansk

Orel

Wittenberg Poznań

Bielostok

Babruysk

Leipzig GERMANY

Operation Barbarossa,
Jun.–Dec. 1941

Gomel

Dresden

Łódź

Kursk

50°N

Breslau

WARSAW

Brest

Prague

GENERAL

BOHEMIA

Lublin

Belgorod

AND

Katowice

GOVERNMENT

Luts'k

Rivne

Kiev

Kharkov

MORAVIA

Ostrava

Kraków

Brno

Zhytomyr

Poltava

VIENNA

SLOVAKIA

Lvov

Lysychan

Ternopol

Vinnytsya

Dnepropetrovsk

BUDAPEST

Chernivtsi

Kremenchuk

HUNGARY

Kirovograd

Zagreb

BESSARABIA

Kryvyy Rih

Nikopol

Ta

Mariupol'

ADRIATIC

CROATIA

Novi Sad

Kishinev

Kherson

SEA OF

AZOV

SEA

BELGRADE

ROMANIA

Galați

Odessa

Kra

ITALY

Sarajevo

BLACK

Novorossisk

ROME

Ploești

SEA Sevastopol

20°E

30°E

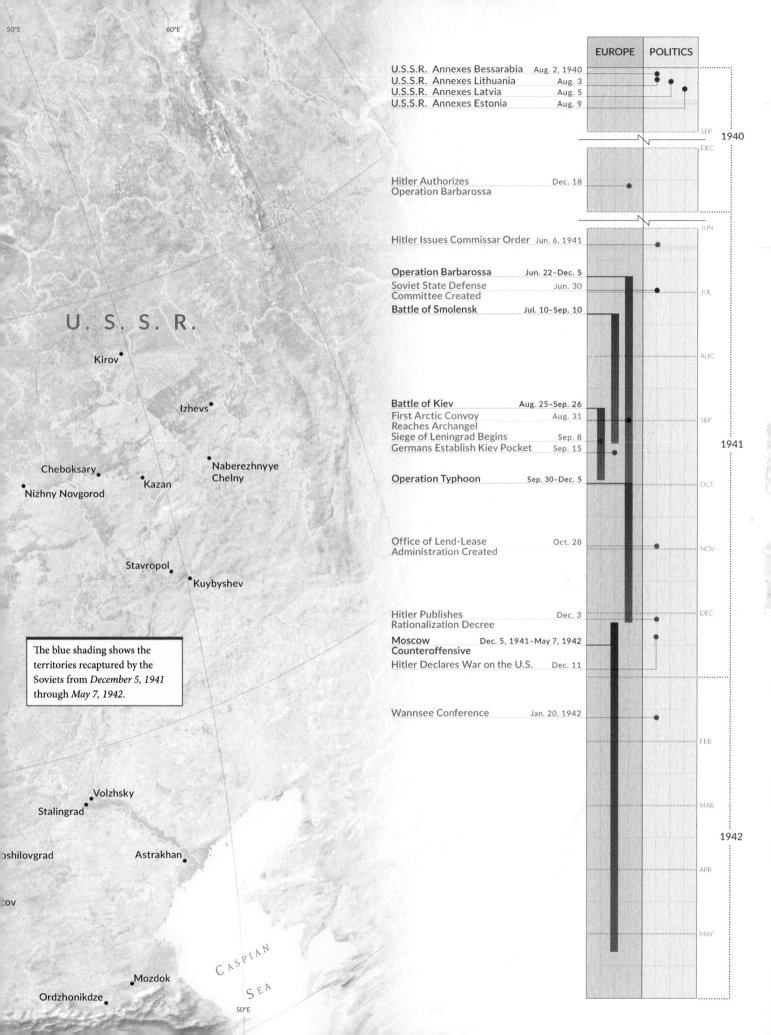

U. S. S. R.

Kirov

Izhevs

Cheboksary
Nizhny Novgorod
Kazan
Naberezhnyye
Chelny

Stavropol
Kuybyshev

The blue shading shows the
territories recaptured by the
Soviets from *December 5, 1941*
through *May 7, 1942*.

Volzhsky
Stalingrad

oshilovgrad
Astrakhan

tov

CASPIAN

SEA

Mozdok

Ordzhonikdze

50°E   60°E

50°E

	EUROPE	POLITICS

U.S.S.R. Annexes Bessarabia Aug. 2, 1940
U.S.S.R. Annexes Lithuania   Aug. 3
U.S.S.R. Annexes Latvia   Aug. 5
U.S.S.R. Annexes Estonia   Aug. 9

Hitler Authorizes   Dec. 18
Operation Barbarossa

Hitler Issues Commissar Order Jun. 6, 1941

Operation Barbarossa   Jun. 22–Dec. 5
Soviet State Defense   Jun. 30
Committee Created
Battle of Smolensk   Jul. 10–Sep. 10

Battle of Kiev   Aug. 25–Sep. 26
First Arctic Convoy   Aug. 31
Reaches Archangel
Siege of Leningrad Begins   Sep. 8
Germans Establish Kiev Pocket Sep. 15

Operation Typhoon   Sep. 30–Dec. 5

Office of Lend-Lease   Oct. 28
Administration Created

Hitler Publishes   Dec. 3
Rationalization Decree
Moscow   Dec. 5, 1941–May 7, 1942
Counteroffensive
Hitler Declares War on the U.S. Dec. 11

Wannsee Conference   Jan. 20, 1942

SEP   1940

DEC

JUN

JUL

AUG

SEP   1941

OCT

NOV

DEC

FEB

MAR

1942

APR

MAY

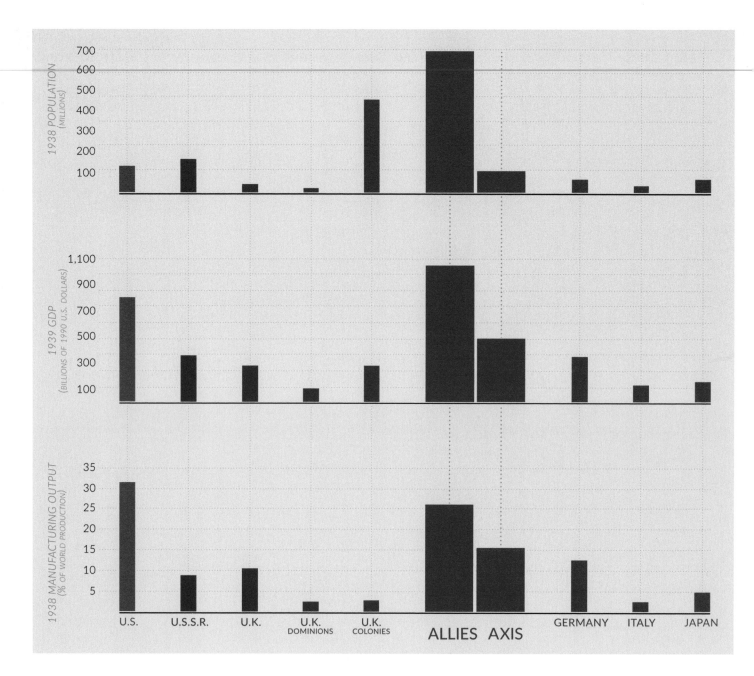

1938 POPULATION (MILLIONS)

1939 GDP (BILLIONS OF 1990 U.S. DOLLARS)

1938 MANUFACTURING OUTPUT (% OF WORLD PRODUCTION)

U.S.   U.S.S.R.   U.K.   U.K. DOMINIONS   U.K. COLONIES   **ALLIES AXIS**   GERMANY   ITALY   JAPAN

THE SOVIET UNION ▲ JOINS THE ALLIES

On the face of it, by attacking the Soviet Union, Hitler was tipping the resource balance decisively against Germany. The Führer, however, expected to quickly overrun the most populous and developed areas of the U.S.S.R., and so to gain more resources for the Reich than he pushed to the Allies.

to pick up territory or influence in Central Europe when no one could oppose him. Instead, he now faced a supremely confident Germany, one in possession of the finest army and air force on the Continent.

Stalin knew that his own forces were far from ready. Their experiences in the 1939 invasion of Poland had demonstrated that the Red Army was deficient in training, equipment, and leadership. The 1939–40 "Winter War" with Finland, in which the much smaller Finnish army held the Soviets at bay for months, underlined the Red Army's weaknesses even more starkly. Stalin's purges of his officer corps, which began in 1937 and continued right through the German invasion, were a major factor. The Soviet regime killed, imprisoned, or dismissed close to 55,000 officers. In their place, it promoted men who were politically reliable rather than militarily skilled, who had far too little experience for the positions they now had to fill, and who were paralyzed into inaction for fear of further purges. Such men were

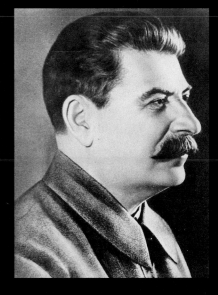
Joseph Stalin was born Iosif Vissarionovich Dzhugashvili, but took "Stalin" ("man of steel") as a nom de guerre. He played a leading role in the 1917 October Revolution and in 1922 became general secretary of the Communist Party of the Union of Soviet Socialist Republics. After Vladimir Lenin's death in 1924, Stalin began to consolidate his power and eventually became the de facto dictator of the Soviet Union. His rule was marked by paranoia and brutal repression. He forced agricultural collectivization and industrialization upon the country, which brought benefits, including the ability to withstand Hitler's attack, but Stalin's regime displaced, incarcerated, or killed millions of Soviet citizens in the process.

The rise of Nazism in 1933 was a direct challenge to the Soviet Union. Stalin spent the subsequent eight years trying to navigate difficult diplomatic waters while building the Soviet Republic's strength. His strategic mistakes in 1941, on top of the purges of the previous four years, cost the country dearly. He evolved into an effective war leader, however. That ability, together with the country's resources, its army's increasing skill, and the Soviet people's almost unbelievable sacrifices, sufficed to first stop and then gradually drive back the Nazi invasion.

Victory did not bring an end to Stalin's oppression. Not only did he maintain one of the world's most viciously totalitarian states, but also his regime established a stranglehold over Eastern Europe, and he helped establish the Cold War that defined the next half century. Thus, though some laud him for his wartime leadership, he is most often remembered as one of history's greatest tyrants.

---

incapable of planning, coordinating, and executing modern, mobile, combined-arms warfare—a style of war that, in any case, Stalin had repudiated at the same time he began the purges.[6]

Now, having seen what the Wehrmacht had accomplished in France, Stalin adopted a two-part strategy. First, he did all he could to maintain friendly relations with Germany. He increased the flow of the raw materials that the Germans needed. He rebuffed British attempts to draw him in on their side, and even reported those attempts to the Germans. And he downplayed German intrusions into the Soviet Union's agreed-upon sphere of interest. The details of Stalin's thinking remain closed to us, but he apparently believed that he could at least delay a German strike by bowing to Hitler's wishes and denying the Führer a reason to break their pact.[7] At the same time, however, with the expectation that war would come eventually, and in reaction to the Red Army's miserable performance in Finland, Stalin brought in new senior leadership, which began to reorganize and modernize the Red Army. Such changes would take time, though, especially as persistent instability and debate within the Soviet senior commands interfered with the program.[8]

On the German side, victory over France put the senior leadership into a state of euphoric uncertainty. The Wehrmacht had achieved, in seven weeks, the victory that had eluded the German Army in four years of fighting during World War I. Britain was in no position to interfere on the Continent for the foreseeable future, and most Germans (and some Britons) expected a negotiated settlement; the Soviets even encouraged it. When the British government opted to keep fighting, Hitler and his generals were at a loss: What to do next? In the coming months, they would consider a number of alternatives, including an air campaign against Britain, possibly followed by an invasion; or attacks in the Mediterranean against Gibraltar and Egypt. On the

EASTERN FRONT

diplomatic front, Hitler considered forming a Napoleon-style Continental bloc with Vichy France, Italy, Spain, and perhaps even the Soviet Union. None of these offered the promise of quick victory, however, and so, in an apparent effort to find a solution, Hitler pursued them all, to varying degrees.[9]

At the same time that Hitler was considering those options, however, his mind kept returning to a bigger one: an attack on the Soviet Union. He had long seen Russia as a potential living space (*Lebensraum*) for Germans, a land peopled by inferior Slavs, and the center of the worldwide "Jewish-Bolshevik" conspiracy. An invasion

WEHRMACHT PLAN ▶

The German invasion plan called for three army groups to advance into the Soviet Union on a broad front. These forces were to surround and destroy Red Army troops defending near the border, which planners expected would cripple Soviet resistance and produce victory in a short campaign.

GERMAN LOGISTICS ▲

The German Army still relied heavily on horse-drawn transport for its supply columns.

offered Hitler a chance to strike out at his greatest racial and political enemies, and to take the land as a German colony. The inhabitants would be enslaved, killed, or expelled.

Hitler also had more immediate, practical reasons for attacking the Soviet Union. Germany's long-term strategic outlook was not good. The territories it had conquered to date were proving more of an economic liability than a treasure trove. Key commodities such as oil, coal, and food were already running short. Britain was hard to get at; the United States, increasingly hostile. Any further aid from the Soviet Union would make Germany dependent, and Hitler would never accept that. On the other hand, if he conquered Russia, he could knock out Britain's last potential ally on the Continent. If that did not lead the British to despair and submission, Germany would still gain the resources it would need to fight against the two great maritime powers.[10] And so, between late June and mid-December, as other options proved unworkable, Hitler gradually made up his mind to attack in the East.[11]

After the war, many of the surviving generals maintained that they had viewed Hitler's decision with deep misgivings. How could he commit them to another two-front war, after the disastrous experience of World War I? The commander in chief of the army, Walther von Brauchitsch, and the chief of the army General Staff, Franz Halder, questioned briefly the campaign's strategic rationale. Other officers worried that the Wehrmacht could suffer the same fate as Napoleon's Grande Armée in 1812.

By this stage in the war, however, no one in the army had enough power to question Hitler's decisions. Another point was just as important, though: most of the senior officers believed that the Wehrmacht would defeat the Red Army easily in a single campaign, leading to the collapse of Stalin's government. Their optimism encouraged Hitler to order the attack. He did not make that strategic mistake by himself.[12]

OPERATIONAL PLANS

Starting in late July 1940, even while air and naval attacks on the British were taking shape, the planners worked out the details.[13] The Wehrmacht would attack with three army groups. Each group's goal was to penetrate the border defenses, and then cut off and destroy the Soviet armies as far to the west as possible. The Wehrmacht could not let the Soviets withdraw into the interior and prolong the campaign. The plan called for a three-week pause after the initial advance, to allow the armies to rest, refit, and resupply before moving on. By then, however, the planners expected most of the serious fighting to be over. The Germans believed that the Soviets could neither stop the attack nor carry out a fighting retreat, and that they did not possess the reserves to keep fighting after losing their armies on the western border.

The German plan contained huge flaws. Its central assumption, that the Soviet

regime would collapse after a military defeat, was doubtful. Beyond that, the Germans grossly underestimated the Soviets' military capabilities. True, the Red Army was not the Wehrmacht's equal qualitatively, but its size and dispositions were going to cause problems. The Germans believed that the Red Army numbered two million men. The true number by June 22 was already over five million. Moreover, the Germans *overestimated* the number of Red Army units in the western military districts by 30 percent to 50 percent.[14] Thus, the Wehrmacht would be unable to catch and defeat the bulk of the Red Army near the frontier. A decisive military victory in the lands west of Moscow was anything but certain.

The Wehrmacht also faced daunting logistical and personnel challenges. The

Heinrich Himmler, who missed his chance to fight in the First World War and failed at agronomy during the postwar years, turned increasingly to the occult, radical anti-Semitism, and German mythology. In August 1923 he joined the Nazi Party; then in 1925 he joined the Schutzstaffel, or SS, which was originally a small personal bodyguard for Adolf Hitler.

Himmler took over as leader of the SS in January 1929, and he strove to turn it into his vision of an utterly loyal, fanatically ideological, and racially pure organization. Eventually it became a dominant and feared force—within the Nazi Party, within Germany, and throughout occupied Europe. Himmler's empire included thousands of concentration camps and forced labor camps; the killing centers of the Final Solution; the Gestapo and other police and intelligence forces, including the Einsatzgruppen (task groups), which shot over two million Jews and other civilians in the East; a network of business enterprises and agricultural colonies; centers of Nazi ideological education; and a powerful armed force, the Waffen-SS. He was also a driving force behind plans to "Germanize" Central and Eastern Europe by eliminating, displacing, or enslaving the people there. In all this, Himmler was the master organizer—and ruthless opportunist—who translated Hitler's wishes into practical steps.

Himmler's reach exceeded his grasp when he took over senior military commands in 1945, however; he was completely unequal to the task. Moreover, when he saw that the war was lost, he attempted to open negotiations with the Western Allies through Sweden. Hitler found out, declared Himmler a traitor, and stripped him of his offices. Himmler committed suicide after the British captured him in May 1945.

HEINRICH LUITPOLD HIMMLER
October 7, 1900–May 23, 1945

invading force would number three million Germans (plus a half million allies), 600,000 vehicles, and 625,000 horses. Their objectives lay between six hundred and one thousand miles from their start lines. The Russian railroads—what few there were of them—were a different gauge than those in Western Europe, so Wehrmacht railroad crews would have to convert them before they would be usable. In the meantime, the Germans would have to use trucks to make up the difference, but they had far too few, and of far too many types; many of them civilian models that the Germans had requisitioned from all over Europe. The roads in the Soviet Union were also too few, and most of them were unpaved: dust bowls in dry weather and quagmires in wet. Then there was the question of the supplies that were to travel over those roads. The planners expected shortages of gasoline and rubber by midyear. Furthermore, the supply of trained soldiers would run out by October, and there was already a serious shortage of officers. The Wehrmacht was running the campaign on a shoestring. If the Germans did not achieve their goals within their stated time frame, they were going to be in deep trouble.[15]

The logistical problems overlapped with weaknesses in German force structure and operational doctrine. Many people still think of the Wehrmacht as a highly mobile force, but, in fact, most of it marched at the same pace as Napoleon's army: its troops on foot, its supplies and artillery horse drawn. The mobile forces had to advance at a rapid pace, but by doing so, they would soon outrun both their supply columns and the infantry armies following them. Two sets of problems would ensue. First, the Red Army was committed to a doctrine of counterattack, so the Germans could not afford to leave significant Soviet forces in their rear. Envelopments took time, and the slower infantry armies would not be available to seal the armored groups' encirclements. The armored forces themselves would have to do it, but that would allow the Soviets

PRISONERS OF WAR ▲

The Germans expected to take millions of Soviet prisoners, and they did, but they never intended to feed or house those prisoners properly. Nearly 60 percent of Soviet prisoners would die in German captivity during the war, with hundreds of thousands murdered outright, and the rest dying from systematic starvation, exposure, and disease.

outside the pocket to fall back and regroup. Second, with supply columns falling behind, supplies would run out in short order. The army's supply administration did its best to overcome that problem with a series of expedients, but the fact remained that the generals were taking an enormous risk. Amazingly, as they confronted their supply and transportation limitations, they reacted not by questioning the operational concept but by shortening their forecast for the time they would need to win.[16]

The question that naturally arises from this litany of problems is: How could a group of highly trained, experienced, and intelligent officers place themselves and their troops in such a precarious position? A complex collection of intellectual and institutional elements was at work. Intellectually, Germany's military leaders saw the Soviet Union in contradictory terms. On the one hand, it seemed a long-standing menace to European civilization, dating back to the Mongols, and Communism's inherent hostility made the threat only worse. On the other hand, Russia appeared to be a colossus with feet of clay: politically unstable, with a mix of ethnic and national groups (many of whom hated Stalin passionately), racially and culturally inferior, and militarily incapable. The generals were aware of many of the same weaknesses in the Red Army that made Stalin so nervous, and, after all, the Wehrmacht had just beaten France. The threat provided a rationale for the attack, while the weaknesses made success seem likely.

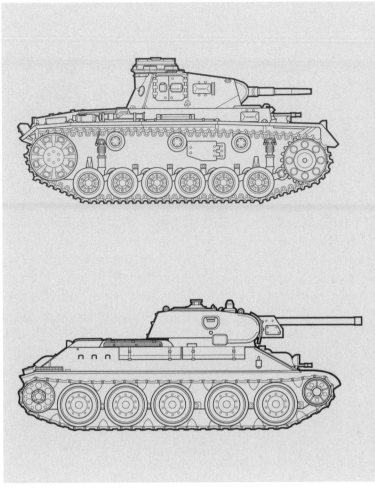

Panzer III (Model G)

Entered Service	1938 (1940)
Weight	20.3 tons
Crew	5
Armament	50 mm main gun. Armor penetration: 43 mm at 500 m (547 yards), 32 mm at 1,000 m (1,094 yards) Two 7.92 mm MG34 machine guns
Armor	12–30 mm
Speed	25 mph
Range	102 miles
Production	5,714

T-34 (Model 41)

Entered Service	1940 (1941)
Weight	26.5 tons
Crew	4
Armament	76 mm main gun. Armor penetration: 60 mm at 500 m (547 yards), 52 mm at 1,000 m (1,094 yards) Two 7.62 mm machine guns
Armor	20–52 mm
Speed	33 mph
Range	250 miles on road, 160 miles in country
Production	57,339 (all variants)

Institutionally, the Wehrmacht's leaders also suffered from several attitudes and practices that blinded them to the realities of the campaign to come. Perhaps the most important of these was a tendency to place the operational concept above all other considerations. That is, their planning process started with the commander and his chief of staff deciding on the scheme of maneuver. They would inform the supply officer of the plan and tell him to support it; then they would inform the intelligence officer and ask about the enemy in their path. At no time did they allow logistical or intelligence considerations to alter their basic intentions. There was also a subtle but pervasive bias against the intelligence function. Even intelligence officers, who received no special training in their field, believed that intelligence assessment was something that any officer could do. All of this contributed to an environment that stifled contrary opinions and produced an overly optimistic groupthink.[17]

▲ **MEDIUM TANKS IN OPERATION BARBAROSSA**

With better speed, a much more powerful main gun, more frontal armor, longer range, and excellent durability, the T-34 easily outperformed the Panzerkampfwagen III and was the best overall tank in use during Operation Barbarossa. The Germans tried to modify their tanks to meet the Soviet T-34 threat, and later German tanks like the Tiger proved equal or better. But the T-34 was much cheaper and more efficient to produce, and was rolled out in far greater numbers.

RACIAL WAR

One further element of German planning requires our attention. More than the Germans' operational concept and strategic assumptions would define the coming campaign. The Germans' ultimate intentions for the land and the people they would

conquer would interact with the conventional campaign to shape the war's nature and outcome.

On March 30, 1941, Hitler addressed the principal commanders and staff officers for Operation Barbarossa. This would be a war of extermination, he said. A race war. The usual rules would not apply. Soviet soldiers were not to be treated as comrades. Bolshevik commissars and intelligentsia were to be eliminated. He was calling on them to violate the norms and international laws of war, but in no contemporary source is there a hint of resistance on their parts.[18] Nor did the leaders of the Army High Command (OKH) or the Armed Forces High Command (Oberkommando der Wehrmacht, or OKW) so much as bat an eyelid. In fact, Brauchitsch had told the senior commanders on March 27 that the troops "have to realize that this struggle is being waged by one race against another, and proceed with the necessary harshness."[19]

In fact, the military, the SS, and other Reich authorities shared many of the same goals and values, which shaped their plans for the war behind the lines. The army obviously wanted to win the campaign as rapidly as possible. It also wanted to control the vast territories it was going to conquer, in order to allow for the free movement of troops and supplies, and to extract resources, especially food, since it knew its logistical apparatus could not bring enough forward. The army and the Reich Food Ministry also wanted food to go to German civilians, to prevent the kind of hardships that had sapped morale during World War I. A so-called Economic Staff East would handle broader efforts at expropriation, while the SS planned for the territories' colonization by Germans. All of these actors shared the desire to destroy Jews and Communists along with an utter disregard for the lives of the other peoples who populated the East. So-called military necessity meshed perfectly with ideological imperatives and

deep-rooted prejudices, such that even men who did not see themselves as Nazis could work toward the same goals.[20]

The resulting plans and orders are terrible to read, even today. The army entered into an agreement with the Food Ministry to starve as many as thirty million Soviet citizens so that German soldiers and civilians could have their food. The army and the SS agreed that special units, including the Einsatzgruppen, would operate behind the lines to eliminate anyone who seemed to pose a threat—especially Communists and Jews—and thus maintain order in the rear. The army issued orders that all Red Army political commissars be shot immediately upon capture, that civilians suspected of resistance ("active or passive") could also be shot out of hand on the authority of any officer, and that German troops need not be punished for crimes against Soviet civilians. The army also failed to make adequate preparations to house or feed the millions of prisoners of war it expected to capture.[21]

▲ "ADVANCE INTO THE UNKNOWN"

The German Army's propaganda magazine, *Signal*, published dramatic color photographs that aimed to portray the advancing Wehrmacht as an unstoppable force.

A column of German armor advances into Lithuania on the first day of Operation Barbarossa. The tanks are of the Czech type 38(t), which the Germans seized and adopted after dismembering Czechoslovakia.

SOVIET PLANS AND PREPARATIONS

The Soviets knew nothing of those plans, of course, but they knew that Germany posed a threat, and they were doing their best to prepare.[22] In April 1941 Stalin declared a "special threatening period of war" and started a secret, partial mobilization (which helps to account for the Germans' underestimation of Soviet strength). At the same time, the Red Army continued its efforts to reorganize and modernize, under the leadership of the defense commissar, Marshal Semyon Timoshenko. Those efforts included extensive modifications to the structure and doctrine of virtually every arm of the Red Army: from infantry and mechanized forces to artillery and airborne units, as well as to the supporting logistical systems. The Red air force underwent a similar program. New equipment, such as the T-34 medium and KV-1 heavy tanks, the Yakovlev Yak-1 fighter, and the Ilyushin Il-2 Sturmovik ground attack aircraft, were in production, and all of them were equal or superior to anything the Germans could field.[23]

Unfortunately for the Soviets, they were trying to do too much, too late. The complexity and scale of the reforms and expansion would have challenged any military organization. There simply was not time to complete them; to create a military force that could compete with the Wehrmacht. That would have been true even without the chaotic political picture, in which personnel switched jobs—or disappeared into the Soviet camp system: the gulag—on a regular basis. (By June 1941, fully 75 percent of Soviet officers had been in their jobs less than one year.)[24] The quality of rank and file only added to the problems: most common soldiers were raw recruits or reservists—uneducated peasants whom even experienced officers could not turn into capable fighters quickly.[25]

And so the Red Army and Red air force were huge but hollow organizations in the spring of 1941. The efforts to man, train, and equip them could not keep up. Most units were at half strength or less. There were shortages in every category of equipment, arms, and supplies, but especially in modern weaponry, communications gear, and transport. Poor maintenance reduced further the availability to use the equipment that was on hand. Tactical training was rudimentary or nonexistent: in the air force, for example, commanders curtailed training because they feared being charged with sabotage for any accidents that might take place. Commanders and staffs did not know how to coordinate the different arms or support them logistically.

Problems with Soviet doctrine, plans, and physical preparations mirrored and exacerbated those with force structure and training. The Soviets' intentions for the coming campaign were essentially offensive. Their central idea was to stop any enemy attack as close to the border as possible and then launch a counteroffensive immediately—to carry the war into the enemy's home territory. The Soviets paid little attention to defensive doctrine. More concretely, their plans contained several weaknesses. Fixed defenses were the key to stopping Germany's initial thrusts, but the Soviets had dismantled the fortifications on the old Polish border and had not yet finished constructing their lines to the west, on the new frontier. As the Poles had done in 1939, Soviet forces deployed evenly all along the border rather than concentrating in depth on likely avenues of attack. The Soviets' operational plan, which they adopted in October 1940, assumed that the main German attack would come south of the Pripet Marshes. Moreover, the Soviet General Staff assumed that the Germans would need ten to fifteen days in which to deploy their main attack, thus giving the Red Army time to prepare. Both of those assumptions proved false. Frontline headquarters also lacked up-to-date orders, because the Red Army's ever-changing leadership kept changing the plans.[26]

The political and diplomatic situations added yet another obstacle to an effective defense.[27] Even while Stalin directed the huge changes to his forces, he also continued his efforts to delay or avoid a German attack. By the spring of 1941, there were plenty of indications of an impending offensive, including the obvious fact of the German buildup, as well as warnings from other governments and from Soviet agents. To be fair, though, the indications were not as clear as they seem in hindsight. The Germans planted false information, agents gave conflicting reports, and Stalin—with some justification—suspected the British and the Poles of trying to bring the Soviet Union into the war. An attack seemed unlikely anyway: Why would Hitler, who had his hands full already, start a new war against a state that was doing everything it could to appease him?[28] For these reasons, Stalin avoided any hint of provocation. Luftwaffe

FINLAND

XXXXX
SOUTHEASTERN

18 x ◫ XXXXX
FINLAND

XXXX
23

HELSINKI ⊙

Gulf of Finland

Leningrad

XXXXX
NORTHERN
POPOV

◫ x17
▭ x4

Narva

Tallinn

ESTONIA

Lake Peipus

Novgorod

STOCKHOLM ⊙

Pskov

Gulf of Riga

Ostrov

XXXXX
MILITARY
DISTRICTS

◫ x32
▭ x8

Moscow

Riga

XXXXX
NORTHWESTERN
F. I. KUZNETSOV

◫ x21
▭ x4

XXXXX
STAVKA
RESERVE

◫ x4
▭ x1

LATVIA

Dvinsk

Vyaz'ma

Vitebsk

Kaluga

BALTIC SEA

XXXX
8

LITHUANIA

Smolensk

Indicates how many infantry
and armor divisions
comprised each army group

XXXX
18

Kovno

XXXX
11

Vilna

Minsk

Mogilev

XXXXX
WESTERN
PAVLOV

◫ x32
▭ x12

Bryansk

Königsberg

XXXX
◫ 4
HOEPNER

XXXX
16

XXXX
13

Ore

◫ x26
▭ x3

Danzig

XXXXX
NORTH
LEEB

XXXX
3

Hrodna

Babruysk

SOVIET

◫ x24
▭ x2

XXXXX
OKH
RESERVE

XXXX
9

XXXX
10

Bielostok

Dnieper

Gomel

Kursk

◫ x38
▭ x9

XXXXX
CENTER
BOCK

XXXX
◫ 3
HOTH

XXXX
4

Pinsk *Pripet*

UNION

Be

WARSAW ⊙

XXXX
◫ 2
GUDERIAN

Brest

Pripet Marshes

Łódź

XXXX
◫ 4

GENERAL

Kh

GOVERNMENT

Lublin

XXXX
6

Kovel'

Kiev

XXXX
5

Luts'k

XXXX
◫ 1
KLEIST

Zhytomyr

Poltava

Katowice

Kraków

XXXX
17

XXXX
6

Lvov

XXXXX
SOUTHWESTERN
KIRPONOS

◫ x42
▭ x16

Cherkassy

Kremenchuk

◫ x42
▭ x5

XXXXX
SOUTH
RUNDSTEDT

XXXX
26

Ternopol

Vinnytsya

Dnepropetrovsk

Tatra Mountains

U K R A I N E

Kirovograd

Kryvyy Rih

SLOVAKIA

Uman

Nikopol

XXXX
12

Chernivtsi

XXXXX
SOUTHERN
TYULENEV

◫ x11
▭ x4

Melit

XXXX
ROM 3

XXXX
11

Kishinev

Kherson

HUNGARY

BUDAPEST ⊙

XXXX
9

Carpathian Mountains

Prut

Odessa

NOTE

To simplify depiction,
many unit symbols are
shown differently from
standard practice.

XXXX
SIXTH = XXXX
REICHENAU   6

XXXX
ROM 4

BLACK SEA

Galați

Sevastopol

0   50   100 Miles

ROMANIA

reconnaissance aircraft penetrated deep into Soviet airspace, unopposed. Soviet units in the frontier zone could not get permission to concentrate or deploy into defensive positions, right up to the moment of the invasion. Not until the late evening of June 21 did Stalin allow a vaguely worded warning to go out to the chain of command. Most units were under attack well before they received it.[29]

If war is the unfolding of miscalculations, as the historian Barbara Tuchman put it, then Operation Barbarossa is one of the best examples. As the sun set on June 21, at least 104 German divisions and 26 more from Germany's allies faced 163 Soviet divisions, the latter echeloned up to 250 miles from the frontier. A Soviet High Command (Stavka) reserve contained an additional 57 divisions that deployed back along the Dvina and Dnieper River lines, and 83 more divisions existed in other districts. In the air, 2,700 Luftwaffe planes—60 percent of German strength—would face 7,133 Soviet aircraft in the western districts. The remaining districts had another 6,155 aircraft.[30] Despite their apparent strength, however, Soviet units were undermanned, underequipped, undertrained, and poorly deployed and led. Nevertheless, they expected to stop their adversary early and throw him back. The Wehrmacht, on the other hand, was experienced, proficient, and confident, assuming that victory would be quick and easy—but running the invasion on a shoestring. Neither side understood what it was in for.

INITIAL OPERATIONS

Operation Barbarossa opened at three fifteen in the morning on June 22, 1941, with bombing raids against key Soviet airfields and a massive artillery bombardment up and down the frontier. Soon the Wehrmacht began its advance, against ineffectual resistance. At dawn, further air raids caught most of the Red air force on the ground, destroying hundreds of planes. Those few that got into the air did not last long because of their technical inferiority and the pilots' inexperience.[31] The Germans quickly achieved complete air supremacy, and turned their attention to attacking headquarters, transportation networks, and troop concentrations. Radio jamming and deep raids by German commandos added to Soviet confusion and disorganization. Headquarters could not communicate with one another, and so could not find out where the enemy was, maintain a coherent defense, or coordinate counterattacks. Soviet troops often fought tenaciously, even suicidally, but without direction, coordination, supplies, or air support, their efforts were doomed.[32]

The Wehrmacht advanced into Russia on three axes. Army Group North headed through the Baltic states to Leningrad (as the Soviets called Saint Petersburg). Army Group Center advanced on Moscow via Minsk and Smolensk. And Army Group South aimed for Kiev and beyond to the Donets Basin. Army groups North and Center made

◀ SOVIET AND GERMAN DEPLOYMENTS, JUNE 22, 1941

Germany calculated that the Soviet forces stationed along the border were not strong enough to halt its invasion force, but were large enough that their destruction would cripple the Red Army.

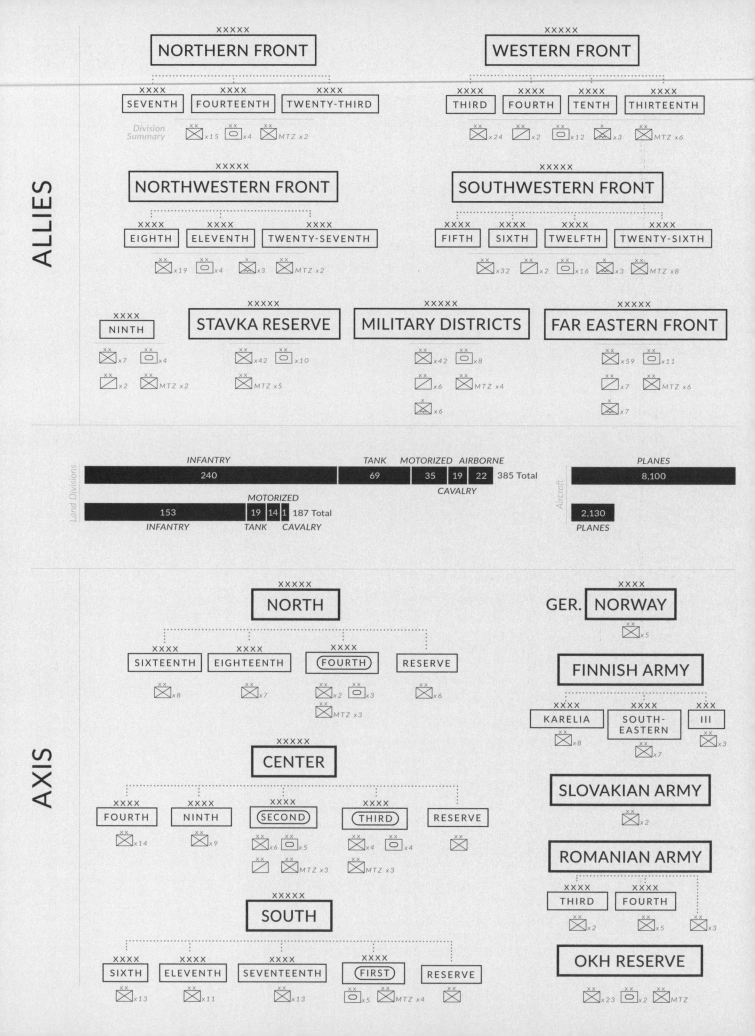

ALLIES

XXXXX
NORTHERN FRONT

XXXXX
WESTERN FRONT

XXXX	XXXX	XXXX
SEVENTH	FOURTEENTH	TWENTY-THIRD

XXXX	XXXX	XXXX	XXXX
THIRD	FOURTH	TENTH	THIRTEENTH

Division Summary ⊠ x15 ▭ x4 ⊠ MTZ x2

⊠ x24 ⊠ x2 ▭ x12 ⊠ x3 ⊠ MTZ x6

XXXXX
NORTHWESTERN FRONT

XXXXX
SOUTHWESTERN FRONT

XXXX	XXXX	XXXX
EIGHTH	ELEVENTH	TWENTY-SEVENTH

XXXX	XXXX	XXXX	XXXX
FIFTH	SIXTH	TWELFTH	TWENTY-SIXTH

⊠ x19 ▭ x4 ⊠ x3 ⊠ MTZ x2

⊠ x32 ⊠ x2 ▭ x16 ⊠ x3 ⊠ MTZ x8

XXXX
NINTH

XXXXX
STAVKA RESERVE

XXXXX
MILITARY DISTRICTS

XXXXX
FAR EASTERN FRONT

⊠ x7 ▭ x4 ⊠ x2 ⊠ MTZ x2

⊠ x42 ▭ x10 ⊠ MTZ x5

⊠ x42 ▭ x8 ⊠ x6 ⊠ MTZ x4 ⊠ x6

⊠ x59 ▭ x11 ⊠ x7 ⊠ MTZ x6 ⊠ x7

Land Divisions

INFANTRY	TANK	MOTORIZED	AIRBORNE	
240	69	35	19	22	385 Total

CAVALRY

INFANTRY		MOTORIZED		
153	19	14	1	187 Total

TANK CAVALRY

Aircraft

PLANES
8,100

2,130

PLANES

AXIS

XXXXX
NORTH

XXXX
GER. NORWAY

⊠ x5

XXXX	XXXX	XXXX	
SIXTEENTH	EIGHTEENTH	FOURTH	RESERVE

⊠ x8 ⊠ x7 ⊠ x2 ▭ x3 ⊠ MTZ x3 ⊠ x6

FINNISH ARMY

XXXX	XXXX	XXX
KARELIA	SOUTH-EASTERN	III

⊠ x8 ⊠ x7 ⊠ x3

XXXXX
CENTER

XXXX	XXXX	XXXX	XXXX	
FOURTH	NINTH	SECOND	THIRD	RESERVE

⊠ x14 ⊠ x9 ⊠ x6 ▭ x5 ⊠ MTZ x3 ⊠ x4 ▭ x4 ⊠ MTZ x3 ⊠

SLOVAKIAN ARMY

⊠ x2

ROMANIAN ARMY

XXXX	XXXX
THIRD	FOURTH

⊠ x5 ⊠ x3

XXXXX
SOUTH

XXXX	XXXX	XXXX	XXXX	
SIXTH	ELEVENTH	SEVENTEENTH	FIRST	RESERVE

⊠ x13 ⊠ x11 ⊠ x13 ▭ x5 ⊠ MTZ x4 ⊠

OKH RESERVE

⊠ x23 ▭ x2 ⊠ MTZ

General Ivan Fedyuninsky was in command of the XV Infantry Corps when the Germans attacked. His headquarters was in Kovel, Ukraine, thirty miles from the border on the main rail line to Kiev. His account of the chaotic Soviet response to the initial phase of Operation Barbarossa reflects just the sort of disruption of command and control arrangements that Blitzkrieg tactics were intended to achieve:

> Railway junctions and lines of communication were being destroyed by German planes and diversionist groups. There was a shortage of wireless sets at army headquarters, nor did many of us know how to use them... Orders and instructions were slow in arriving, and sometimes did not arrive at all... The liaison with neighbouring units was often completely absent, while nobody tried to establish it. Taking advantage of this, the enemy would often penetrate into our rear and attack the Soviet headquarters... despite German air supremacy, our marching columns did not use any proper camouflage. Sometimes on narrow roads, bottlenecks were formed by troops, artillery, motor vehicles, and field kitchens, and then the Nazi planes had the time of their life... Often our troops could not dig in, simply because they did not even have the simplest implements. Occasionally trenches had to be dug with helmets, since there were no spades.[33]

excellent progress from the start. The former gained crossings over the Dvina River within a few days, and moved on into Estonia and across the border into Russia, advancing two-thirds of the way to Leningrad. Army Group Center carried out a successful pincer movement at Minsk, followed by another at Smolensk. Army Group South had more trouble, since the Soviets had placed their strongest forces there, and since their commander, Colonel General Mikhail Kirponos, had risked drawing Stalin's ire by deploying his forces in expectation of the German attack, contrary to orders. Still, by the end of July, the Germans were threatening Kiev and had advanced far to the southeast.

By late July, as the Germans were considering their next moves, they appeared to have every reason for confidence. The Wehrmacht was at the peak of its effectiveness. German columns had broken through Soviet defenses and advanced deep into the enemy's rear, encircling the Soviet combat forces, cutting them off from their supplies, disrupting attempts to organize, and taking advantage of the tactical defense as the Soviets tried to break out. Tactically, the Reich's armor, infantry, artillery, and air force communicated and fought as a team, under the direction of officers whose knowledge, common training, and drive put them at the top of their profession.

The Red Army, meanwhile, was fighting badly. In the initial confusion, all the Soviets could think to do was to implement their prewar plans for immediate counterattacks, but these were clumsy affairs, uncoordinated, unsupported, and thus ineffective and enormously costly. In the first six weeks of the campaign, the Soviets suffered losses of men, equipment, and territory that most observers considered unsurvivable. Entire field armies had ceased to exist. In the border battles alone—from June 22 through about July 10—the Red Army lost approximately 750,000 men, 10,000 tanks, 14,600 guns and mortars, and 4,000 aircraft. The first phase of the Battle of

◀ ORDER OF BATTLE FOR OPERATION BARBAROSSA, JUNE 22, 1941

BLITZKRIEG TO THE EAST ▲

This photograph, taken near Brest, captures the combination of energy and ruthlessness that characterized the Wehrmacht in the initial stages of Operation Barbarossa. Even in the Panzer divisions, however, most of the mechanized infantry units moved on trucks rather than armored half-tracks like the one shown here.

Smolensk—up to early August—cost perhaps another 500,000 casualties; hundreds of thousands more fell or became prisoners in the northern and southern sectors.[34] Little appeared to stand between the Wehrmacht and Leningrad, Moscow, and the material riches of the Ukraine and the Caucasus. Franz Halder remarked that the campaign had been won in the first two weeks.[35]

That is not to say, however, that all was going well for the Germans. Predictably, the infantry was not keeping up with the armor, and the transport system was proving inadequate. Railroad conversion proceeded far behind schedule, and railheads lay hundreds of miles behind the front. The poor state of the roads was taking an enormous toll on German motor vehicles. Dust clogged air filters and destroyed engines, and the rutted surfaces led to fuel consumption and tire damage that exceeded all expectations. The number of functional transport vehicles dropped by 25 percent to 30 percent in the first month alone. Horses were wearing out too, and not enough replacements were available. By late July, the armies were beginning to complain of shortages of fuel and ammunition. Personnel losses too were more serious than the planners had anticipated; by August 3, Halder had recorded total casualties of 179,500.[36] At that rate, the Wehrmacht would use up its replacements in short order.

The situation would have been worrisome to anyone not convinced of the Red Army's impending military and political demise.

The uncomfortable truth, however, was that no such demise was in the offing. The Germans had reached the point in the campaign when they expected serious fighting to come to an end. But the Soviets refused to give up, and they were performing miracles of mobilization and reorganization. By July 1, they had called up an astounding 5.3 million additional men. By August 1, they had formed 17 new field armies, with 144 new divisions; their strength stood at 401 divisions, despite having lost 46 since June 22.[37] They also created a new high command system and simplified the structure of their field forces to adapt to their lack of equipment and qualified officers. They even managed to dismantle and move 1,500 factories far to the east, out of the Germans' reach. These were emergency measures that did not yet allow the Red Army to compete with the Wehrmacht on a unit-to-unit basis. The Russians might have started to realize, though, that their only hope lay in hanging on and prolonging the fight as long as possible. As Halder had to admit on August 11, "[I]f we smash a dozen [divisions], the Soviets simply put up another dozen."[38] The Germans were not getting the period of rest and refurbishment for which they had planned. Instead, they had to fend off a

▲ GERMAN MOTOR CONVOY ON THE EASTERN FRONT

A motor convoy navigates a typical road on the Eastern Front: rutted, dusty when dry and a quagmire when wet. Conditions such as these took a heavy toll on German vehicles and slowed supply deliveries.

FINLAND

20°E   40°E

Vologda

⊙ STOCKHOLM

⊙ HELSINKI

Gulf of Finland

Tallinn

KHIUMA

ESTONIA   Lake Peipus

SAAREMAA

Tartu

Gulf of Riga

GOTLAND

Riga

BALTIC SEA

LATVIA

Pskov

Ostrov

Dvinsk

LITHUANIA

Leningrad

XXXX 23

XXXX 42

XXXX 7

XXXXX NORTHERN POPOV

XXXX 8

XXXX 55

XXXX 54

XXXX 48

Novgorod

XXXX 52

XXXXX NORTHWESTERN F. I. KUZNETSOV   Yaroslav

XXXX 11

SOVIE UNIO

XXXX 34

XXXX 27

XXXXX STAVKA RESERVE BOGDANOV

XXXX 22

⊙ Mosco

XXXX 19

XXXXX WESTERN TIMOSHENKO

Vyaz'ma

Jul. 18

Vitebsk

19 20

300k

Smolensk

Kaluga

XXXX 24

Tul.

Königsberg

XXXX 18

XXXX 4 HOEPNER

XXXXX NORTH LEEB

XXXX 16

Danzig

Kovno

Vilna

Minsk

3 13

3

3

2

Mogilev

Jun. 27

Babruysk

2

300k

XXXX 28

Bryansk

XXXX 50

XXXXX BRYANSK YEREMENKO

Orel

XXXX 13

Kursk

20

Aug. 16

Dnieper

Aug. 25

Gomel

XXXX 40

XXXX 2

OKH RESERVE

XXXX 9

XXXX 3 HOTH

XXXXX CENTER BOCK

XXXX 2 GUDERIAN

⊙ WARSAW

Bielostok

10

300k

Vistula

Brest

XXXX 4

Pinsk   Pripet

Pripet Marshes

Jul. 16

XXXX 21

XXXXX XXXXX

Belgorod

Łódź

GENERAL

XXXXX SOUTH RUNDSTEDT

GOVERNMEN

Lublin

XXXX 6

Kovel'

XXXX 5

XXXX 37

XXXXX SOUTHWESTERN KIRPONOS

Kharkov

Katowice

Kraków

XXXX 17

Luts'k

6

Zhytomyr

Kiev

XXXX 26

XXXX 38

Poltava

Lvov

1

Jul. 9

Cherkassy

Kremenchuk

XXXX 6 (RECONSTITUTE

Ternopol

17

Vinnytsya

1

Aug. 2

Dnepropetrovsk

XX 1 (RECONS

Tatra Mountains

SLOVAKIA

Chernivtsi

UKRAINE

6

12

18

Uman

Kirovograd

17

Kryvyy Rih

100k

Nikopol

XXXX 18

HUNGARY

ROM 3

⊙ BUDAPEST

Carpathian Mountains

Prut

ROM 3

11

Kherson

XXXX 9

XXXXX SOUTHERN TYULENEV

Kishinev

Odessa

XXXX 11

XXXX COASTAL

50°N

ROM 4

BLACK SEA

CRIMEA

ROM 4

30°E

ROM

XXXX 4

Galați

ROMANIA

Sevastopol

continuing series of Soviet attacks, which, while poorly executed and hugely costly to the Red Army, still caused casualties, held up advances, and forced the Wehrmacht to expend fuel and ammunition. The Germans desperately needed to deliver a knockout blow, but how? Where they were strong, they won; but they could not be strong everywhere.[39]

ADVANCE IN THREE DIRECTIONS

By early August, the German high command also finally had to deal with a conflict that had been hanging over it for months. Although the original operational plan had called for simultaneous thrusts toward Leningrad, Moscow, and the Ukraine, Halder and his staff had believed from the start that Moscow was the place where the Soviets would make their last stand, if they had anything left after the battles on the frontiers. A staff exercise early the previous December had indicated that a final drive on Moscow would succeed only if the northern and southern army groups supported it. However, on December 5, when Halder presented this idea to Hitler, the Führer rejected it out of hand. He believed, largely for economic reasons, that Leningrad and the Ukraine had to be the priority targets. At the time, the two men failed to resolve the issue: Hitler had stated his intentions, but Halder quietly disregarded them and shaped the plan of operations around his own ideas, perhaps with the hope or expectation that, when push came to shove, his concept would win out.[40]

Now the decision point had arrived, but Hitler would not give in, despite opposition from his top generals. Neither Brauchitsch nor Halder could persuade him. Nor could Fedor von Bock, commander of Army Group Center. General Alfred Jodl, Hitler's primary military advisor in the armed forces high command, tried to trick the Führer into believing that the Soviets were concentrating in front of Moscow, and recommended that the Wehrmacht eliminate the threat. Hitler countered that they should strike where the Soviets were weak, and continued to maintain that Germany needed resources more than it needed the Soviet capital. The two sides argued and exchanged memoranda through much of August. Halder and the other generals still believed that the best way to force the Red Army into a climactic battle of annihilation was to attack the capital. Still Hitler would not budge. He finally ordered half of Army Group Center's tank forces to reinforce Army Group North, which had failed to make satisfactory progress toward Leningrad. Then he ordered the other half to attack southward and link up with forces from Army Group South, thus encircling and destroying the mass of Soviet forces that were defending Kiev and driving deep into the Ukraine. Moscow would have to wait.[41]

The operation to cut off Kiev was a huge success. Stalin had expected the attack against Moscow to continue, and so the Soviets were poorly deployed to block the

◀ OPERATION BARBAROSSA, JUNE 22–AUGUST 25, 1941
German forces made dramatic gains in the first weeks of Operation Barbarossa, destroying dozens of divisions and inflicting about a million casualties by August. But in that same period, the Soviet Union called up over 5 million men to fight and formed more than 140 new divisions.

A Panzer III medium tank of the 18th Panzer Division fords a river in the Soviet Union. The division operated as part of Guderian's Second Panzergruppe, in Army Group Center's sector.

southward thrust when it came. The attack began on August 25, and Soviet counterattacks could not stop it. Stalin ignored his generals' requests to pull back, and on September 15 the ring closed. Within another ten days, most of the fighting in the pocket was over. The Soviets had lost over 700,000 more men. Four field armies, consisting of forty-three divisions, were gone.[42] In the meantime, other forces from Army Group South took all the territory west of the Dnieper River, while Army Group North advanced to the gates of Leningrad, despite heavy resistance.

With actions on the flanks completed to Hitler's satisfaction, attention now returned to the central axis and Moscow. Planning had begun in early September for a new offensive, Operation Typhoon, to encircle Moscow. By the end of the month, the Germans had assembled nearly 2 million men in 78 divisions, with 14,000 artillery pieces, over 1,000 tanks, and nearly 1,400 aircraft, organized in three armies and three armored groups. They faced a Soviet force consisting of three *fronts* (army groups), comprising 1.25 million men, 990 tanks, 7,600 guns and mortars, and 667 aircraft. Impressive though these numbers were, however, they belied the two sides'

The Germans Advance, August 26–December 5, 1941 ▸

Starting in late August, Hitler ordered German forces to concentrate attacks north toward Leningrad and south toward Kiev. In October, after four Soviet armies were encircled and eliminated in the Ukraine, the Germans began a renewed drive on Moscow: Operation Typhoon.

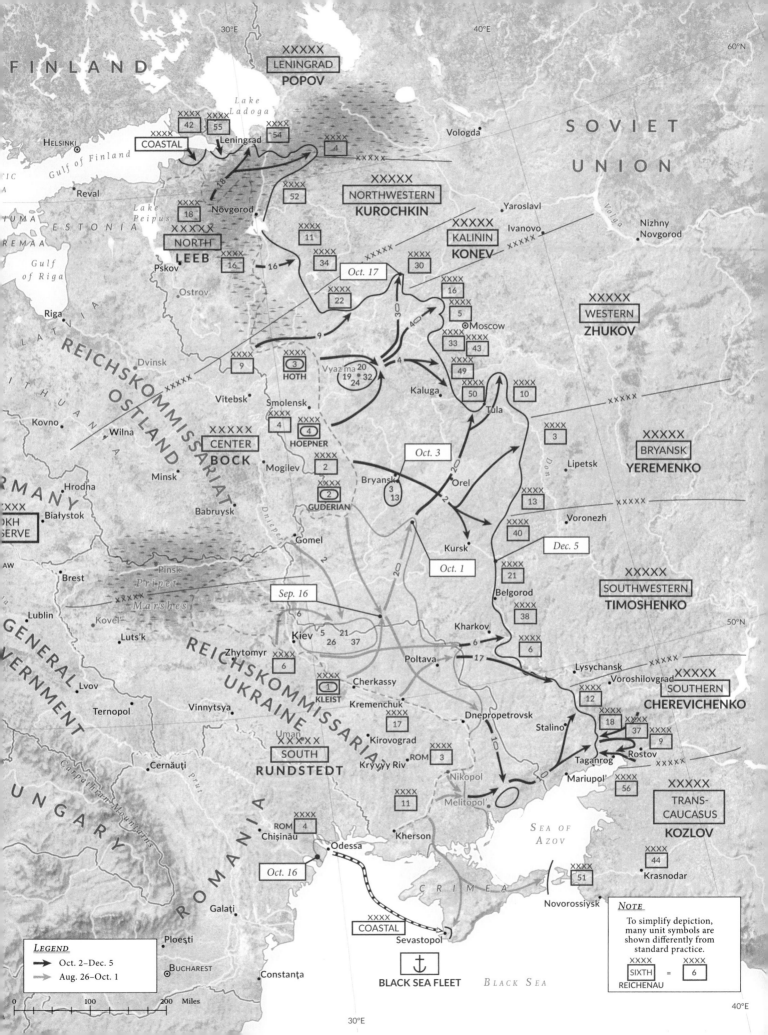

FINLAND

SOVIET UNION

XXXXX
LENINGRAD
POPOV

Lake Ladoga

Vologda

XXXX · 42 · | XXXX · 55 ·
Leningrad
XXXX · COASTAL ·
XXXX · -54 ·
XXXX · 4 ·
xxxxx

Helsinki

Gulf of Finland

Reval

ESTONIA

Lake Peipus

Novgorod

XXXX · 52 ·

XXXXX
NORTHWESTERN
KUROCHKIN

Yaroslavl

Ivanovo

XXXXX
KALININ
KONEV

Nizhny Novgorod

Volga

60°N

XXXX · 18 ·

REMAA

Gulf of Riga

XXXXX
NORTH
LEEB

Pskov

Ostrov

XXXX · 11 ·

XXXX · 16 · → · 16

XXXX · 34 ·

Oct. 17

XXXX · 30 ·

XXXX · 16 ·

XXXX · 5 ·
⊙Moscow

XXXXX
WESTERN
ZHUKOV

Riga

LATVIA

Dvinsk

XXXX · 22 ·

9

XXXX · 33 ·

XXXX · 43 ·

LITHUANIA

Vitebsk

Smolensk

XXXX · 9 ·

XXXX · ③ ·
HOTH

Vyaz'ma 20
19 · 32
24

4

Kaluga

XXXX · 49 ·

XXXX · 50 ·

XXXX · 10 ·

Kovno

Wilna

XXXX · 3 ·

Lipetsk

XXXXX
BRYANSK
YEREMENKO

Minsk

XXXXX
CENTER
BOCK

Mogilev

XXXX · 4 ·

XXXX · ④ ·
HOEPNER

Oct. 3

Tula

Don

REICHSKOMMISSARIAT OSTLAND

GERMANY

Hrodna
Białystok

XXXX
OKH RESERVE

XXXX · 2 ·

XXXX · ② ·
GUDERIAN

Bryansk
③
13

Orel

Voronezh

XXXX · 13 ·

XXXX · 40 ·

XXXXX
SOUTHWESTERN
TIMOSHENKO

Babruysk

Gomel

Dnieper

2

*Pinsk
Pripet
Marshes*

Kursk

Oct. 1

Dec. 5

Brest

xxxxx

Kovel'

Sep. 16

6

XXXX · 21 ·

Belgorod

XXXX · 38 ·

50°N

GENERAL GOVERNMENT

Lublin

Luts'k

5 · 21
26 · 37
Kiev

Kharkov

6

XXXX · 6 ·

Zhytomyr

XXXX · 6 ·

Lvov

Ternopol

Vinnytsya

XXXX · ① ·
KLEIST

Cherkassy

Poltava

17

Lysychansk
Voroshilovgrad

XXXXX
SOUTHERN
CHEREVICHENKO

REICHSKOMMISSARIAT UKRAINE

Kremenchuk

Dnepropetrovsk

XXXX · 17 ·

Uman
XXXXX
SOUTH
RUNDSTEDT

Kirovograd

Kryyÿy Riv

ROM · 3 ·

Stalino

Taganrog

XXXX · 12 ·

XXXX · 18 ·

XXXX · 37 ·

XXXX · 9 ·

Rostov

Mariupol'

XXXX · 56 ·

XXXXX
TRANS-
CAUCASUS
KOZLOV

Cernăuţi

HUNGARY

Carpathian Mountains

Prut

Nikopol'

Melitopol'

10

XXXX · 11 ·

ROM · 4 ·
Chişinău

ROMANIA

Galaţi

Oct. 16

Odessa

Kherson

Sea of Azov

XXXX · 44 ·

Krasnodar

XXXX · 51 ·

Ploeşti

⊙Bucharest

CRIMEA

Novorossiysk

NOTE

To simplify depiction,
many unit symbols are
shown differently from
standard practice.

XXXX
SIXTH
REICHENAU
=
XXXX · 6 ·

Constanţa

XXXX · COASTAL ·
Sevastopol

⚓
BLACK SEA FLEET

Black Sea

40°E

LEGEND
→ Oct. 2–Dec. 5
→ Aug. 26–Oct. 1

0 · 100 · 200 Miles

30°E

THE OUTSKIRTS OF MOSCOW, ▲
DECEMBER 1941
As German Army Group Center neared Moscow, masses of Soviet citizens mobilized to dig immense tank traps around the city. The German drive stalled, and winter helped level the playing field for the Soviets.

weaknesses. The Soviet troops were a mix of worn-down veterans and green recruits. Most divisions were at half strength, and the counteroffensives of the previous weeks had left them ill-prepared to conduct an effective defense. Even the most basic equipment was scarce, and defensive lines were incomplete.

On the German side, losses had been high, the men were tired, and the equipment was failing. More than half the tanks were out of action. Continued fighting against Soviet counterattacks, together with the inadequate railroad network and vehicle shortages, had precluded a buildup of ammunition and fuel.[43] Moreover, the supplies that did get through for the drive toward Moscow came at the expense of the clothing and building materials that the troops would need when winter arrived. The Germans still had an edge over their foes, but only a small one. They were taking an enormous gamble.

Initially, the offensive was another stunning victory for the Wehrmacht. The Germans broke through the Soviet lines, advanced up to 125 miles, and completed two encirclements, at Vyaz'ma and Bryansk. The Soviets lost another million men, including over 685,000 prisoners, along with 6,000 guns and 830 tanks. A gap three hundred miles wide now existed in the Soviet line, and nothing seemed to stand between the Germans and Moscow.

At that moment, however, three things happened. First, the Soviets mobilized

Halder entered the army as a cadet in 1902 and attended the Bavarian War Academy from 1911 to 1914. He served in various staff positions throughout the First World War, mostly on the Western Front, and ended the war as a captain. He stayed on active duty, serving as a General Staff officer. In February 1938 he achieved the rank of general of artillery, and on September 1 he took over from Ludwig Beck as chief of the General Staff. Halder's time in that position is the subject of controversy. He was extremely hardworking, and technically proficient at tactics and operational maneuver; he helped direct the Wehrmacht to its greatest victories, including the conquests of Poland, the Low Countries and France, and the Balkans—but not the invasion of Denmark and Norway, which he opposed. During Operation Barbarossa, he unsuccessfully pushed Hitler to focus German efforts on the drive to Moscow. He also came to realize that the resilient Red Army would be more difficult to defeat than Hitler believed.

Like most of his comrades, however, he was unable to grasp the fundamental strategic weakness of Germany's position. Before and during the war, he maintained a passive-aggressive relationship with Hitler; he toyed with political opposition and then gave it up, but later tried to undermine Hitler's military plans in favor of his own. Halder also played a much greater role in the regime's crimes than he admitted later. In any case, by September 1942, his disagreements with Hitler had reached the point where the Führer forced him out of active service. After the coup attempt of July 20, 1944, he was arrested and placed in a concentration camp; American troops freed him in May 1945. Halder went on to lead the Historical Liaison Group, a cell of former German officers working for the U.S. Army Historical Division. Halder's group helped establish the dual myths of the German Army's military genius and moral correctness.

440,000 civilians to dig defenses in front of Moscow, and thousands of men—local militia and NKVD (internal security) troops—to man them. Second, the Germans, with an excess of confidence, began to broaden their front instead of concentrating on taking or surrounding the city. And third, it began to rain. This happens every year in Russia, as the Germans should well have known. It is called the fall *rasputitsa*: literally, "the time without roads." (It happens again in the spring, when the snow melts.) For the Soviets, this was a problem, but one they were anticipating, and they were closer to their bases of supply. For the Germans, it was a disaster. Supplies could not get through, units could not move, aircraft could not fly. The Germans tried to resume their advance, and made good progress at first, but stiffening Soviet resistance and the awful weather conditions forced them to halt by mid-October. They would have to wait for the ground to freeze before trying again.

This was another point at which the Germans would have benefited from taking a good hard look at their situation, with an eye toward going over to the defensive. Despite recent German victories, there was no sign that the Soviets were going to give up or run out of soldiers. The strength of the average German infantry division stood at 65 percent; for armored divisions, it was 35 percent. Supplies of every kind were short. Winter was coming. Everyone—even Hitler—now recognized that the campaign would last into 1942. Arguably, the best opportunity to take up a defensive stance had already passed, but such a move still might have made sense, rather than further exhausting the available forces. The army's senior leadership was determined to press on, however, sure that the Soviets had to be on their last legs. As late as November 23,

Halder was insisting that the army should make a "minimum" advance to a line that started well to the east of Leningrad, passed east of Moscow by 150 miles, and went on to Rostov, on the Don River.

In the meantime, on November 15, 1941, the Germans resumed their attack. Again they made good initial progress along some axes. But the fighting was grinding them down; they were at the end of their strength. By early December, the offensive had stalled. Now the Germans were in a bind. They could no longer advance. They were not holding defensible terrain, nor had they constructed any field fortifications or cold-weather quarters. Construction materials and winter clothing, as well as reserves of fuel and ammunition, sat in depots in Poland, and the means to move them forward were lacking. As the temperatures sank well below freezing and the snow fell, the men had their hands full just trying to survive; any thought of attacking was gone.

If there was one bit of good news for the Wehrmacht, it was that the Soviets were exhausted as well and in no position to attack. That, at least, was the assessment of German intelligence—but they were mistaken. On November 24 the Soviet high command ordered the deployment of its newest strategic reserve, and many of the new divisions consisted of battle-tested Siberian troops: Stalin had learned that the Japanese did not intend to attack in the East, so he had released forces to join the defense

of Moscow. Soviet forces in the west now numbered 343 divisions and 98 separate brigades, totaling over four million. The best estimate is that the Soviets had lost more than two million troops just since the end of September. Even so, they had fought the Wehrmacht to a standstill at last and were about to turn the tables.

THE FRONT BEHIND THE FRONT

This is a good moment to turn aside from the battlefront and consider what was going on behind the lines. Here the struggle was every bit as brutal, and in some ways even more so. Neither Stalinism nor Nazism was a system that cared much about the lives of ordinary people. On the contrary: people, individually or collectively, were either tools of the state, to be used in any way the state saw fit, or enemies of the state, to be repressed or eliminated. Each side was responsible for death and suffering on an almost unimaginable scale. Comparing their relative degrees of evil is a highly subjective exercise, although one should bear in mind that the Nazis were the aggressors, and their intent was genocidal to an extent that the Soviets' was not.

Such comparisons, as complicated as they are for us today, were even more so for

The Wehrmacht made only the most minimal provision for the millions of Red Army soldiers captured in the first phases of Operation Barbarossa. One of the relatively few who survived to the end of the war describes the conditions that the Soviet POWs faced:

In the camp itself at Roslavl' there were several barracks. The majority of them were of the semidugout type, with earth floors below ground level. Water from above and below the ground flooded these barracks, and in October 1941 their floors were a filthy mire, in which the prisoners were ankle-deep. There were no plank beds, boards, or straw, and the prisoners were compelled to lie right in the dirt. In winter, the floor was an icy surface, covered with snow that was wafted in and carried in by people's feet . . . People were crammed in there, packed in like sardines. A living wall of prisoners swayed from side to side. The weakened hearts of many comrades could not withstand it. The crushed and lifeless corpses swayed, like live men, in the mass of the living, and in the morning they fell to the ground, no longer held upright by the bodies of their comrades who were still alive.[44]

people on the ground at the time. When German soldiers arrived in some parts of Soviet territory, such as eastern Poland, the Baltic states, Byelorussia (now Belarus), and the Ukraine, some of the local people—at times a large majority—welcomed them as liberators. Some of them remembered the German occupation during the First World War, which had been, on the whole, strict but relatively benign. More of them simply hated the Soviet government, and with good reason.

Stalin's regime was responsible for widespread destruction and death. Over three million people died in a manmade famine in the Ukraine in 1932 and 1933, as the regime forcibly extracted food from the region. Millions more from across the country were imprisoned or killed in the Great Terror and other purges in the late 1930s. In eastern Poland, which the Soviets took over in 1939 as part of their pact with the Nazis, the new rulers carried out a ruthless offensive against any real or imagined enemies, usually the educated, influential, and well-off. Hundreds of thousands of men, women, and children were arrested and put into the Soviet gulag camp system or were deported to Siberia or Kazakhstan. Tens of thousands died from the conditions there; thousands more were shot out of hand. Similar actions took place in the Baltic states, which the Soviets annexed forcibly in 1940. A year later, as the Wehrmacht advanced into the newer Soviet lands, NKVD jailers shot thousands of prisoners whom they could not evacuate.[45] Stalin's paranoia and cynicism had permeated the Soviet system, bringing suffering and death on an unprecedented level. Many of its people believed that the Germans would bring relief from such horror.

The shock and disappointment must have been so much the greater, then, when the Germans proved to be even worse than the Soviets. On the strategic level, one wonders why the Germans did not take better advantage of anti-Stalinist feelings to gain support for the campaign against the regime. Several broad factors were at play. First, the Germans believed that they were going to win the campaign easily, so there seemed to be no compelling reason to take the local inhabitants' desires (for independence, or justice, or even for sustenance) into account. Second, as far as the Wehrmacht was concerned, military necessity overruled those desires—as well as the laws of war. The need for a rapid campaign, together with the limitations of the logistical

system, meant that the army would have to live off the land, and that it could not afford any disruptions from guerilla attacks against its lines of supply. Nazi ideology, the military's traditionally harsh approach to partisan warfare, and broader German racism toward Jews and Slavs filled in the gaps: there would be no leniency.

The violence took on several aspects. German soldiers, acting on the orders they had received, shot many Red Army political commissars upon capture. Military authorities, in cooperation with the SS, also culled about a half million Jews, Communists, and "Asiatics" from the prisoner-of-war pens and murdered them. The rest of the POWs—some 2.8 million—suffered such levels of starvation, exposure, exhaustion, disease, and abuse that approximately 1.8 million of them died by the spring of 1942. As for the civilian Jews, as the Wehrmacht advanced, SS Einsatzgruppen and other police units (as well as army security divisions, military police, and some regular troops, and often with the aid of local auxiliaries) shot Jewish men, women, and children en masse. By the end of the year, the Germans had murdered about a million Jews as part of that program. They forced the remaining Jews into ghettos, where they performed labor and lived under ghastly conditions until such time as the authorities decided to kill them too.[46] The Wehrmacht justified its participation by stating that it was fighting Communist partisans.

Such reasoning also left a trail of dead non-Jewish civilians and burned villages across the land, despite the fact that no significant partisan movement had yet arisen.

▲ MASS SHOOTING

Men of an unidentified German unit—possibly Wehrmacht, more likely SS or police—carry out a mass shooting. Note the large group of spectators in the background. Such killings were impossible to keep secret. In autumn 1941, senior commanders circulated orders that authorized such actions.

FORCED LABOR ▲

Wehrmacht soldiers round up Jews in Mogilev, Byelorussia, for forced labor. The army played a key role in the detention, employment, and execution of millions of Jews.

In any case, the murder of the very old and the very young hardly qualified as a battle against partisans. Finally, as planned, the Germans took massive quantities of food to supply the Wehrmacht and the homeland, as well as requisitioned housing and even clothing. Uncounted millions died from starvation, exposure, and disease. The Soviet regime's scorched-earth program, which tried to destroy anything that might be of use to the Germans, only added to the civilians' woes.

Not all German soldiers participated in these crimes: many were never in a position to do so, and others found ways to avoid the more disturbing duties. Apparently, some senior commanders even became concerned that their soldiers' support for Nazi policies was not as firm as it should be. In October and November of 1941, those commanders sent out a series of orders that attempted to explain and justify the shootings and other criminal policies, which were common knowledge in the ranks by that point.[47] On the whole, however, the Third Reich's leaders had little trouble seeing their intent put into practice. Thus, trapped between the two sides, the peoples of Eastern Europe suffered a terrible fate.

ПАРТИЗАНЫ БЕЙТЕ ВРАГА БЕЗ ПОЩАДЫ!

GUERRILLA FIGHTERS OF 1942—NO MERCY TO THE ENEMY
Poster by Koretzky

▲ "No Mercy to the Enemy!"

Nazi Germany and the Soviet Union fought the war on the Eastern Front with staggering ferocity and ruthlessness, which Germany engendered as a matter of policy.

The Nazis believed that their racial mission and "military necessity" trumped all international laws of war. This order by Field Marshal Walter von Reichenau, commander of the Sixth Army, was intended to instill that idea in ordinary soldiers. When he received a copy, Hitler liked it so much that he ordered it distributed to every unit on the Eastern Front.

The most important goal of the campaign against the Jewish-Bolshevik system is the complete destruction of its instruments of power and the eradication of the Asiatic influence in the European cultural realm.

In this connection there also exist tasks for the troops that go beyond the traditional, one-sided definition of a soldier. The soldier in the east is not only a combatant according to the rules of warfare, but also the bearer of an inexorable racial idea and the avenger of all the bestialities that have been committed against the German and related peoples.

Therefore the soldier must have full understanding for the necessity of the harsh but justified punishment of the Jewish subhumans. It has the further purpose of forestalling uprisings in the rear of the armed forces, which experience shows were always instigated by Jews.

The battle against the enemy behind the front is still not being taken seriously enough. Insidious, cruel *partisans* and degenerate women are still being taken as prisoners of war; snipers and tramps, half-uniformed or in civilian clothes, are being handled like decent soldiers and taken away to the detention camps . . .

Feeding of local inhabitants and prisoners of war who are not in service with the Wehrmacht, at troops' kitchens, is exactly as misplaced a human gesture as is giving away cigarettes and bread. What the homeland spares, what the leadership brings forward under great difficulties, the soldier is not to give away to the enemy, also not when it comes from booty, which is a necessary part of our supply . . .

The complete *disarmament of the population* in the rear of the fighting troops is urgent, considering the long, vulnerable supply chain . . . If it is established that individual partisans are acting under arms in the rear of the army, drastic measures are to be taken. These are also to extend to the male population that would have been in a position to hinder or report attacks. The nonparticipation of many allegedly anti-Soviet elements, which springs from a "wait-and-see" attitude, must be turned to a clear decision for active collaboration against Bolshevism. If not, then no one can complain of being judged and handled as a follower of the Soviet system. The terror of German countermeasures must be stronger than the threat from fragmentary Bolshevik elements that are wandering around.

. . . The soldier has to fulfill two different goals:

1. *The complete destruction of misleading Bolshevik doctrine, the Soviet state and its armed forces;*

2. *The merciless eradication of foreign insidiousness and cruelty, thereby securing the life of the German Wehrmacht in Russia.*

Only thus will we do justice to our historic task, to *free* the German people from the *Asiatic-Jewish danger once and for all.*[48]

SOVIET COUNTERATTACK

On December 5, 1941, the Soviets launched another massive counteroffensive against Army Group Center, striking first at the wings that threatened to encircle Moscow. The Red Army had concentrated a force that outnumbered the Germans by two to one at their chosen points of attack, with a slightly lesser superiority in artillery and near parity in tanks—all without arousing any suspicion.[49] The attack came in temperatures of negative 5 degrees Fahrenheit, with more than three feet of snow on the ground. Many of the Soviet units were themselves still very weak from the fighting of

SOVIET WINTER OFFENSIVE, DECEMBER 5–MAY 7, 1942 ▶

On December 5, Soviet troops launched a counterattack to drive German forces away from Moscow. About two weeks later, more assaults were added along a broader front. The Germans were pushed back but retired in good order.

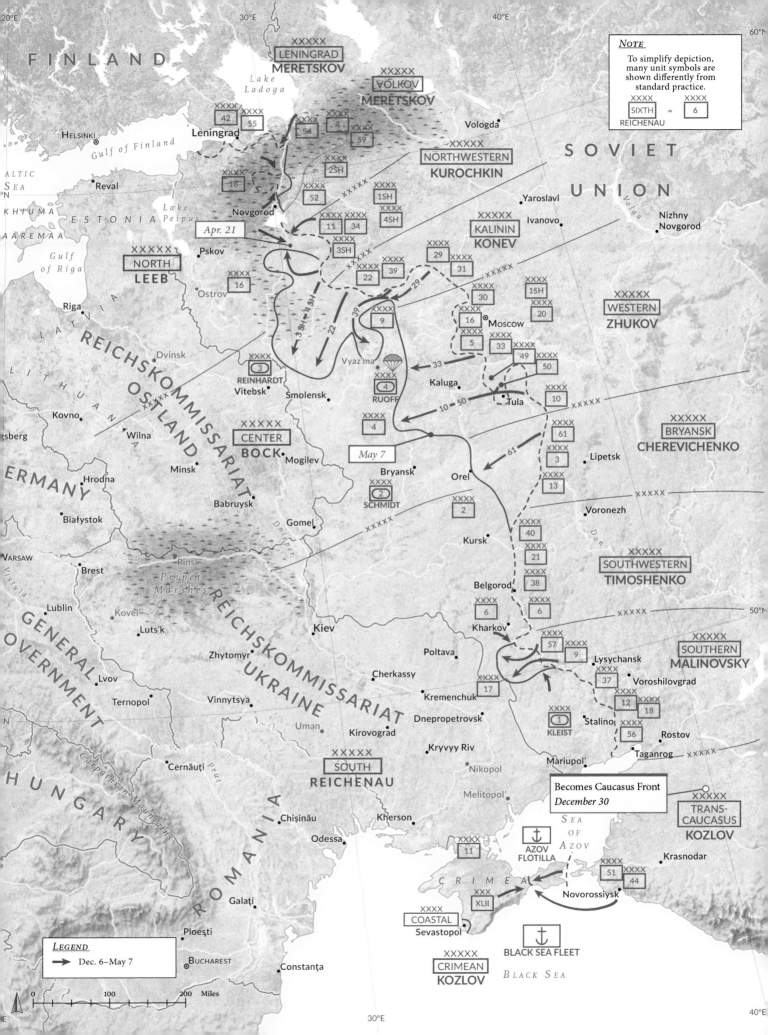

Camouflage Coveralls

The idea of using disruptive patterns for camouflage was introduced in WWI, and in the 1920s to early 1930s, the Italian and German armies introduced camouflage shelter sections that could be worn as ponchos. In 1937 the Germans developed the first printed textile jackets employing the principle. The next year the Soviets, who were particularly attuned to the value of all forms of military deception (*maskirovka*), began issuing the MK "deception coveralls" to snipers, paratroopers, and certain reconnaissance units.

Sniper Rifle

The most common Soviet sniper rifle was a standard model 1891/30 7.62 mm Mosin-Nagant bolt-action infantry weapon, modified with a longer bolt that was bent downward so that it would not strike the scope when operated. Rugged and accurate to about one minute of angle (sufficient for a head shot at 400 yards), the Mosin-Nagant proved more effective in the field than the semiautomatic SVT-40 used by some snipers, despite the high rate of fire offered by the latter.

PU Sniper Scope

Like most Soviet military hardware of WWII, the PU scope was designed for a combination of good performance, durability, and ease of mass production. Shorter and lighter than most military scopes, the PU provided a relatively low 3.5x magnification, a windage dial, and an elevation dial calibrated for shots at up to 1,300 meters (over 1,400 yards). Since it lacked a focusing mechanism, it was only suitable for snipers with perfect vision.

the previous weeks, but they pressed the Germans hard, and often succeeded in penetrating far to the rear to attack headquarters and disrupt supply lines. Several days passed before the German high command recognized the seriousness of the situation, and then there was little it could do. Significant reinforcements would not reach the front for weeks. The senior commanders, with a distinct note of panic to their messages, proposed pulling back; they worried that the Soviets might surround and destroy the Wehrmacht's forward elements. As Hitler pointed out, however, the armies had not prepared any positions in the rear, and given the extreme shortages of fuel, vehicles, and horses, there was no way to pull out the heavy weapons. He approved a few local withdrawals but otherwise insisted that the troops hold where they were. On December 18 the Soviets broadened their offensive to include attacks against the middle of Army Group Center and soon penetrated the lines there as well. The elimination of an entire German army group loomed.[50]

The Germans did hang on, if only barely—and arguably in large part because of Hitler's determination.[51] Stalin unintentionally assisted them by issuing an order that broadened the counteroffensive against Army Group Center to include the entire front. The Germans were weak, but not that weak; the Red Army could not destroy them all at once. The Soviet offensive went on for two months but finally sputtered out in the mud of the spring *rasputitsa*, and the Wehrmacht held on. Though it had been pushed back, and despite the loss of more than 700,000 men since October, the German Army was still firmly on Soviet soil. In the aftermath, Hitler dismissed a number of his generals, including Brauchitsch. He now took command of the army personally and began preparing its next big effort.[52]

Three Turning Points

With the failure of the German invasion in 1941, the war now entered a new phase, in at least two respects. First, and most immediate, the Soviets had blocked the Germans' strategic effort to crush Russia in one campaign. They had suffered enormous losses: up to 40 percent of the Soviet population, 35 percent of its productive capacity, half of its agriculture, and two-thirds to three-quarters of key raw materials supplies either had been destroyed or were now under German control.[53] In the end, though, the Soviet Union had stopped the Germans cold, and it still had enormous potential. It had the human and material resources to keep fighting, and its political system, as well as the will of its people, had never reached the breaking point.[54] From here on, the Red Army would become increasingly well armed and skillful, until it outmatched the Wehrmacht in more than just numbers.

◀ Soviet Sniper

During the Winter War of 1939–40, the Red Army suffered severely at the hands of Finnish snipers. In response, Soviet military leaders developed improved doctrine and training, and by June 1941, the U.S.S.R. had the best-trained, largest, and arguably best-equipped sniper force in the world. After the initial battles of Operation Barbarossa decimated the Red Army, women were increasingly allowed into frontline combat roles. Some early volunteers were so effective as snipers that in 1943 the Soviet Union established a Central Women's School for Sniper Training, which ultimately graduated 407 instructors and 1,061 snipers.

БЬЕМСЯ МЫ ЗДОРОВО
КОЛЕМ ОТЧАЯННО —
ВНУКИ СУВОРОВА,
ДЕТИ ЧАПАЕВА.

MOBILIZING HISTORY ▲

Prior to World War II, Soviet propaganda trumpeted the modernity of Communist ideology and Comrade Stalin's leadership. With the existential threat posed by the Nazi invasion, the Soviets reverted to their history. This poster highlights that the current soldiers of the Red Army follow in the footsteps of the great Russian military heroes: Alexander Nevsky, who ruled Russia in the thirteenth century; eighteenth-century field marshal Aleksandr Suvorov; and Vasily Chapayev, a famous commander during the Russian Civil War.

The second turn in the war came with Germany's declaration of war against the United States on December 11, four days after Japan attacked Pearl Harbor. Hitler had believed for years that war with the United States was inevitable.[55] He knew that his navy was too weak to take on the Americans directly, but with Japan in the war, that point seemed moot. Most of the Wehrmacht's leaders believed, like their Führer, that America's entry would make no great difference. So long as Germany could win in the East in 1942, it would have all the resources it would need to hold off the United States and Great Britain indefinitely. To that end, and with the knowledge that the Wehrmacht could not again summon the resources it had deployed against the Soviet Union the previous June, Hitler would concentrate his forces on the southern part of the Soviet front, driving for the Caucasus—and Stalingrad.

The Germans made one more momentous decision as the first campaign in the East reached its climax. Its exact timing remains a matter of debate, but at some point in the latter half of 1941, almost certainly by late fall, the Germans decided on the so-called Final Solution to the Jewish Question: the physical annihilation of every Jew within their sphere of influence and, ultimately, throughout the world. There was no written order, and probably no single decision point; instead, a series of incremental decisions led up to the awful conclusion. Obviously, shooting Jewish men, women, and children behind the lines in the East was a big step in that direction. In the months that followed, other milestones appeared: mobile gas vans, and then killing centers, to which the Germans could bring Jews for mass execution while keeping the program secret. Then, by the end of November, the Final Solution became a unified governmental policy. The head of the SS Reich Security Main Office, Reinhard Heydrich, scheduled a meeting with representatives of other governmental agencies to establish his authority over the program and to begin the process of coordination. The meeting took place in the Berlin suburb of Wannsee on January 20, 1942, by which time the first of the killing centers, at the Polish town of Chelmno, was already in operation. The Holocaust was now fully under way: roughly three million Jews would die in 1942, half of the total number of victims who would die as a result of the Final Solution.

CONCLUSION

The German invasion of the Soviet Union demonstrates how interconnected ideology, culture, politics, economics, and warfare are. The Germans based their strategy, military operations, and occupation policies upon their perceived racial and military superiority. They assumed that they would win the campaign easily and that military victory would lead to the collapse of the Soviet system. That assumption allowed them to paper over the weaknesses in their plan and removed any tendency to compromise in their treatment of the people whom they conquered. Ultimately, however, their weaknesses caught up with them. They could not sustain their offensive, could never quite destroy the Red Army, could never force the Soviets to give up. Their fundamental assumption failed them, and all that they had built upon it backfired. The Germans left themselves no options, deep in a foreign land, facing an enemy whose strength and hatred would only grow.

On the Soviet side, the role of victim placed a veneer of respectability onto a regime that was nearly as bad as the Nazis'. Whether its totalitarian nature helped or hurt in its struggle for survival is hard to say, but either way, the regime held fast. It endured military and economic losses that would have crippled most other states. The standing forces with which it started the war, including millions of men and huge quantities of equipment, were mostly gone. Some of its most valuable territories, containing vast amounts of raw materials, agricultural land, and people, were now under German occupation. Recovering from such setbacks required immense political will and control. The Soviet people made nearly unimaginable sacrifices—sacrifices that their own government and the nature of their enemy demanded of them. In the end, they won. The course of the war, and the world's future, would be different as a result.

INTRODUCTION

Before the outbreak of the Second World War in Europe, the most likely Great Power foe for the expanding Japanese Empire was not the United States or Britain, but rather the Soviet Union. The Japanese takeover of Manchuria in 1931 and the creation of the puppet state of Manchukuo the following year brought Japan and the Soviet Union eyeball-to-eyeball along an ill-defined, three-thousand-mile-long border. Numerous border disputes escalated to a significant regimental-size clash in 1938. A substantial faction within the IJA (Imperial Japanese Army) wanted a war with the Soviets, thinking that the Communist state was weak and that Japan could quickly eliminate its traditional enemy. Border violations in the late spring of 1939 along the Outer Mongolian–Manchukuoan border in the region of the Khalkhin Gol River erupted into a full-scale battle. Soviet forces under General Georgy Zhukov, making liberal use of tanks and airplanes, practically destroyed an entire Japanese division. But even while the fighting was under way, the international strategic situation was changing rapidly. As Zhukov's pincers were closing the ring behind the Japanese, Stalin signed the Nazi-Soviet Non-Aggression Pact with Germany. Tokyo was taken by surprise: Hitler had not informed his Axis partners of his plans, and Japanese leaders could no longer depend on Germany to check Soviet ambitions in Asia. Japan negotiated a cease-fire with Russia and turned its attention increasingly toward the south instead of the north.

The German conquest of Western Europe in May 1940 further encouraged that shift in focus. The Nazi triumph isolated European colonies in Asia, weakened Great Britain, and seemed to offer Japan the opportunity to break the military stalemate in China by blocking outside aid from reaching Chiang Kai-shek's Guomindang (Nationalist) regime through British Burma and French Indochina. The Japanese advance into northern French Indochina in September 1940, however, increased tensions with the United States, which responded by imposing a series of economic sanctions on Japan between September 1940 and June 1941. The Japanese reacted in late September by signing the Tripartite Pact among Germany, Italy, and Japan to pressure the Americans, and toward the end of 1940, the Japanese military began serious study for a possible war against the Western powers. To secure their northern flank, the Japanese opened negotiations with the Soviets that culminated in the signing of the Japan-Soviet Neutrality Pact in Moscow in April 1941. Japan's military planning for the seizure of the oil-rich Netherlands East Indies accelerated.

The German invasion of the Soviet Union in June 1941 again surprised Tokyo, and created a dilemma. Should Japan join with its German ally and attack its traditional enemy the Soviet Union, or should Tokyo strike south to secure the natural resources that the military and the nation required? Japan's leaders hedged their bets. The army mobilized for a northern offensive, contingent upon German success, but it also moved into southern French Indochina in mid-July, prompting further economic restrictions from the United States. On July 26 America, Britain, and the Netherlands

5

JAPAN STRIKES: FROM PEARL HARBOR TO MIDWAY

EDWARD J. DREA

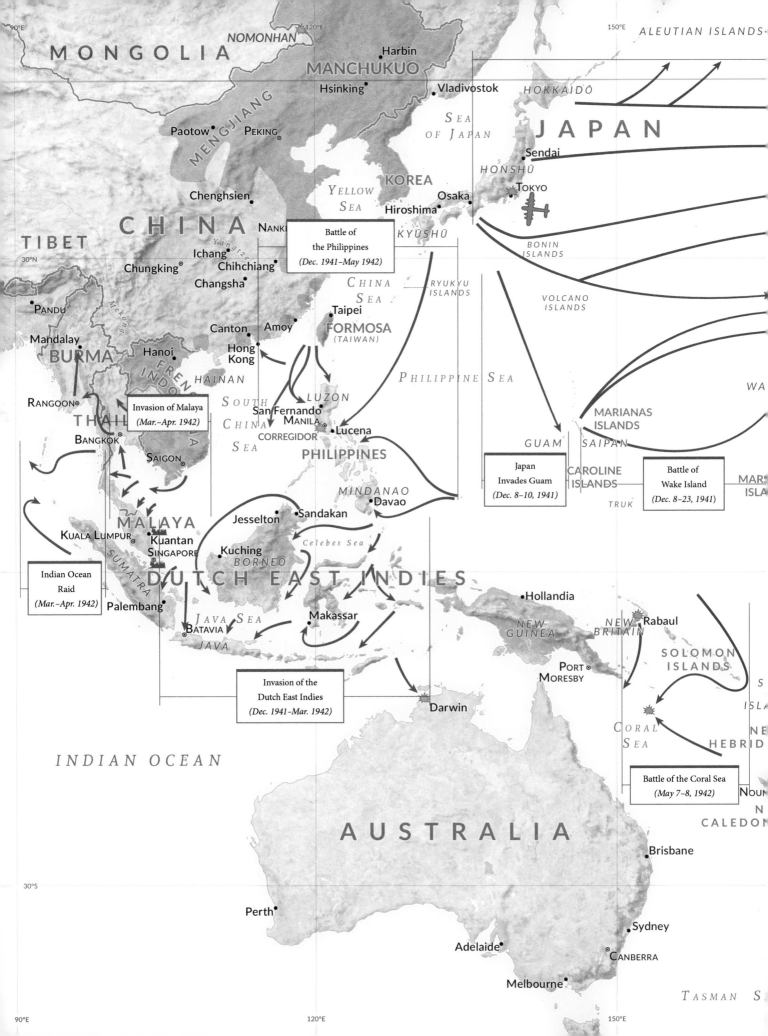

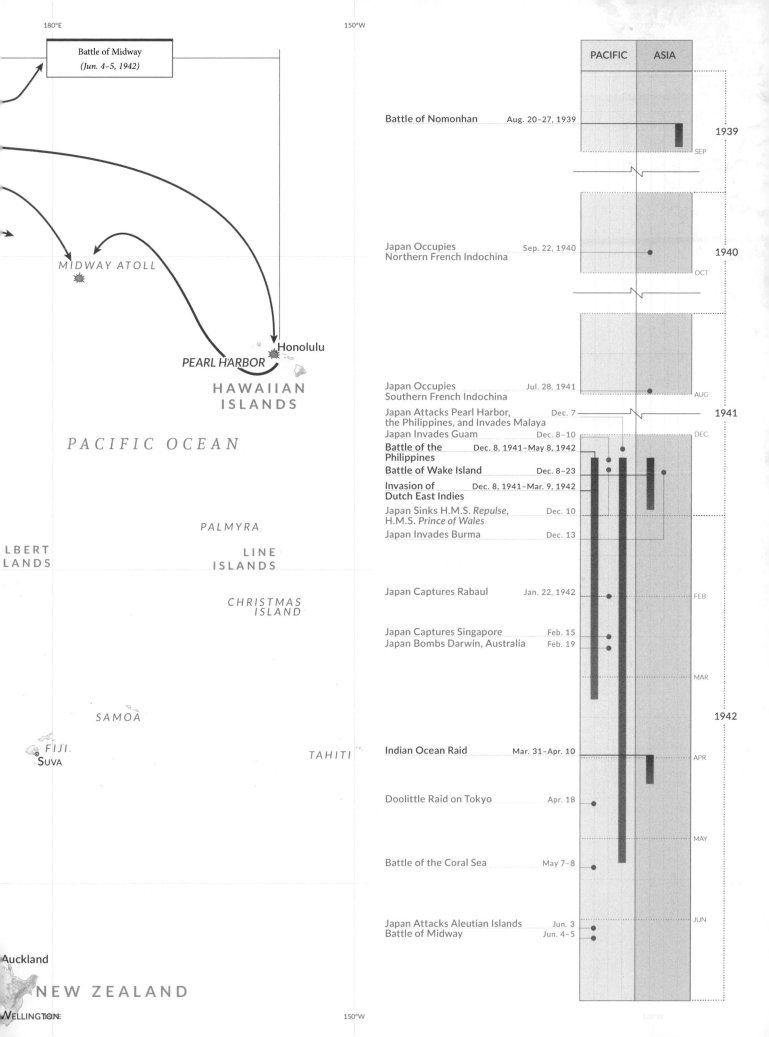

180°E

Battle of Midway
(Jun. 4–5, 1942)

150°W

MIDWAY ATOLL

Honolulu
PEARL HARBOR

HAWAIIAN
ISLANDS

PACIFIC OCEAN

PALMYRA

LBERT
LANDS

LINE
ISLANDS

*CHRISTMAS
ISLAND*

SAMOA

FIJI
SUVA

TAHITI

Auckland

NEW ZEALAND

WELLINGTON

150°W

PACIFIC	ASIA

Battle of Nomonhan — Aug. 20–27, 1939 — 1939 — SEP

Japan Occupies
Northern French Indochina — Sep. 22, 1940 — 1940 — OCT

Japan Occupies
Southern French Indochina — Jul. 28, 1941 — AUG — 1941

Japan Attacks Pearl Harbor,
the Philippines, and Invades Malaya — Dec. 7 — DEC

Japan Invades Guam — Dec. 8–10

Battle of the Philippines — Dec. 8, 1941–May 8, 1942

Battle of Wake Island — Dec. 8–23

Invasion of Dutch East Indies — Dec. 8, 1941–Mar. 9, 1942

Japan Sinks H.M.S. *Repulse*,
H.M.S. *Prince of Wales* — Dec. 10

Japan Invades Burma — Dec. 13

Japan Captures Rabaul — Jan. 22, 1942 — FEB

Japan Captures Singapore — Feb. 15

Japan Bombs Darwin, Australia — Feb. 19

MAR

1942

Indian Ocean Raid — Mar. 31–Apr. 10 — APR

Doolittle Raid on Tokyo — Apr. 18

MAY

Battle of the Coral Sea — May 7–8

Japan Attacks Aleutian Islands — Jun. 3 — JUN

Battle of Midway — Jun. 4–5

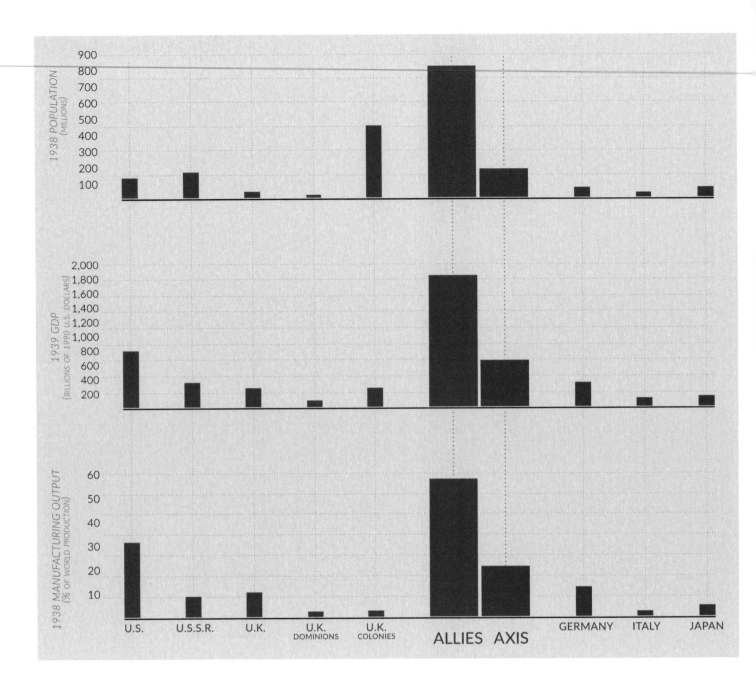

The Pacific War Begins ▲

The huge disparity in economic power between the United States and Japan meant that the latter could not win a long war, even if the bulk of U.S. production went to the European theater—unless the Americans could be persuaded that the cost of seeking victory would be too high to pay.

put in place an oil embargo, which backed Japan into a corner. Without oil, Japan's industry and war machine, still fully engaged in the fighting in China, would grind to a halt by late 1942.

After a month of watchful waiting, interagency discussions, and official meetings, on September 6 an imperial conference decided to continue its advance south and to seize the raw materials Japan needed.[1] War began on December 7, 1941, without a declaration of hostilities when Japanese surprise attacks struck British Malaya and Pearl Harbor, Hawaii.

These attacks were meant to cripple American and British air and sea power in the region, clearing the way for offensive operations with the dual purpose of gaining swift control of the economic resources of southern Asia (especially the oil fields of the Netherlands East Indies) and eliminating British and American bases that barred the

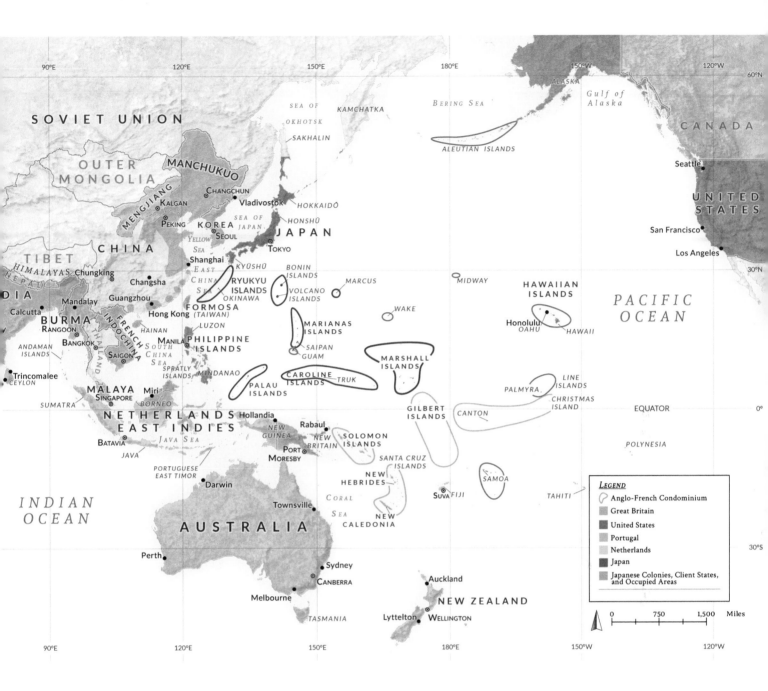

way to these resources, and that could otherwise be used as counteroffensive spring-boards against Japan.

The five-month first stage of Japanese operations would seize Malaya, the Philippines, British Borneo, the Dutch East Indies, the Bismarcks, Guam, the Gilberts, Wake Island, and Burma. Establishing a perimeter from the Western Pacific to the Indian Ocean allowed the Japanese to fight a protracted war, which would lead, they hoped, to a negotiated settlement with the Allies.[2] This "centrifugal offensive" proved extraordinarily successful, and the Allies fared no better in the first stages of the Pacific War than they had in the early campaigns in Europe. It would take until the middle of 1942, and the crucial Battle of Midway, for the Allies to regain a foothold in the Pacific and begin to turn the tide against Japan.

▲ JAPAN AND THE PACIFIC, SEPTEMBER 1, 1939

Much of Southeast Asia was divided up among European colonial powers before Japan rose to Great-Power status. In the 1930s, the Japanese fought to expand their own zone of imperial control on the Asian mainland. After the fall of France, Japan occupied French Indochina and began to contemplate an attack on the oil-rich Netherlands East Indies (modern Indonesia).

JAPANESE CARRIER PLANES ▲

In 1941, few if any nations had sailors or naval pilots as skilled as the personnel of the Imperial Japanese Navy (IJN).

FIRST STRIKES

The six-carrier task force raid on Pearl Harbor caught the bulk of the U.S. Pacific Fleet at anchor and completely unaware. Only the fleet's carriers avoided attack, simply because they were at sea at the time. Two waves of Japanese aircraft sank or damaged 19 U.S. warships, including all 8 battleships. Almost 350 American planes were destroyed or damaged, and 3,649 Americans were killed or wounded. In retrospect, many considered the Japanese failure to launch a third wave to destroy shore installations and oil tanks a grave error. Denied fuel and repair facilities, the U.S. Pacific Fleet would have been forced to withdraw to the U.S. West Coast. But the Japanese objective was to cripple the U.S. fleet for six months, clearing the way to carry out their plan to seize Southeast Asia. That accomplished, Admiral Chuichi Nagumo—who knew that the American carriers were away but not when they would return—placed the preservation of his force above the opportunity for a third attack and turned his fleet back toward Japan.[3]

Admiral Husband Kimmel, the commander in chief of the U.S. Pacific Fleet,

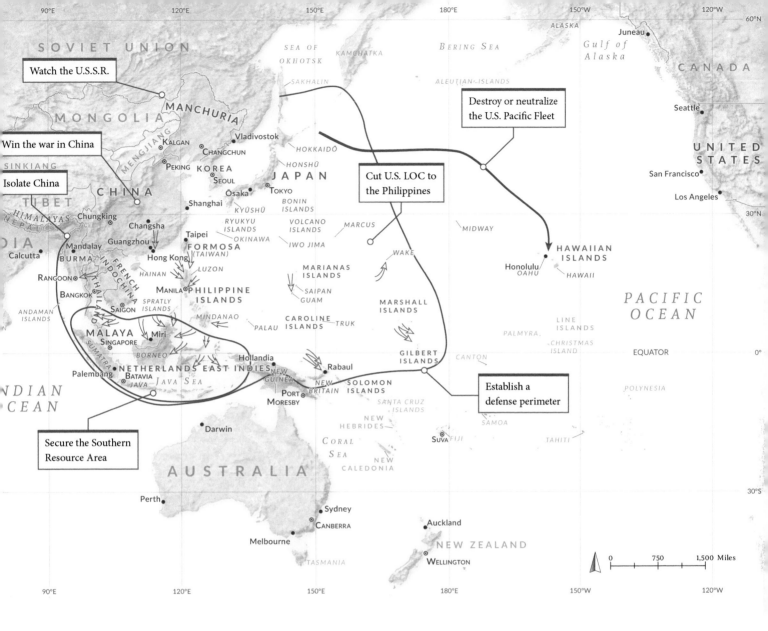

Watch the U.S.S.R.

Win the war in China

Isolate China

Secure the Southern
Resource Area

Cut U.S. LOC to
the Philippines

Destroy or neutralize
the U.S. Pacific Fleet

Establish a
defense perimeter

and Lieutenant General Walter Short, the commander of the fleet's Hawaiian Department, were responsible for the defense of Pearl Harbor. Despite repeated war games, fleet exercises, studies, plans, and discussions concerning a surprise air attack, American army and navy leaders did not believe that the Japanese would undertake such a risky venture. On December 16 both Kimmel and Short were relieved for cause.[4]

Ten hours after the Pearl Harbor attack, Japanese naval aircraft flying from bases on Taiwan still managed to surprise and destroy half of the U.S. Army's aircraft on the ground in the Philippines. General Douglas MacArthur, commander of the U.S. Army Forces, Far East, was aware of the attack on Hawaii, but for reasons that remain unclear even today, he neither dispersed his aircraft nor ordered them to strike the Japanese air bases on Taiwan (where, as it happened, Japanese pilots had been temporarily grounded by thick fog).[5] This strike "removed in one stroke the greatest single obstacle" to Japan's southward advance. Without airpower, U.S. naval operations in the area would have to be extremely limited. Control of air and sea allowed

▲ JAPANESE PLANNED OPENING ATTACKS, 1941

The initial Japanese attacks on Pearl Harbor, the Philippines, and Malaya were not ends in themselves but rather a means to gain a free hand for an attack on the resource-rich Netherlands East Indies. The Japanese also wanted to cut off China from American and British aid, without which the Chinese war of resistance could hardly continue.

the Japanese to isolate the remaining American force in the Philippines and to move unchecked throughout the Pacific.[6]

Next, on December 10, an estimated 5,000 Japanese struck from Truk, in the Caroline Islands, to overwhelm the 365 U.S. Marines on Guam, who surrendered to prevent reprisals against the local population. The lightly defended Gilbert Islands fell the same day. The following day, the American defenders of Wake Island managed to beat back an attempted landing. But on December 23 a reinforced Japanese assault force renewed the attack and, after savage hand-to-hand fighting near the beaches, captured Wake.[7]

Approximately one hour before the Pearl Harbor attack and almost seven thousand miles to the west, Japanese troops fought their way ashore at Kota Baharu in northern Malaya. This was the beginning of four major Japanese land campaigns spread over thousands of miles of land and sea—the Malayan operation, the conquest of the Netherlands East Indies, the advance into Burma, and the subjugation of the Philippines—all of which served to secure the Indies' resources and a safe maritime line of communication between the Indies' resources and Japan's factories.

In these operations, Japanese military forces proved more than a match for the colonial armies they faced. The invading Japanese soldiers were veterans of the China campaigns. They were well trained, equipped, indoctrinated, and ruthlessly efficient, though their triumphs were soiled by atrocities in China, including the murders of civilians and prisoners of war alike. Japan's navy was arguably the best in the world in late 1941, and its air arm was lethal. Its Mitsubishi Zero fighter was the best aircraft in the region.[8] And while the army's air force had less prestige, it too boasted veteran pilots flying first-line fighters and bombers.

The impact of the skill and aggressiveness of the initial Japanese attacks was redoubled by the fact that these qualities were so completely unexpected by their targets. Racist attitudes contributed to British and American military forces being caught flat-footed. For example, Air Chief Marshal Sir Robert Brooke-Popham, commander in chief of the British Far East Command and responsible for Malaya, had dismissed Japanese soldiers as "subhuman" and unable "to form an intelligent fighting force."[9] These attitudes on the Allied side interacted with Japanese atrocities and violations of the laws of war to make the fighting in the Pacific War especially brutal. Right from the beginning, "Remember Pearl Harbor" became a rallying cry that demanded revenge for the sneak attack.[10] Later, Japanese determination to fight to the death was viewed by many Allied combatants as justifying a no-prisoners approach to combat.[11] The war in the Pacific became a "war without mercy," not just because of racial and racist ways of thinking on both sides but also due to the style of combat that the Pacific theater demanded, combining close combat in jungle-covered terrain with the increased lethality of mid-twentieth-century warfare.[12]

ORDER OF BATTLE FOR THE PACIFIC THEATER, DECEMBER 7–8, 1941 ▶

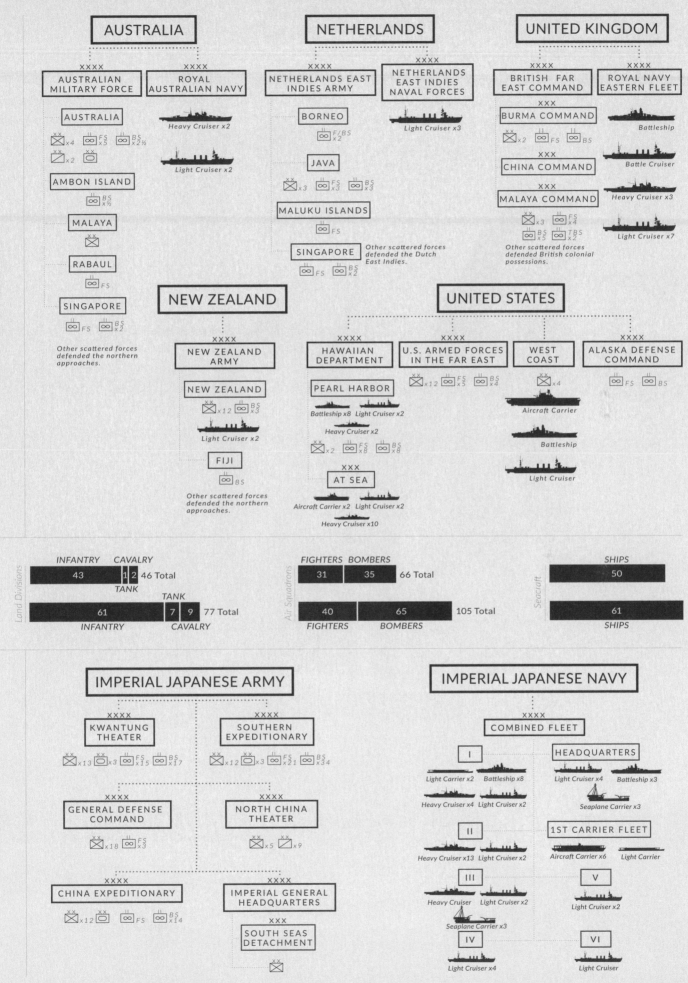

ALLIES

AUSTRALIA

xxxx AUSTRALIAN MILITARY FORCE
xxxx ROYAL AUSTRALIAN NAVY

Heavy Cruiser x2

Light Cruiser x2

AUSTRALIA
⊠ x4   ⊡ FS x5   ∞ BS x2½
⊠ x2   ⊡

AMBON ISLAND
∞ BS x½

MALAYA
⊠

RABAUL
∞ FS

SINGAPORE
∞ FS   ∞ BS x2

Other scattered forces defended the northern approaches.

NETHERLANDS

xxxx NETHERLANDS EAST INDIES ARMY
xxxx NETHERLANDS EAST INDIES NAVAL FORCES

Light Cruiser x3

BORNEO
∞ F/BS x2

JAVA
⊠ x3   ⊡ FS x3   ∞ BS x3

MALUKU ISLANDS
∞ FS

SINGAPORE
∞ FS   ∞ BS x2

Other scattered forces defended the Dutch East Indies.

UNITED KINGDOM

xxxx BRITISH FAR EAST COMMAND
xxxx ROYAL NAVY EASTERN FLEET

xxx BURMA COMMAND
⊠ x2   ⊡ FS   ∞ BS

Battleship

xxx CHINA COMMAND

Battle Cruiser

xxx MALAYA COMMAND
⊠ x3   ⊡ FS x4
∞ BS x5   ⊡ TBS x2

Heavy Cruiser x3

Light Cruiser x7

Other scattered forces defended British colonial possessions.

NEW ZEALAND

xxxx NEW ZEALAND ARMY

NEW ZEALAND
⊠ x12   ∞ BS x3

Light Cruiser x2

FIJI
∞ BS

Other scattered forces defended the northern approaches.

UNITED STATES

xxxx HAWAIIAN DEPARTMENT
xxxx U.S. ARMED FORCES IN THE FAR EAST
xxxx WEST COAST
xxxx ALASKA DEFENSE COMMAND

⊠ x12   ⊡ FS x5   ∞ BS x4
⊠ x4
∞ FS   ∞ BS

PEARL HARBOR

Battleship x8   Light Cruiser x2
Heavy Cruiser x2

⊠ x2   ⊡ FS x8   ∞ BS x8

Aircraft Carrier

Battleship

Light Cruiser

xxx AT SEA

Aircraft Carrier x2   Light Cruiser x2
Heavy Cruiser x10

Land Divisions

INFANTRY | CAVALRY | | TANK
43 | 1 | 2 | 46 Total

INFANTRY | | TANK | CAVALRY
61 | | 7 | 9 | 77 Total

Air Squadrons

FIGHTERS | BOMBERS
31 | 35 | 66 Total

FIGHTERS | BOMBERS
40 | 65 | 105 Total

Seacraft

SHIPS
50

SHIPS
61

JAPAN

IMPERIAL JAPANESE ARMY

xxxx KWANTUNG THEATER
⊠ x13   ⊡ x3   ∞ FS x15   ∞ BS x17

xxxx SOUTHERN EXPEDITIONARY
⊠ x12   ⊡ x3   ∞ FS x21   ∞ BS x34

xxxx GENERAL DEFENSE COMMAND
⊠ x18   ∞ FS x3

xxxx NORTH CHINA THEATER
⊠ x5   ⊠ x9

xxxx CHINA EXPEDITIONARY
⊠ x12   ∞ FS   ∞ BS x14

xxxx IMPERIAL GENERAL HEADQUARTERS

xxx SOUTH SEAS DETACHMENT
⊠

IMPERIAL JAPANESE NAVY

xxxx COMBINED FLEET

I
Light Carrier x2   Battleship x8
Heavy Cruiser x4   Light Cruiser x2

HEADQUARTERS
Light Cruiser x4   Battleship x3
Seaplane Carrier x3

II
Heavy Cruiser x13   Light Cruiser x2

1ST CARRIER FLEET
Aircraft Carrier x6   Light Carrier

III
Heavy Cruiser   Light Cruiser x2
Seaplane Carrier x3

V
Light Cruiser x2

IV
Light Cruiser x4

VI
Light Cruiser

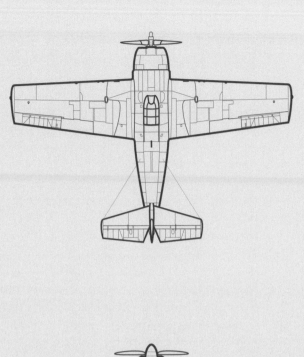

Grumman F4F Wildcat F4F-3

Entered Service	1940
Armament	Four .50 caliber (12.7 mm) M2 machine guns
Bombs	Two 100 lb bombs
Engine	1,200 hp Pratt & Whitney R-1820 Radial Engine
Maximum Speed	325 mph
Maximum Range	845 miles
Rate of Climb	2,040 ft per minute
Ceiling	35,000 ft
Span	38 ft
Length	28 ft 9 in
Height	11 ft 11 in
Weight	4,425 lbs empty, 5,876 lbs loaded
Produced	7,898

Mitsubishi A6M2 Zero

Entered Service	1940
Armament	Two 20 mm cannon and two 7.7 mm machine guns
Bombs	Two 132 lb bombs
Engine	925 hp Nakajima Sakae 12 Radial Engine
Maximum Speed	316 mph
Maximum Range	1,160 miles, or 1,940 miles with drop tanks
Rate of Climb	2,750 ft per minute
Ceiling	33,790 ft
Span	39 ft 5 in
Length	29 ft 9 in
Height	9 ft 7 in
Weight	3,704 lbs empty, 5,313 lbs loaded
Produced	10,450 (all variants)

▲ Zero Versus F4F Wildcat

The Zero was more maneuverable and had greater range than the Wildcat. However, the rugged nature of the Wildcat's design, with armor plating and self-sealing fuel tanks, and its ability to dive away from trouble, often gave the F4F the edge over the more flimsily built and unarmored Zero. The U.S. Navy used better-trained pilots and better tactics to create a kill-to-loss ratio of nearly 6 to 1 in 1942 and almost 7 to 1 for the entire war.

◀ Pearl Harbor

The Japanese attack at Pearl Harbor destroyed or seriously damaged all eight American battleships in port. The U.S.S. *Tennessee* and the U.S.S. *West Virginia* are shown here sitting on the bottom of the harbor. However, with the American aircraft carriers away at the time of the attack and the U.S. submarine force undamaged, the fleet's most vital assets remained intact.

Though tensions between the two nations had escalated over the preceding months, Japan's attack on Pearl Harbor came as a shock to the United States. The next day, President Franklin Roosevelt addressed Congress:

Yesterday, December 7, 1941—a date which will live in infamy—the United States of America was suddenly and deliberately attacked by naval and air forces of the Empire of Japan.

The United States was at peace with that Nation and, at the solicitation of Japan, was still in conversation with its Government and its Emperor looking toward the maintenance of peace in the Pacific. Indeed, one hour after Japanese air squadrons had commenced bombing in the American Island of Oahu, the Japanese Ambassador to the United States and his colleague delivered to our Secretary of State a formal reply to a recent American message. And while this reply stated that it seemed useless to continue the existing diplomatic negotiations, it contained no threat or hint of war or of armed attack.

It will be recorded that the distance of Hawaii from Japan makes it obvious that the attack was deliberately planned many days or even weeks ago. During the intervening time the Japanese Government has deliberately sought to deceive the United States by false statements and expressions of hope for continued peace.

The attack yesterday on the Hawaiian Islands has caused severe damage to American naval and military forces. I regret to tell you that very many American lives have been lost. In addition, American ships have been reported torpedoed on the high seas between San Francisco and Honolulu.

Yesterday the Japanese Government also launched an attack against Malaya.

Last night Japanese forces attacked Hong Kong.

Last night Japanese forces attacked Guam.

Last night Japanese forces attacked the Philippine Islands.

Last night the Japanese attacked Wake Island. And this morning the Japanese attacked Midway Island.

Japan has, therefore, undertaken a surprise offensive extending throughout the Pacific area. The facts of yesterday and today speak for themselves. The people of the United States have already formed their opinions and well understand the implications to the very life and safety of our Nation.

As Commander in Chief of the Army and Navy, I have directed that all measures be taken for our defense.

But always will our whole Nation remember the character of the onslaught against us.

No matter how long it may take us to overcome this premeditated invasion, the American people in their righteous might will win through to absolute victory. I believe that I interpret the will of the Congress and of the people when I assert that we will not only defend ourselves to the uttermost but will make it very certain that this form of treachery shall never again endanger us.

Hostilities exist. There is no blinking at the fact that our people, our territory, and our interests are in grave danger.

With confidence in our armed forces—with the unbounding determination of our people—we will gain the inevitable triumph—so help us God.

I ask that the Congress declare that since the unprovoked and dastardly attack by Japan on Sunday, December 7, 1941, a state of war has existed between the United States and the Japanese Empire.[8]

MALAYA

Since December 1940, Imperial Japan's army and navy had independently planned and war-gamed their southern advance toward a common strategic goal of seizing the natural resources of Java, the most populous of the Netherlands East Indies islands. To reach the oil of the Indies, the Japanese operational objective was to capture the British naval base at Singapore, the key to unlocking the entire region. They decided to attack Singapore overland from the north beginning the same day that they struck Pearl Harbor.

The thirty-second president of the United States, Franklin D. Roosevelt served for twelve years, from 1933 to 1945, and was elected president four times. He led the United States through the Great Depression and the Second World War.

The nation elected FDR president at the height of the Great Depression in 1932. He took immediate steps to address the crisis, promising a New Deal designed to ease the suffering of the American people. Although domestic issues remained paramount, the rise of Fascism in Italy, Nazism in Germany, and militarism in Japan throughout the 1930s made diplomacy and foreign policy ever more important.

With the outbreak of World War II in September 1939, Roosevelt worked diligently to aid the Allies while maintaining the support of the American public, which remained isolationist. As the Axis threat increased, FDR gained increasing support from Congress and the American people. The president worked with Congress to amend the Neutrality Acts, institute the first peacetime draft in America, and approve Lend-Lease aid.

Following the Japanese attack on Pearl Harbor, FDR led the American war effort and worked closely with the Allied powers. He established a strong working relationship with British prime minister Winston Churchill and Joseph Stalin of the Soviet Union. The "Big Three" met several times over the course of the war to coordinate strategy. The resulting strong Allied coalition focused on the major task of defeating the Axis. The differences between the Big Three remained muted until the last days of the war, when the defeat of Germany and Japan appeared assured and the primary focus of discussion shifted to the future of the postwar world.

FDR did not live to see the end of the war. He passed away in Georgia on April 12, 1945. Vice President Harry S. Truman succeeded him as president. FDR remains one of the United States' greatest wartime presidents.

The Japanese Army's plan called for the 5th Division of Lieutenant General Tomoyuki Yamashita's Twenty-Fifth Army to land in Thailand, move rapidly south into Malaya, and then continue south along the west coast. Yamashita's 18th Division would land at Kota Baharu, seize the airfields in the vicinity, and then drive south along the east coast. The Imperial Guards Division[14] would follow the 5th Division's advance. The army's 3rd Air Division and the navy's 25th Air Flotilla would provide more than 600 aircraft, operating from bases in southern Indochina. The Japanese had about 60,000 troops, 183 guns, 230 tanks, and 1,500 trucks for west coast operations.[15]

Yamashita's main worry was getting ashore. "If we can land," he told planners, "we will succeed." The general emphasized speed and aggressiveness, intending to drill straight through his opponents and let follow-on units mop up the disorganized enemy stragglers. "Ride anything that moves, friendly or enemy," he ordered subordinates, "but keep pushing the advance. Even if you're fired on from flanks or rear, don't stop to engage in a fight."[16] Troops without motorized transport were provided with bicycles to keep pace with a fast-moving advance. Along the east coast, the 18th Division would rely on horse-drawn transport.

The British were aware of Singapore's vital importance and prepared the northern defenses. The defending forces far outnumbered the Japanese. At the time of the invasion, Lieutenant General Arthur Percival, General Officer Commanding (GOC) Malaya, had almost 90,000 troops: 20,000 British, 15,000 Australians, 37,000 partially trained Indians, and 16,000 locally recruited Asians. Reinforcements were also en route. But units were understrength, and many of the troops were of poor quality.

Most of the units from India were poorly trained and equipped, and they had lost many of their better officers and NCOs as cadre for the new units mobilized for the wartime expansion of the Indian Army.[17] Staff training was poor, and communications were complicated by a lack of signal equipment and a plethora of languages, from English to Urdu.

Until the late 1930s, it was assumed that the long sea passage from Japan to Malaya would permit British warships the time to detect and intercept a Japanese invasion fleet at sea. But after defeats by the Germans in 1940 and 1941, Britain was fighting for survival, and East Asia was not the priority theater for ships or planes. So ground reinforcements were dispatched until sufficient aircraft to defend the peninsula could arrive.[18]

Percival had 158 operational aircraft, with 88 in reserve, but most were obsolete. There were no tanks, because the British high command had deemed tanks unsuitable for jungle warfare. But despite these weaknesses, the British expected their forces to be sufficient to defeat the Japanese; after all, the ragtag Chinese had held them at bay for four years.[19]

The British force's operational planning was ad hoc. There was indecisiveness about a preemptive ground attack into Thailand, and requirements to defend northern airfields led Percival to adopt a wide area defense without the corresponding ability to deploy mobile forces to counter enemy penetrations.[20] Percival's troops were never meant to fight a major battle in northern Malaya. They were part of a long-range defense of Singapore, and sooner or later would be needed to defend that island until a battle fleet and relief convoys could arrive. Meantime, they were to defend the airfields. But the key to the defense of northern Malaya was not defending the airfields per se, but denying their use to the enemy.[21]

If advanced forces were driven back, then they would retreat southward to the next defensive position, all the while aiming to delay the Japanese advance on Singapore. Thus, British commanders had to preserve their forces, which made them anxious about being cut off and surrounded—and, consequently, liable to retreat before it was absolutely necessary. This produced a pattern of "relentless withdrawal": the British had ceded the initiative to the Japanese before the fighting started.[22]

But a delaying action is not a rout, and the British ground commanders expected that they would enjoy air and naval support throughout the campaign. Because of the great distances separating Japanese air bases in French Indochina from Singapore (over six hundred miles) British strategists doubted that Japan could muster sufficient

JAPANESE SOLDIER ▶

The campaigns of the winter of 1941–42 demonstrated that the Japanese soldier was skilled, tough, and very brave. Militarists in Japan had hijacked the samurai concept of Bushido (literally "the way of the warrior") to present war as a purifying event for the nation, and death as the duty of all soldiers. Surrender was considered a betrayal of the emperor. In the Field Service Code issued in 1941, General Hideki Tōjō wrote: "Do not live in shame as prisoner. Die and leave no inglorious crime behind you." Training inculcated brutality, with conscripts harshly beaten, and Japanese soldiers were told to expect torture by the Allies if they were captured. Japan suffered over 2 million military deaths during the war, but there were only 20,000 to 50,000 Japanese prisoners captured.

Type 90 Helmet

Japanese helmets were specifically designed to be lightweight. Because of their thinner metal, they offered significantly less protection than U.S. or British helmets.

Type 97 Fragmentation Grenade

At just one pound, the main Japanese hand grenade was about 25 percent lighter than the American equivalent, but still lethal. It was somewhat complicated to use: the soldier had to screw down the firing pin, then pull the safety pin, then smack the fuse head against a solid object (such as a helmet) before throwing. The four- to five-second fuse was somewhat unreliable, so it was recommended to throw it immediately, even against close-in targets.

Type 99 Rifle

Like every major belligerent except the United States, Japan provided its infantrymen with bolt-action magazine rifles. Many soldiers were equipped with older weapons that fired light 6.5 mm cartridges, but in 1939 these started to be replaced with the more powerful 7.7 mm Arisaka Type 99. The Type 99 models issued early in the war had two unusual features: a wire monopod intended to allow for steadier shooting, and a sight with horizontal prongs to guide antiaircraft firing.

Type 30 Sword Bayonet

At an overall length of over twenty inches, the Type 30 was far longer than the fourteen-inch American bayonet designed for use with the M1 Garand. American forces in the Pacific consequently tended to prefer the older bayonet that was designed for the M1903 Springfield, because it was also twenty inches.

Footwear

Japanese soldiers wore heelless boots and long wrapped leggings or puttees. One purpose of the leggings was to minimize the skin exposure to malaria-carrying mosquitoes. Japanese troops were also issued lightweight cotton mittens to protect their hands from mosquitoes.

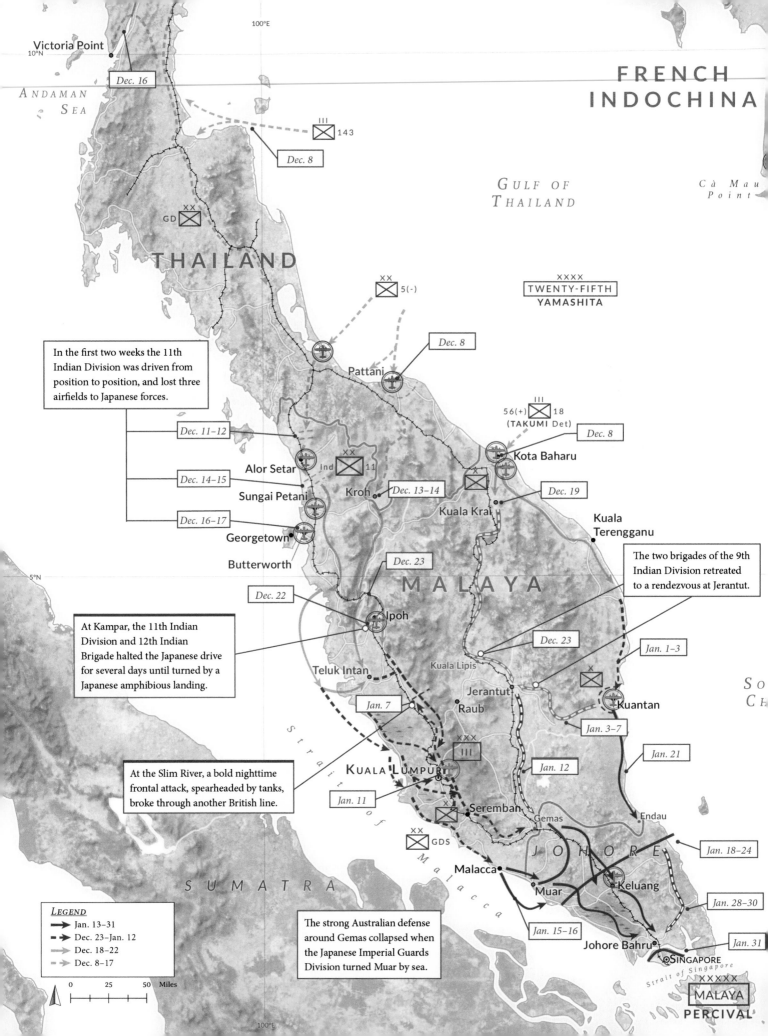

Victoria Point
Dec. 16

ANDAMAN SEA

FRENCH INDOCHINA

GULF OF THAILAND

Cà Mau Point

III 143
Dec. 8

GD XX

THAILAND

TWENTY-FIFTH
YAMASHITA

XX 5(-)

Dec. 8

Pattani

56(+) III 18
(TAKUMI Det)

Dec. 8

Kota Baharu

In the first two weeks the 11th Indian Division was driven from position to position, and lost three airfields to Japanese forces.

Dec. 11–12

Alor Setar

Ind XX 11

Dec. 14–15

Sungai Petani

Kroh

Dec. 13–14

Dec. 16–17

Kuala Krai

Dec. 19

Georgetown

Butterworth

Kuala Terengganu

MALAYA

The two brigades of the 9th Indian Division retreated to a rendezvous at Jerantut.

Dec. 23

Dec. 22

Ipoh

At Kampar, the 11th Indian Division and 12th Indian Brigade halted the Japanese drive for several days until turned by a Japanese amphibious landing.

Teluk Intan

Kuala Lipis

Dec. 23

Jan. 1–3

X

Kuantan

SO CH

Jan. 7

Jerantut

Raub

Jan. 3–7

Jan. 21

Strait of Malacca

At the Slim River, a bold nighttime frontal attack, spearheaded by tanks, broke through another British line.

III

KUALA LUMPUR

Jan. 12

Jan. 11

X

Seremban

Gemas

Endau

JOHORE

Jan. 18–24

XX GDS

Malacca

Muar

Keluang

Jan. 28–30

SUMATRA

LEGEND
→ Jan. 13–31
▪▪▶ Dec. 23–Jan. 12
→ Dec. 18–22
▪▪▶ Dec. 8–17

0   25   50 Miles

The strong Australian defense around Gemas collapsed when the Japanese Imperial Guards Division turned Muar by sea.

Jan. 15–16

Johore Bahru

Jan. 31

SINGAPORE

Strait of Singapore

XXXXX
MALAYA
PERCIVAL

▲ JAPANESE SOLDIERS, MALAYA

Japanese soldiers use inflatable rubber rafts to cross a Malayan river. The British often tried to use river lines to halt the Japanese advance, but always unsuccessfully.

◀ THE JAPANESE INVASION OF MALAYA, DECEMBER 8, 1941–JANUARY 31, 1942

Beginning with landings on December 8, Japanese forces advanced quickly down the Malay Peninsula toward Singapore.

aircraft to achieve air superiority. As Anglo-Japanese relations continued to deteriorate, the arrival at Singapore on December 4 of two new capital ships, the battle cruiser *Repulse* and the battleship *Prince of Wales*, was expected to deter enemy landings on the east coast because the warships could wreak havoc on troop transports and merchantmen. But the aircraft carrier *Indomitable*, which was to accompany them, had struck a reef in transit and was undergoing emergency repairs, leaving the two surface ships without integrated air cover.[23]

Percival, nicknamed Rabbit because of his receding chin and protruding teeth, is often depicted as a weak, schoolmasterly type of general. Although not particularly articulate or inspirational, he was a perceptive officer who understood, perhaps obsessively, that the defense of Singapore hinged on holding air bases in northern Malaya.[24] His superior, Air Chief Marshal Brooke-Popham, dreadfully underestimated the Japanese soldier, mainly on racist grounds. Officially, he was optimistic, but he had private doubts about Singapore's ability to withstand a Japanese invasion and understood Malaya's low overall priority.[25] Brooke-Popham lacked the resources to defend Malaya, a condition exacerbated by a command arrangement that made the Royal Navy responsible to London and not the British Far East commander.

Aerial sightings of Japanese convoys on December 6 had alerted the British to a Japanese invasion, but they were uncertain of the target. Japanese landings at Kota Baharu on the night of December 7–8 met resistance ashore. Despite effective British air attacks at dawn, enough of the landing force came ashore to be able to push the outnumbered Indian defenders off the beaches.[26] In the first day's air action, Japanese forces slashed RAF strength in northern Malaya from 110 to 50 aircraft.[27] The speed of the Japanese advance confused the defenders. Indian troops were preparing to defend one airfield when British troops blew up buildings at the same airfield. This had a disastrous effect on the Indian soldiers' morale, and on December 11 orders forbade further demolition using explosives. Instead, buildings were to be demolished as much as possible, and fuel tanks were to be emptied. Two days later, the ground commander abandoned the other two airdromes, the ground staff of which had already fled, leaving the airfields intact.[28] Despite Percival's emphasis on protecting the northern air bases, they fell quickly and disastrously. The Japanese 5th and 18th Divisions had secured their first major objectives at the cost of just 500 casualties.

After word of the attack, the *Prince of Wales* and *Repulse*, escorted by three destroyers, steamed north from Singapore toward the invasion beaches.[29] On December 9 a Japanese submarine spotted the warships and relayed their positions to Saigon, French Indochina. The next morning, ninety-six high-level bombers and torpedo planes flew from Saigon the then-unheard-of distance of 430 miles to attack the ships. Four torpedo hits sunk the *Repulse*. *Prince of Wales* survived five torpedoes,

SINKING OF THE H.M.S. *PRINCE OF WALES* AND H.M.S. *REPULSE* ▶

The *Prince of Wales* (above) and the *Repulse* (below) seen under attack from Japanese planes off the coast of Singapore, December 10, 1941.

but, dead in the water, suffered a direct bomb hit. Within an hour, the battleship keeled heavily to port and disappeared inside a minute. More than 800 British seamen perished; three Japanese aircraft were lost and twenty-eight damaged.[30] Within the first four days of the Japanese invasion, the British had lost control of the air and the sea.

On the ground, when the Japanese hit strongpoints, they did one of two things: they smashed through with tanks and infantry or searched out enemy flanks in shallow envelopments and deep turning movements to get behind enemy linear defensive positions and take them from the rear.[31] Combat engineers advanced with infantry and armor to repair bridges or build new ones to support the rapid advance. To sustain the momentum of the advance, bicyclists would wade the peninsula's numerous shallow streams—holding their bikes aloft—or cross on crudely cut log bridges supported by the shoulders of the engineers.

With Japanese forces advancing on both sides of the peninsula, the retreat of one British unit left the others' flanks exposed and forced their withdrawal as well. The relentless tempo of the Japanese advance left the British unsure of where each next attack would fall, and Japanese control of the skies restricted British movement during daylight hours.[32]

British leaders worried that the disaster at Pearl Harbor, followed by the overrunning of U.S. Pacific possessions and the rapidly deteriorating situation in Malaya, might alter the Americans' current Germany-first strategy and shift American resources to the Pacific. British prime minister Winston Churchill and U.S. president Franklin Roosevelt met in Washington, D.C. During a series of meetings between December 22, 1941, and January 14, 1942, which included their respective senior military staffs, they reaffirmed the Germany-first strategy. It called for a largely defensive effort in the Pacific until the war in Europe was won. Once the Nazis were defeated, Japan would inevitably also succumb to Allied material superiority, but the reverse was not necessarily true. Still, the Arcadia Conference (the code name for the meetings) could not ignore the Japanese thrust. Among other major decisions, participants created the American-British-Dutch-Australian Command, or ABDACOM, on December 31 as the single unified command for the threatened area, with General Sir Archibald Wavell as overall commander. The complexities of commanding military and naval forces of four nations without a common doctrine were mind-boggling. The immensity of the new theater did not help in the slightest. Wavell's HQ on Java, for instance, was 2,000 miles from Rangoon and 1,100 miles from Singapore, and signal communications were unreliable.[33] Wavell was also profoundly ignorant of the Japanese military and scornful of non-European armies.[34] Once his defensive plans began to fail, he invariably attributed defeats to his generals' incompetence rather than to Japanese skill.

On January 7 General Wavell flew into Singapore. The previous night, twenty Japanese tanks supported by a few hundred infantrymen and combat engineers had burst through the front lines of the 11th Indian Division to cross the strategic Slim River Bridge less than 250 miles from Singapore. Two Indian brigades disintegrated, and the advancing Japanese seized numerous abandoned heavy weapons and hundreds of

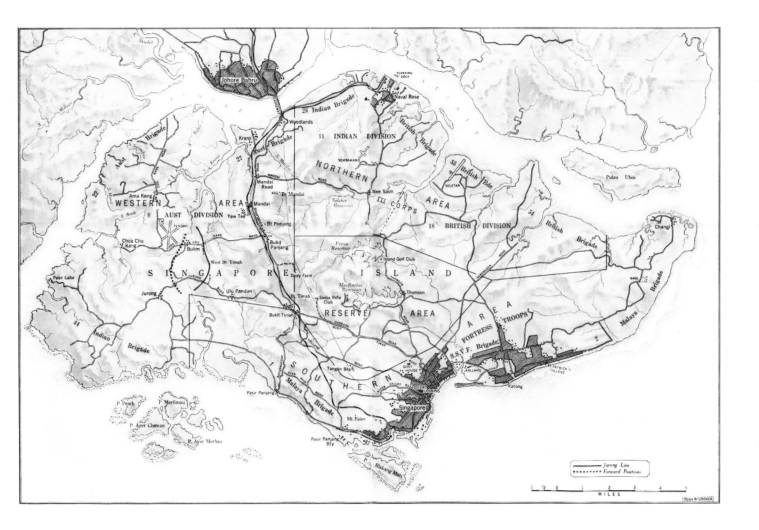

British commander Arthur Percival spread his troops along Singapore's coast, with insufficient forces held in reserve. This map comes from the twenty-two-volume *Australian Official History of the Second World War*, an excellent resource particularly for the history of the Pacific War and the war in North Africa. The entire work is available online.

vehicles.[35] Wavell saw the results and ordered a withdrawal 150 miles south to Jahore Province. Without coordinating with Percival, Wavell appointed the commander of the Australian 8th Division, Major General Gordon Bennett—whom Wavell believed showed greater fighting spirit—to defend Jahore.

Described as "ambitious, bellicose, and obnoxious," Bennett deployed the barely trained 45th Indian Brigade along a twenty-five-mile front—one-third of it north of the Muar River; the rest south—to protect the coastal road. On January 16 Yamashita's Imperial Guards hit the divided brigade from the north while a battalion turned it from the sea. The entire line collapsed, and withdrawing troops had to fight their way through Japanese roadblocks thrown up in their rear.[36] The British frontline troops, reinforced only by newly arrived, inadequately trained Indian units and by 2,000 Australian reinforcements described as so undisciplined as to be a danger to their own side, were unable to regroup. The relentless retreats continued.[37] By January 31, the last Allied troops had withdrawn to Singapore Island.

Percival tried to defend the entire island's coast—twenty-eight miles from east to west—leaving him weak everywhere, with no reserves available to counterattack against a landing. Without a defense in depth, if the Japanese were able to overcome the shoreline defenses, they could drive unchecked deep into the center of the island without meeting further resistance. On the evening of February 8, Yamashita launched a two-division assault on Singapore. A demonstration by the Guards attracted Percival's forces' attention, allowing the 5th and 18th Divisions to cross the straits in barges and landing craft and overrun 2,500 Australian defenders. Ten minutes after the start of the assault, blue flares popped over the landing beach signaling that the Japanese were ashore. By dawn, 15,000 Japanese were on the island, supported by tank-infantry teams and artillery. When Wavell flew back to Singapore on February 10, the Japanese controlled the northern third of the island, had captured one of its three airfields, and were advancing toward the main British supply dumps.[38] Wavell berated Percival and Bennett, telling the Australian to "get the hell out" and take his "bloody Aussies" with him.[39]

Bennett did get out, but he left his troops behind. On February 15, with Singapore in its death throes, Bennett decided that it was his duty to escape rather than surrender. Without authorization, he handed over command of the 8th Division to his deputy, commandeered a sampan at gunpoint, crossed the Strait of Malacca, and eventually made his way to Australia. Wavell had already flown out of Singapore on February 11 from the one airfield remaining in British hands. By that time, all other key areas, including the island's crucial water reservoirs, had been lost to the Japanese.

Yamashita, however, was worried. His ammunition and rations were running dangerously low, and the stiff resistance encountered on Singapore Island surprised him. As a last resort, he threatened to annihilate the Singapore garrison unless Percival capitulated promptly. With all hope gone, on February 15 Percival surrendered his roughly 100,000 troops on Singapore. Altogether the Japanese took 130,000 British Empire troops prisoner—one-third of whom would end up dying during captivity. During the overall campaign, British forces suffered more than double the battle casualties of the Japanese: about 25,000 to 9,600, respectively.[40]

Java

Singapore's capture broke open the gateway to the Netherlands East Indies (NEI), the outer islands of which were already under Japanese attack. With successes in Malaya and the Philippines securing the Japanese flanks, Imperial General Headquarters (IGHQ) moved up the date of its NEI operation by one month. Lieutenant General Hitoshi Imamura, commander of the Sixteenth Army, set March 1 for the invasion of Java, where he expected to meet strong resistance. Japanese planners and commanders had two concerns: first, that the Allies would concentrate their defenses on Java, resulting in heavy Japanese losses; second, that the Dutch would destroy the oil fields, the prize the Japanese sought. War games conducted at Imperial headquarters had concluded that NEI would be the most costly of all the southern operations, and Japan didn't want to give the Allies time to make it any more difficult.[41]

The Japanese plan involved sequencing air, naval, and ground units to seize the outer islands—Borneo, Amboina, Timor, Sumatra—in order to isolate Java. First, they would aim to achieve local air superiority early. Then the navy would destroy Allied warships, enabling ground troops to land and overrun small, isolated Dutch garrisons and seize advance air bases for army and navy aircraft. With airfields in southern Sumatra and on Borneo and Celebes, the Japanese would be able to guarantee air cover for a two-pronged invasion of Java.

The Royal Netherlands Indies Army numbered about 38,000 men, with 25,000 concentrated on Java. About 10,000 were Europeans or Eurasians; the rest were indigenous soldiers—some of questionable loyalty, serving under European officers. A 40,000-man militia drawn from the European population was short on training and equipment. There were also on Java 6,500 British soldiers with 25 light tanks, 1,000 Australian troops, and 500 American field artillerists. The air arm was a mixture of Dutch, British, Australian, and American units consisting of perhaps 200 operational but worn and mainly obsolete aircraft. The Allied navies' heaviest ships were eight light cruisers.[42]

On the other hand, the Japanese Sixteenth Army had 40,000 troops organized in three divisions, two independent mixed brigades, and two tank regiments. The army's 3rd Air Division had 140 combat aircraft, while the navy's 11th Air Flotilla added 185 more. The 1st Carrier Division in support contributed another 190 aircraft. The invasion fleet was organized around two battleships and two heavy cruisers that far outgunned and outranged the more numerous Allied warships.

Most of the initial ground operations in the NEI were small-scale affairs, with numerically superior Japanese forces quickly overrunning Dutch garrisons of a few dozen or several hundred men. Allied pilots, despite being outnumbered and flying inferior aircraft, persisted in attacking Japanese shipping and ground targets, with mixed results. More apparent was the Japanese success in a series of naval engagements that ended in the almost complete destruction of the ABDA navies.

By January 12, a strong Japanese naval-ground task force had seized the oil fields, airfield, and harbor at Tarakan, Dutch Borneo. They overwhelmed the 1,300 defenders, but not before the Dutch sank two minesweepers, set fire to the oil fields and oil storage areas, and destroyed the airfield. The day before, the Japanese had captured lightly defended Menado chiefly for its airdromes. Within two weeks, the airfields at both places were again operational under the Japanese flag.

The Japanese struck next on January 23–24, 1942, against Balikpapan. A Dutch submarine sank one transport, and later a second attack by four U.S. destroyers of World War I vintage put three more transports on the bottom. The Dutch ground commander burned the oil wells, and his 200-man force withdrew into the interior.

One week later, the Japanese invaded Amboina in order to secure their left flank for the Java operations. Nighttime amphibious landings on January 31 along Amboina's northwest and southeast coasts encircled the mixed 3,600-man Dutch-Indonesian and Australian garrison. Understrength, outmaneuvered, and overwhelmed,

INITIAL JAPANESE OPERATIONS, DECEMBER 1941 ▶

Wide-ranging Japanese attacks on Malaya, the Philippines, and Singapore set the stage for a concerted thrust against the Netherlands East Indies. Operations to secure the colony's outer islands, in turn, cleared the way for an assault on Java, the main Japanese objective (off map, south of Borneo).

BAY OF
BENGAL

BURMA

THAILAND

FRENCH

INDOCHINA

CHIN

Nanning

Hanoi

HAINA

Calcutta

Chittagong

Cox's Bazar

Maungdaw

Akyab

Agartala

Brahmaputra

Bhamo

Shwebo

Mandalay   Maymyo

Sagaing

Meiktila

Magwe

Loikaw

Prome   Toungoo

Pegu

RANGOON

Moulmein

Namsang

Lashio

Mekong

Mekong

Mekong

ANDAMAN
ISLANDS

Port Blair

ANDAMAN SEA

Tavoy

Mergui

Victoria Point

Gulf of
Thailand

BANGKOK

××××
FIFTEENTH
IIDA

××
⊠

××××
SOUTHERN
TERAUCHI

××
⊠∞ 3

SAIGON

|||
⊠

|||
⊠

|||
⊠

Rendezvous point at
midnight on *December 7*

|||
⊠

|||
⊠

|||
⊠

NICOBAR
ISLANDS

×
⊠ Pattani

Alor Setar

Georgetown

Butterworth

×
⊠

×
⊠ Kota Baharu

MALAYA

××××
TWENTY-FIFTH
YAMASHITA

××××
SOUTHERN
FORCE
KONDO
(Support)

Ipoh ××××

MALAYA
PERCIVAL ×

×
⊠

Teluk Intan

KUALA LUMPUR

Seremban

×
⊠

Malacca   Muar

××
⊠

SINGAPORE

INDIAN OCEAN

SUMATRA

Pemangkat

|||
⊠

Pontianak

0°

LEGEND

→ After Dec. 24
▶ Dec. 17–23
→ Dec. 8–16
▶ Before Dec. 7

0   150   300   Miles

N ET HE
EAST

|||
⊠

Palembang

JAVA

90°E   100°E   110°

▲ WAR DAMAGE

In Java, as in the rest of the "Southern Resource Area," the Japanese hoped to win the support of the native peoples against European colonialism. They had little success, partly because of the damage inflicted by Japanese air raids.

AUSTRALIAN PROPAGANDA ▶

Before the war, the prevailing attitude toward the Japanese military in Europe and Australia was closer to contempt than fear. After the many Allied defeats of the first six months of the Pacific War, however, the threat to Australia was not taken lightly.

THE JAPANESE SEIZE JAVA, ▲
MARCH 1–8, 1942

Considering that the Allies had numerical superiority and the advantage of fighting on home ground, some Japanese leaders expected the conquest of Java to be difficult. In fact, it took only a week for the invaders to win a complete victory and to force the surrender of the remaining defenders.

the Allies surrendered on February 3. Then Japanese naval air units attacked an Allied fleet in the Makassar Strait, seriously damaging two U.S. cruisers. The fleet turned back out of range of Japanese aircraft.[43]

Next, the Japanese struck at Palembang, the center of Sumatra's oil industry. On the fourteenth of February, 350 army paratroopers jumped near the airfield and refinery. They lost most of their heavy equipment and were scattered in the drop. But in hastily reorganized three- to six-man groups armed with light weapons, they attacked under cover of army and navy air support and succeeded in seizing the airfield. Although suffering more than 40 percent casualties, they, with the aid of another 100 paratroops dropped the next day, were able to hold the airfield against Dutch counterattacks until regular Japanese ground units arrived on February 18. By then, the 38th Division had landed and was in complete control of south Sumatra.[44]

That isolated Java from the west. Subsequent operations—the bombing of Darwin, Australia, on the nineteenth; the invasion of Bali on the twentieth; and the invasion of Timor the same day—cut off Java from the east. American B-17s did damage a Japanese transport off Bali, and on February 18–19, 1942, an ABDA force of two light

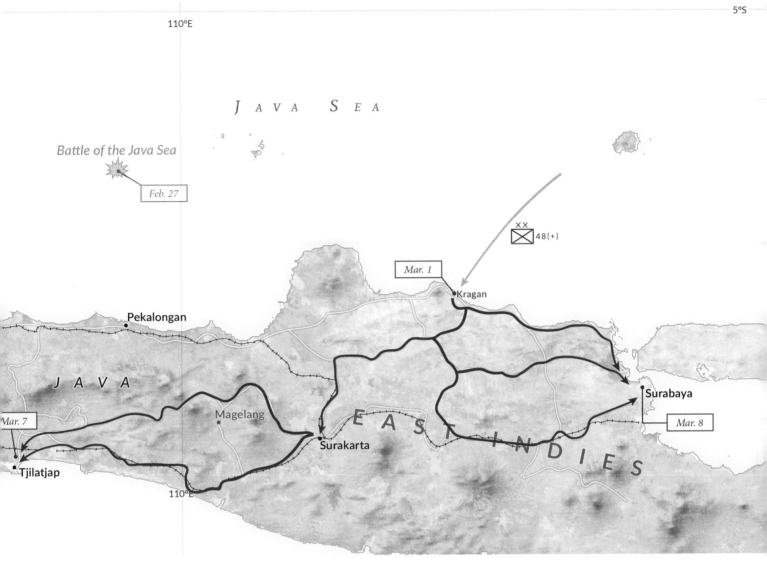

cruisers and three destroyers sallied into the Lombok Strait. In a night action off the Bali anchorage, the Allied fleet counterattacked the landing site, which was defended by a Japanese destroyer squadron. The Japanese, who were especially skilled at night gunnery, sank one Dutch destroyer and heavily damaged a Dutch cruiser as well as one American destroyer, in exchange for one badly damaged destroyer. Now Java was isolated from the east. Once again, Japanese aggressiveness and the Allies' inability to concentrate forces had resulted in a stinging defeat, and another blow to Western prestige in Asia.

Aware that a combined Allied fleet was waiting in Java, General Imamura, the Sixteenth Army commander, anticipated hard fighting for his invasion force. He had about 23,500 troops, while his opponents mustered about 27,000. Imamura's February 28 order of the day read: "We are landing in the face of the enemy. If the army commander [Imamura] is lost at sea, the division commander should replace him. Furthermore, if the division commander drowns, a replacement should be available." [45]

Wavell, however, was resigned to defeat. On February 22 he signaled Churchill that

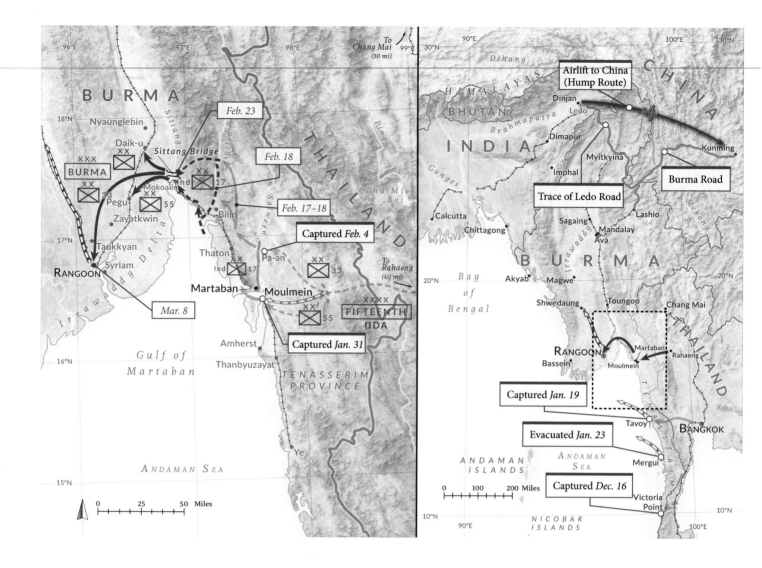

BURMA, DECEMBER 8, 1941– MARCH 8, 1942 ▲

Although Victoria Point was captured on December 16, the main Japanese thrust into Burma began the following month. Japanese forces advanced from the Thai border and captured Rangoon in less than two months.

the defense of Java was hopeless, and he departed the island on February 25. The next day, the Allies detected the Japanese western and eastern convoys approaching Java. The Dutch headquarters ordered Rear Admiral Karel Doorman to sail from Surabaya with his fifteen Allied warships and attack the eastern convoy. But with no common doctrine, language, communications, codes, or tactics, the result was four courageous but small and separate task forces. After a fruitless search, they returned to Surabaya the morning of the twenty-seventh only to learn that an enemy convoy (the eastern convoy) had been sighted ninety-five miles to the north.

Doorman immediately raised steam and soon encountered the Japanese 5th Cruiser Division in the Java Sea. During a two-hour gunnery duel conducted at long range, the Allies lost two destroyers, suffered damage to other ships, and retreated. Japanese cruisers had launched more than 120 "Long Lance" torpedoes, almost all of which were set incorrectly and exploded prematurely. Seeing the waterspouts caused by the detonations, the Japanese admiral thought they were enemy mines and withdrew northwestward: a rare case of victor and vanquished both retreating from the same engagement.[46]

But at five o'clock, the Japanese cruiser division launched three observation aircraft to spot and correct gunfire, and then attacked again. A British destroyer was sunk and a British cruiser damaged. The British destroyer *Jupiter* then hit a drifting Dutch mine and sank. The Japanese cruiser fleet closed in after full darkness, sinking two Dutch cruisers with torpedoes. The Battle of the Java Sea was the greatest naval surface engagement since the Battle of Jutland in 1916. Admiral Doorman lost three destroyers, two light cruisers, and his life; the Japanese, not a single ship.[47] Superior night combat training and tactics, better optics and gunnery skills, and effective cooperation between air and naval units accounted for the lopsided Japanese victory.[48]

At eight o'clock the next evening, the heavy cruiser U.S.S. *Houston* and Australian light cruiser *Perth* tried to escape to Australia through Sunda Strait but ran into the western invasion force. The Allied cruisers found themselves between General Imamura's transports, already at anchor in Bantam Bay, and Japanese cruisers attacking the Allied ships from the northwest. Naval gunfire sank the *Perth*, and damaged the *Houston*, but eight torpedoes launched at *Houston* missed and continued to run into Bantam Bay, sinking four transports, including the one carrying Imamura. Naval gunfire then pummeled the crippled *Houston*, leaving her dead in the water and sinking. Imamura, wet and covered with oil slick, reached shore safely. The navy later sent apologies, but Imamura's chief of staff told the naval aide to keep quiet and hushed up the friendly fire incident.[49]

At dawn on March 1, Japanese troops simultaneously went ashore in eastern, central, and western Java. The bulk of Dutch forces were deployed in western Java to defend both the colonial capital and port at Batavia (modern Jakarta) on the northwest coast, and the commercial and administrative city of Bandung about seventy-five miles southeast, the center of resistance. The Dutch experienced the inevitable fog of war. An Australian pioneer battalion requested intelligence on Japanese movements from the Dutch headquarters only to learn that because the morning newspapers had not yet been distributed, the headquarters did not know.[50] A Dutch unit about twenty-five miles inland reported on March 3 that the Japanese had not landed on Java. Five minutes later, a Japanese tank appeared on their front.

On March 1 the vanguard of a 1,200-man Japanese detachment that had landed at Eretan Wetan moved by truck twenty-five miles southwest and, employing six light tanks, seized the Kalidjati airfield. The subsequent heavy fighting for the airfield decided the campaign. A 3,500-man Dutch counterattack spearheaded by twenty light tanks on March 3 surprised the Japanese near Kalidjati and drove them back with heavy casualties. Hastily summoned airpower broke the Dutch attackers' momentum. For five hours, Japanese air units bombed and strafed Dutch assembly areas and Dutch motorized convoys moving north from Bandung. Dutch forces were so badly mauled and lost so much equipment and transport that further resistance on Java became impossible.[51]

The next few days were anticlimactic. Batavia was captured on March 5, and two days later, Bandung surrendered under a two-pronged Japanese attack from the north and the west. On March 9 the NEI surrendered unconditionally. Imamura insisted that the Dutch broadcast their surrender decision to all Allied units on Java because he worried that otherwise he would have to defeat each national force in turn. American, British, and Australian forces on Java surrendered on the twelfth. The conquerors swept up 37,000 military prisoners of war, of whom about 8,500 died during their captivity. It had taken just sixty days and about 2,600 Japanese casualties from the first landings at Menado and Tarakan to conquer the Indies—two months less time than anticipated in prewar plans.[52]

BURMA

If Java was the centerpiece of Japanese objectives, Burma was an afterthought. The country's strategic location, however, made it important to the Allies, especially the United States, which regarded Burma as vital to the effort to keep China in the war. The strategic implications of isolating China by cutting the Burma Road to the north and threatening India (Britain's most important colony) to the west gave the Burma campaign far greater significance than the Japanese had originally considered.

In the shorter term, the Japanese had to secure Burma to protect their northwest flank and prevent interference in the Twenty-Fifth Army's operations in Malaya.[53] All of Burma eventually would be occupied, but because of the commitments during the first stage of operations, only the airfields of southern Burma would be taken initially. Lieutenant General Shōjirō Iida's Fifteenth Army, composed of elements of the 33rd and 55th divisions—about 20,000 troops—would accomplish this mission. His force multiplier was the 5th Air Division, with 145 combat aircraft plus reconnaissance and transport planes, reinforced in mid-January 1942 by 80 aircraft redeployed from the Philippines.

The British Empire's forces in Burma consisted of perhaps 20,000 troops in all: two understrength regular British battalions, two Indian brigades, and local Burmese units. Like their comrades in Malaya, they suffered from poor training, lack of jungle field craft, shortages of ammunition and equipment, and inadequate air support—just sixteen obsolete aircraft. Burma had barely entered into British strategic planning, which was concerned with the defense of Hong Kong and Malaya.[54] In an ABDA command that was already stretched on resources and manpower, nothing could be spared for Burma.

Even two weeks after the Pearl Harbor attack, General Wavell believed that he had several months in which to prepare Burma's defenses, due to Japanese operations elsewhere. He sought outside support, negotiating with China's Generalissimo Chiang Kai-shek to send a squadron of the American Volunteer Group (nicknamed the Flying Tigers), then operating under Chinese control, to defend Rangoon and reinforce another Flying Tigers squadron already training in Burma. Wavell also appointed a new commander, Lieutenant General Thomas Hutton, to organize the resistance. Much like Percival in Malaya, Hutton believed that he would have to fight the Japanese forward—to allow time for reinforcements to land at Rangoon and for the Chinese to move south in the event of an attack. He decided to block northern entry from Thailand by denying the Japanese the railroad and road network in the mountainous Shan

Japanese infantry combined aggressiveness with infiltration tactics to defeat the British in Burma.

States region and hold the line along the Salween River. Most of the reinforcements that Prime Minister Churchill promised Wavell, however, were diverted to Malaya. The 17th Indian Division did arrive, but it consisted of raw, poorly trained troops. Hutton deployed the unit to southernmost Tenasserim Province, where he saw no direct threat to Rangoon. It became responsible for almost 450 miles of front, and its division commander, in opposition to Hutton, wanted to withdraw to defend the Sittang River crossing.[55]

On December 13, small elements of Japan's 55th Division seized Victoria Point in southernmost Burma and its airfield, preventing the British from staging reinforcements by air from India to Malaya. The move surprised the British, who expected any Japanese invasion to come from farther north. Nine days later, sixty Japanese heavy bombers escorted by more than fifty fighters flying from bases in Thailand and Indochina bombed Rangoon, aiming to prevent reinforcements from using the port and to terrorize the population in an effort to make essential workers flee. A combined British Empire–Flying Tigers force of thirty fighter planes shot down six Japanese bombers; two more fell to antiaircraft artillery fire. On Christmas Day more than sixty bombers again struck Rangoon; the Japanese lost another six bombers and fighters.

OIL FIELDS ▲

The Japanese push into its strategic South was influenced by a need for war materials and natural resources. Burmese oil fields such as this one were prime targets for Japanese aggression.

The heavy losses caused a temporary cessation to the big raids, but they had already sown panic throughout Rangoon.[56]

On January 20, 1942, the 55th Division struck northern Tenasserim Province with the objective of seizing the Sittang Bridge, the easiest way to reach the capital at Rangoon, as quickly as possible. Simultaneously, a parallel advance by the Japanese 33rd Division crossed the Salween River at Pa-an to threaten the flanks and rear of the 17th Indian Division. Burma army headquarters underestimated the scale of this effort and initially considered it a diversion; after all, the unprepared 17th Division had been deployed to Tenasserim because the area was deemed unlikely to see combat.

Japanese aggressiveness, combined with infiltration tactics, spooked the untested recruits of the 17th Division. They fled their outpost positions, leaving open the way to Moulmein, a key road junction and port on the mouth of the Salween River that was already under continuous Japanese air attack. Heavily outnumbered and in danger of encirclement, the division commander withdrew. Wavell was incredulous that 5,000 troops (2,000 of them service personnel) could not hold Moulmein. He refused to send

On April 16, 1942, as Lieutenant General William Slim's Burma Corps withdrew from Rangoon toward Mandalay, a large portion of his 1st Burma Division was cut off by Japanese roadblocks to its north and south near Yenangyaung, where the oil fields had been set on fire to deny them to the advancing Japanese. On the 17th, when the temperature reached 114 degrees Fahrenheit, a Chinese division with attached British armor and artillery failed to break through to the isolated forces.

The situation was grave. At half-past four in the afternoon, [Major General Bruce] Scott [the commander of 1st Burma Division] reported on the radio that his men were exhausted from want of water and continuous marching and fighting. He could hold that night, he thought, but if he waited until morning, his men, still without water, would be so weakened they would have little or no offensive power to renew the attack. He asked for permission to destroy his guns and transport and fight his way out in the dark . . .

I could not help wishing that he had not been so close a friend. I thought of his wife and of his boys. There were lots of other wives, too, in England, India, and Burma, whose hearts would be under that black cloud . . .

I told Scott he must hang on. I had ordered a Chinese attack with all available tanks and artillery the next morning. If Burma Division attacked, then we ought to break through, and save our precious guns and transport . . . He said "All right, we'll hang on and we'll do our best in the morning, but, for God's sake, Bill, make those Chinese attack."

I stepped out of the [radio] van feeling about as depressed as a man could. There, standing in a little half-circle waiting for me, were a couple of my own staff, an officer or two from the Tank Brigade, [Lieutenant General] Sun Li-jen [the Virginia Military Institute–educated commander of the Chinese 38th Division], and the Chinese liaison officers. They stood there silent and looked at me. All commanders knew that look. They see it in the eyes of their staffs and their men when things are really bad, when even the most confident staff officer and the toughest soldier want holding up, and they turn to where they *should* turn for support—to their commander. And sometimes he does not know what to say. He feels very much alone.

"Well, gentlemen," I said, putting on what I hoped was a confident, cheerful expression, "it might be worse!"

One of the group, in a sepulchral voice, replied with a single word:

"How?"

I could cheerfully have murdered him, but instead I had to keep my temper.

"Oh," I said, grinning, "it might be raining!"

Two hours later, it was—hard.[57]

reinforcements and blamed local commanders for the loss of the town on January 31.[58] Wavell was also incensed by Hutton's handling of the situation, and on February 6 he flew to Rangoon to order him, "Take back all you have lost!"[59]

By now, the 33rd Division had crossed from Thailand and on February 10 attacked Pa-an, near the left flank of the British line defending the west bank of the Salween River. The British battalion holding the town was overwhelmed and lost 500 of its 700 effectives. It estimated that it had killed 600 of 2,000 Japanese in what the battalion war diary termed "a glorious action."[60] Nevertheless, Pa-an fell, and the 33rd Division began crossing the Salween River.

Realizing that the 33rd Division might roll up his scattered forces, on February 19 Hutton finally authorized a retreat to Sittang. Two days later, Wavell signaled him that the enemy too must be tired and have suffered heavy casualties: "No sign that he is in superior strength. You must stop all further withdrawal and counterattack whenever possible. You have little air opposition . . . and should attack with air forces available." Practical advice included using colored umbrellas to coordinate air strikes on enemy targets in the jungle.[61]

The 17th Division commander followed Hutton's orders to fight on the west bank of the Bilin River, southeast of Sittang. This made tactical but not operational sense because fighting forward meant that the Sittang Bridge could not be properly prepared for defense. The Japanese 55th Division, in overwhelming strength, cracked the Bilin River line by February 18. The 33rd Division had already advanced farther inland, moving through jungle terrain under cover of darkness along paths marked by advance scouts. Suddenly it burst out of the rugged terrain north of Bilin—again turning the defenders' inland flank—and headed for the Sittang Bridge.[62] The road-bound, slow-moving British division tried to conduct an orderly withdrawal but was accidentally bombed and strafed by its own airplanes, forcing the unit to stop and regroup. The delay allowed the surging Japanese time to swing behind the 17th and reach the Sittang River Bridge. Unable to defend the bridge, on February 23 the British destroyed it, leaving most of the Indian division trapped on the wrong side of the river.

Given the magnitude of the British defeat, General Iida remarked, everyone assumed that command of Japanese Fifteenth Army functioned smoothly. In fact, he explained, his headquarters had difficulty controlling the two understrength divisions that were operating in rough terrain with little logistic support. Iida feared that the enemy might slip away from under their noses right up until the moment the Japanese trapped the 17th Indian Division at the Sittang River.[63]

By late February, the Japanese were across the river and threatening Rangoon. Wavell, now commander in chief, India, flew 1,400 miles from New Delhi to meet Hutton in Burma on March 1. He publicly berated Hutton and subsequently cashiered the 17th Division's commander.[64] A few days later, Wavell signaled London to say that despite some disorganization, morale was sound. He then ordered counterattacks to blunt the Japanese advance, but these failed, and the Japanese closed in on Rangoon. The British withdrew north to Mandalay in order to save what was left of the Burma Army. Rangoon was taken on March 8, by which time special stay-behind demolition parties had already destroyed much of the critical port infrastructure, as well as oil refineries and the power station. As operations in Malaya and the NEI wrapped up, Japanese units redeployed from those areas to reinforce Burma against Chinese troops moving from the north, setting the stage for the conquest of the entire country. This left only the American forces in the Philippines to contend with.

THE PHILIPPINES

At the end of November 1941, the regular strength of the American and Filipino ground forces had been about 31,000, including the Philippine Division, composed of American and Filipino troops. A military buildup had been under way since mid-1941, but the quality of the ten reserve Filipino divisions (all but three deployed on Luzon) was low, as the recruits lacked training and equipment.[65] Prewar defense plans called for the Americans to deny the use of Manila Bay to the Japanese by concentrating forces for a defensive stand on the Bataan Peninsula. However, General Douglas MacArthur, the commander of the newly established U.S. Army Forces, Far East, aimed to fight the Japanese invaders on the landing beaches on Luzon and defend the

Douglas MacArthur was an American general who played a prominent role in the American military and politics throughout the first half of the twentieth century. He attended West Point, graduating in 1903 as the first captain. MacArthur served with distinction during World War I as a divisional chief of staff. During the interwar years, he was the superintendent of the Military Academy and later the chief of staff of the U.S. Army. In 1937 MacArthur retired from the army and became a military advisor to the Philippine government. He was recalled to active service in the U.S. Army in 1941, as the threat of war grew imminent.

During World War II, MacArthur was the U.S. Army's senior commander in the Pacific theater. He oversaw the defense of the Philippines until he was ordered by the War Department to leave. He orchestrated the army-led "island hopping" campaign across the southwestern Pacific and back to the Philippines. He was promoted to five-star rank in December 1944 and assumed command of all U.S. Army forces in the Pacific the following April. It was MacArthur who received the Japanese government's official surrender aboard the U.S.S. *Missouri*.

Even after the end of World War II, MacArthur continued to play an influential role in the Pacific Rim. From 1945 to 1951, he oversaw the occupation and rebuilding of Japan, effectively acting as an American viceroy. After North Korea invaded South Korea in 1950, MacArthur was given command of all United Nations forces in that conflict. He conceived the brilliant amphibious landing at Inchon that ensured the defeat of the invaders in South Korea, then pushed for an expansion of the war into North Korea. After the Chinese intervened, he continued to advocate for an escalation of the war, despite President Harry Truman's determination to limit the conflict. MacArthur lost his command in April 1951. As Truman later explained, "I fired him because he wouldn't respect the authority of the president."

entire island. He argued successfully to the War Department that the islands could be held if more U.S. weapons and equipment were made available to the Filipino divisions then beginning to mobilize. A highly visible result of his efforts was the deployment of thirty-five B-17 heavy bombers to the islands, intended as a deterrent to Japanese aggression. Twelve of these were destroyed on the ground during the attacks of December 8, and two days later, only fourteen heavy bombers remained.[66]

Over the rest of December, experienced Japanese naval pilots flying superior aircraft followed up their initial attacks and steadily whittled away at MacArthur's surviving air force in the Philippines. When the main Japanese landings in Lingayen Gulf north of Manila began on December 22, only a handful of aircraft remained, and all naval forces, except for small gunboats and motor torpedo boats, had been ordered south to join ABDACOM.[67] Lieutenant General Masaharu Homma led the Japanese Fourteenth Army, a two-division force, in the main assault southward from Lingayen Gulf. He targeted Manila, where poorly trained and ill-equipped Filipino troops of the North Luzon Force proved no match for the invaders. Homma's 16th Division, meanwhile, executed a secondary landing the night of December 23–24 at Lamon Bay, about 125 miles southeast of Manila, and began moving toward the capital against light resistance.

MacArthur declared Manila an open city and moved his headquarters to the island fortress of Corregidor at the entrance to Manila Bay. His remaining forces would withdraw to the mountainous Bataan Peninsula, fighting a phased delaying action to allow for food and supplies to move to Bataan. The bravery of small units of determined

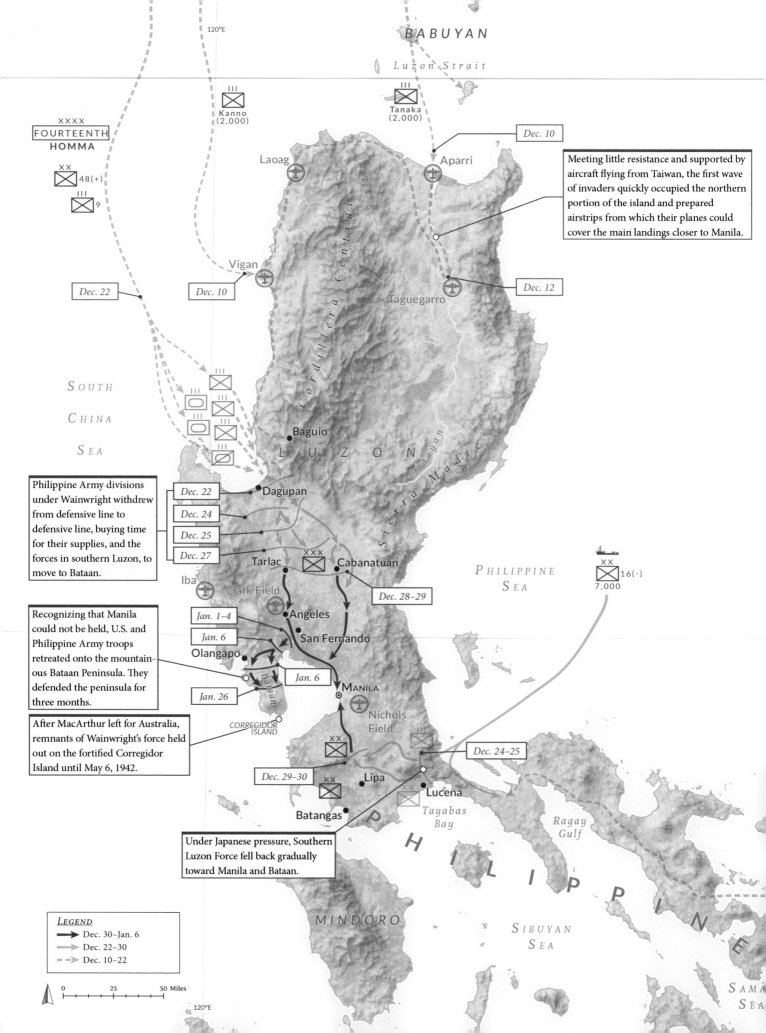

BABUYAN

Luzon Strait

xxxx
FOURTEENTH
HOMMA

xx 48(+)

iii 9

iii Kanno (2,000)

iii Tanaka (2,000)

Laoag

Aparri

Dec. 10

Meeting little resistance and supported by aircraft flying from Taiwan, the first wave of invaders quickly occupied the northern portion of the island and prepared airstrips from which their planes could cover the main landings closer to Manila.

Vigan

Dec. 22

Dec. 10

Taguegarro

Dec. 12

Cordillera Central

SOUTH

CHINA

SEA

iii

iii

iii

iii

Baguio

LUZON

Sierra Madre

Cagayan

Philippine Army divisions under Wainwright withdrew from defensive line to defensive line, buying time for their supplies, and the forces in southern Luzon, to move to Bataan.

Dec. 22

Dec. 24

Dec. 25

Dec. 27

Dagupan

Tarlac

xxx

Cabanatuan

PHILIPPINE SEA

xx 16(-) 7,000

Dec. 28–29

Iba

Clark Field

Angeles

San Fernando

Jan. 1–4

Jan. 6

Recognizing that Manila could not be held, U.S. and Philippine Army troops retreated onto the mountainous Bataan Peninsula. They defended the peninsula for three months.

Olangapo

Bataan

Jan. 6

Jan. 26

MANILA

Nichols Field

iii

Dec. 24–25

After MacArthur left for Australia, remnants of Wainwright's force held out on the fortified Corregidor Island until May 6, 1942.

CORREGIDOR ISLAND

xx

Dec. 29–30

xx

Lipa

Lucena

Tayabas Bay

Ragay Gulf

Under Japanese pressure, Southern Luzon Force fell back gradually toward Manila and Bataan.

Batangas

PHILIPPINE

MINDORO

SIBUYAN SEA

SAMA SEA

American and Filipino soldiers enabled the main force to escape to Bataan, but MacArthur had previously distributed supplies and equipment to the forward beaches, and these stores could not so easily be transferred to Bataan. By the end of the first week, the defenders of Bataan were already on half-rations, ammunition and medical supplies were lacking, and equipment wearing out.

Homma's original objective was Manila, which he captured on January 2, 1942. The IGHQ believed that with the fall of Manila, the rest of the Philippine campaign would simply be a mopping-up operation. Accordingly, as soon as Homma took Manila, IGHQ transferred the elite 48th Division to the Indies.[68]

Bataan, however, would be defended in depth. The twenty-mile-long main line of resistance extended from Mabatang on the east coast to Mauban on the west, separated in the middle by mountainous terrain. On January 9 Homma's reduced forces attacked the eastern defenses and suffered heavy losses. They regrouped, and by the thirteenth had pushed a salient into the American-Filipino line. Counterattacks by the weakened defenders could not dislodge them and instead opened more gaps between units. The Japanese exploited these openings to turn the defenders' inland flank on the 17th, forcing a general withdrawal.

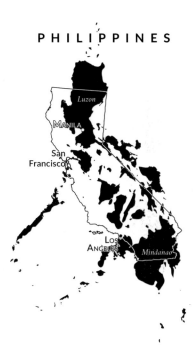

The next day, the Japanese struck the western defenses while a smaller detachment secretly circled the American right flank via the supposedly impassable peaks of Mount Natib and established a roadblock, cutting off I Corps from the southern peninsula. Repeated U.S. counterattacks failed, and Lieutenant General Jonathan Wainwright, commander of North Luzon Force, had to withdraw, leaving behind most of his artillery.[69] By the end of January, the defenders of Bataan were at their last line of resistance. The Japanese too were exhausted, and in early February, Homma swallowed his pride and called for reinforcements. On February 22 General Marshall ordered MacArthur to leave the Philippines, at a time of his choosing, to take command of a new American force in Australia. In doing so, Marshall acknowledged the hopelessness of the Philippine resistance. MacArthur departed Corregidor on March 12 by PT boat and arrived in Australia five days later to a hero's welcome.

Homma's reinforcements brought in the 14th Division, as well as strong artillery and air units recently available following the conclusion of the campaigns against Singapore and Hong Kong. They launched a strengthened offensive on April 3, grinding down the sick and exhausted defenders. Finally, on April 8, U.S. forces on Bataan surrendered. Only Corregidor Island still held out, until a Japanese nighttime amphibious assault on May 5 managed to get ashore, despite fearsome losses and strong American counterattacks. On May 6 Wainwright, now in command of all forces in the Philippines, surrendered.

Then ensued the "March of Death," as the Japanese marched their weakened

◀ **ATTACK ON LUZON, DECEMBER 10, 1941–MAY 6, 1942**
Contrary to prewar plans, General Douglas MacArthur attempted to repel a Japanese attack on Luzon by deploying troops to the beaches rather than concentrating on the Bataan Peninsula. The defenders were pushed back anyway, but in the retreat lost many of the supplies that had been moved out to coastal positions.

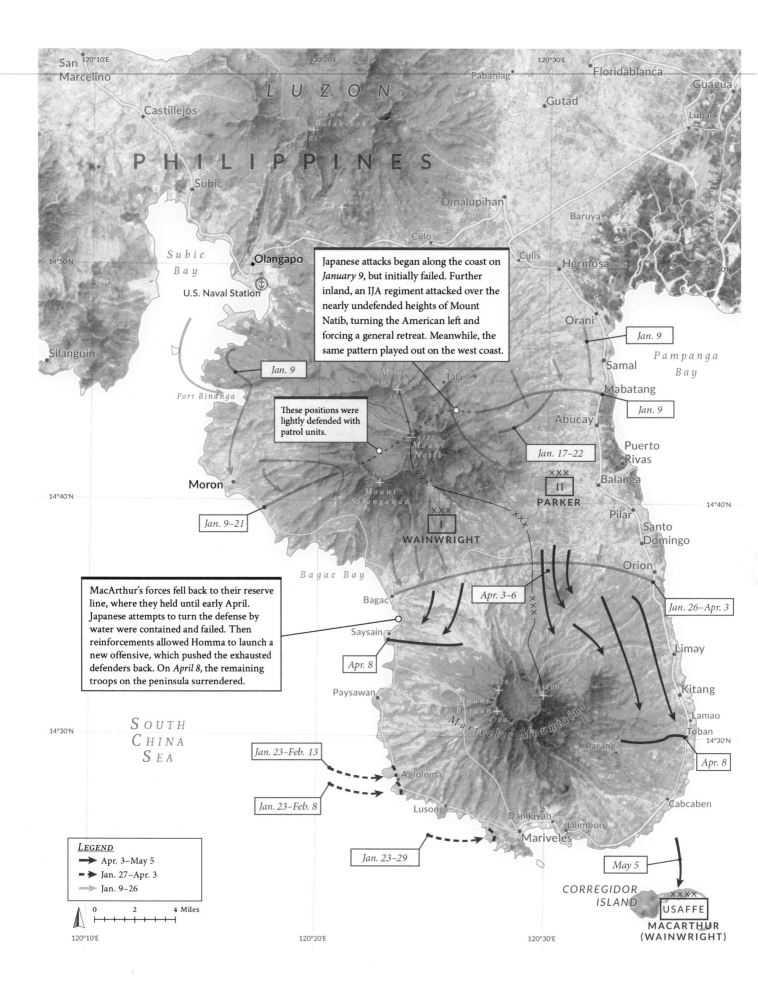

San Marcelino

120°10'E · 120°20'E · 120°30'E

Pabanlag · Floridablanca

Gutad · Guagua

L U Z O N

Castillejos

Mount Balakibok 3057

Subic

P H I L I P P I N E S

Dinalupihan · Baruya

Pampanga River

Mount Susongdalaga

Culo

Culis · Hermosa

14°50'N

Olangapo

Subic Bay

U.S. NAVAL STATION

Japanese attacks began along the coast on *January 9*, but initially failed. Further inland, an IJA regiment attacked over the nearly undefended heights of Mount Natib, turning the American left and forcing a general retreat. Meanwhile, the same pattern played out on the west coast.

Orani

| Jan. 9 |

Pampanga Bay

Samal

Silanguin

Port Binanga

| Jan. 9 |

Mount Santa Rosa 3052 · Tala

These positions were lightly defended with patrol units.

Mabatang

| Jan. 9 |

Abucay

Puerto Rivas

4222 · *Mount Natib*

| Jan. 17–22 |

×××

| II |
PARKER

Balanga

Moron

3620

Mount Silanganan

| Jan. 9–21 |

×××

×××

| I |
WAINWRIGHT

Pilar

Santo Domingo

14°40'N

14°40'N

Bagac Bay

Orion

Bagac

| Apr. 3–6 |

×××

| Jan. 26–Apr. 3 |

MacArthur's forces fell back to their reserve line, where they held until early April. Japanese attempts to turn the defense by water were contained and failed. Then reinforcements allowed Homma to launch a new offensive, which pushed the exhausted defenders back. On *April 8*, the remaining troops on the peninsula surrendered.

Saysain

Limay

| Apr. 8 |

Paysawan

1420

Mount Bataan 1200

Kitang

Lamao

Mariveles Mountains

4700

Toban

14°30'N

S O U T H
C H I N A
S E A

Parang

14°30'N

| Jan. 23–Feb. 13 |

| Apr. 8 |

Agloloma

| Jan. 23–Feb. 8 |

Lusong

Danikiyan

Lilimbon

Cabcaben

Mariveles

| Jan. 23–29 |

| May 5 |

LEGEND
→ Apr. 3–May 5
⇢ Jan. 27–Apr. 3
→ Jan. 9–26

0 · 2 · 4 Miles

CORREGIDOR ISLAND

××××
USAFFE
MACARTHUR
(WAINWRIGHT)

120°10'E · 120°20'E · 120°30'E

captives sixty miles under a hot sun, denied them food and water, and subjected them to random and often fatal brutality. About 500 Americans and 2,500 Filipinos died during the notorious march.[70]

The drawn-out fighting in the Philippines did not alter Japan's timetable of conquest. Stage one of its operational plan, with the exception of the Philippines, was completed ahead of schedule with spectacular results. During these operations, the Imperial Japanese Navy had sunk thirty-four Allied warships and lost just three

▲ **BATAAN DEATH MARCH**

After the surrender of U.S. and Filipino forces on Bataan, the Japanese marched the prisoners over sixty miles to detention camps. Roughly 3,000 men died on the brutal trek through the jungle terrain.

◀ **BATAAN, JANUARY 9–MAY 5, 1942**

The defenders of the Bataan Peninsula had no real hope of avoiding defeat, but their determined and prolonged resistance tied down substantial Japanese forces, to the benefit of Allied forces in New Guinea and Burma.

destroyers.[71] Japanese forces captured more than 300,000 Allied troops and gained control of Southeast Asia and the Western Pacific. Stage Two commenced when the Japanese Navy pushed into the Solomon Islands and Papua New Guinea in order to cut the line of communication between the United States and Australia. These Japanese moves shifted the U.S. Navy's attention to the South Pacific.

CORAL SEA AND MIDWAY

The defense of the Philippines kept American attention riveted on the land fighting until the surrender of Corregidor on May 6. But on the very day that the Japanese landed on the little island fortress, the first of two naval battles that, taken together, marked the turning point of the Pacific War began far to the south. This was the result of a confluence of events that began shortly after the loss of Bataan. First, on April 18 Lieutenant Colonel James H. Doolittle led sixteen U.S. Army Air Forces B-25 medium bombers, flying from the deck of the U.S. Navy carrier *Hornet*, in one-way attacks on major Japanese cities.[72] Stunned by the unexpected air strikes, the Japanese Combined Fleet insisted that to prevent future air raids it had to lure out and destroy the American carrier forces near Midway Island in the Central Pacific. It was a controversial plan already under consideration.[73] The naval General Staff had grudgingly agreed to Combined Fleet's Midway plan prior to the Doolittle Raid, but insisted an attack against the Aleutian Islands and a limited incursion into the Southwest Pacific precede it.[74] The army General Staff initially regarded a Midway operation as overreach, but following the Doolittle Raid, it formally approved the plan.[75]

Earlier, on January 22, Japanese naval and ground forces had seized the massive natural harbor at Rabaul, on the large island of New Britain (an Australian territory in the Bismarck Archipelago). The naval base they established there had great value, simultaneously protecting the southern approach to Truk, Japan's major fleet anchorage in the Caroline Islands, and providing an advance base for operations against Australia. The navy then insisted that to protect Rabaul, it would have to occupy strategic points in the Solomon Islands and on Papua New Guinea (another Australian territory), including Port Moresby on the southern side of the island. In mid-March U.S. cryptanalysts broke the main Japanese naval cipher, JN-25. Decrypted communications (code-named Ultra intelligence) then made clear to the Allies that a major enemy amphibious thrust against Port Moresby was imminent, to be spearheaded by two fleet carriers.[76]

Admiral Chester W. Nimitz, commander in chief of the Pacific Fleet since December 31, 1941, quickly positioned two carriers, *Lexington* and *Yorktown*, in the Coral Sea. He was looking for a showdown with the Japanese fleet.[77] (After Pearl Harbor, the U.S. Pacific Fleet had been reorganized into four task forces, each with a carrier as its center and screened by cruisers and destroyers.)[78] On May 7, search planes, Japanese and American, scoured the Coral Sea looking for the opposing carriers. A Japanese pilot mistook an American oiler for a carrier, which Japanese aircraft then attacked and heavily damaged. The Americans had little better luck, striking two old Japanese

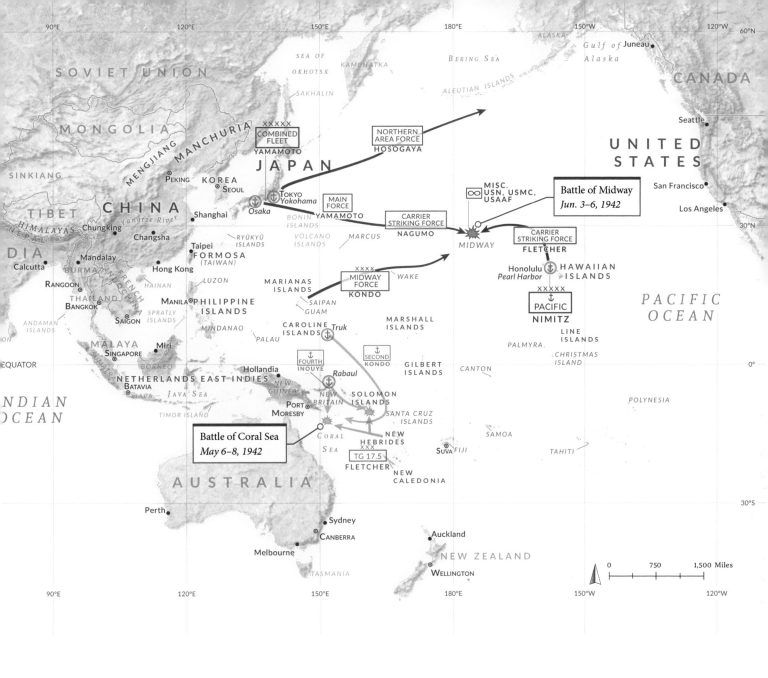

light cruisers mistakenly thought to be carriers. Fortune changed when an American pilot en route to attack the cruisers spotted the light carrier *Shōhō*. Bomb and torpedo attacks delivered by more than ninety U.S. Navy aircraft sank the carrier. Three U.S. aircraft were lost. A second Japanese strike force of twenty-seven bombers, directed against an Australian force covering the Jomard Passage, lost more than half its numbers after first being ambushed by American fighters and subsequently losing its bearings in bad weather and darkness.[79]

The next morning, the opposing carrier search planes found one another, and the flattops launched their dive-bombers and torpedo bombers. *Yorktown*'s and *Lexington*'s aircraft heavily damaged the fleet carrier *Shōkaku*. Meanwhile, planes from the *Shōkaku* and *Zuikaku* struck the two U.S. carriers, hitting the *Lexington* with torpedoes and a bomb and the *Yorktown* with a single bomb. A few hours later, internal explosions caused by leaking gasoline set *Lexington* ablaze from stem to stern. The

▲ CORAL SEA AND MIDWAY:
MAY 6–JUNE 6, 1942

The twin Allied victories of Coral Sea and Midway in May and June 1942 reversed a long run of Japanese successes in the Pacific War.

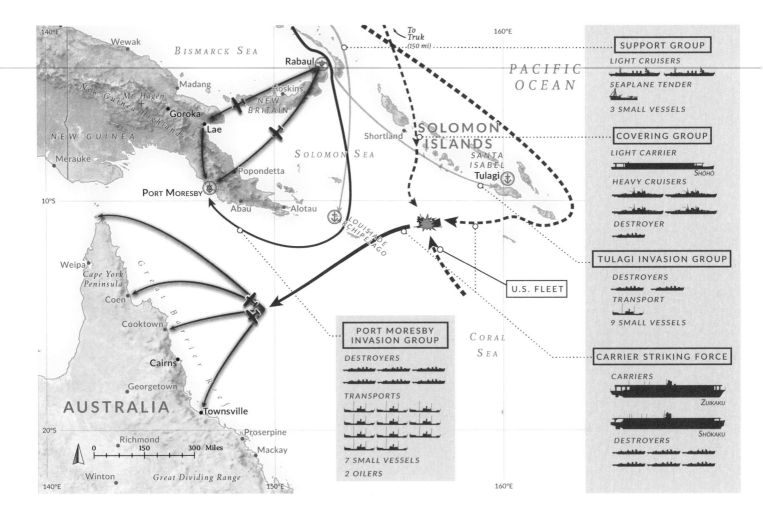

CORAL SEA: ▲
THE JAPANESE PLAN,
MAY 1942

American and Japanese fleets had both had enough, and each withdrew, ending the first naval engagement where opposing ships never sighted each other and aircraft did all the fighting.[80] The battle was a tactical draw: each fleet had one carrier sunk and another damaged. But in the broader picture, the outcome favored the Americans: the Japanese had to postpone their amphibious assault on Port Moresby and, more important, had to weaken the size of their carrier task force at the subsequent battle of Midway by one-third.

"Miracle at Midway" has popularly described the U.S. Navy victory that followed. But closer examination of the naval battle of June 4–5 suggests that the American success was less the result of divine intervention (or luck) than of the institutional and organizational deficiencies of the Japanese Navy. On paper, the Japanese enjoyed overwhelming superiority, but Admiral Isoroku Yamamoto, commander in chief of the Combined Fleet, scattered his forces among widely separated commands.[81] There was the strike force, set to attack Midway from the northwest, which had four fleet carriers, two battleships, and two cruisers. It would neutralize Midway's defenses, enabling a separate invasion force—with one light carrier, two battleships, and eight heavy cruisers—to approach Midway from the southeast. The reserve, divided into a main force and a guard force, had three battleships and a light carrier, but was six hundred miles west of the strike force.

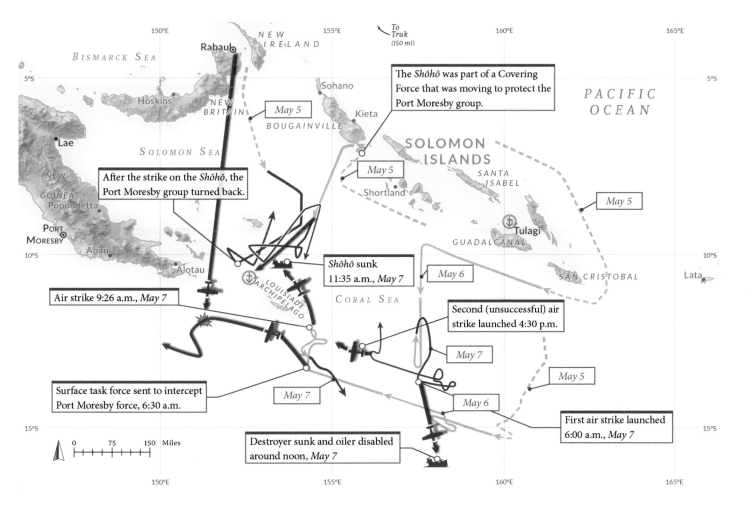

The *Shōhō* was part of a Covering Force that was moving to protect the Port Moresby group.

After the strike on the *Shōhō*, the Port Moresby group turned back.

Air strike 9:26 a.m., *May 7*

Shōhō sunk 11:35 a.m., *May 7*

Second (unsuccessful) air strike launched 4:30 p.m.

Surface task force sent to intercept Port Moresby force, 6:30 a.m.

First air strike launched 6:00 a.m., *May 7*

Destroyer sunk and oiler disabled around noon, *May 7*

▲ CORAL SEA: THE ACTION OF MAY 6-7, 1942

Decrypted Japanese messages had again revealed to the U.S. Navy the imminence of a major enemy fleet operation. Although the Imperial Japanese Navy had introduced a new cipher that made almost all messages after late May unreadable, by then the Americans had advance knowledge of the Japanese objectives, the composition of the various Japanese task forces, the likely date of attack, and the enemy's general approaches to Midway.[82] Knowing a showdown was imminent, Nimitz had set 1,700 men working around the clock in the Pearl Harbor drydock to repair the damage the *Yorktown* had suffered at Coral Sea. Draining the electricity from the Honolulu grid to provide sufficient lights and welding power, they made the carrier seaworthy—barely—in three days, rather than the ninety days initially estimated to be necessary. Consequently, when the battle off Midway arrived, the odds favored the Americans. They had 3 carriers (including *Yorktown*) with 234 aircraft, 22 other warships, plus 127 aircraft flying from Midway Island—96 sent as reinforcements in response to Ultra intelligence—against Japan's 4 carriers with 229 aircraft and 17 other surface combatants.[83]

The Japanese diversionary attack on the Aleutians opened on June 3, but—knowing that the main attack was headed toward Midway—Nimitz ignored it. When the Japanese carrier aircraft struck Midway the next morning, the Americans were ready. Their search aircraft had already spotted the Japanese fleet, and as the Japanese raiders

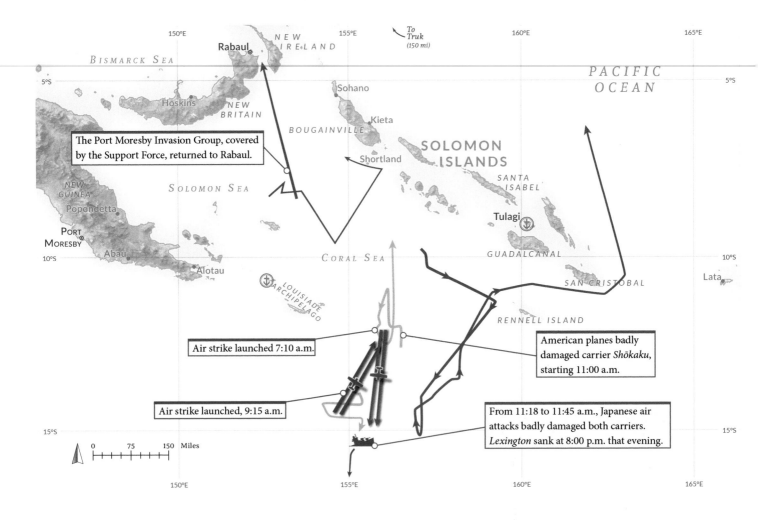

The Port Moresby Invasion Group, covered by the Support Force, returned to Rabaul.

Air strike launched 7:10 a.m.

Air strike launched, 9:15 a.m.

American planes badly damaged carrier *Shōkaku*, starting 11:00 a.m.

From 11:18 to 11:45 a.m., Japanese air attacks badly damaged both carriers. *Lexington* sank at 8:00 p.m. that evening.

0   75   150   Miles

CORAL SEA: ▲
THE CONCLUSION OF
THE BATTLE, MAY 8, 1942

left Midway and returned to their ships, they were followed by strike aircraft from the *Yorktown*, launched at seven o'clock a.m. One hour later, Admiral Raymond Spruance's Task Force Sixteen, organized around the carriers *Hornet* and *Enterprise*, sent its planes into the air—a risky move, since the Japanese flattops were barely within strike range. During this interval, Army Air Forces B-26s flying from Midway's still-operational runways attacked the Japanese carrier force, as did U.S. Navy torpedo planes. Around eight o'clock, B-17s and sixteen U.S. Marine dive-bombers from Midway plus two torpedo squadrons from the carrier *Hornet* launched high-level bombing, dive-bombing, and low-level torpedo attacks against the enemy carriers. These were futile despite great bravery and loss of life. Torpedo Squadron Eight, for example, lost all fifteen of its aircraft, and half the marine planes were shot down, mostly by veteran Japanese pilots in swift, high-performance Zero fighters.[84]

The American torpedo attack, having occurred an hour before the arrival of the U.S. Navy dive-bombers, did not, as commonly asserted, bring the Japanese carriers'

U.S. NAVAL AVIATOR ▶

In 1941, the U.S. Navy had only 5,900 pilots, but in 1942, more than 10,000 were trained. In 1942, 20,000 earned their wings, and in 1944, another 21,000 learned to fly. Furthermore, over the course of the war, the duration of pilot training increased from seven to eleven months—a marked contrast with the situation in Germany and Japan. As the quality of Axis pilots declined, the skill of their American adversaries rose.

M450 Summer Flight Helmet with Ear Cups

In the Pacific theater the U.S. Navy used cloth flight helmets rather than leather because of the heat. The AN-6530 goggles were used both by the army and the navy. Pilots liked the comfort and protection of these goggles, which used exchangeable yellow, green, and clear optical glass lenses and a rubber eye cushion. The ear cups held a radio headset and helped block exterior noise.

Type B-4 Life Preserver

Before 1928, life preservers were ring buoys or cork life belts, and then balsa wood and foam. That year a Minnesota fisherman patented a new type of lightweight life vest that used carbon dioxide cartridges to inflate airtight rubberized pockets. The new vest gained widespread renown in 1935, when the U.S.S. *Macon*, a dirigible, crashed in the Pacific. All but two crew members survived because they wore the vest. During WWII, the U.S. Navy provided life vests for every sailor and aviator, and these vests saved countless lives. Sailors nicknamed the vest the "Mae West" after the popular and famously buxom actress.

AN-S-31 Flying Suit

Bomber pilots often wore their regular officer uniforms under the famed A2 leather bomber jacket. Fighter pilots (like the one shown here) needed a uniform specially designed for the cramped spaces of the cockpit. The AN-S-31 was used by the Army Air Forces and the Navy. It was a one-piece garment made of lightweight fabric suitable for all weather.

The B8 Parachute

Parachutes for pilots made their debut in the American military after World War I. During the Great War, high-ranking American officers resisted providing them, thinking that having a parachute might make flyers ditch their planes too often. The B8 model, introduced in 1942, was more comfortable on the back than earlier parachutes.

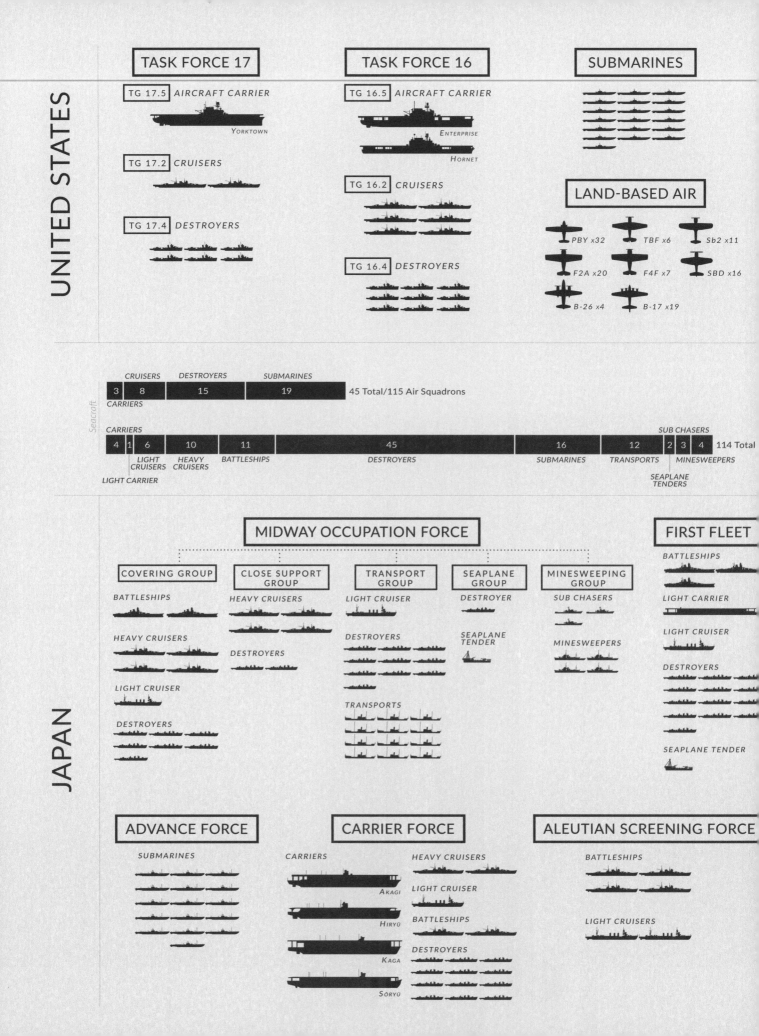

UNITED STATES

TASK FORCE 17

TG 17.5 *AIRCRAFT CARRIER*
Yorktown

TG 17.2 *CRUISERS*

TG 17.4 *DESTROYERS*

TASK FORCE 16

TG 16.5 *AIRCRAFT CARRIER*
Enterprise
Hornet

TG 16.2 *CRUISERS*

TG 16.4 *DESTROYERS*

SUBMARINES

LAND-BASED AIR

PBY x32   TBF x6   Sb2 x11

F2A x20   F4F x7   SBD x16

B-26 x4   B-17 x19

Seacraft

CARRIERS | CRUISERS | DESTROYERS | SUBMARINES
| 3 | 8 | 15 | 19 | 45 Total/115 Air Squadrons

CARRIERS | LIGHT CARRIER | LIGHT CRUISERS | HEAVY CRUISERS | BATTLESHIPS | DESTROYERS | SUBMARINES | TRANSPORTS | SEAPLANE TENDERS | SUB CHASERS | MINESWEEPERS
4 | 1 | 6 | 10 | 11 | 45 | 16 | 12 | 2 | 3 | 4 | 114 Total

JAPAN

MIDWAY OCCUPATION FORCE

COVERING GROUP

BATTLESHIPS

HEAVY CRUISERS

LIGHT CRUISER

DESTROYERS

CLOSE SUPPORT GROUP

HEAVY CRUISERS

DESTROYERS

TRANSPORT GROUP

LIGHT CRUISER

DESTROYERS

TRANSPORTS

SEAPLANE GROUP

DESTROYER

SEAPLANE TENDER

MINESWEEPING GROUP

SUB CHASERS

MINESWEEPERS

FIRST FLEET

BATTLESHIPS

LIGHT CARRIER

LIGHT CRUISER

DESTROYERS

SEAPLANE TENDER

ADVANCE FORCE

SUBMARINES

CARRIER FORCE

CARRIERS
Akagi
Hiryū
Kaga
Sōryū

HEAVY CRUISERS

LIGHT CRUISER

BATTLESHIPS

DESTROYERS

ALEUTIAN SCREENING FORCE

BATTLESHIPS

LIGHT CRUISERS

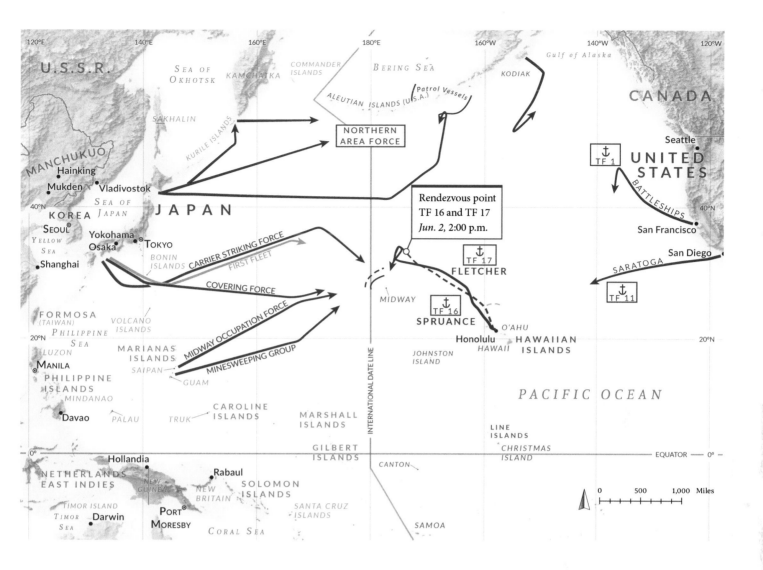

The Japanese plan for the Battle of Midway was typically elaborate. The Americans' ability to read Japanese codes, however, prevented them from being distracted by the secondary movement against Alaska.

fighter cover or combat air patrol (CAP) to wave-top levels. But although the American attacks were ineffective, the continual assaults from different directions did force the CAP to dash about the sky to meet the latest threat, leaving gaps at higher altitudes for the U.S. dive-bombers to exploit. The uncoordinated but unrelenting American attacks also forced the carriers to take high-speed evasive maneuvers. While the CAP pilots were re-forming, the approaching American dive-bombers from *Yorktown* and *Enterprise* bore down on the scattered and individually vulnerable carriers.[85]

Those planes almost missed the Japanese carriers, which were not where the pilots expected to find them. Dangerously low on fuel, the planes were just minutes from having to turn back when pilots fortuitously spotted a lone Japanese destroyer moving northwest at high speed.[86] The Americans headed in the same direction and within ten minutes sighted the carriers. By chance, another American formation, including fighters, bombers, and torpedoes, was approaching simultaneously from the southeast, in effect placing the disorganized Japanese carriers between the two attacking forces.[87] Without centralized command and control, the Japanese CAP pilots had no

THE BATTLE OF MIDWAY, ▶
JUNE 4–5, 1942

Despite the advantages of forewarning and of the "unsinkable aircraft carrier" provided by Midway Island, the Americans did not do well in the first phases of the battle.

THE BATTLE OF MIDWAY, ▶
JUNE 4, 1942

Lucky timing was a major factor in the dramatic success of the American dive-bombers, which destroyed four Japanese fleet carriers—three of them in a matter of just a few minutes.

◀ ORDER OF BATTLE FOR THE BATTLE OF MIDWAY, JUNE 4–5, 1942

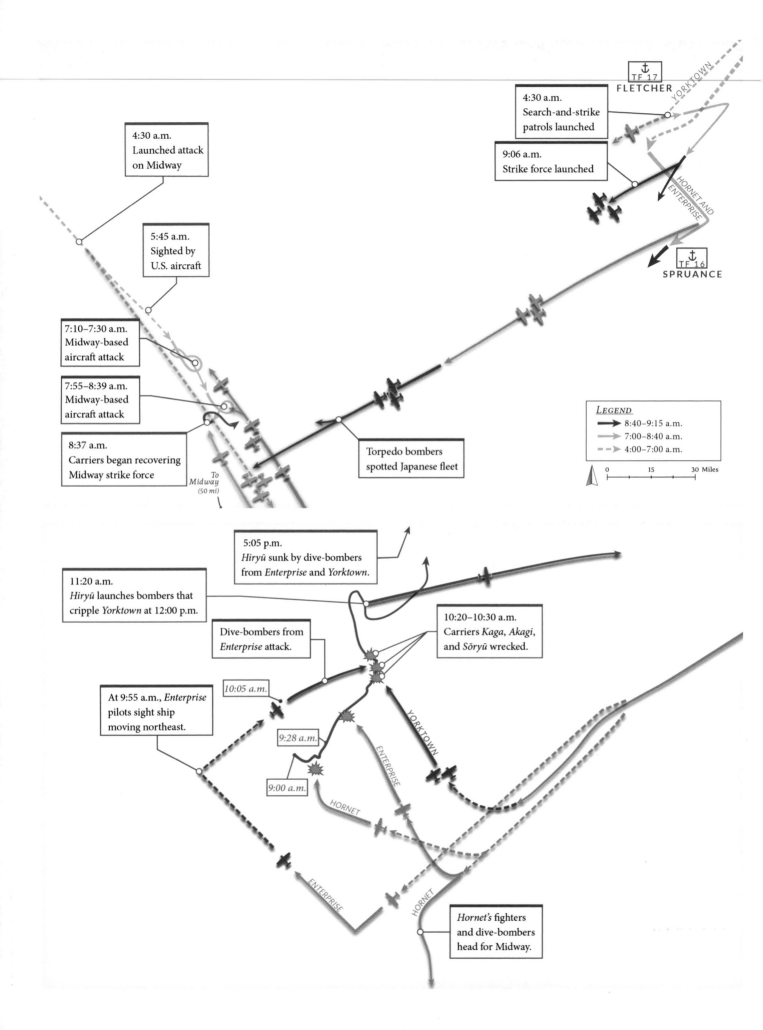

4:30 a.m.
Launched attack
on Midway

5:45 a.m.
Sighted by
U.S. aircraft

7:10–7:30 a.m.
Midway-based
aircraft attack

7:55–8:39 a.m.
Midway-based
aircraft attack

8:37 a.m.
Carriers began recovering
Midway strike force

*To
Midway
(50 mi)*

Torpedo bombers
spotted Japanese fleet

TF 17
FLETCHER
YORKTOWN

4:30 a.m.
Search-and-strike
patrols launched

9:06 a.m.
Strike force launched

HORNET AND
ENTERPRISE

TF 16
SPRUANCE

LEGEND
8:40–9:15 a.m.
7:00–8:40 a.m.
4:00–7:00 a.m.

0   15   30 Miles

5:05 p.m.
Hiryū sunk by dive-bombers
from *Enterprise* and *Yorktown.*

11:20 a.m.
Hiryū launches bombers that
cripple *Yorktown* at 12:00 p.m.

10:20–10:30 a.m.
Carriers *Kaga*, *Akagi*,
and *Sōryū* wrecked.

Dive-bombers from
Enterprise attack.

10:05 a.m.

At 9:55 a.m., *Enterprise*
pilots sight ship
moving northeast.

9:28 a.m.

9:00 a.m.

YORKTOWN

ENTERPRISE

HORNET

ENTERPRISE

HORNET

Hornet's fighters
and dive-bombers
head for Midway.

NAVAL WARFARE

Torpedoes

Torpedoes played an important role in naval war in the Pacific. They were dropped from aircraft, launched from surface ships, and fired from submarines. The Japanese had the best torpedo during the war: the Type 93, known by the Americans as the "Long Lance." It had a larger warhead and much longer range than American torpedoes, and was still faster. Both American and Japanese destroyers had torpedoes, but the Japanese included torpedo launchers on their light and heavy cruisers as well, and they used them very effectively during surface engagements.

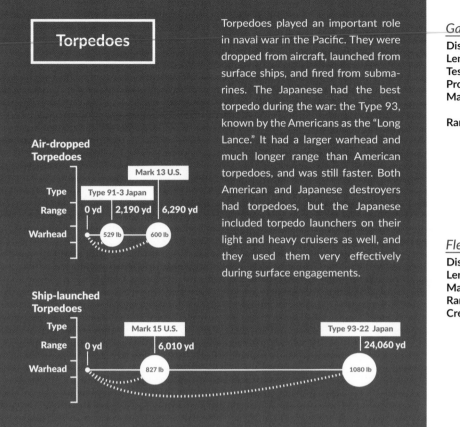

Air-dropped Torpedoes

Type	Type 91-3 Japan	Mark 13 U.S.
Range	0 yd	2,190 yd	6,290 yd
Warhead	529 lb	600 lb

Ship-launched Torpedoes

Type	Mark 15 U.S.	Type 93-22 Japan
Range	0 yd	6,010 yd	24,060 yd
Warhead	827 lb	1080 lb

Gato Class Submarine

Displacement	1,525 tons	Crew	60
Length	104 yd	Endurance	48
Test Depth	98 yd		75
Propulsion	Diesel-electric	Armament	6 f
Maximum Speed	21 knots surfaced, 9 knots submerged		24
Range	12,400 mi surfaced at 10 knots		1

Fletcher Class Destroyer

Displacement	2,050 tons	Armament	5
Length	126 yd		6–
Maximum Speed	36.5 knots		7–
Range	5,500 mi at 15 knots		2x
Crew	329		6
			2

Northampton Class Heavy Cruiser

Displacement	9,200 tons	Armament	3x3 8"/55 caliber guns
Length	200 yd		8 5"/25 caliber guns
Maximum Speed	32.5 knots		6 21" torpedo tubes
Range	14,900 mi at 15 knots		24 40 mm (1.57 in) AA guns
Crew	1,100		28 20 mm (.79 in) AA guns
			2 catapults
			4 float planes

Brooklyn Class Light Cruiser

Displacement	9,767 tons	Armament	5x
Length	202 yd		8
Maximum Speed	32.5 knots		8
Range	11,800 mi at 15 knots		2
Crew	868		4

South Dakota Class Battleship

Displacement	37,970 tons	Armament	3x3 16"/45 caliber guns
Length	230 yd		8x2 5"/38 caliber dual-purpose guns
Maximum Speed	27 knots		5x4 1.1" AA guns
Range	14,100 mi at 15 knots		34 20 mm (.79 in) AA guns
Crew	2,257		8 .50 caliber machine guns
			2 catapults
			3 float planes

Yorktown Class Aircraft Carrier

Displacement	19,800 tons	Crew	2
Length	275 yd	Armament	8
Maximum Speed	32.5 knots		5x
Range	14,400 mi at 15 knots		3,
		Aircraft	9(

F4F Wildcat Fighter

Entered Service	1940
Armament	4 .50 caliber machine guns
Bombs	2 100 lb bombs
Engine	1,200 hp Pratt & Whitney R-1820 radial engine
Maximum Speed	325 mph
Maximum Range	845 miles
Rate of Climb	3,300 ft per minute
Ceiling	35,000 ft
Span	38 ft
Length	28 ft 9 in
Height	11 ft 11 in
Weight	4,425 lbs empty, 5,876 lbs loaded
Produced	7,898

SBD Dauntless Dive-Bomber

Entered Service	1940
Armament	2 .50 caliber machine guns
	2 .30 caliber machine guns
Bombs	Up to 2,250 lbs
Engine	1,200 hp Wright R-1820-60 radial engine
Maximum Speed	225 mph
Maximum Range	1,115 miles
Rate of Climb	1,700 ft per minute
Ceiling	25,530 ft
Span	41 ft 6 ⅜ in
Length	33 ft 1 ¼ in
Height	13 ft 7 in
Weight	6,404 lbs empty, 9,359 lbs loaded
Produced	5,936

TBF Avenger Torpedo Bomber

Entered Service	1942
Armament	3 .50 caliber machine guns
	2 .30 caliber machine guns
	Up to 8 rockets
Bombs	Up to 2,000 lbs of bombs or
	1 2,000 lb Mark 13 torpedo
Engine	1,900 hp Wright R-2600-20 radial engine
Maximum Speed	275 mph
Maximum Range	1,000 miles
Rate of Climb	2,060 ft per minute
Ceiling	30,100 ft
Span	54 ft 2 in
Length	40 ft 11 ½ in
Height	15 ft 5 in
Weight	10,545 lbs empty, 17,893 lbs loaded
Produced	9,839

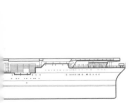

PBY Catalina Flying Boat

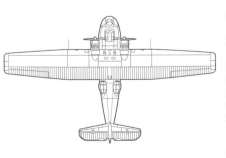

Entered Service	1936
Armament	2 .50 caliber machine guns
	3 .30 caliber machine guns
	Up to 8 rockets
Bombs	Up to 4,000 lbs of bombs, depth charges, or torpedoes
Engine	2 1,200 hp Pratt & Whitney R-1830-92 radial engines
Maximum Speed	196 mph
Maximum Range	2,520 miles
Rate of Climb	1,000 ft per minute
Ceiling	15,800 ft
Span	104 ft
Length	63 ft 10 in
Height	20 ft 2 in
Weight	20,910 lbs empty, 35,420 lbs loaded
Produced	4,051

NAVAL WARFARE

Although the U.S. and Japanese navies both considered the battleship to be the measuring stick of sea power when the war began, the carrier battle group came to dominate the war in the Pacific. Carrier planes provided aerial reconnaissance and the main offensive strike capability, while supporting warships helped defend the flattops from enemy aircraft and submarines. The battleships rarely fought ship-versus-ship engagements, but the carriers and their fighter, dive-bomber, and torpedo aircraft were involved in all the major engagements of the Pacific war.

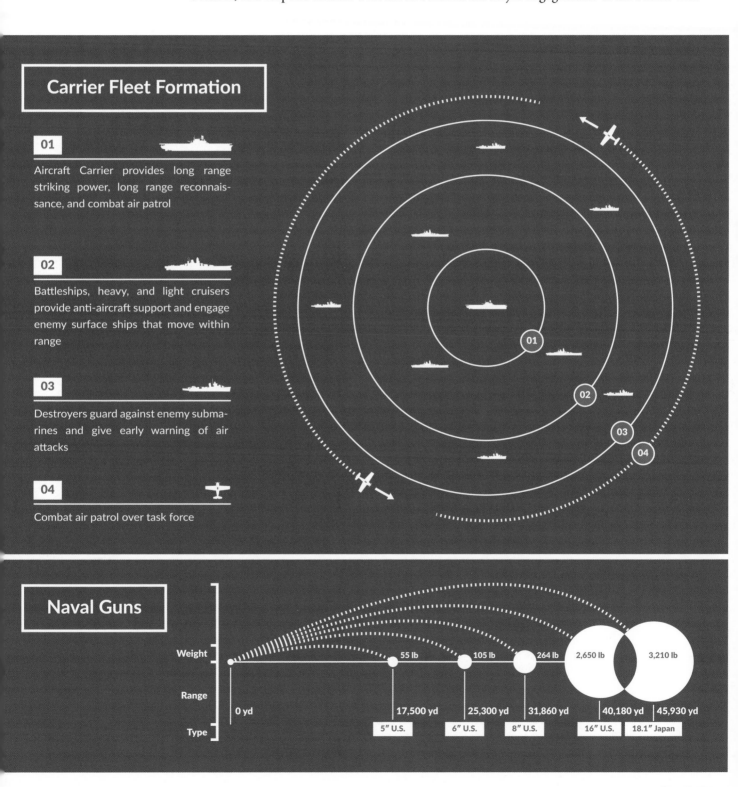

Carrier Fleet Formation

01
Aircraft Carrier provides long range striking power, long range reconnaissance, and combat air patrol

02
Battleships, heavy, and light cruisers provide anti-aircraft support and engage enemy surface ships that move within range

03
Destroyers guard against enemy submarines and give early warning of air attacks

04
Combat air patrol over task force

Naval Guns

Weight	55 lb	105 lb	264 lb	2,650 lb	3,210 lb
Range	0 yd	17,500 yd	25,300 yd	31,860 yd	40,180 yd	45,930 yd
Type		5" U.S.	6" U.S.	8" U.S.	16" U.S.	18.1" Japan

sense of the overall battle. Instead of an aerial umbrella over the carriers, the CAP was a cheesecloth that left the big ships exposed to attack.[88]

Between 10:20 a.m. and 10:30 a.m., U.S. Navy dive-bomber strikes left three Japanese carriers blazing wrecks.[89] Planes from the surviving carrier, *Hiryū*, exacted a measure of revenge early that afternoon with two attacks that crippled the *Yorktown* with two 550-pound bombs and three torpedo hits. A Japanese submarine would sink the stricken carrier the next day. A few hours later, around 5:00 p.m.,

ISOROKU YAMAMOTO
April 4, 1884–April 18, 1943

A bold and farsighted naval professional, Isokoru Yamamoto both shaped and executed Japanese naval strategy in the first years of the Pacific War.

Shortly after he graduated from the Japanese naval academy, Yamamoto participated in the 1905 decisive defeat of the Russian navy off Tsushima. He studied English at Harvard from 1919 to 1921 and was naval attaché in Washington, D.C., from 1926 to 1928. Although he viewed the U.S. Navy as qualitatively inferior to the Imperial Japanese Navy (IJN), he fully appreciated the immense potential of American shipyards and industry, and had no confidence that Japan could prevail in a long war. Once he decided that war was inevitable, however, he concluded that Japan's best hope was to cripple the American fleet at Pearl Harbor with a surprise attack.

Such a preemptive strike was only conceivable because the IJN was a global leader in naval aviation, thanks in part to Yamamoto's time at the Naval Air Corps headquarters (1930–1933) and as vice-minister of the navy (1936–1939). A firm believer in the value of aircraft carriers, Yamamoto argued that "in modern warfare battleships will be as useful to Japan as samurai swords."

As commander-in-chief of the Combined Fleet, Yamamoto planned the Pearl Harbor strike and received much of the credit for its success. But the American carriers had not been destroyed, and Yamamoto persuaded his hesitant colleagues to support another attempt to knock out the U.S. Navy's operational capability before more ships could sail from American dockyards and it would be too late. The result was the Japanese defeat at Midway (June 1942), though this outcome was due at least as much to luck and ULTRA intelligence as it was to the complexity of Yamamoto's operational plan.

In April 1943, an American aircraft killed Yamamoto while he was flying to the Solomon Islands on an inspection tour.

CHESTER WILLIAM NIMITZ
February 24, 1885–February 20, 1966
Fleet Admiral

Chester Nimitz was a prominent U.S. naval officer who attained the five-star rank of fleet admiral of the United States Navy during World War II. He originally applied to attend the U.S. Military Academy, but with no appointments available, he enrolled at the Naval Academy instead. After graduating seventh in his class, Nimitz held a number of positions throughout World War I and the interwar years. Most notable was his experience as one of the navy's lead submariners.

Ten days after the attack on Pearl Harbor, Nimitz was appointed to command the entire Pacific Fleet. Nimitz soon defeated the Japanese at the pivotal battles of Coral Sea, Midway, and the Solomon Islands. Nimitz's forces led the westward drive across the Central Pacific that competed with Douglas MacArthur's more southwestern forces for supplies and recognition.

After the war, Nimitz became chief of naval operations and oversaw the postwar naval reforms. The most important of these was Nimitz's full support in the construction of the U.S.S. *Nautilus*, the first nuclear-powered submarine. Thanks in part to Nimitz's leadership, the U.S. Navy remained the most powerful and capable navy in the world throughout the twentieth century, despite its dramatic decrease in size.

Hiryū suffered catastrophic damage from four 1,000-pound bomb hits on her forward deck.[90] The Japanese would lose more ships as the battle petered out, and the loss of 25 percent of their naval aviators engaged was serious.[91] But their biggest loss was the four carriers: the Japanese still had six operational carriers, but had no new fleet carriers scheduled for delivery until 1944, while the Americans had a dozen fleet carriers already under construction.[92] What Midway did accomplish, according to a Naval War College study, was to "put an end to Japanese offensive action" and restore the naval balance in the Pacific.[93] The Japanese thrust was spent.

CONCLUSION

For the Allies, prewar unpreparedness, indecision, wishful thinking, and poor operational decisions added up to a series of humiliating defeats in the first half year of the Pacific War. But thanks in large part to Ultra intelligence, the Allies were able to at least partially redress the balance in the naval air actions at Coral Sea and Midway. For the Japanese, on the other hand, careful planning, decisive execution, and calculated daring had produced a string a victories in the short run, based on quantitative and qualitative air and naval superiority as well as qualitatively superior ground forces. The Japanese Empire, however, lacked the industrial capacity required for a protracted conflict and, ultimately unable to sustain these advantages, sought a decisive fleet engagement to end the war. This fanciful concept brought the Japanese to Midway—where instead they found only defeat.

ATTACKING AT MIDWAY ▶

A low-flying Douglas TBD Devastator torpedo bomber makes its run at a Japanese carrier during the Battle of Midway.

MAJOR NAVAL VESSELS SUNK ▶

The results of the first six months of naval warfare in the Pacific were very one-sided in favor of the Japanese. Midway went a long way toward redressing the balance.

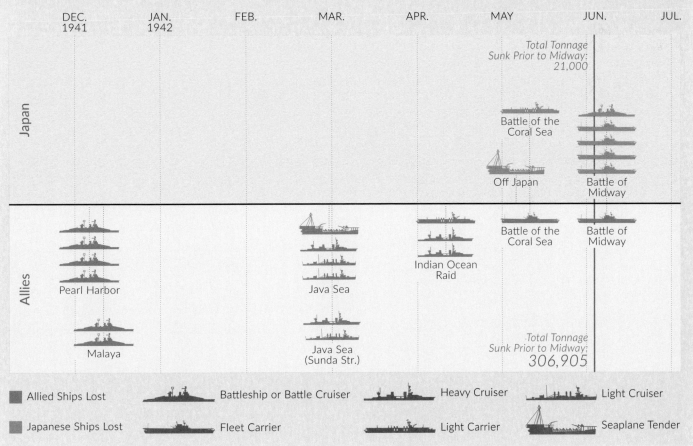

	DEC. 1941	JAN. 1942	FEB.	MAR.	APR.	MAY	JUN.	JUL.

Japan

Total Tonnage Sunk Prior to Midway: 21,000

Battle of the Coral Sea

Off Japan

Battle of Midway

Allies

Pearl Harbor

Malaya

Java Sea

Java Sea (Sunda Str.)

Indian Ocean Raid

Battle of the Coral Sea

Battle of Midway

Total Tonnage Sunk Prior to Midway: 306,905

■ Allied Ships Lost

■ Japanese Ships Lost

Battleship or Battle Cruiser

Fleet Carrier

Heavy Cruiser

Light Carrier

Light Cruiser

Seaplane Tender

INTRODUCTION

World War II was the only truly total war, in which nearly every combatant power was forced to mobilize its population and economic and manpower resources to the full in pursuit of victory. National mobilization was a complex process, and it raised an obvious issue: on the one hand, the armed forces wanted as many men (and women) and as many weapons as they could get; on the other hand, the economy needed all the manpower and finance it could find to meet the demands for military output while still providing enough goods for the home population. In the end, these goals could be met only by increasing military and industrial efficiency, while at the same time imposing tough discipline on labor and sacrifices on civilian living standards.

This chapter examines how the various belligerents sought to overcome the problems of wartime mobilization, and their degrees of success. The simple possession of large economic and human resources did not in itself guarantee victory. Ultimately, what mattered was the way those resources were utilized and the extent to which each state was willing and able to extract the maximum from its population.

MOBILIZATION AND ITS PROBLEMS

Based on the experience of World War I, the idea of "total war" was widespread in the lead-up to the Second World War. From the outset, it was assumed that large-scale mobilization would be necessary, even if the war proved to be shorter or less total than expected. For every country involved, two questions—How many men and women should be mobilized? And how best to use them?—would prove to be among the most important and complex strategic considerations of the entire conflict.

The foremost wartime priority was to mobilize men for the armed forces. But the question of how many men to enlist depended on many variables, not least of which was the importance of keeping enough skilled male industrial laborers at work rather than sending them to the front. In a total war, the effective functioning of the domestic economy had to be sustained, so it made little sense to mobilize all the young skilled workers or administrators. In Germany, some 4.8 million men (26 percent of the male workforce) were given exempted status by 1941 because their labor was essential to the armaments industry; in Britain, some 6 million men (40 percent of the workforce) were exempted by 1941, leaving the armed forces to rely on a smaller pool of manpower than in World War I.[1] Draft boards in the United States likewise exempted workers who could demonstrate that their labor was vital for the domestic war economy. Only in the Soviet Union, where men could be recruited from all age groups (including their fifties), was the level of exemption significantly lower. As a result, the Soviet Union relied more on other sources of labor—women, juveniles, and prisoners—from the start of the war.

As the war progressed, mobilization into the armed forces also depended on the extent of casualties and losses. Where the casualty rate could be kept low, the need

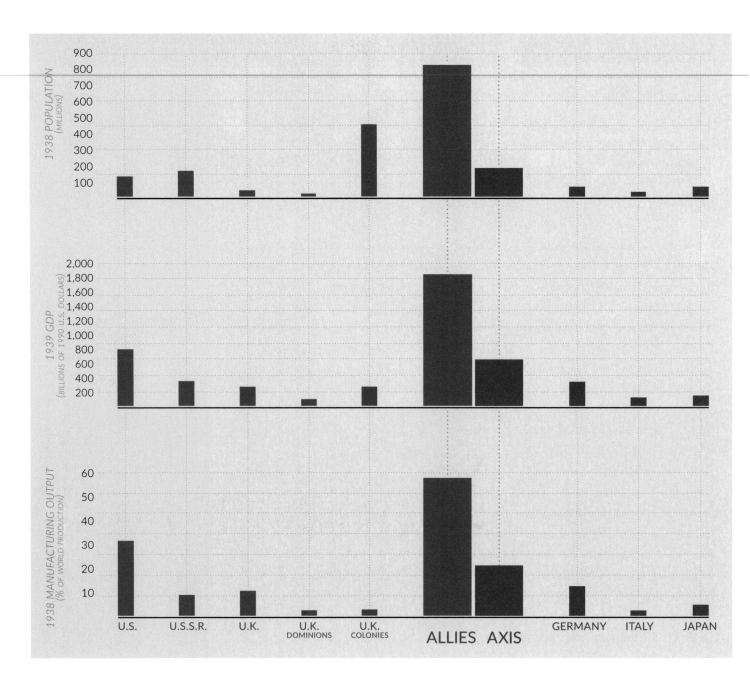

RESOURCES OF THE ▲
PRINCIPAL BELLIGERENTS

War production depended on two main factors: resources and efficiency. The Allies had a large advantage in the former, which was magnified by a substantial superiority in the latter.

for replacements was reduced not just directly but also indirectly. The longer soldiers or pilots survived in service, the more skilled and experienced they became, which allowed them to fight more effectively. This increased further their chances of surviving longer, again lowering the need for replacements. This was particularly true among air force pilots and crew; novice airmen were the most vulnerable in any unit, while pilots who survived their first ten or fifteen sorties were more likely to survive further missions.[2] Where casualty rates were high and remained high—for example, in ground combat on the German-Soviet front—the strength of the armed forces had to be constantly replenished by drawing on younger or older age groups or reducing periods of leave or rest.[3] In general, the states committed to large-scale and continuous ground warfare had to mobilize their male population to a much greater extent; these included Germany and the Soviet Union, but also Japan, with its large area of territorial conquest in mainland Asia and the Pacific. Japanese armed forces numbered 1.6 million in 1939, but by 1945, over 10 million men (14 percent of the population) had been mobilized, and 2 million men had died.[4] Britain and the United States, by contrast, used more specialized service personnel in the air force and navy, while sustaining a smaller ground army in relation to population size. Neither British nor American armed forces suffered the kind of losses incurred by their Soviet ally or the Axis enemies. The United States lost 291,000 men in combat; Britain, 270,000.[5] The figure for Germany was 5.3 million, while Soviet military losses totaled 8.67 million.[6]

These figures help to explain why the numbers recruited into the armed services in proportion to the population varied widely among the different combatant powers. In the United States, 16.1 million men and women were recruited into the armed forces, representing 11.3 percent of the 1938 population; in Britain, 5.3 million men and women were recruited, representing 11.2 percent of the 1938 population.[7] In the Soviet Union, by contrast, 29.5 million were mobilized during the war into the armed forces. This figure represented 17.4 percent of the prewar population, though in practice the proportion was much higher. By 1941, around 60 million former Soviet citizens were located in the German-occupied area, leaving a population of only 120 million to supply all the military and industrial labor for the Soviet war effort. Relative to this smaller pool, the military recruited over 25 percent of the population.[8] In the German armed forces, a total of 17.2 million served at some point during the war, including approximately 1.5 million recruited from annexed areas and occupied states. The two groups together represented almost 18 percent of the population of so-called Greater Germany.[9] High losses in combat on the Eastern Front meant that heavy recruitment continued in Germany and the Soviet Union throughout the war, whereas the peak of British and American mobilization came in the first wave of recruitment and then tailed off. In Germany, 6 million new recruits were called up between 1942 and 1945. As the pool of younger men declined, the age limits were loosened; though initial recruitment was limited to men aged nineteen to twenty-eight, by the war's end, 36 percent of total German recruits were men in their thirties or older.[10] In the Soviet Union, there was no

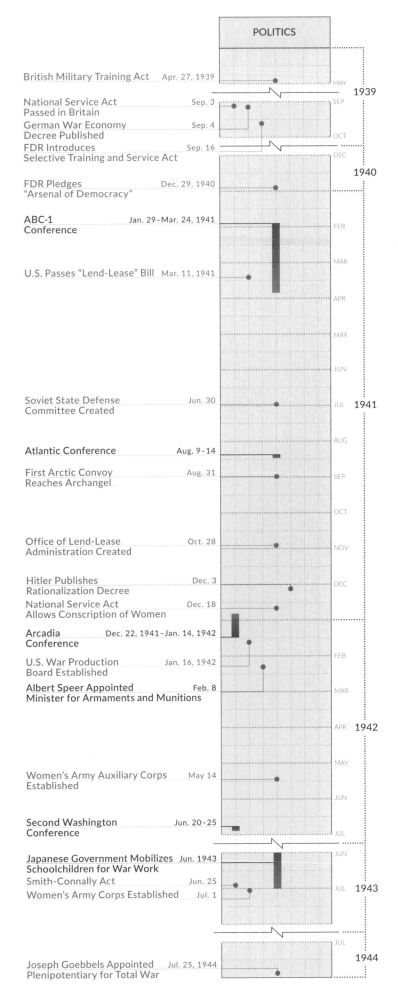

▲ ATTACK JAPAN

In order to defeat skilled and determined enemies on two fronts, the United States needed to produce high-quality munitions in immense quantities. This poster was created to motivate home-front workers to do their part in the effort to knock out Japan and Germany.

◀ "THIS IS *YOUR* FIRING LINE!"

All belligerents used propaganda to encourage home-front workers to view themselves as essential contributors to the war effort.

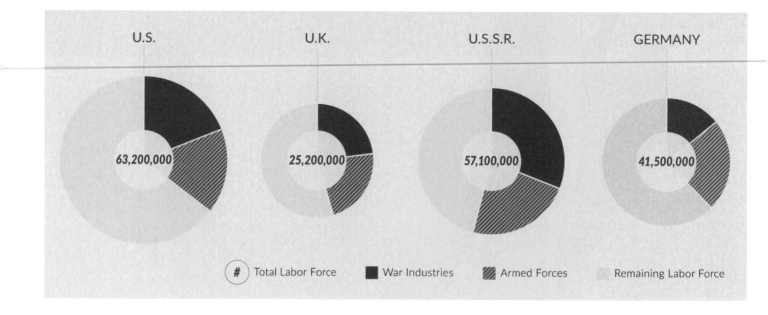

U.S.	U.K.	U.S.S.R.	GERMANY
63,200,000	25,200,000	57,100,000	41,500,000

(#) Total Labor Force   ■ War Industries   ▨ Armed Forces   Remaining Labor Force

MOBILIZATION OF THE ▲ WORKFORCE, 1942

Each belligerent nation made different choices about how to allocate its available manpower among war industries (mainly the armaments, shipbuilding, metalworking, engineering, and chemical sectors), uniformed service, and other occupations. For example, Germany put a much higher proportion of its population into shooting guns than into making them—partly because Germany could divert some of the effort of arms production to foreign laborers forced to work in the munitions factories of the Reich.

alternative but to recruit from across the male population, since the early wartime casualties in 1941–42 wiped out a large portion of the younger-age cohorts.[11]

It is important to remember that these figures of total recruitment do not represent the size of the fighting forces, which at any one point in the war would be much smaller. This is due partly to losses (prisoners; missing in action; dead; seriously injured; disabled or killed by disease; and psychiatric casualties), which continuously reduced the number of servicemen available for combat. And it was due partly to the large segments of the armed forces that, at any given point, were undergoing training or engaged in the administrative and logistical services necessary for an effective war effort.

Training was an essential factor for all armed forces, since poorly trained forces were completely ineffective in modern warfare, with its high reliance on technology. The American and British emphasis on airpower required recruits with higher educational qualifications and technical skills. Training for ground troops could take a year or more, and for highly technical services like the air force, it often took even longer. However, as is especially visible in the German air forces, a high casualty rate at the front could speed up the flow from training units—though only at the cost of putting combat personnel into battle before they were fully equipped to cope. Explanations for the defeat of the Luftwaffe in 1944 have emphasized the declining number of hours spent in flying training by German pilots, which fell from 210 hours in 1942 to only 112 hours in 1944—if there was enough aviation gas. Not only were pilots sent to the front with much shorter training time, but also the lack of fuel meant that they spent less time in the air and more time in simulator training.[12]

The administrative, support, and logistics elements in the armed forces were also essential for effective functioning. Each soldier, airman, or sailor in action was supported by a large number of noncombatants and rear-echelon personnel. At times soldiers outside the frontline units might also find themselves having to fight—for example, in the famous Bastogne pocket during the Battle of the Bulge in 1944—but in general the long tail behind each combat element performed its services at little

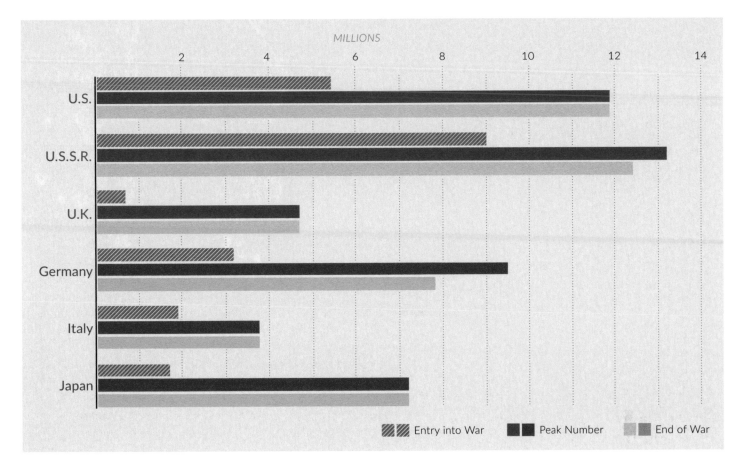

MILLIONS

2	4	6	8	10	12	14

U.S.

U.S.S.R.

U.K.

Germany

Italy

Japan

⬛ Entry into War ⬛ Peak Number ⬛ End of War

risk. The German armed forces had around 2 million at the front line in 1943, but an estimated 8 million engaged in a wide variety of other service roles. The American Army in the Pacific War had *18* support personnel for every soldier in combat.[13] The ratio between the combat personnel and support personnel in the air forces was also remarkably low. The Eighth Air Force, for example, had 283,000 personnel in December 1943, of whom only around 25,000 were flying crew.[14] The vast size of the armed forces reflected the inflated number of personnel in rear areas and support roles alongside those actually fighting: for example, the German Army at its maximum size was 4.67 million; the Soviet Army was 5.55 million; the U.S. Army, 5.9 million.[15]

In all the combatant powers, any males who were not in military service were employed in the war industry and agriculture. Here Britain and America proceeded quite differently from Germany and the Soviet Union. Because of the Great Depression, the Western Allies had many unemployed or underemployed workers willing and able to transfer to war production. In both Britain and the United States, unemployment dropped dramatically as rearmament accelerated and the war began. In Britain, registered unemployment stood at 1.7 million in 1938 but fell to just 54,000 by 1944, by which time the total domestic workforce had expanded by 2.8 million.[16] In the United States, the expansion was even more remarkable, given the huge numbers out of work: unemployment stood at 9.5 million in 1939 but was only 670,000 by 1944. Over the same period, the overall size of the workforce swelled from 44 million to 65 million, an exceptional increase made possible only by bringing large numbers

▲ MILITARY MOBILIZATION

It has been said that World War II was won by American arms and Russian blood. The extraordinary total for the military manpower raised by the U.S.S.R., as shown here, offers some justification for the latter part of that claim. Data visualizations presented later in the chapter will make the case for the first half of the statement.

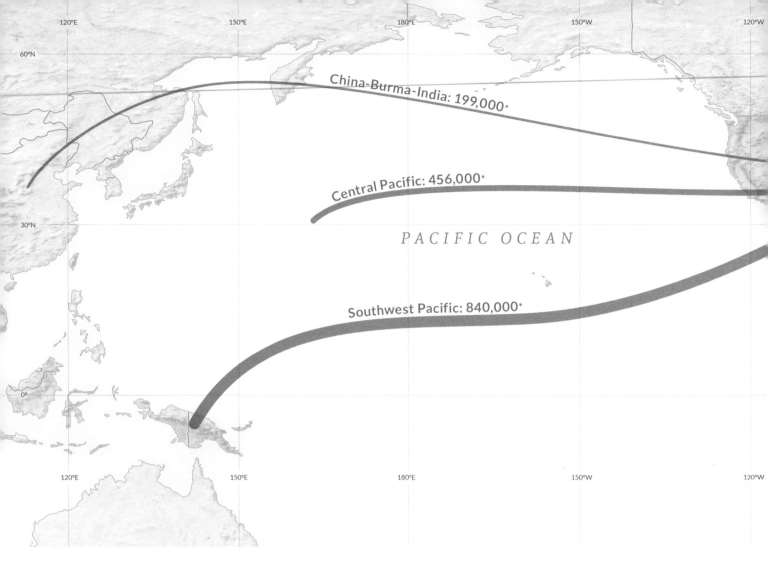

China-Burma-India: 199,000*

Central Pacific: 456,000*

PACIFIC OCEAN

Southwest Pacific: 840,000*

THE DEPLOYMENT OF U.S. ▲ ARMY (INCLUDING AIR FORCES) PERSONNEL IN WORLD WAR II, 1939–45

The thick line flowing to northwest Europe reflects the strategic logic of the Germany-first strategy adopted by the United States and Great Britain at the Arcadia Conference of December 1941– January 1942: "Germany is still the prime enemy, and her defeat is the key to victory. Once Germany is defeated, the collapse of Italy and the defeat of Japan must follow."

of women, African Americans, and juveniles into productive employment.[17] The additional workforce was directed chiefly to armaments production and war contracts. It was the United States' "Group 1" industries (engineering, capital goods, munitions) that drove much of the growth, rising faster than other sectors, from 4.7 million in 1939 to 11 million in 1943.[18] At peak, the United States devoted 45 percent of its gross national product (GNP) to the war, and Britain devoted some 55 percent.[19]

For the Soviet and German dictatorships, it was markedly more difficult to ramp up war production. Both states were already at full employment in the late 1930s, and labor shortages in Germany had already led to an inflow of migrant labor from other European states.[20] The proportion of the national economic effort devoted to defense purposes was already very high in Germany before the outbreak of the war: 23 percent of GNP, 60 percent of capital investment, and almost 30 percent of labor in manufacturing and construction.[21] But since there were almost no unemployed resources to be transferred to the war effort, finding labor and factory capacity for expanded war production required closing down much of the civilian sector, increasing productive efficiency, and finding resources from the occupied areas. By 1941, almost

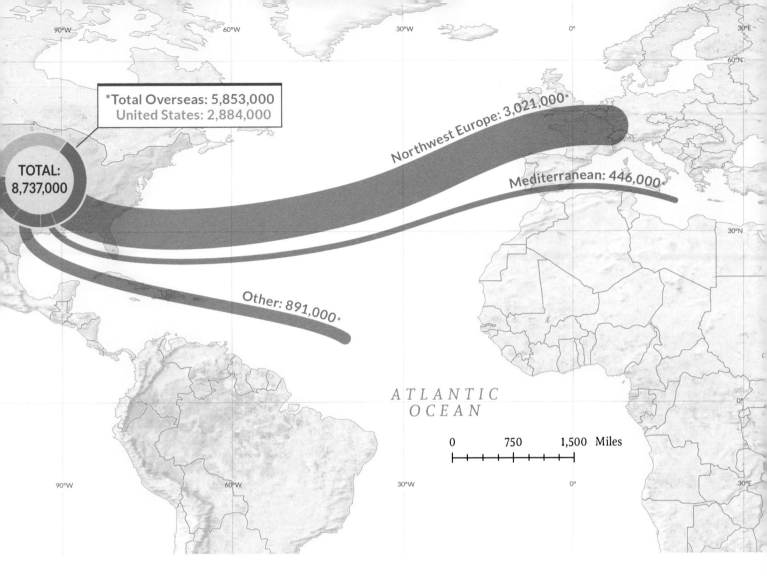

*Total Overseas: 5,853,000
United States: 2,884,000

TOTAL: 8,737,000

Northwest Europe: 3,021,000*

Mediterranean: 446,000*

Other: 891,000*

ATLANTIC OCEAN

0   750   1,500   Miles

two-thirds of German labor was working directly for the war: millions of workers had been switched from inessential trades to work on war production, while additional material resources were looted from the conquered areas.[22] Already by this stage of the war, there were labor shortages in all sectors of the economy, making it difficult to expand production quickly. The three armed services competed with each other to retain scarce labor resources in the industries working for them, but the effect was to make industry less efficient by reducing the possibility for developing standard products and mass-production methods.[23]

The labor problem for the Soviet Union was even more complicated. Here rapid industrialization in the 1930s had already involved a major social upheaval, relocating 30 million rural workers to new industrial centers, where they had to be trained hastily to meet the urgent demands of Stalin's Five-Year Plans. Prewar defense spending was almost as extensive as in Germany, reaching 17 percent of GNP by 1939.[24] But the Axis invasion of June 22, 1941, produced a profound crisis in the Soviet economy. German advances cut off the Soviet regime from two-thirds of its industrial and mining capacity, almost one-third of the Soviet population, and the nation's main grain

"Cut the Line!" ▲

American shipyards produced over a thousand LSTs (Landing Ships, Tank) during the war. These large vessels were specifically designed to land tanks and vehicles during amphibious operations. The majority were built along inland waterways rather than in seaboard ports; this one is being launched into the Ohio River in Pittsburgh.

surplus area in the Ukraine. Industrial employment fell sharply, from 13.8 million in 1940 to 8.7 million in 1942, rising to a wartime peak of just 10 million in 1944.[25] The portion of the shrunken economy devoted to war production increased to around 60 percent of GNP; the country's labor deficit meant that additional war workers had to be taken from the existing population at the expense of civilian output; and at the same time, the workforce expanded, drawing upon old, young, and female laborers as well as the large prisoner population.

EXPANDING THE LABOR POOL

Even in the states least affected by labor shortages, it was necessary during the war to extend recruitment for the armed forces, war industry, and agriculture to sectors of the population (including occupied or colonized areas) previously unemployed or underrepresented in the military and civilian workforce. Since women made up approximately half of the adult population, it was inevitable that they would be involved in fulfilling the demands of total war. For a small segment of the female population, this meant service in the armed forces or in their supporting services and administration.

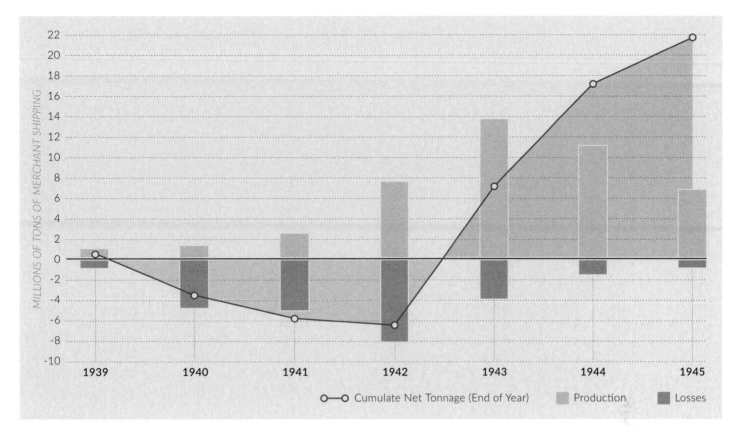

MILLIONS OF TONS OF MERCHANT SHIPPING

○—○ Cumulate Net Tonnage (End of Year) █ Production █ Losses

For a far larger portion, war work consisted of replacing or supplementing male labor in all areas of economic activity.

The recruitment of women into the armed forces was universal, but it followed differing patterns among the major combatant states. There remains a persistent myth that German women were not recruited to serve in the armed forces, based on the argument that National Socialist ideology preferred women to remain at home, leaving men to do the work of war. In reality, the ideology was more ambiguous. As long as women recruited to do work for the armed forces retained their femininity, the recruiting propaganda stressed the need for all "racial comrades," men or women, to do their part for the war effort. In total, around 500,000 women worked formally as Armed Forces Auxiliaries (*Wehrmachtshelferinnen*), serving in antiaircraft posts, in radar stations and military telecommunications, or as administrators and military welfare personnel, thus allowing more men to serve on the front lines. In addition, some 200,000 worked for the principal civil defense organization.[26] The only stipulation was that women could not actually fire weapons, though this restriction seems to have been relaxed once shortages of antiaircraft personnel became acute in 1944–45.

The ban on bearing arms also applied to female recruits in the British and American armed forces, who could come close to the front line as nurses or radio operators but were not expected to fight. The combined strength of British women in the Women's Royal Naval Volunteer Reserve, the Auxiliary Territorial Service (army), and the Women's Auxiliary Air Force (WAAF) reached 453,000 in September 1943, all of them volunteers.[27] They served in a wide range of administrative roles; the WAAFs

▲ **ALLIED PRODUCTION AND LOSSES OF MERCHANT SHIPPING**

To win the war, the United States had to keep Britain and the Soviets fighting, and had to ship its own military forces across the ocean. This would not have been possible if the navies and shipyards of the Allies had not together won the Battle of the Atlantic.

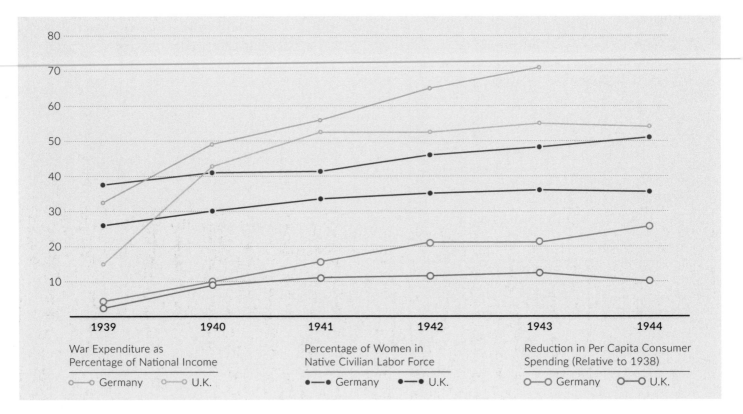

80
70
60
50
40
30
20
10

| 1939 | 1940 | 1941 | 1942 | 1943 | 1944 |

War Expenditure as
Percentage of National Income

o——o Germany   o——o U.K.

Percentage of Women in
Native Civilian Labor Force

●—● Germany   ●—● U.K.

Reduction in Per Capita Consumer
Spending (Relative to 1938)

o——o Germany   o——o U.K.

ECONOMIC MOBILIZATION ▲ FOR TOTAL WAR

For both Germany and Britain, by 1941, more than half the nation's economic production went directly to support the war effort. Even though more women joined the paid workforce, so much expenditure on guns meant that families had to make do with less butter.

played an especially critical part in running communications and operations rooms for the large British air effort. Like their German counterparts, some British women in the ATS did serve in antiaircraft units and occasionally defied regulations by firing the guns. British women were also represented strongly in the civil defense organizations. By the summer of 1940, there were already 309,000 women employed full-time or part-time in air-raid protection duties, and over 1 million in the Women's Voluntary Service, a uniformed welfare organization set up in 1938 to enroll women for relief work in the event of a bombing war.[28]

The United States recruited almost 400,000 women into the various branches of the armed services, 63,000 of them into the Women's Army Auxiliary Corps (which became part of the army proper as the Women's Army Corps, or WAC, in July 1943), and by the end of the war, around 90,000 served in the navy's auxiliary branch, Women Accepted for Volunteer Emergency Service (WAVES).[29] The decision to recruit women into the armed forces was not without argument, since the all-male services had to be persuaded that the presence of women would not undermine military discipline or compromise the masculine image of the military profession. The U.S. Army and U.S. Army Air Forces refused to define women as *in* the service—instead, they were only *with* the service—until it became clear that the distinction was undermining

MASS PRODUCTION AT WILLOW RUN

Modern war required large quantities of rubber. For example, a Sherman tank used nearly a ton of rubber, and a heavy bomber used half a ton. Demand rose as the American economy mobilized for war: the U.S. military required over 500,000 tons of rubber in 1943. But following their seizure of Southeast Asia in early 1942, the Japanese controlled most of the world's supply of natural rubber. The solution for the Allies was to produce synthetic rubber from petroleum byproducts. The four major rubber companies, Firestone, Goodyear, United States Rubber, and Goodrich, shared information and began a comprehensive program to expand production. In 1942 the four produced just 2,241 tons of synthetic rubber. Following a massive plant construction program similar to the one that built aviation fuel refineries, the U.S. output rose to 920,000 tons of synthetic rubber in 1945. Synthetic rubber was a crucial component of the Allied war effort and a key to victory.

Size

Plant and Airport	1,878 acres
Main Plant Length	3,200 feet
Main Plant Width	1,450 feet
Assembly Line Length	5,460 feet
Total Floor Area	4,734,617 sq ft
Concrete	1,575,356 sq yd
Steel	38,000 tons

Government Investment

Land & Improvements	$5,075,500
Buildings	$58,762,800
Machinery & Equipment	$32,648,700
Total	$96,487,000

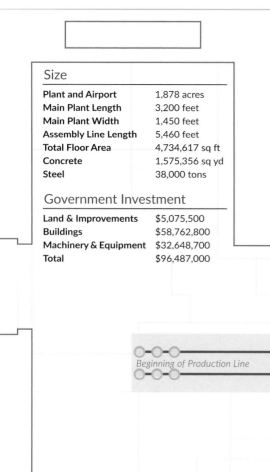

Beginning of Production Line

1 Alumium

Durable, lightweight aluminum is a key material for aircraft production. Fortunately for the Allies, the United States produced 10.7 percent of the world supply of bauxite ore and had sufficient power supply and mills to mass-produce aluminum from that ore. In 1942 the U.S. produced 751,900 metric tons of aluminum, while Germany produced 420,000 and Japan 103,000 metric tons. The expansion of U.S. production facilities increased output to 1,092,900 metric tons in 1944. Alcoa, the Aluminum Company of America, built eight smelters, eleven fabricating plants, and four refineries, and operated them for the government during the war. Even with access to over 50 percent of the world's supply of bauxite in Germany, Italy and occupied Europe, German production peaked at 470,000 tons in 1944 due to limited production facilities and electric power, and the effect of the Allied strategic bombing campaign.

2 Aircraft Engine

Winnin
possible
high-pe
Motors
produce
Pratt &
ers. Bo
German
from 1
benefite
ers, and
tane av
ble of p
that of

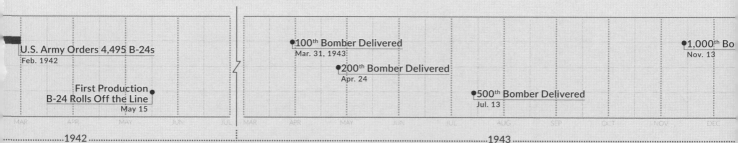

U.S. Army Orders 4,495 B-24s
Feb. 1942

First Production
B-24 Rolls Off the Line
May 15

100th Bomber Delivered
Mar. 31, 1943

200th Bomber Delivered
Apr. 24

500th Bomber Delivered
Jul. 13

1,000th Bo
Nov. 13

1942

1943

4 High-Octane Aviation Fuel

The U.S. government invested a billion dollars to finance the construction of nearly two hundred new petroleum refineries. The large-scale production of 100-octane aviation fuel made high-performance engines possible. Fuel additives such as tetraethyl lead were developed, increasing the performance of 100-octane fuel even further. With additives, the standard American 100-octane fuel was rated 130, indicating 30 percent better performance. The U.S. refined 73,000 barrels per day of aviation fuel in 1942, rising to 600,000 barrels per day in September 1945. In contrast, German output averaged 13,600 barrels per day in 1939, and fell in August 1944 to just 3,476 barrels per day of greatly inferior aviation fuel.

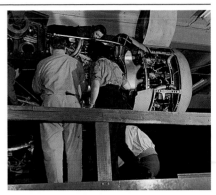

An Eyewitness at Willow Run

"The Liberator bomber grows around its center wing—support of an arsenal, and storage place for fuel. Bombs will be carried under its long, wide belly; gasoline tanks will be built into the wing itself. In a central bay of the plant, well down the line, it is joined by fore and aft sections of the fuselage; by the empennage, or tail section; by the outer wings. The four engines descend from a balcony overhead, and are put in place. Here, at the meeting place of a few great streams, is something that begins to look like a bomber. Equipped at length with landing gear and wheels, . . . [a] little later it is patiently beneath a traveling crane. From the crane's hook hangs a sling holding a new propeller; and within a few minutes, a four-man crew has adjusted the propeller to one of the engines."

e air war would have been im-
thout adequate production of
mance aircraft engines. General
t 206,000 during the war. Ford
32,179, of which 57,851 were
itney engines for heavy bomb-
mpanies easily outproduced all
ms combined: 111,529 engines
to 1944. U.S. engines, which
rom better design, turbocharg-
e use of higher quality high-oc-
on fuel, were on average capa-
ucing higher horsepower than
man or Japanese engines.

Only Five B-24s Remained in
the U.S. Army Air Force Inventory
Dec. 31, 1946

●er Delivered

●1,500ᵗʰ Bomber Delivered
Jan. 14, 1944

●2,000ᵗʰ Bomber Delivered
Mar. 18

●3,000ᵗʰ Bomber Delivered
Jun. 16

4,000ᵗʰ Bomber Delivered ●
Aug. 29

Last B-24 Rolls Off the
Willow Run Assembly Line
Jun. 28

Willow Run Awarded the Army-Navy
"E" Award for Production Excellence
Apr. 1945

1944   1945   1946

MASS PRODUCTION AT WILLOW RUN

Willow Run

Covering nearly three square miles, the Willow Run plant was the largest factory building in the world at the time of its construction. To support the plant's mile-long assembly line, the facility included everything a small city needed: power and sewer plants, a medical facility, forty-four eating places, wells providing five million gallons of water per day, security personnel, fire personnel, and its own radio station. The plant also had a complete airfield with six runways, three large hangers (two of which could each house twenty B-24s at a time), a control tower, a café, refueling facilities, and emergency equipment.

President Roosevelt Calls for 50,000 Planes for the
Air Forces and Production Capacity of 50,000 per Year
May 16, 1940

Ford Accepts $200 Million Contract to
Build Fuselage Assemblies for 1,200 Planes
Feb. 1941

First Machinery Installed
Sep. 1

Ground Broken for the Willow Run Factory
Apr. 18

Officially Named the
Willow Run Bomber Plant
Oct. 8

FDR Endorses Plan for 500 Heavy Bombers per Month
May 4

Last of Eight Miles
of Concrete Poured
Dec. 3

JUN   FEB   MAR   APR   MAY   JUN   JUL   AUG   SEP   OCT   NOV   DEC   FEB

1940   1941

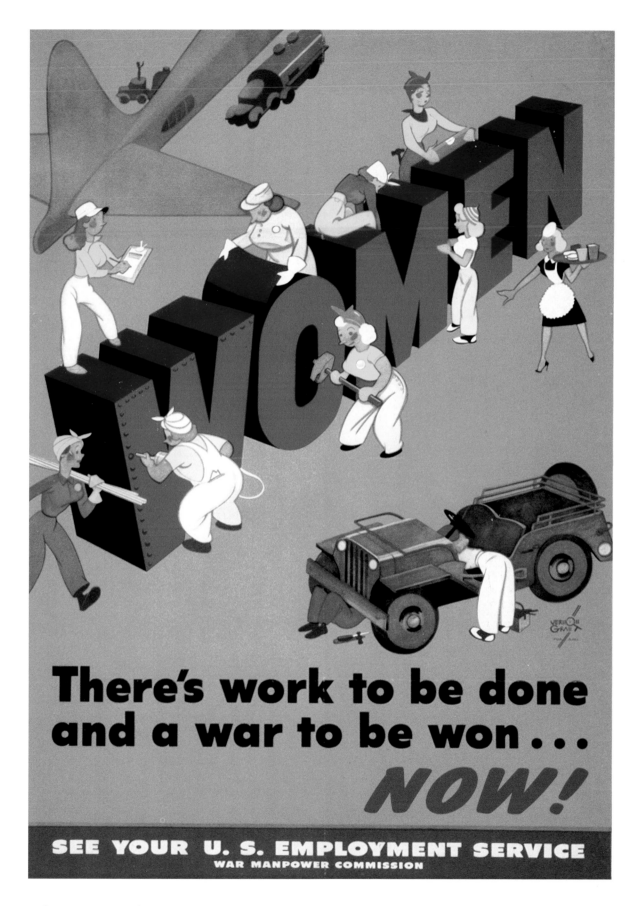

▲ "Women: There's Work To Be Done"

Every country in the war needed to mobilize its economy to increase war production even while pulling large numbers of men out of the workforce and into uniform. This was possible only because so many women moved into traditionally male jobs.

▲ War Work

Millions of African American women and men joined the skilled labor force in America even though the factories were often segregated. Here a real-life "Rosie the Riveter" operates a hand drill while working on an A-31 Vengeance dive-bomber at the Vultee plant in Nashville.

German Welder ▶

Like many others, this German woman learned a traditionally male skill in order to work in the family business, taking the place of a brother killed in combat.

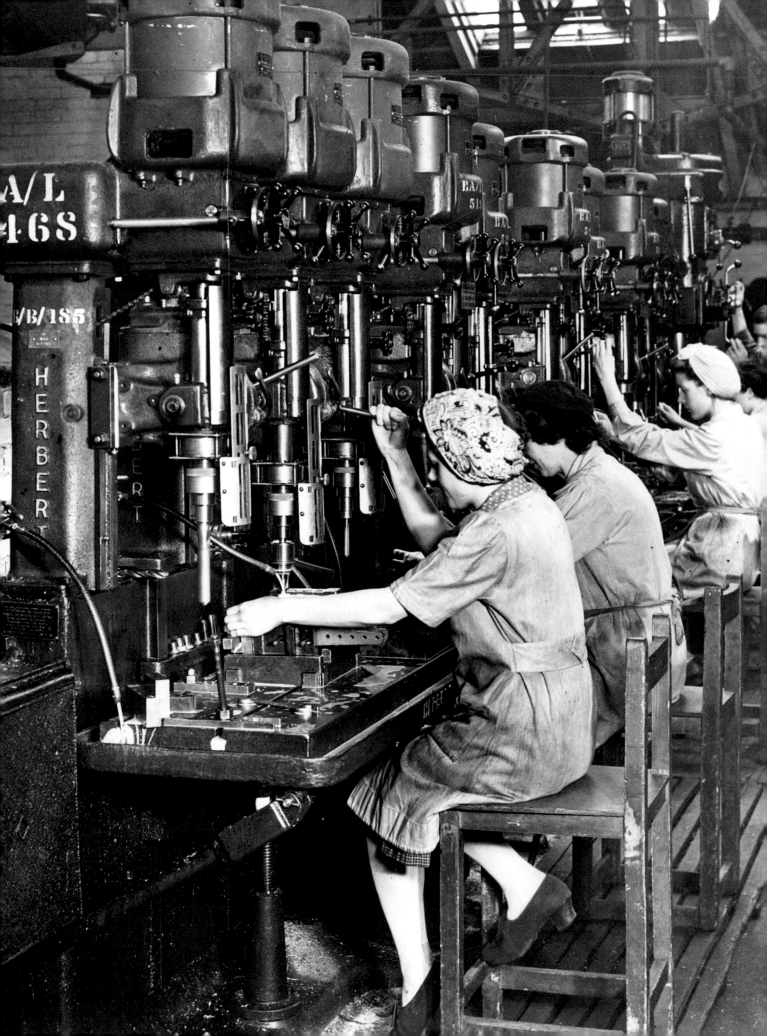

This is our war...

Join the WAAC

WOMEN'S ARMY AUXILIARY CORPS
UNITED STATES ARMY

APPLY AT ANY U. S. ARMY RECRUITING AND INDUCTION STATION

▲ WOMEN'S ARMY AUXILIARY CORPS

Though initially enlisted as "auxiliaries" (helpers) of the army rather than actual army soldiers, women served in a variety of military roles starting in 1942. The next year, the WAAC became the Women's Army Corps—officially a branch of the United States Army rather than a separate organization. The head of Pallas Athena, visible in the background, was the insignia of the WAAC.

◀ BRITISH WAR WORKERS

Many British women served in the military; many more, such as these women working for Blackburn Aircraft in Leeds, contributed to the war effort by joining the industrial labor force.

A WAC Nurse Wades ▲ Ashore in Normandy

American women did not serve in combat units during World War II, but they did serve in combat zones—especially in North Africa and Europe, where field hospitals staffed by army nurses closely followed the frontline units.

the effective use of female recruits in essential military support roles. Legislation in July 1943 (the Rogers Bill) introduced full integration of women into the army, a step already achieved in European armies. This resulted in a simpler organization and encouraged a wave of new volunteers, though a quarter of the existing WAACs chose to return to civilian life because they did not want to be integrated fully into the forces. The change did allow women to hold commissioned rank in the army, from second lieutenant to colonel.

The U.S. Navy, on the other hand, refused to recruit women at all until the sheer scale of the mobilization needs made it evident that women were needed for a wide range of auxiliary roles. The WAVES program was established on July 30, 1942, and because of the pressure to change the army's attitude toward female recruits, the navy insisted from the start that the women would count as serving personnel—*in*, rather than *with* the navy—and that there would also be a cohort of women officers.[30] By 1945, some 81,000 WAVES had graduated from the women's training school. Among the most challenging activities for women was the work of ferrying and testing aircraft, carried out by 1,074 women who qualified as Women Airforce Service Pilots (WASPs), of whom 38 were killed in accidents. Congress refused to grant them military status throughout the war, and they were awarded veterans' benefits only in 1977. This example shows that the distinction between being with or in the military lingered on after the war in continuing arguments about gender roles in the armed forces.

The recruitment of women was not just a result of shortages of male labor. In both Britain and the United States, women exerted strong pressure throughout the war for duties that went beyond the nursing and welfare work that were traditionally assigned

to women in wartime. Since the Western nations viewed the war as a genuinely democratic effort, the inclusion of women played a part in cementing domestic solidarity for the war effort and distributing responsibilities more broadly.

In the Soviet Union, women made direct contributions to the military war effort from the early stages of the German-Soviet war. In part, female recruitment was made necessary by the shocking level of casualties that the Red Army and the air force suffered in the first year. Another factor was the Communist ideology, which dictated that all Soviet citizens, male or female, had a responsibility to defend the revolutionary state in any way they could, including service in the armed forces.[31] By the end of 1943, there were 800,000 women in the armed forces, many of them in combat roles. When the war ended, there were 246,000 women serving at the front, and an estimated 25,000 as partisans. Much of the night bombing of German Army communications or Luftwaffe bases in Russia was carried out by women pilots, including the legendary

46th Guards Night Bomber Aviation Regiment, whose members flew 24,000 missions and won twenty-three medals as Heroes of the Soviet Union.[32]

Women on the Soviet home front also had a vital role to play. Women constituted half the overall labor force by 1945, and four-fifths of all workers on the collective farms, where many pulled the ploughs in teams because of the shortages of tractors and animals. Almost all of their produce was requisitioned by the state, leaving them constantly short of food even as they were forced to grow it.[33] Teenage schoolgirls were also expected to work in factories with little supervision, risking industrial accidents or harsh punishment if production norms were not met. By 1944, some 53 percent of the industrial labor force consisted of women and girls.[34]

As in the Soviet Union, all major combatant powers ameliorated labor shortages by employing a higher proportion of women. In Japan, there existed a large prewar female workforce, which switched from producing consumer goods to producing war-related products as military mobilization accelerated. It proved difficult to recruit many more women during the war, and by 1944, secondary education was suspended to release 3.43 million schoolchildren into the labor market.[35] In Germany, there was already a large female workforce when war broke out, much of it employed on the millions of small German farms. But the proportion of women in the native German labor force increased from 37 percent in 1939 to 51 percent at the end of the war. Many women who had been employed full-time in clerical roles or inessential manufacture were switched to essential war production positions. To allow women with families to participate, state-run nurseries provided child care. They supplied places for 1.2 million infants by 1944, enabling 3 million married women with families to serve six-hour shifts as part-time labor.[36]

The United States also established state-run nurseries for women with children, but only 120,000 places were ultimately available. Nonetheless, from 1942 onward, 4.6 million American women entered the workforce; this brought the proportion of female workers from 25 percent in the prewar labor force to 35 percent in 1945, though this was still below the level in Germany before the start of the war. In Britain, the proportion rose to a wartime peak of 37 percent, the same percentage as in Germany in 1939.[37] In both the democracies, a great many older or married women were not expected to work; the lower level of male mobilization into the armed forces ensured that the demands made of the female population would be less severe than in Germany or the Soviet Union.

Even as millions of women were recruited to new opportunities during the war, this advancement did not end gender discrimination or guarantee greater gender equality. Women seldom assumed supervisory or managerial roles, and pay disparities between male and female laborers lingered even when they performed the same work. In manufacturing industries in Britain, women's average weekly earnings were still only half of men's in 1945, as before the war.[38] From the view of the men organizing war industry, the female labor force was easier to discipline and less likely to strike, where striking was possible. In factories, the supervisors were usually men, while the subordinate or routine jobs on the factory floor were more likely to be taken by women. In Britain, there was strong resistance from the male workforce in some industries, notably shipbuilding, to the dilution of the workforce, and to ensure trade

Diana Murray Hill, a British woman who volunteered for war work, describes a typical day's schedule for a worker in a British war factory. It is taken from Hill's 1944 book based on her experiences, *Ladies May Now Leave Their Machines*:

7:50 a.m. Having had breakfast, set off for the bus park and get into waiting works bus.

8:15. Arrive at factory gates. Produce identity card disc at Police Checking Station and pass through into factory grounds. Enter shop, giving groan under stale yellow atmosphere, take time-card out of rack and clock-in.

8:30. At place on machine. Start up machine. If job is in progress, find job-book form from inspection-wall, fill in name and date and join queue at time-office for clocking on job. Operator then starts on job, getting setter to adjust the machine as soon as he is free, till a good enough component is produced to be placed in the queue on inspection-wall, together with respective job-book, route-card and gauges, to be passed for a First-Off [initial inspection].

The operator then gets to work, turning them out, and putting them on the wall, till, with one eye on the clock and the other up the bay, she sees the welcome approach of the tea-trolley, about 10 a.m. Here there is a ten minutes' respite from handle-turning, and the operators rush with their mugs—and often those of the [male] setters—to collect a liquid that tastes like a mixture of oil with a touch of tannin, also to eat some cake if she has brought any. She then resumes the handle-turning, with usual interruptions from inspection, and appeals to setter, till lunch-time.

At 10:30, "Music While You Work" blares forth from a loudspeaker which has to be strident enough to be heard above the noise of the machinery.

12:55 [p.m.]. Girls leave machines to get ready for lunch.

1:00–2:00. Lunch interval. Queuing up "first," outside canteen doors; inside canteen to obtain lunch tickets at shop, and then again at food-hatches, followed by a scramble for space at table.

1:55. Clock-in and make-up in the cloakroom.

2:00. Start up machine and resume work.

3:00. "Music While You Work."

4:15. Tea for girls in canteen (more queuing up).

4:30. Resume work.

7:20. Clean down machines. Clock off job. Repeat morning program in cloakroom, reversed.

7:30. Clock out and pass through checking station. Queue for bus and home by 8.[39]

unions' cooperation, guarantees had to be given that after the war, the work would again become exclusively male.[40] In the Soviet Union, the female workforce was already an accepted part of the industrialization process, but here too women were generally subjected to a tough discipline imposed by male officials who displayed little sympathy for workers who had to struggle to find food and, in many cases, look after a family. The many pressures faced by the female workforce meant higher levels of absenteeism because of illness or exhaustion, a comprehensible consequence of the wartime demands of juggling job, family, and household, but one that encouraged persistent male prejudice about the unreliability or feebleness of female labor.[41]

MOBILIZING MINORITIES

In the United States and Britain, the search for additional or substitute labor also included nonwhite minorities. The British were happy to recruit local labor in British colonial territories to service their global military commitments. Britain's African empire supplied 663,000 black laborers and soldiers, who worked chiefly in the

African and Mediterranean theaters. Military units were generally officered by whites, but there was a long tradition of black service to the Crown that could be mobilized without provoking severe racial tensions.[42] The United States also had a tradition of using nonwhite military personnel that went back to the American Revolution and the Civil War. But although 13 percent of draftees in World War I had been black, there was strong official prejudice against recruiting black men in any number for combat in World War II. President Roosevelt insisted that the army and navy mobilize black recruits, and it was agreed that their number should be at least 10 percent—the proportion of blacks in the population. But the armed forces would not alter their view that once recruited, the black servicemen would be segregated from whites as much as was feasible, and they established separate training facilities, camp amenities, and units.[43] This situation led to strange paradoxes: segregation was reintroduced into northern states that had abandoned it decades before, while the War Department thought that southern white officers would be better commanders of black units because they were more familiar with the black community. The result was to provoke occasional violent protests among black volunteers against forms of discrimination they were no longer accustomed to, and, in response, some military facilities were desegregated by 1943.[44]

Black enlisted men did ultimately reach about 10 percent of army strength, with 642,000 enlisted black men. But this disguised the fact that most black servicemen were employed in simple service and laboring roles rather than in combat. The army justified this discrimination by arguing that black recruits scored poorly on the Army General Classification Test. (By 1943, around half of black draftees failed the test, for which many of them had little educational preparation.) A small number of black army and air force units did see combat and fight with distinction, and 5,718 black men became officers, though this figure amounts to only 1.9 percent of the officer corps.

The navy, too, accepted black recruits reluctantly and allowed very few to become officers. In 1943, 71 percent of black personnel served in the stewards' branch, providing service staff for the ships' wardrooms and cookhouses, and even by 1945, only 6 percent of the navy's strength was black.[45] The extent of discrimination in the armed forces was perhaps best exemplified by the fate of black recruits into the army air forces. High-grade recruits were trained at a separate facility at Tuskegee, Alabama, not far from the white air force base at Maxwell, but few of them were allowed to fly in combat despite the fact that they exhibited all the skills that white pilots acquired. Four squadrons of fighters were eventually shipped to the Mediterranean theater in 1943 and 1944, where the pilots were constantly scrutinized by white commanders in case their performance confirmed established prejudices. Once in combat, the black pilots were able to demonstrate their capability, but that did not end the criticism from senior white airmen that a black pilot was not the equal of a white one. In reality, the black airmen in Italy proved just as effective as the white aircrews, whether escorting the bombing raids against northern Italy and Austria, or in dogfights with the limited number of Luftwaffe fighters left in the theater. The Tuskegee Airmen came to symbolize the limits of military integration in the face of persistent white prejudice. On their return to New York at the end of the war, they had to disembark down a gangplank for blacks while their white companions went down the one reserved for whites only.[46]

Ironically, despite their being perceived as potential fifth-columnists and despite the forced internment of 120,000 U.S. citizens and residents of Japanese descent into displacement camps in 1942, Japanese Americans made an important contribution to the U.S. war effort. Some 22,500 of them volunteered for military service, and 18,000 were recruited into segregated military units, some of which saw combat and won extensive praise for valor.[47] Indeed, the 100th Battalion, 442nd Regimental Combat Team, composed entirely of Japanese Americans, was and remains the most decorated unit in U.S. military history.

The mobilization of minorities in the face of labor shortages also took much more coercive and violent forms. In mainland Japan, 320,000 Korean and Chinese laborers were forced to work in industry and construction, while throughout the Japanese Empire, thousands of young girls were forced into prostitution as "comfort women" for Japanese soldiers.[48] In Germany, where there were real limits to mobilization by 1941, the decision was made to exploit the labor resources of occupied Europe and the large prisoner-of-war intake, Polish, French, and Soviet. In March 1942 a Nazi Party leader, Fritz Sauckel, was made plenipotentiary for labor supply, and tasked to find additional resources outside Germany. Backed by German armed forces and the Gestapo, he rounded up millions of Europeans in periodic sweeps and transported them to the

▲ AMERICAN MILITARY POLICE SERGEANT IN COLUMBUS, GEORGIA

The United States armed forces were segregated throughout World War II. The military reintroduced segregation into northern and western states.

Spencer Moore was a junior officer in the 92nd Infantry Division, the only African American infantry division committed to combat in World War II. It fought in Italy from September 1944 to May 1945. In November 1944 he wrote to his parents about the conditions the 92nd faced on the fighting front:

Dear Mom and Pop,

The Jerry artillery and firing keeps you very jumpy and you are not so at ease of mind. Five officers (Colored) have been killed in action so far. Two were my classmates at OCS. Has the 92nd published any casualty lists in the colored papers? We are all getting a raw deal. We have been in the line 82 days and we don't know when we are going to get relieved. We thought the election [Roosevelt's fourth term election] would change it but it hasn't. The men are lousy, sick, frost-bitten, shell-shocked, and scared. It's good Jerry doesn't know the condition of some of us or we would be in a lot hotter water. I wish some of the colored papers could get a hold of this and ask the War Department when we are going to get relieved. It looks as if they want to annihilate the all colored 92nd. The all means all colored on the line and a few on the staffs. I don't know what the papers are saying but it's really tough. A couple of the colored officers have been or are up for courts-martial because they refuse to lead troops into death traps. I just wish some of us here could get back and tell what we know. I guess they are all afraid if some of us get turned loose there will be too many "mulattos" in the world. I am really disgusted with the whole setup. It looks as if they don't even expect to give us a break. We can look right out of the hole and see Jerry parading around on the skyline and it takes half of the day to get artillery on it, because we have to conserve ammunition and yet Jerry shells the hell out of us. It's no joke to see men you have known, lived with, eaten with, and slept with blown up or shot down before your eyes. The majority of the men are too tired to fight. Well, Mom, I've blown off enough steam for now. The NAACP should know this situation. Jerry is beginning to shell again so I'll sign off for now.

Your loving son, Spencer[49]

Reich, where they were compelled to work in German industry and agriculture.[50] This program of forced labor was the only way that Germany could continue to expand its war production, and it laid the heaviest sacrifices of total war—longer hours of work, poor working conditions, limited health care—upon the backs of non-Germans. Germany also began to rely upon labor from the concentration camps (including the notorious labor facility at Auschwitz), which housed a prisoner population of 714,000 by January 1945. Conditions for camp prisoners were considerably worse than for other foreign laborers, designed in many cases so that prisoners would be worked to death.[51] There is no certainty about the aggregate number of laborers and prisoners of war who worked for the German war effort. The global figure by the peak, in 1944, was almost 9 million, but the mortality rate was high for all categories of forced or camp labor, resulting in an estimated 2.5 million deaths. The global addition to the German labor pool may have been as high as 13.5 million over the whole war period.[52]

In most respects, the forced labor regime was self-defeating, since it imposed atrocious conditions on the recruits, reducing their capacity to work effectively. Workers died regularly and had to be replaced, while poor diet and minimum health care meant

TUSKEGEE AIRMEN ▶

The government was proud enough of the African American aviators of the 332nd Fighter Group and the 447th Bombardment Group (which trained at an airfield near Tuskegee, Alabama) to enlist their images for use in wartime propaganda, even though the military remained segregated until after the war. The 332nd was commanded by Lieutenant Colonel Benjamin O. Davis Jr.—who in 1936 had been the first black cadet to graduate from West Point since 1889.

M1 Helmet

The M1 helmet was a significant improvement over the old trench helmet. Made from a single piece of Hadfield manganese steel, it originally had a liner designed to emulate football helmets of the era. That fiber-and-rayon shell proved too flimsy in the field and was replaced with a molded resin liner. A leather-and-cloth adjustable headband clipped to the internal suspension webbing.

Pistol

Private soldiers were not usually issued pistols, but often acquired them by one means or another.

Browning Automatic Rifle

The .30 caliber Browing Automatic Rifle, or BAR, was used in small numbers late in the First World War. During WWII, it provided American infantry squads with an automatic weapon capable of laying down a base of fire to cover advances by the riflemen. Its primary weakness was its use of twenty-round box magazines, which limited the volume of fire available to the squad. The Germans' use of the MG34 and later MG42 belt-fed machine gun as their standard squad automatic weapon gave German infantry a significant advantage in firepower over their American adversaries.

BAR Ammunition Belt

Despite a rate of fire that was low for an automatic weapon, the BAR consumed ammunition voraciously. The BAR man's ammunition belt had six pouches holding twelve box magazines, but 240 rounds was not enough. An assistant gunner carried additional magazines to sustain the squad's capacity to deliver automatic fire.

We French workers warn you... defeat means slavery, starvation, death

that productivity was always consistently lower than that of German workers. Foreign laborers were not allowed to use air-raid shelters when the heavy bombing started, unless there was room once Germans had taken their places, and as a result suffered heavy casualties from air raids. The German labor system was a combination of expediency and irrationality. By October 1944, some 37 percent of employment in German war industry was non-German, and a high proportion of the laborers were women from enemy nations, chiefly Poland and the Soviet Union. The forced workers and camp prisoners were parceled out into smaller subcamps, and then divided up further to supply the needs of local industrialists, who sent in their demands for labor quotas to the central authorities. The exception was agricultural labor, which was sent to work on farms singly or in small groups, and had to be disciplined by the local farmers. By

▲ "WE FRENCH WORKERS WARN YOU"

The French fared much better under German occupation than did the populations of Slavic countries conquered by the Nazis—but even under the "independent" Vichy regime, French citizens were subjected to compulsory labor requirements to support the German war effort, and suffered from hunger and repression. This poster was intended to remind an American audience that the sacrifices of war were outweighed by the potential consequences of defeat.

◀ U.S. INFANTRYMAN WITH BROWNING AUTOMATIC RIFLE

The soldier depicted here is a Nisei (second-generation Japanese American) of the 442nd Regimental Combat Team. After Pearl Harbor, worried about sabotage and espionage, the U.S. government ordered more than 120,000 American citizens and residents of Japanese descent moved out of the West Coast to internment camps in the interior. Nonetheless, overruling the recommendation of a War Department board, President Roosevelt in 1943 authorized the formation of a Nisei unit commanded by white officers. The 442nd RCT fought in Italy, France, and Germany. Its soldiers earned almost ten thousand Purple Hearts and twenty-one Medals of Honor, and won General George C. Marshall's praise for their "tremendous fighting spirit."

1945, the compulsory labor system extended throughout the German Reich, the only way in which the German war effort could be sustained for as long as it was.

The fate of European Jews differed from the rest of the program of forced migration and labor. Instead of using Jewish labor as fully as possible, the Nazis shipped millions to extermination camps and killed them. Only 20 percent of Jewish prisoners, those deemed most fit for labor, were spared execution—though in many cases, they were then worked to death. A network of workshops or building sites was set up around the camps to make use of the surviving Jews for as long as they could still work despite meals of thin soup, tattered prison clothing, and the sadistic discipline that marked life in the camps.[53] Even here, in the inhuman conditions of the genocide of the Jews, the German authorities tried to extract a quota of labor to feed their war machine while completing their program of mass murder.

▲ **GERMAN FACTORY**

Large factories such as this one, photographed in 1940, allowed for efficient production of tanks. Later in the war, under Allied strategic bombing, the Germans had to shift toward more decentralized production facilities—but managed to increase total output despite that handicap.

◄ **"I WORK IN GERMANY . . . FOR FRANCE"**

The Germans required large numbers of French workers for the German armaments industry. Initially the Vichy government tried to recruit volunteers, appealing to patriotism and emphasizing that the Nazis would release French POWs in exchange for willing workers. When this failed, compulsory labor laws sent hundreds of thousands of Frenchmen to work camps in Germany.

▲ **Working for the Wehrmacht**

This fourteen-year-old Ukrainian boy was shipped to Berlin to undertake compulsory labor for the German armed forces.

Most people are familiar with the names of a few Nazi concentration camps, such as Auschwitz and Buchenwald. Few realize how many camps there were or how widespread throughout Germany they were.

GUNS OR BUTTER?

The purpose of large-scale domestic mobilization was to supply the goods needed to wage war, in sufficient quantities and of sufficient quality, to secure ultimate victory. This aim posed two questions: How could military output be organized efficiently? And how could the domestic population cope with the reduction of consumer production that would inevitably accompany the expansion of the military economy? The answer to these questions varied a good deal from one country to another, but, more often than not, it boiled down to a choice between military and consumer production: the question of "Guns or butter?"

Nowhere was this trade-off felt more heavily than in the Soviet Union. After the initial German invasion, with steel production reduced by half, coal production cut by more than half, and the industrial labor force down by 35 percent, the only course left

PRISON CAMPS ▲

The Germans used the inmates of their notorious concentration camps to supplement wartime production. These women are returning to Auschwitz after a day working in the arms factory outside the camp.

for the rump Soviet economy, now based on the industrial areas of the central Urals region, was to focus all production on guns, to the virtual exclusion of butter.[54] Output in the civilian industrial sector (which, in fact, included many goods destined for the army) fell by 1943 to only 46 percent of what it had been in 1937, itself a low level.[55] The restructuring of the economy, carried out by the state planning agency Gosplan under the young economist Nikolai Voznesensky, left only the slenderest of margins for civilian consumption. Living standards, already comparatively low, shrank to the lowest level compatible with sustaining the labor force's ability and willingness to carry on working. To supplement food supply, Soviet factories established millions of small allotments on which workers and their families could grow food (chiefly potatoes); factories were allowed to distribute one or two hot meals a day, so that work also promised survival. For those who did not or could not work—the disabled, the elderly, the very young—there were no rationed supplies, and an unknown number perished during the war from hunger, cold, and disease.[56] This was a directly coercive system in which work was the key to survival, and those who shirked or stole from the state factory or collective farm would be sent to the gulag labor camps, where prisoners also worked on war orders.[57] The overall result of the Soviet war effort was a remarkable revival of military output following the disaster of 1941. Between 1942 and 1945, the Soviet Union exceeded German production of almost all major classes of army weapons and aircraft, despite possessing an economy only a fraction of the size of the German New Order.

SLAVE LABOR

Paul Steinberg, a Jewish prisoner in the Auschwitz concentration camp in 1944–45, describes work in the vast I. G. Farben chemical complex built there during the war, where he and thousands of other camp prisoners were made to work for the German war effort:

I. G. Farben pays the SS a daily flat rate per slave laborer. Under the direction of an Austrian conductor, the band accompanies the departing procession of *Kommandos* [work details].

We walk toward Buna (the factory for making synthetic rubber) in ranks of five, dragging our clogs in the mud or snow, carrying our bowls for the noon soup clamped under our arms. It's raining. An icy rain with gusts of wind that have the run of this flat, dreary plain in Silesia. The *Kommando* is one of the benign sort. Cleaning, readying materials for heavy labor, stacking bricks at the very worst. It's still too much.

After ten o'clock you have to husband your energy every minute. A moment lingering near a brazier. A trip to the latrines, which doesn't need to be faked: almost all of us are suffering from larval dysentery. The *Kapo* [a prisoner charged with supervising other prisoners] usually turns a blind eye. Every now and then the arrival of a *Meister*— a German foreman—or even an SS officer provokes a spasm

of feverish activity, urged on by the theatrical shouts of the *Kapo*.

When the bad moment has passed we catch our breath. Brief pause at noon, when the siren blows.

The German and Polish workers and foremen, the volunteer workers, the prisoners of war, the forced laborers— the whole scurrying mass collected from the four points of the compass to feed the German war machine—now gets out its lunch . . . Back to work: we still have three and a half hours to go. Two hundred and ten minutes that crawl by slowly, so slowly. The blessed days when we work indoors are vacations we enjoy to the fullest. Other times, you have to try getting a turn at slipping into the tool shed, where the *Kapo* takes shelter.

Darkness falls early around four o'clock. The cold becomes more gripping, especially since hunger and fatigue are taking their toll. At last the signal for *Feierabend*, time to knock off work. The factory empties out, the *Kommandos* form up and begin the walk back. The prospect of hot soup and sleep, after the trial of the evening roll call, gives even the weakest among us some strength.[58]

The Soviet Union was also helped greatly by aid from the United States. Roosevelt extended aid in the summer of 1941, and the Soviet Union received a total of $10.7 billion of aid—convoyed to the Arctic at Murmansk, or across the Pacific to Vladivostok, or through the southern highway route from Persia (Iran). As the Soviet economy focused on military production, the U.S. aid provided large quantities of other supplies, largely food. Industrial goods and food amounted to 55 percent of aid in 1944 and 60 percent in 1945, easing the domestic food production crises that followed the German seizure of the Ukraine. Railroad equipment, trucks, field telephones, phone wire, and radios also proved immensely helpful.[59] American supplies were vital to the Soviet war effort, though Soviet leaders were seldom grateful and proved to be tough negotiators. The standard Soviet line after the war was that America's Lend-Lease aid did not matter much. But since the fall of Communism, new evidence has emerged to show that Stalin really did understand its significance, saying at one point that without Western aid, the Soviet Union "could not have continued the war."[60]

Of all the combatant nations, only the United States proved able to provide both guns *and* butter in plenty for the war effort.[61] The American experience resulted from what might be called the economics of superabundance. It made little difference how

ПОД ЗНАМЕНЕМ ЛЕНИНА
— ВПЕРЕД К ПОБЕДЕ!

▲ "Under the Flag of Lenin, March to Victory" (1941)

Especially early in the war, Soviet propaganda appealed to Marxist ideological principles. Here the war against Germany is presented as a struggle to preserve the fruits of the Bolsheviks' October Revolution of 1917.

◀ "Everything for the Front!"

The existential threat posed by Germany pushed the Soviet Union to emphasize wartime production over food, declaring that everything was needed for the front lines.

LEND-LEASE FOOD FOR THE ▲
SOVIET UNION, CINCINNATI
Preparing canned pork for Lend-Lease shipment to the U.S.S.R. at the Kroger grocery and baking company. While the tanks, trucks, and planes the United States sent to the Soviets garnered more attention, the food and raw materials allowed more Soviets to carry arms in the fight against the Nazis.

efficiently the war economy was managed because there were ample supplies of raw materials, food, capital goods, and labor not only for the needs of the home population and the U.S. armed forces, but also to provide generous quantities of supply for America's allies. The Roosevelt government did not institute a rigid system of state control but instead relied on a number of federal agencies—most important of which was the War Production Board established under the Sears Roebuck director, Donald Nelson—which supervised and controlled the distribution of key resources and tried to reduce waste or inefficiency in the system.[62] There were examples of poorly planned production, duplication of effort, and misallocation of resources, but these did little to dent the entrepreneurial enthusiasm exhibited by American industry when invited to fulfill contracts. Traditions of mass production, effective management training, and a considerable depth of technical proficiency were ideal for the transition to large-scale war production. So effective did these qualities prove that by 1943, the Ford Motor Company alone was producing more military equipment than Italy. By the middle of the war, the United States was producing more war goods than the rest of the world put together.[63] The remarkable upsurge of economic activity meant that America's

GNP expanded by 87 percent between 1938 and 1945, almost doubling aggregate output and exceeding the growth performance of any other war economy.

The United States' immense economic resources made it possible for the country to supply substantial quantities of military equipment, food, and materials to the other Allied states even while building up and supplying its own armed forces. The roots of America's vast program of assistance lay in the initial requests for military equipment from Britain and France in 1939–40.[64] By the winter of 1940–41, Britain was effectively bankrupt, having liquidated most overseas assets in an effort to purchase American supplies.[65] Roosevelt was initially limited by Congress in what he could offer, but in early 1941 he formulated the idea of leasing or lending the supplies on extended credit. "Lease-Lend" (the scheme soon came to be called "Lend-Lease") was passed into law in March 1941, and thereafter a strong flow of goods crossed the Atlantic. Britain was the principal beneficiary, taking over the war $30 billion of goods, 64 percent of it military equipment and 12 percent of it food. Without this aid, Britain, itself struggling with the guns-or-butter dilemma, would have had to impose much stricter limits on consumption for the home population. Instead, consumer spending fell by only 13 percent during the war, while some goods remained nonrationed. In return, the British Empire supplied America with $7.5 billion of reciprocal aid, most of it in the form of base facilities, depots, and services.[66]

The idea that guns should be preferred to butter originated in a speech made in the 1930s by Hermann Göring, head of the German Luftwaffe, who proclaimed that "guns will make us powerful; butter will only make us fat." Nevertheless, the German economic mobilization during World War II has presented historians with a number of paradoxes. At the end of the war, the United States Strategic Bombing Survey unearthed statistical evidence about consumer production in Germany that seemed to suggest that Germany had enjoyed what came to be called a "peace economy in wartime"; not until 1943 or 1944, so the Survey team argued, did Germany convert its economy to total war and cut back on civilian living standards.[67] This argument was used to explain how the German war economy reached its peak military output in September 1944, even after two years of intensive bombing had already destroyed much of the urban landscape.[68] This view of the German economy has been undermined from several perspectives. Using more reliable statistical evidence, historians have discovered that a high proportion of German resources and labor were diverted to war production from the first months of the war, and that by 1941, there was a growing crisis in the war economy as spare resources were used up. Far from a "peace economy in wartime," the result was a stringent rationing system imposed in 1939 for all categories of civilian goods and food, the shutdown of much nonessential production, and a lengthened working week. As goods disappeared, the state increased taxation and introduced a system of voluntary saving to help siphon away the potential consumer demand. By 1942, per capita consumption had already fallen by 25 percent, and was cut further as the war went on.[69]

Germany seemed to have addressed its guns-or-butter question firmly in favor of guns even before the war. But if the German economy had already been restructured for a large-scale war effort, why did military production remain surprisingly low in

HENRY J. KAISER
May 9, 1882–August 24, 1967

The businessman Henry J. Kaiser typified the ambitious twentieth-century American entrepreneur who carved out an industrial empire from his own efforts. He became famous in World War II for starting up shipyards from scratch and mass-producing vital cargo vessels and escort carriers for the American war effort. A second-generation German American who had dropped out of school in eighth grade, Kaiser founded his first construction company in 1914. His success brought him a share in the construction of the Hoover Dam. When the Second World War broke out, he followed his business philosophy of "find a need and fill it"; although he had never built a ship, he established an immense new shipyard in Richmond, California. Kaiser Shipyard won the order to produce a standard cargo vessel, nicknamed the Liberty Ship.

Kaiser management set out to design a production line for ships much like that for automobiles. A mile-long assembly line stretched back from the coast, and here prefabricated sections of the ships were brought and welded together. The decks and bulkheads were added to the keel as it moved along a continuous construction line, with each ship finally arriving at the coast for launching. At the start of the program, each ship took 1.4 million man-hours and 355 days to build; by 1943, the figures were 500,000 man-hours and an average of 41 days per ship. In 1942 a demonstration was made to see how fast a ship could be built. The *Robert E. Peary* was completed in just four days. Other shipyards adopted Kaiser's methods, and productivity in the shipbuilding industry increased by 25 percent each year. In 1945 Kaiser moved into automobile manufacture, taking over Ford's no-longer-necessary Willow Run airplane plant near Ypsilanti, Michigan, which in 1944 had an output of one bomber every sixty-three minutes. Rationalization and scientific management were major assets for the American war effort and help to explain the remarkable American production performance during the war.

the early years of the war, as the Bombing Survey discovered in 1945? With access to not only domestic resources but also the resources of all the occupied areas in Europe, why wasn't Germany's war production booming? The principal answer lies in the failure of the dictatorship to establish a clear political and administrative structure for the war economy. Since the German economy was in effect a command economy, the absence of a central committee or office for issuing commands fostered widespread confusion. In the absence of firm direction and with limited opportunities for high profits, industrialists pursued their own interests as best they could—hoarding stocks, retaining labor, overcharging for their products. Meanwhile, the military leadership insisted that the tactical demands of the front should take priority in all questions of production, so that instead of large-scale mass production, assembly lines were constantly interrupted to introduce new technical features or modifications of design.

This prevented Germany from reaping the full benefits of the large investment programs in military industry, engineering, and raw materials production that had been undertaken during the 1930s and early 1940s, and reduced the possibility of rationalized mass production characteristic of Soviet or American factories. Instead, the demand for military innovation and tactical improvements overrode the demand for

A TOTAL EFFORT ▶

Government officials attempted to maximize war production by minimizing waste in all other parts of the economy. Free labor, motivated by patriotism, proved far more productive than the unwilling workers who filled many German factories.

When you ride ALONE you ride with Hitler!

Join a Car-Sharing Club TODAY!

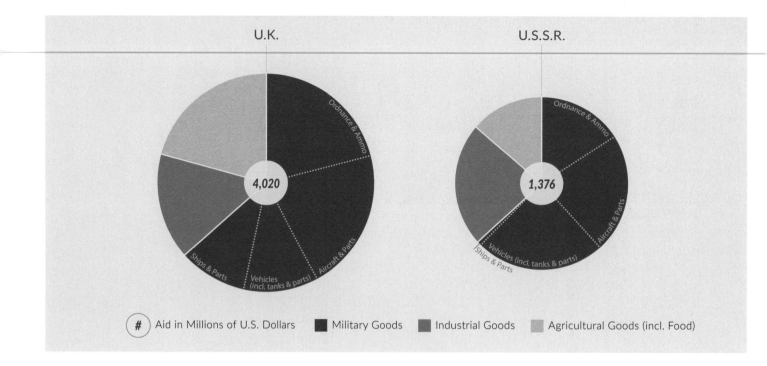

U.K.

U.S.S.R.

4,020

1,376

Ordnance & Ammo

Aircraft & Parts

Vehicles (incl. tanks & parts)

Ships & Parts

Aid in Millions of U.S. Dollars   ■ Military Goods   ■ Industrial Goods   ■ Agricultural Goods (incl. Food)

U.S. LEND-LEASE AID TO ▲
THE BRITISH COMMONWEALTH
AND TO THE U.S.S.R.

large numbers of weapons, resulting in a wide variety of different models of aircraft, armored vehicles, and guns that were inefficiently produced because they were built in small batches. As battlefield losses rose rapidly in 1941–42, equipment and weaponry proved difficult to replace. Following demands from Hitler, expressed in a decree on industrial rationalization in December 1941, greater efforts to streamline production were made by Albert Speer, minister for armaments and munitions from February 1942 until the end of the war, but also by other officials, including the secretary of the Air Ministry, Erhard Milch, who played an important role in reducing waste and duplication in aircraft production. This was, as historian Adam Tooze has argued, not so much a production miracle as the final realization of what had up until now been a large but inefficiently mobilized war potential.[70]

This also explains the second paradox about German production reaching its peak in 1944, when bombing was at its most destructive. The reforms and centralization of planning begun in late 1941—coupled with the willingness to exploit non-German labor with ever-greater ruthlessness, and an intelligent program of industrial dispersal to cope with the bombing threat—allowed Germany to reach its available optimum production by 1944.[71] Even then, much more might have been produced given the resource base available and the expansion of synthetic and substitute production had it not been for the shift in American bombing strategy in 1944 to focus on oil, transport, and chemicals as decisive targets (a topic that will be discussed in the next volume). Unlike the Soviet Union, where severe shortages necessitated rigorous economic

MORE FROM LESS ▶

For every tank or plane Germany produced in 1942, it drew on a national resource base of 655 industrial or foreign workers and 1,161 tons of steel production. For the Soviet Union, which both devoted more of its resources to war production and used them far more efficiently, the figures were 162 workers and 145 tons of steel. American factories too were much more efficient than German or Japanese ones.

Output Compared to Economic Base

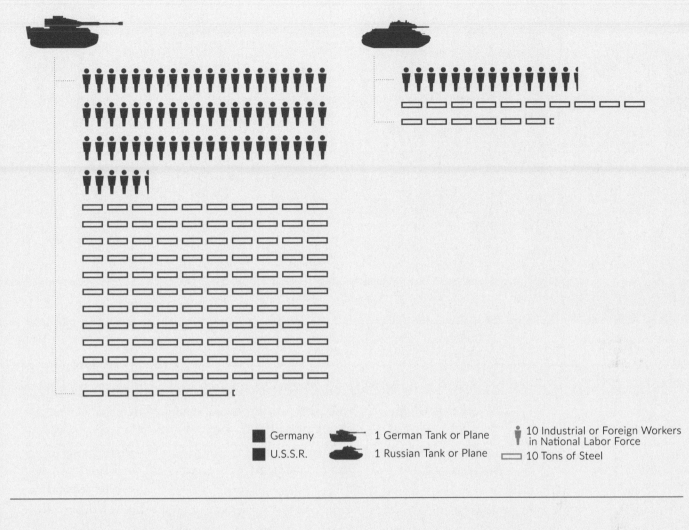

■ Germany	[tank] 1 German Tank or Plane	[person] 10 Industrial or Foreign Workers in National Labor Force
■ U.S.S.R.	[tank] 1 Russian Tank or Plane	[bar] 10 Tons of Steel

Output of Aircraft in Pounds per Man-Day

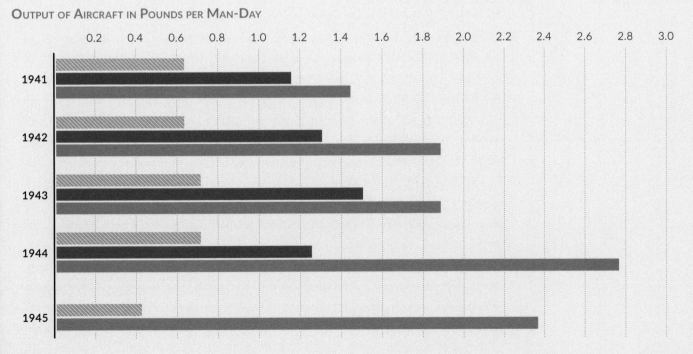

■ Germany	▨ Japan ■ U.S.

Albert Speer was the leading National Socialist architect during Hitler's Third Reich (1933 to 1945). He was appointed minister for armaments and war production in 1942 and played a key role in sustaining German war production during the last three years of World War II.

Speer trained as an architect in the 1920s but found it difficult during the economic recession of 1929–32 to find work. After hearing a Hitler speech, he decided to join the NSDAP in March 1931 and worked on Party commissions. Hitler authorized him to design the new Reich Chancellery building in Berlin, which opened early in 1939. When Fritz Todt, the first minister for armaments and munitions, died in a plane crash, Hitler appointed Speer to head a Ministry of Armaments and War Production. Speer continued a number of reforms already begun under Todt, the most important of which was the centralization of war production under a system of main committees, one for each major class of weapon. In March 1942 Speer also introduced a central planning organization to oversee the distribution of key materials. Under his direction, the German war economy tripled the output of military equipment between 1941 and 1944, despite the onset of heavy Allied bombing. He found that it was possible to expand production with a coordinated dispersal program and the unscrupulous use of slave and forced labor. Speer was captured at the end of the war and put on trial at Nuremberg. He was found guilty of exploiting forced labor but was sentenced to twenty years in jail rather than execution. He wrote the best-selling *Inside the Third Reich* when he emerged from prison in 1966.

discipline and tight centralization, the technical strength of German industry and the wide availability of conquered resources created an unwarranted confidence that German production would match strategic requirements. Balancing economic performance and military strategy was a difficult judgment to make for every fighting power, but in Germany, the balancing act was a relative failure.

CONCLUSION

In total war, states strive to extract as much as possible from the economy to serve the war effort, limited only by the amount of resources available, the capacity of the civilian population to accept tougher working conditions and reduced living standards, and the need to strike a balance between military mobilization and economic production. In this sense, simply possessing an abundance of resources did not guarantee that they would be utilized fully or efficiently for the war effort. The organization of production, propaganda directed at the home front, deliberate damage (such as bombing) to the enemy economy, and the extent and nature of military intervention in the running of the war economy all played parts in determining the eventual success or failure of mobilization. These are all factors that help explain the wide differences visible in the major war powers' economic performance and mobilization.

The civilian population's willingness to put up with the demands of war production, or to accept high levels of casualties, was only indirectly related to the military success of national forces. In the Soviet Union in 1941–42, facing the threat of defeat, the regime mobilized the population for supreme efforts against the Fascist invader through a mixture of coercion and patriotic propaganda; in Germany in 1944–45, even though

defeat seemed inevitable, the regime coerced and cajoled the labor force (including the millions of compulsory workers) and the armed forces to continue the fight to the bitter end.[72] Mobilization in both these cases was not only an organizational question but also a question of morale. Although dissenters and protesters were shot or imprisoned, and there existed no public space for the population to discuss or argue, or even strike, both populations displayed a stoical and fatalistic patriotism in the face of the threat of national extinction, which was vividly presented in German and Soviet propaganda.

In contrast, mobilization in the United States and the British Commonwealth produced fewer sacrifices, and a strong sense of moral commitment to a progressive cause, which, by 1943, thanks to American economic power, seemed likely to result in an Allied victory. Neither state was occupied; the United States was not attacked by bombers, while Britain was bombed heavily only during the winter of 1940–41, with little long-term economic effect. Strikes and limited protest occurred; strategy could be discussed and criticized; demands for greater racial integration or gender equality

▲ NAZI RALLY IN BERLIN, FEBRUARY 1943

"Total War Is the Shortest War," proclaims the giant banner in the background. The message was simple: harder work and more sacrifice would bring quicker victory and allow soldiers to return to their families sooner.

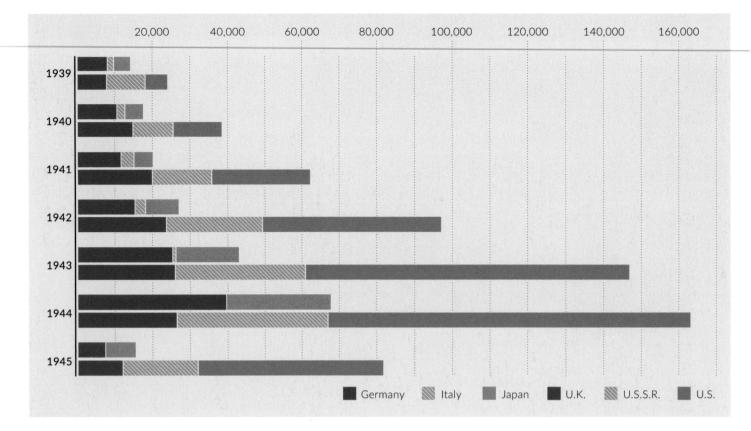

▲ PRODUCTION OF AIRCRAFT

▼ PRODUCTION OF AIRCRAFT CARRIERS (ALL TYPES)

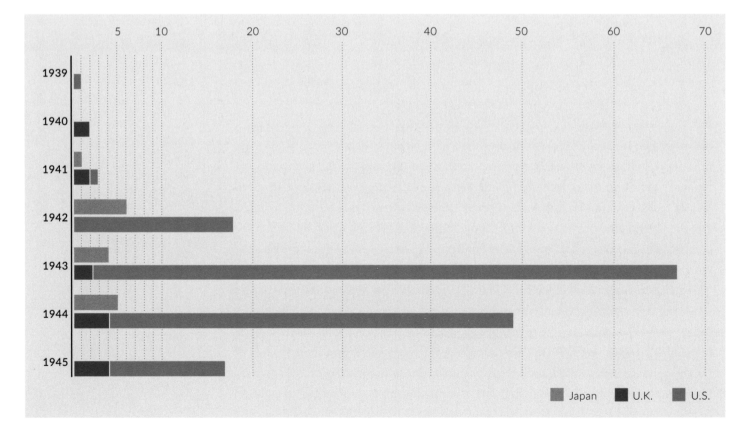

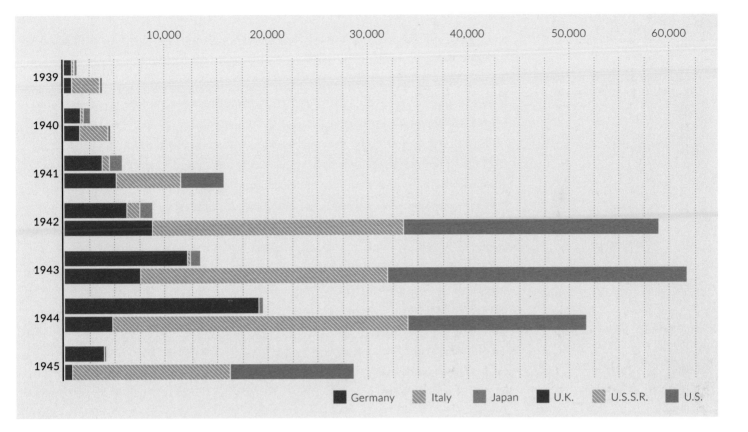

▲ PRODUCTION OF TANKS AND SELF-PROPELLED GUNS

▼ PRODUCTION OF MILITARY TRUCKS

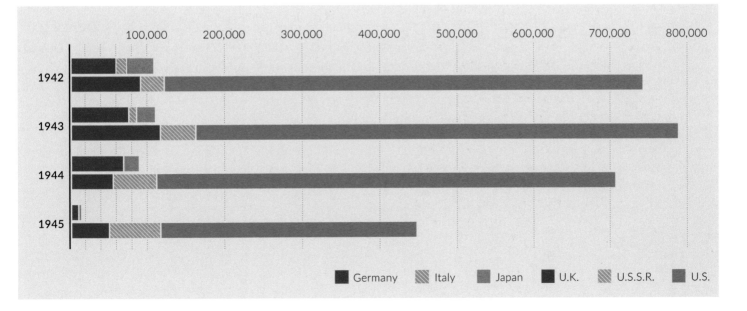

were made and debated. Moreover, both Western powers, and the other Allied states, benefited from agreements to share economic resources and to keep open trade and supply routes to all the powers fighting the Axis enemy—including China, where efforts to supply Chinese forces by an airlift operation over the Himalayan "Hump" helped to keep alive Chinese resistance to the Japanese invasion. The logistical and trading effort, supported by the two largest navies in the world, gave the Allies a flexibility that the Axis states lacked. There was little collaboration among Germany, Italy, and Japan. Italian requests for raw materials and machinery from Germany were met only partway due to a creeping sense of distrust between the two Axis partners. German officials thought they could make better use of them—not an entirely unreasonable belief given the poor record of the Italian war effort.[73]

This chapter has also shown that there were major differences in the level and nature of military mobilization among all the combatant powers. The large numbers of potential recruits in the Soviet Union, for example, meant little if they could not be trained effectively because they lacked basic educational skills. The immense losses experienced by the Soviet Army owed something to poor levels of training and technical competence. High casualty rates on the Eastern Front also meant that experienced or more highly trained men were lost first, leaving the new echelons more open to further heavy losses, as had happened in World War I, and forcing the Soviet authorities to mobilize a higher and higher proportion of the male population. The potential manpower crisis was solved only by increasing the output of weapons to a level that could swamp the enemy. On the other hand, the more modest levels of mobilization in Britain and the United States reflected a desire to focus on strategies where manpower could be optimized by insisting on high standards of training and allocating men (and women) to military roles for which they were best equipped. This was done to try to reduce losses and to maximize the efficiency of Western forces at the battlefront, and it contributes to the explanation of why casualty rates were so much lower in the West than elsewhere. The German case lies somewhere between these two extremes. German servicemen were generally highly trained and technically competent, but the sheer scale of the war that Germany tried to fight resulted in high levels of attrition of skilled military manpower and ever more extreme mobilization policies. These differences in national mobilization, both for the armed forces and for the economy, play a central part in explaining how the Allied side eventually triumphed over the Axis in World War II.

▲ "United We Are Strong"

The combined industrial strength of the Allies was vastly greater than that of the Axis nations. But as the poster suggests, Allied success owed as much to effective coordination as to raw strength.

Im Namen
des
Deutschen Volkes
verleihe ich

Gisela

geb.

Königsberg (Pr)

die dritte Stufe
des
Ehrenkreuzes
der Deutschen Mutter

Berlin, den 1. Oktober 1939

Der Führer

▲ "THE CROSS OF HONOR OF THE GERMAN MOTHER"

Hitler created this medal to encourage German women to have more Aryan babies. The Gold Cross went to morally "worthy" women who bore eight or more "genetically fit" children. Recipients were given social privileges similar to those traditionally reserved for injured war veterans.

Nothing in all of human history equaled the tide of Axis conquests in the first three years of World War II.

The shockingly rapid defeat and occupation of Poland in 1939 set the pattern for what followed. Fast-moving, seemingly unbeatable offensives by Hitler's Wehrmacht knocked out Denmark and Norway in a matter of days. In a lightning five-week campaign, Germany not only seized the Netherlands and Belgium but also completely defeated the powerful French Army, compelled the surrender of the French government, and swept the British Expeditionary Force into the sea. In a single stroke, the Wehrmacht achieved the objectives that four years of unrelenting struggle had failed to accomplish from 1914 through 1918.

German arms reversed Italian setbacks in the Mediterranean, occupying Yugoslavia, Greece, and Crete, recovering Libya from the British, and threatening Egypt and the vital Suez Canal. The Wehrmacht then smashed into Russia, destroying the frontline Soviet armies along the border. In short order, it advanced all the way to the gates of Leningrad and Moscow, occupying Latvia, Lithuania, Byelorussia, Moldova, and much of the Ukraine. Hitler crowed on October 3, 1941, "Behind our troops [in Russia] . . . there already lies . . . a territory twice the size of the German Reich when I came to power in 1933."[1] With Romania, Hungary, Bulgaria, and (de facto) Finland having joined the Axis, and Spain and Sweden remaining in cooperative neutrality, by late 1941, Hitler had established domination over Europe that surpassed even that of Charlemagne in the ninth century or Napoleon in the nineteenth.

True, by that time, the German surge had seemingly reached a crest. Britain remained out of reach in the West; Rommel had been thrust back onto the defensive in North Africa; and now on the Eastern Front, it had become clear that the Soviets were a much tougher enemy than Hitler had expected. Moscow and Leningrad remained in Soviet hands, and it was now becoming clear that Hitler's objective of forcing the Soviet Union out of the war before the end of 1941 would not be met. Still, the Führer remained confident that he would win the war in Russia soon enough. The Wehrmacht's hammer blows had cost the Red Army four million men, eight thousand aircraft, and seventeen thousand tanks; how could any state, much less the "rotten structure" that Stalin's regime had imposed on a restive population, survive such losses for long?[2] Winter was the Russians' friend, and the German troops needed some time to regroup, refit, and ready themselves for a renewed push in the spring. But a pause in Hitler's drive to conquer "living space" in the East for the German people was not a defeat. Victory delayed would still be victory.

Neither was Hitler much worried about Britain. Yes, the RAF had succeeded in blocking his planned invasion of England, and the Blitz had failed to break the British will to fight on. Planes flying from England were now bringing the air war to the Reich, dropping some thirty-five thousand tons of bombs on Germany in 1941.[3] But no matter: the damage they did was small, and German air defenses had improved to the point where they were inflicting horrific losses on Bomber Command's aircraft and crews. Besides, the Luftwaffe was still, for the moment, having to fight a two-front war. Once the Bolshevik state finally collapsed and the Reich could turn its full might—backed by the resources of all Europe, from the Atlantic to the Urals—against

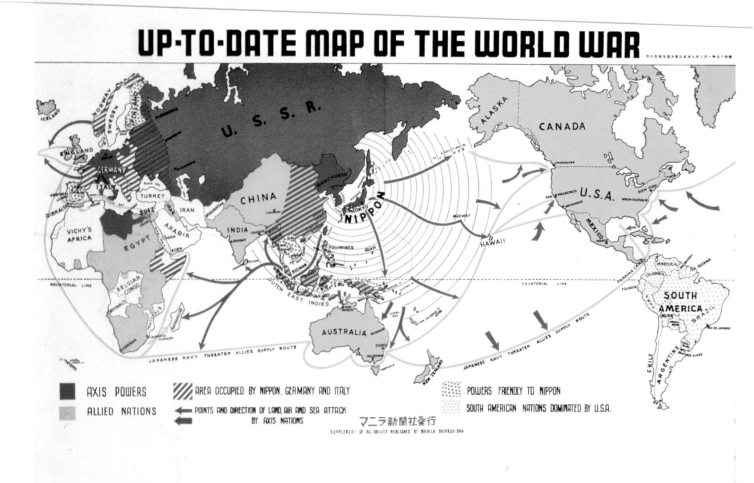

UP-TO-DATE MAP OF THE WORLD WAR

AXIS POWERS

ALLIED NATIONS

AREA OCCUPIED BY NIPPON, GERMANY AND ITALY

POINTS AND DIRECTION OF LAND, AIR AND SEA ATTACK BY AXIS NATIONS

POWERS FRIENDLY TO NIPPON

SOUTH AMERICAN NATIONS DOMINATED BY U.S.A.

マニラ新聞社發行

SUPPLEMENT OF ALL DAILIES PUBLISHED BY MANILA SHIMBUN-SHA

JAPANESE PROPAGANDA MAP ▲

Printed in Manila by the Japanese in January 1942, this poster was intended to persuade Filipinos that the Axis was poised to win the Second World War. It somewhat exaggerates the extent of the Japanese conquests in China and even more so the Japanese naval operations in the Indian Ocean and eastern Pacific—but the overall visual impression it gives of the rising tide of Axis conquests is not far from the truth.

the British, they would see reason and make peace. If not, the growing number of U-boats prowling the Atlantic would cut off Britain from its empire and starve its people into submission.

Hitler was not worried about Britain or the Soviet Union—not on their own. What troubled him was America. Even though the United States still maintained its neutrality, the possibility of American entry into the war was what gave the British hope and kept them fighting. Hitler understood that U-boats sinking American ships had helped bring the United States into World War I, and from the beginning of the war in September 1939, he had ordered his naval commanders to avoid provoking the Americans. But his admirals were constantly pressing him for more freedom to attack U.S.-flagged vessels. They told him that it was impossible to fight an effective torpedo war if they had to check the nationality of targeted ships before shooting. The commander of the submarine fleet, Admiral Karl Dönitz, believed that if his U-boats were given free rein they could starve Britain of food and vital raw materials and win the battle of the Atlantic before the United States could mobilize sufficiently to stop them. In that case, the Americans' potential would not matter: However many divisions they raised, however many tanks and bombers they built, they would not be able to use them

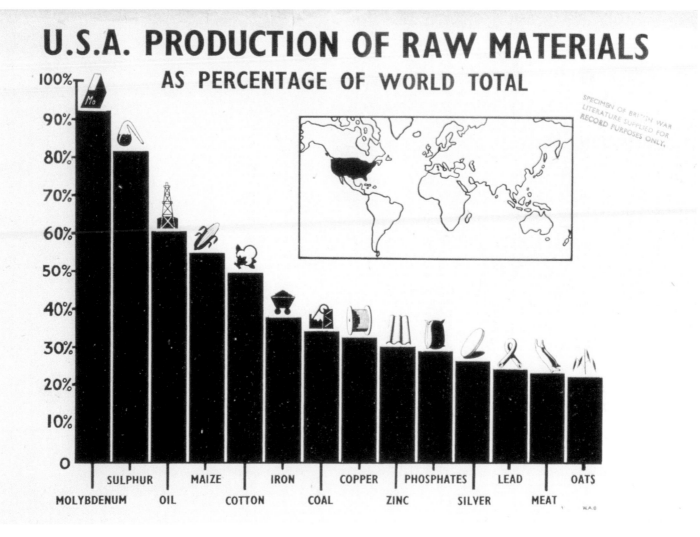

U.S.A. PRODUCTION OF RAW MATERIALS
AS PERCENTAGE OF WORLD TOTAL

SPECIMEN OF BRITISH WAR LITERATURE SUPPLIED FOR RECORD PURPOSES ONLY.

MOLYBDENUM · SULPHUR · OIL · MAIZE · COTTON · IRON · COAL · COPPER · ZINC · PHOSPHATES · SILVER · LEAD · MEAT · OATS

against the Reich if Great Britain had already surrendered and German submarines dominated the Atlantic.

Still, America's immense industrial potential and wealth of natural resources were enough to give any potential enemy pause. The United States produced nearly two-thirds of the world's oil and possessed 58 percent of the global petroleum refining capacity; the combined Axis nations controlled just 4 percent.[4] The year before the war, overall U.S. manufacturing was 50 percent greater than that of the three principal Axis powers *combined*.[5] American factories turned out 26,277 aircraft in 1941—compared with 11,776 for Germany and 5,088 for Japan. And as large as this disparity was in 1941, it would grow larger still in 1942 and then again in 1943.

Hitler concluded it would be best to let that sleeping dog lie—to cultivate isolationist sentiment in the United States, to avoid sinking American ships, and to buy time, thus ensuring that the latent strength of the United States would not be brought to bear until it was too late.

Paradoxically, it was Hitler's nagging trepidation over the dangerous potential of the United States that caused him to react with almost unalloyed joy to the news of Pearl Harbor. His exclamation that "we can't lose the war at all; we now have an

▲ THE RESOURCES OF AMERICA

The British government printed this poster to highlight the significance of gaining America as an ally at the end of 1941, but from the beginning of the war, both Churchill and Hitler were very much aware of the material wealth of the United States.

Sieg Heil!

„ Ein Jahr grösster Entscheidungen steht vor uns . . ."
(Hitler, 11. XII. 1941.)

ÖSTERREICH · TSCHECHOSLOWAKEI · MEMEL · POLEN
NORWEGEN · HOLLAND · BELGIEN · FRANKREICH
JUGOSLAWIEN · GRIECHENLAND

— das waren alles nur lächerliche Kleinigkeiten, ein paar
hunderttausend Tote und Krüppel für Deutschland — nicht
der Rede wert. Jetzt erst geht es richtig los! Jetzt erst beginnt

DER ZWEITE, GRÖSSERE WELTKRIEG

Jetzt muss Deutschland
RUSSLAND,
ENGLAND,
DAS BRITISCHE WELTREICH,
DIE VEREINIGTEN STAATEN
besiegen.

**Vier Fünftel der Bewohner
dieser Erde sind noch frei.**

DER FÜHRER RUFT:
„Dieser Kampf muss bis zur letzten
Konsequenz durchgeführt werden."

VIEL FEIND', VIEL EHR'!

532

„VIEL FEIND', VIEL EHR'!"

Aber was bedeutet das im Licht der nackten Tatsachen?

GEGEN HITLER	FÜR HITLER
Bevölkerung	
	350 Millionen
	davon Bevölkerung der besetzten Gebiete 109 Millionen
1,389 Millionen	
Kriegführende Mächte	
ohne die freien Streitkräfte der von Deutschland besetzten Gebiete	
17	7
Stahl	
110 Millionen Tonnen	50 Mill. Tonnen
Öl und Benzin	
270 Millionen Tonnen	11·75 Mill. Tonnen
Erzeugung der chemischen und Schwerindustrie (im Frieden)	
69.9 Milliarden RM.	38.8 Milliarden RM.

▲ ALLIED PROPAGANDA LEAFLET

Leaflets intended to undermine home-front morale were dropped on Germany by the thousands. This one mocks the Nazi adage "Many Enemies, Much Honor!" by pointing out the long odds against an ultimate Axis victory after the United States joined the war. The "naked facts," according to the flyer, were that the contest was between seventeen nations with a total population of 1,389 million against seven nations with a total population of 350 million (plus a smaller number of unwilling slave laborers). The Axis powers were also badly outclassed in steel production, in the chemical industries, and especially in oil and gasoline output.

◀ AMERICAN OUTRAGE

The Japanese were demonized in American propaganda art in a way the Germans were not. This had something to do with racism but also much to do with the Japanese attack "from out of the blue," which inspired shocked fury as well as grim determination to prevail.

Hoping to enlist the willing cooperation of the native populations of the areas they occupied, or at least to tamp down resistance, the Japanese portrayed themselves as liberating Asian countries from Western colonialism. This was not very effective, however, since Japan's purpose was clearly to establish a colonial regime of its own in the so-called Greater East Asia Co-Prosperity Sphere. The "A, B, C, D" in the broken chain here refers to the alliance of Americans, British, Dutch, and Chinese.

ally which has never been conquered in three thousand years!" may have been meant partly for public consumption and to reassure those less sanguine about adding the United States to Germany's list of adversaries. But the sentiment was surely genuine and shared widely by his military staff at OKW.[6] The crucial fact was not that Japan had attacked Britain, which would divert British resources, nor that Japan's substantial strength would now be added to the fight against the British Empire. What mattered most to Hitler and his staff was that the Japanese attack on Hawaii ensured that as America's potential strength transformed into actual military might, much of its growing power would be directed to the Pacific instead of the Atlantic. Half of America's slowly developing strength, Hitler reasoned, would not be enough to prevent him from finishing off the Soviet Union and then knocking out Britain. Under these circumstances, the Führer concluded, the benefits of war with America outweighed the risks. On December 11 he declared war on the United States. Italy soon did the same.

Hitler's action pleased the Japanese, who calculated that the success of their surprise attack had bought them sufficient time to seize and fortify a strong outer perimeter of defenses almost without interference. Once that was accomplished, the Americans, forced to divide their resources against two ascendant opponents and hindered by the immense distances they would have to cross, would not—or at least might not—be able to muster the moral or material wherewithal to undo Japan's conquests.

In London, the reaction to Pearl Harbor was surprisingly muted. The British had been desperately hoping for America to enter the war, and now they had their wish. But many Britons now worried that too much of their ally's war effort would go to fight Japan. So much American assistance was already needed to defeat the U-boats, to keep British factories and shipyards supplied with the raw materials vital to the war effort, and to keep the hard-pressed Soviet Union on its feet. Now Australia, New Zealand, and India would have to look to their own defenses, while the United States would have to recover from the loss of its entire force of battleships in the Pacific—and it would surely pour its heart and energy into avenging what Secretary of State Cordell Hull called a "treacherous and utterly unprovoked attack upon the United States."[7] That might not leave Britain and the Soviet Union with enough help to sustain the brunt of the fighting against Germany and Italy.

So thought many. But the prime minister, the half-American Sir Winston Churchill, calculated differently. On the evening of December 7, he had been "tired and depressed."[8] But when he learned of the attack, he was filled with relief. "So we had won after all," he thought. "We should not be wiped out. Our history would not come to an end . . . Hitler's fate was sealed. Mussolini's fate was sealed. As for the Japanese, they would be ground to powder. All the rest was merely the proper application of overwhelming force. The British Empire, the Soviet Union, and now the United States bound together with every scrap of their life and strength, were, according to my lights, twice or even thrice the force of their antagonists. No doubt it would take a long time. I expected terrible forfeits in the East; but all this would be merely a passing phase. United we could subdue everybody else in the world."[9]

As he later admitted, though, Churchill had badly underestimated the skill and drive of the Japanese military. His early optimism was challenged often through the winter of 1941–42 and into the spring, as the surge of Japanese conquest flowed rapidly outward. The first blow to his confidence came just two days after Pearl Harbor, when Japanese planes sank the two strongest Royal Navy vessels in the Pacific, the H.M.S. *Prince of Wales* and *Repulse*. "In all the war, I never received a more direct shock," he later wrote. "There were no British or American capital ships [left] in the Indian Ocean or the Pacific . . . Over all this vast expanse of waters, Japan was supreme, and we everywhere weak and naked."[10] Many Japanese military leaders had considered war with the United States a desperate gamble justifiable only because the sole alternative was to bow to America's will, give up a decade's hard-won conquests in China, and surrender Japan's honor without a fight. But by the start of 1942, the gamble seemed to have paid off. "The future is filled with brightness," wrote the chief of staff of the Combined Fleet in his diary. "We surely will win."[11]

For the Allies, disaster followed on disaster in the first stage of the Pacific War.

From French Indochina, which Japan had occupied in 1940, the Imperial Japanese Army quickly overran Malaya, including Singapore, the bastion of British strength in Asia. Sixty-two thousand soldiers of the British Empire were captured—the worst military defeat in all of England's history, at least since Hastings in 1066.[12] Burma fell; the Philippines fell; Borneo, Sumatra, and Java, with their oil fields, fell; New Guinea, and the Gilbert and Solomon Islands all fell. By mid-1942, Japanese forces even threatened Australia, three thousand miles from Tokyo.

At the same time, the Axis forces in Europe seemed to have gotten their second wind. On the Eastern Front (as we will see in chapter 1 of the next volume of *The West Point History of World War II*), the Wehrmacht had checked the Soviet winter counteroffensive of December 1941 and then in the spring smashed ahead in a second Blitzkrieg drive. It was no Barbarossa, but by midsummer of 1942, the Germans had pushed another 150 miles into Russian territory. They occupied the Don Basin and came within striking distance of the Volga River, the vital artery that carried oil from the Caucasian oil fields to fuel Soviet industry and the Red Army's tanks and planes. By late summer, Hitler's armies were deep in the Caucasus and at the gates of Stalingrad. Even in the Mediterranean, Axis forces were back on the roll. Rommel's victories over General Claude Auchinleck in North Africa might have been relatively small in scale, but they were good for German morale, and they threatened the important British lifeline through the Suez Canal to India and Burma.

Perhaps more important than any of the Axis land campaigns was that the Battle of the Atlantic also went well for Germany in the first six months of 1942. In what became known to German submarine crews as the Second Happy Time, U-boats roamed the East Coast of the United States, sinking ships with impunity as the Americans scrambled to organize convoy systems, air patrols, and coastal blackouts. In the first half of 1942, German subs and planes in the Atlantic sank 601 merchant vessels, totaling over three million tons of shipping, much of which went down within sight of the American coast.

If all of these developments made the Axis leaders increasingly confident, they did not, by any means, lead the Allied leaders to despair. Roosevelt and Churchill appreciated better than their adversaries the truly immense industrial might of the United States. America was strong enough to roll back the flow of Japanese conquest; to keep millions of tons of aid flowing to the Soviet Union and Britain; to fight off the U-boats in the Battle of the Atlantic; to send thousands and ultimately tens of thousands of planes to conduct strategic bombing campaigns against Germany and Japan; and to build up its own land and sea forces for an eventual all-out effort against Fortress Europe itself—and to do it all at once.

Churchill and Roosevelt also knew, as Hitler and Hideki Tōjō, the Japanese prime

◀ MOBILE MACHINE SHOP

Two American soldiers work in a mobile machine shop. Although the racism widespread in American society limited the opportunities for black soldiers to serve in combat roles, the effectiveness of frontline U.S. forces rested on plentiful support by rear-echelon troops. By 1945, the number of African American men and women serving in uniform passed 1.2 million.

minister who led his nation into war with the United States, did not, that the diversity of the American population did not equate to weakness. And Stalin knew that despite the heavy blows the Soviet Union had suffered, his people and his regime still held deep reserves of manpower and resolve—reserves that Hitler, with his worldview distorted by his pernicious racial ideology, could hardly conceive of. Further, American and British leaders also realized that they had a key ace in the hole for future operations: the Ultra and Magic intelligence that flowed forth from enemy sources following Allied achievements in breaking the "unbreakable" ciphers of the German Enigma and Japanese Purple encryption machines.

At the midpoint of the war in 1942, then, both sides had good reasons to hope for eventual success. It was difficult to dispute Churchill's calculation that the combined strength of the British Empire, the Soviet Union, and the United States would be too great for the Axis to withstand once America was fully mobilized. The key question was whether England and Russia could stay in the fight long enough to allow for that overwhelming preponderance of force to develop. If Soviet resistance collapsed, the task for America and Britain would become immeasurably more difficult: the German Army and Air Force would be able to concentrate their forces in the West, making an amphibious assault on the Continent practically impossible. Or if the British were forced out of the war by the Battle of the Atlantic, there would be no base from which to launch the cross-Channel invasion anyway—and even the possibility of victory by airpower would practically disappear.

In the Pacific, Japanese defeat was perhaps inevitable, given the great weight of American industrial capacity. In 1942 the Americans built 112 major fighting ships, while the Japanese built 21. In 1943 the figures were 206 to 19.[13] But then, perhaps a complete American victory was *not* guaranteed. Japan's great offensive had carried Imperial forces to the gates of India and within striking distance of Australian territory. If they could go just a little farther, if they could pressure Australia into neutrality or cut off her lines of communication across the Pacific, they would deprive the Americans of the staging areas necessary to roll back Japanese conquests.[14]

And then there was the question of will. The people of the United States were furious with Japan over Pearl Harbor, and prepared for great sacrifices to defeat the Rising Sun. But how great? Would they spend a hundred thousand casualties for revenge, or to return the Netherlands East Indies and French Indochina to their European masters? A million casualties? If faced with a sufficiently determined and skillful defense in the Pacific, and if the Germans succeeded in knocking the Soviets out of the war, would the Americans not come to some compromise with Germany and Japan? Or might the United States be forced to devote so many resources to the struggle with Germany that the American forces in the Pacific would be insufficient to prevail?

The Axis tide had reached its high-water mark. But though the Allies had so far managed to stave off defeat, they were still a very long way from victory, either in Europe or in the Pacific. The ultimate outcome of this titanic world war remained uncertain.

1. David F. Burg and L. Edward Purcell, *Almanac of World War I* (Lexington: University of Kentucky Press, 1998), 239.

2. According to the calculation of Ernest L. Bogart, *Direct and Indirect Costs of the Great World War*, Carnegie Endowment for International Peace, Preliminary Economic Studies of the War, No. 24 (New York: Oxford University Press, 1919), 299.

3. Goldsworthy Lowes Dickinson, "The Foundation of a League of Peace," in *World Peace Foundation pamphlet series*, vol. V (Boston: World Peace Foundation, 1915), 12.

4. In 1920 the United States had *double* the iron and steel production of the other six combined, and consumed about 60 percent more energy. By 1928, its "total industrial potential" was more than double the three Axis powers combined. Paul Kennedy, *The Rise and Fall of the Great Powers: Economic Change and Military Conflict from 1500 to 2000* (New York: Random House, 1987), 200–201.

5. For additional details on the Washington Conference, see Erik Goldstein and John Maurer, eds., *The Washington Naval Conference, 1921–1922: Naval Rivalry, East Asian Stability and the Road to Pearl Harbor* (London: Routledge, 1994). The various naval treaties are also available online.

6. For additional details on the 1930 London Naval Conference, see John H. Maurer and Christopher M. Bell, eds., *At the Crossroads Between Peace and War: The London Naval Conference of 1930* (Annapolis, MD: Naval Institute Press, 2014).

7. The Kellogg-Briand Pact is printed in *The Statutes at Large of the United States of America*, vol. 46, pt. 2 (Washington, D.C.: GPO, 1931), 2343–48.

8. Haruko Taya Cook and Theodore F. Cook, *Japan at War: An Oral History* (New York: New Press, 1992), 41–42.

9. J. M. Roberts, *Europe, 1880–1945*, 3rd ed. (London: Routledge, 2000), 489.

10. For a detailed examination of Hitler's rise to power in Germany, see Richard J. Evans, *The Coming of the Third Reich* (New York: Penguin Press, 2004), and *The Third Reich in Power, 1933–1939* (New York: Penguin Press, 2005).

11. Allan R. Millett and Williamson Murray, eds., *Military Effectiveness*, vol. 2 (Boston: Unwin Hyman, 1988), includes essays focusing on the military effectiveness of each of the major powers. Williamson Murray and Allan R. Millett, eds., *Military Innovation in the Interwar Period* (Cambridge: Cambridge University Press, 1996), includes essays comparing various national experiences dealing with military innovations such as armored warfare, amphibious warfare, strategic bombing, close air support, aircraft carriers, submarines, radio, and radar.

12. For additional details on German military reform in the interwar period, see James Corum, "A Comprehensive Approach to Change: Reform in the German Army in the Interwar Period," in Harold R. Winton and David R. Mets, eds., *The Challenge of Change: Military Institutions and New Realities, 1918–1941* (Lincoln: University of Nebraska Press, 2000).

13. For a detailed examination of the Japanese Army in the interwar period, see Edward J. Drea, *Japan's Imperial Army: Its Rise and Fall, 1853–1945* (Lawrence: University Press of Kansas, 2009).

14. A detailed examination of French Army doctrine and military planning can be found in Robert A. Doughty, *The Seeds of Disaster: The Development of French Army Doctrine, 1919–1939* (Hamden, CT: Archon Books, 1985), and Eugenia C. Kiesling, *Arming Against Hitler: France and the Limits of Military Planning* (Lawrence: University Press of Kansas, 1996).

15. Diary of Captain L. Twomey, The [British] National Archives, Kew, War Office Records, W.O. 217/7, entries for March 5 and 9, 1940, as transcribed online at http://ww2talk.com/forums/topic/36283-private-diary-58-med-regt-ra-march-1940-capt-l-twomey.

16. For additional details on British interwar defense issues, see Harold R. Winton, "Tanks, Votes, and Budgets: The Politics of Mechanization and Armored Warfare in Britain, 1919–1939," in Winton and Mets, *Challenge of Change: Military Institutions and New Realities, 1918–1941*.

17. The Civilian Conservation Corps began as a New Deal program to put young men to work on national conservation projects. They worked in national parks and other remote locations building trails and roads, planting trees, constructing park facilities, and so on. The U.S. Army was put in charge of the program and had to organize these remote camps and provide them with food, shelter, medical care, and equipment. The use of reserve officers to run these camps provided valuable leadership experience for the thousands of officers involved from 1933 to 1942. For additional information on the role of the U.S. Army in the CCC program, see Charles William Johnson, "The Civilian Conservation Corps: The Role of the Army" (PhD dissertation, University of Michigan, 1968).

18. The concept of "Deep Battle" and "Deep Operations" developed by General Vladimir Triandafillov and General M. N. Tukhachevsky emphasized firepower and speed to conduct successful operations, turning tactical success into strategic victories. The Red Army 1936 Field Regulations detail the various parts of their Deep Battle doctrine. An English translation, *U.S.S.R. Report, Military Affairs, Provisional Field Regulations for the Red Army* (Springfield, VA: National Technical Information Service, 1986), is available online at http://1.usa.gov/1D6l0Fu.

19. For a more detailed examination of Soviet interwar military doctrine, see Jacob W. Kipp, "Military Reform and the Red Army, 1918–1941: Bolsheviks, Voyenspetsy, and the Young Red Commanders," in Winton and Mets, *Challenge of Change: Military Institutions and New Realities, 1918–1941*; and Mary R. Habeck, *Storm of Steel: The Development of Armor Doctrine in Germany and the Soviet Union, 1919–1939* (Ithaca, NY: Cornell University Press, 2003).

CHAPTER 2: GERMAN YEARS OF VICTORY

1. For a more recent discussion of the "war of choice" as it relates to U.S. foreign policy and the wars against Iraq in 1991 and 2003, see Richard N. Haass, *War of Necessity, War of Choice: A Memoir of Two Iraq Wars* (New York: Simon & Schuster, 2009).

2. "In a conflict with Great Britain and France, both of which were sea powers, the most important component of the armed forces would have been the navy." Karl-Heinz Frieser, *The Blitzkrieg Legend: The 1940 Campaign in the West* (Annapolis, MD: Naval Institute Press, 2005), 13.

3. The word *Blitzkrieg* had already been floating around for some time in the late 1930s. Sometimes credited to Western, specifically American, correspondents writing about the dramatic German victories in the war's early years, it can actually be found here and there in pre-1939 professional literature. It signified any rapid and complete victory, and the Germans never did use it in any precise sense—yet another supposedly crucial German term used far more in the West than in Germany itself. For the earliest printed use of the term that the authors have found, see Lieutenant Colonel Braun, "Der strategische Überfall," *Militär-Wochenblatt* 123, no. 18 (October 28, 1938): 1134–36, although the sense is that the word had already been in use: "Nach dem Zeitungsnachrichten hatten die diesjährigen französischen Manöver den Zweck, die Bedeutung des strategischen Überfalls—auch 'Blitzkrieg' genannt—zu prüfen" [According to the newspaper reports, the French maneuvers of this year had the goal of testing out the implications of a strategic surprise attack—also called blitzkrieg.] (1134). See also William J. Fanning Jr., "The Origins of the Term 'Blitzkrieg': Another View," *Journal of Military History* 61, no. 2 (April 1997): 283–302.

4. For Case White, begin with the belated "official history" commissioned by the *Militärgeschichtliches Forschungsamt, Das Deutsche Reich und Der Zweite Weltkrieg*, vol. 2, *Die Errichtung der Hegemonie auf dem Europäischen Kontinent* (Stuttgart: Deutsche Verlags-Anstalt, 1979), especially "Hitler's Erster 'Blitzkrieg' und seine Auswirkungen auf Nordosteuropa," 79–156. Robert M. Kennedy, *The German Campaign in Poland, 1939*, Department of the Army Pamphlet no. 20-255 (Washington, D.C.: Department of the Army, 1956), continues to

be useful, and so does Matthew Cooper, *The German Army, 1933–1945: Its Political and Military Failure* (Chelsea, MI: Scarborough House, 1978), 169–76. See a pair of articles written for the popular audience: Pat McTaggart, "Poland '39," *Command* 17 (July/August 1992): 57; and David T. Zabecki, "Invasion of Poland: Campaign That Launched a War," *World War II* 14, no. 3 (September 1999): 26ff. See also the pertinent sections in the memoir literature: Heinz Guderian, *Panzer Leader* (New York: Dutton, 1952), 46–63; Erich von Manstein, *Lost Victories* (Novato, CA: Presidio, 1982), 22–63; and F. W. von Mellenthin, *Panzer Battles: A Study of the Employment of Armor in the Second World War* (New York: Ballantine, 1956), 3–9. A good revisionist work, drawn from Polish sources, is Steven Zaloga and W. Victor Madej, *The Polish Campaign, 1939* (New York: Hippocrene, 1991).

5. Zaloga and Madej, *Polish Campaign*, 15–27, offer a meticulous discussion of the various Polish deployment options in 1939.

6. For the dispute over the German operational plan, see *DRZW*, vol. 2, *Die Errichtung der Hegemonie*, 92–99; and Kennedy, *German Campaign in Poland*, 58–63 and 73–77.

7. Kennedy, *German Campaign in Poland*, 62.

8. *DRZW*, vol. 2, *Die Errichtung der Hegemonie*, 96.

9. Kennedy, *German Campaign in Poland*, 83. It was this breakout attempt that may well have given rise to the ridiculous notion that Polish cavalry "charged" German tanks in the course of this campaign. Zaloga and Madej, *Polish Campaign*, 110–12, put the tale to rest once and for all. They describe a successful charge by the 18th Lancer Regiment and its commander, Colonel Kazimierz Mastelarz, against a weak German infantry position that later came to grief when several German armored cars happened on the scene. They also note that Polish cavalry was well acquainted with the capabilities of tanks, since each cavalry brigade had an armored troop attached to it. For the origins of the story, see Guderian, *Panzer Leader*, 52, although we should note that Guderian mentions only a charge by Polish cavalry against positions of the German 2nd (Motorized) Infantry Division.

10. The Light divisions originated in plans to motorize the German cavalry. Each consisted of four mechanized infantry battalions and a single tank battalion, with an overall strength of ninety light tanks.

11. Hans von Luck, *Panzer Commander: The Memoirs of Colonel Hans von Luck* (New York: Random House, 1989), 28–29.

12. Still the best account of the operations in Poland: see B. H. Liddell Hart, *History of the Second World War* (New York: Putnam, 1970), 27–32. For an account that emphasizes the Polish side, see Zaloga and Madej, *Polish Campaign*, 103–56.

13. For the battle of the Bzura, see Zaloga and Madej, *Polish Campaign*, 131–38, the only English-language source to mention it in much detail.

14. James Sidney Lucas, *Battle Group!: German Kampfgruppen Action of World War Two* (London: Arms and Armour, 1993), 10–24, focuses on the operations of the 4th Panzer Division in Warsaw and on the Bzura.

15. Zaloga and Madej, *Polish Campaign*, 158, address the "myth of the 'eighteen-day war,'" pointing out that Army Group South "lost more men killed in the final half of the war than in the first two weeks."

16. The figures are from Zaloga and Madej, *Polish Campaign*, 156. Based on the German primary sources, *DRZW*, vol. 2, *Die Errichtung der Hegemonie*, 133, gives a figure of 1 million Polish prisoners: 700,000 to Germany and 300,000 to the Soviet Union.

17. D. Barlone, *A French Officer's Diary (23 August 1939–1 October 1940)*, trans. L. V. Cass (Cambridge: Cambridge University Press, 1942), 26–27.

18. For the role of the Luftwaffe in the Polish campaign, see James S. Corum, *The Luftwaffe: Creating the Operational Air War, 1918–1940* (Lawrence: University Press of Kansas, 1997), 272–75.

19. For *Weserübung*, see Adam R. A. Claasen, *Hitler's Northern War: The Luftwaffe's Ill-Fated Campaign, 1940–1945* (Lawrence: University Press of Kansas, 2001), a definitive portrait of German combined operations in the north, ranging far beyond Luftwaffe activity to include

land and naval combat, not to mention the interplay of all three arms. Another important work by a contemporary scholar is James S. Corum, "The German Campaign in Norway as a Joint Operation," *Journal of Strategic Studies* 21 (1998): 50–77, which looks carefully not only at the successes of German interservice cooperation in the campaign but also at Allied failures in the same area. "In Norway, it was less a question of German brilliant planning and mastery of the operational art than it was of a mediocre plan executed energetically versus a bad plan executed poorly," he concludes (74). For a new edition of a venerable primary source, see Erich Raeder's memoir, *Grand Admiral* (New York: Da Capo Press, 2001), especially 300–318.

20. For a fine operational summary of the Danish campaign, see Major Macher, "Die Besetzung Dänemarks," *Militär-Wochenblatt* 125, no. 45 (May 9, 1941): 1791–93, written on the occasion of the campaign's first anniversary. For a summary of the rise and development of the German airborne forces, see F. Stuhlmann, "Fallschirmjäger," *Militär-Wochenblatt* 125, no. 25 (December 20, 1940): 1191–92.

21. See Claasen, *Hitler's Northern War*, 62–65.

22. Macher, "Die Besetzung Dänemarks," 1793.

23. Still useful for the initial German landings and the Norwegian response to them, see two articles in the *History of the Second World War* series (London: Marshall Cavendish, 1973): J. L. Moulton, "Hitler Strikes North," no. 3, 68–74; and Leif Bohn, "The Norwegian View," no. 3, 77–78.

24. Claasen, *Hitler's Northern War*, 43–44, discusses the immense difficulty of coordinating these various bodies—the "Export Group," the "First Naval Transport Group," and a group of three tankers—and getting them to their destinations on time.

25. Claasen, *Hitler's Northern War*, 68–69.

26. For the sinking of the *Blücher*, see Carl O. Schuster, "Coastal Defense Victory: *Blücher* at Oslo," *Command* 39 (September 1996): 30–31. Schuster argues that the disaster was due to poor tactical decisions, and that the Germans should have entered Oslo Fjord with either a landward thrust against the fortress by assault troops or, failing that, a damn-the-torpedoes run by a "lighter, faster, and more expendable ship" instead of a "vessel with VIPs aboard." See also Claasen, *Hitler's Northern War*, 66. Richard D. Hooker Jr. and Christopher Coglianese, "Operation *Weserübung*: A Case Study in the Operational Art," in Richard D. Hooker Jr., ed., *Maneuver Warfare: An Anthology* (Novato, CA: Presidio Press, 1993), point out that, as disastrous as the loss of the ship was, it held up the capture of Oslo only by a half day (380).

27. For Fornebu, see Claasen, *Hitler's Northern War*, 68–69.

28. For the operational details of this little-known phase of the Norwegian campaign, see Earl F. Ziemke, *The German Northern Theater of Operations, 1940–1945* (Washington, D.C.: Department of the Army, 1959), 63–86.

29. For the Namsos-Aandalsnes landings, and the devastating impact of Luftwaffe bombing, see Claasen, *Hitler's Northern War*, 100–117.

30. David G. Thompson, "Norwegian Military Policy, 1905–1940: A Critical Appraisal and Review of the Literature," *Journal of Military History* 61, no. 3 (July 1997): 503–20, www.jstor .org/stable/2954034, has done the great service of investigating the campaign from the Norwegian perspective. For the Norwegian view of the Allied forces in Norway, see 518–19.

31. For Hitler's decree, see Claasen, *Hitler's Northern War*, 108–9.

32. See "Grossdeutschlands Freiheitskrieg 1940, 'pt. 39,' Englands diplomatische und militärische Niederlage in Norwegen," *Militär-Wochenblatt* 124, no. 45 (May 10, 1940): 2041–44.

33. Some 3,000 sailors survived the sinking of their vessels and joined General Dietl's land force in the defense of Narvik. Raeder, *Grand Admiral*, 310.

34. For a discussion of how Hitler handled the bad news out of Narvik, see the memoirs of General Walter Warlimont of the high command of the Wehrmacht (OKW), *Inside Hitler's Headquarters, 1939–45* (Novato, CA: Presidio Press, 1964), 76–81. Warlimont describes "Hitler

hunched on a chair in a corner, unnoticed and staring in front of him, a picture of brooding gloom . . . I turned away in order not to look at so undignified a picture." He could not help but make a comparison to "Moltke's imperturbable calm and self-assurance on the battle-fields of Bohemia and France" (79–80).

35. See Corum, *Luftwaffe: Creating the Operational Air War*.

36. For Case Yellow, the scholarly work of choice is Frieser, *Blitzkrieg Legend*, a very welcome English-language edition of the original German-language work from 1995. For the planning of the offensive, see the still-crucial article by Hans-Adolf Jacobsen, "Hitlers Gedanken zur Kriegführung im Western," *Wehrwissenschaftliche Rundschau* 5, no. 10 (October 1955): 433–46. All subsequent work on the topic has been a commentary on this article, including the same author's own *Fall Gelb: der Kampf um den deutschen Operationsplan zur Westoffensive 1940* (Wiesbaden: F. Steiner, 1957). See also *DRZW*, vol. 2, *Die Errichtung der Hegemonie*, 233–327. The standard works in English remain Jeffrey A. Gunsburg, *Divided and Conquered: The French High Command and the Defeat in the West, 1940* (Westport, CT: Greenwood Press, 1979), and especially Robert A. Doughty, *The Breaking Point: Sedan and the Fall of France, 1940* (Hamden, CT: Archon Books, 1990). For the role of Guderian's Panzers in the campaign, see the fine but relatively short monograph by Florian K. Rothbrust, *Guderian's XIXth Panzer Corps and the Battle of France: Breakthrough in the Ardennes, May 1940* (New York: Praeger, 1990). Finally, even with all these scholarly riches, there will always be those who turn to the fine popular account by Alistair Horne, *To Lose a Battle: France 1940* (Boston: Little, Brown, 1969).

37. For the primary source on the battle over the operational plan, see Manstein, *Lost Victories*, 94–126, although his memoirs must be read with care. For useful correctives, see Marcel Stein, *Field Marshal von Manstein, a Portrait: The Janus Head* (Solihull, U.K.: Helion & Co., 2007), and Mungo Melvin, *Manstein: Hitler's Greatest General* (London: Weidenfeld & Nicolson, 2010).

38. For a discussion of the Mechelen incident, including detailed analyses of the actual documents taken by the Belgians, see Jean Vanwelkenhuyzen, "Die Krise vom Januar 1940," *Wehrwissenschaftliche Rundschau* 5, no. 2 (February 1955): 66–90.

39. For a good personality portrait of Manstein, see Dana V. Sadarananda, *Beyond Stalingrad: Manstein and the Operations of Army Group Don* (Mechanicsburg, PA: Stackpole Books, 2009), 8–12.

40. Manstein, *Lost Victories*, 113.

41. *DRZW*, vol. 2, *Die Errichtung der Hegemonie*, 254.

42. Rothbrust, *Guderian's XIXth Panzer Corps and the Battle of France*, 29.

43. For these "Sonderunternehmen," see *DRZW*, vol. 2, *Die Errichtung der Hegemonie*, 259–60.

44. For the campaign in the Netherlands, see E. H. Brongers, *The Battle for the Hague, 1940: The First Great Airborne Operation in History* (Soesterberg: Aspekt, 2004). David Meyler, "Missed Opportunities: The Ground War in Holland," *Command* 42 (March 1997): 58–69, offers detailed orders of battle for the Dutch Army.

45. For Eben Emael, see James E. Mrazek, *The Fall of Eben Emael* (Novato, CA: Presidio, 1970). It is a popular work that emphasizes vivid writing yet is also well grounded in the sources, including interviews with General Kurt Student and Colonel Rudolf Witzig.

46. Known as the *Hohlladung*. See Mrazek, *Fall of Eben Emael*, 56, for a cross-sectional diagram.

47. Jeffrey A. Gunsburg, "The Battle of the Belgian Plain, 12–14 May 1940: The First Great Tank Battle," *Journal of Military History* 56, no. 2 (April 1992): 207–44, www.jstor.org/stable /1985797. See especially 222–23.

48. For the Dyle Plan, see Gunsburg, *Divided and Conquered*, 119–46 and 265–92, which argues that the plan was potentially a "strategy for victory," but that it also "carried the risk of degenerating into an encounter battle in which the enemy, operating under unified command from nearby bases with air superiority, would have the advantage" (270), a sound judgment. See also Doughty, *Breaking Point*, 12–14.

49. For the Breda variant, see Doughty, *Breaking Point*, 14–17, and Gunsburg, *Divided and Conquered*, 138–39 and 270–71, which argues that it "siphoned off almost all of the mobile reserves" (138) and "strained the limits of French doctrine" (270).

50. Copyright © March 22, 1982, B. H. Liddell Hart. Reprinted by permission of Da Capo Press, a member of the Perseus Books Group.

51. Doughty, *Breaking Point*, 102.

52. For the primary source on the Sedan crossing, see Guderian, *Panzer Leader*, 75–82.

53. The best overview and analysis of the crossing is found in Frieser, *Blitzkrieg Legend*, 145–97.

54. For the Allied counterattacks at Montcornet, Crécy, and Arras, see Gunsburg, *Divided and Conquered*, 231–34, 245–46, and 249–50.

55. For the "reconnaissance in force," see the primary source, Guderian, *Panzer Leader*, 87–88.

56. Hugh Sebag-Montefiore, *Dunkirk: Fight to the Last Man* (Cambridge, MA.: Harvard University Press, 2006), 425.

57. Frieser, *Blitzkrieg Legend*, 291–319, offers the most detailed and persuasive analysis of Hitler's "halt order," the tensions within the German officer corps, and the entire operational sequence around Dunkirk.

58. A welcome addition to the literature that finally gives the British side at Dunkirk is Sebag-Montefiore, *Dunkirk: Fight to the Last Man*.

59. Churchill uttered the famous phrase in a speech to Parliament on June 4, 1940. For the relevant extracts, see Winston S. Churchill, *The Second World War*, vol. 2, *Their Finest Hour* (Boston: Houghton Mifflin, 1949), 115–18.

60. For an analysis of this opening year of the war that places German operations in a long-term historical context, see Robert M. Citino, "The Prussian Tradition, the Myth of the Blitzkrieg and the Illusion of German Military Dominance, 1939–1941," in Frank McDonough, ed., *The Origins of the Second World War: An International Perspective* (London: Continuum, 2011).

CHAPTER 3: BRITAIN STANDS ALONE

1. Churchill's speech can be found in Churchill College Archive Centre, Cambridge, U.K.

2. See Ashley Jackson, *The British Empire and the Second World War* (London: Hambledon Continuum, 2006), for a thorough analysis of the contribution of the Empire and Commonwealth. On the African contribution, see David Killingray, *Fighting for Britain: African Soldiers in the Second World War* (Woodbridge: James Currey, 2010). The total number of black soldiers was 658,000 during the war. There were also 221,000 white Rhodesians and South Africans.

3. See Alex Kershaw, *The Few: The American "Knights of the Air" Who Risked Everything to Save Britain in the Summer of 1940* (New York: Da Capo Press, 2006). On Polish air force recruits, see Michael Peszke, "The Polish Air Force in the United Kingdom, 1939–1946," *Royal Air Force Power Review* 11 (2008): 54–75.

4. David Reynolds, *The Creation of the Anglo-American Alliance 1937–41: A Study in Competitive Co-Operation* (London: Europa, 1981), 121–31. The deal was based on the delivery of fifty older U.S. destroyers in return for new U.S. bases, six in the Caribbean, one at Bermuda, one in Newfoundland. The destroyers were not fully delivered until spring 1941, and all of them needed modification before they could be operated. A more favorable interpretation of the deal can be found in Warren Kimball, *Forged in War: Churchill, Roosevelt and the Second World War* (London: HarperCollins, 1997), 56–58.

5. The standard history of SOE is M. R. D. Foot, *S.O.E.: The Special Operations Executive, 1940–1946* (London: Pimlico, 1999); see too David Stafford, *Britain and European Resistance 1940–1945: A Survey of the Special Operations Executive, with Documents* (Toronto: University of Toronto Press, 1983), 16–17, 25.

6. The National Archives (TNA), Kew, London, FO 898/457, PWE Annual Dissemination of Leaflets by Aircraft and Balloon 1939–1945.

7. Michael Stenton, *Radio London and Resistance in Occupied Europe: British Political Warfare 1939–1943* (Oxford: Oxford University Press, 2000). See chaps. 1 and 2 for the origins of the Political Warfare Executive.

8. Winston Churchill, "We Shall Fight on the Beaches," June 4, 1940, reproduced with permission of Curtis Brown, London, on behalf of the Estate of Winston S. Churchill. Copyright © The Estate of Winston S. Churchill.

9. Details on the raiding in Martin Middlebrook and Chris Everitt, *The Bomber Command War Diaries: An Operational Reference Book 1939–1945* (Leicester: Midland Publishing, 2000), 42–80.

10. These plans are printed in Charles Webster and Noble Frankland, *The Strategic Air Offensive Against Germany*, vol. 4 (London: Her Majesty's Stationery Office, 1961), 99–102.

11. Winston Churchill, *The Second World War*, vol. 2 (London: Cassell, 1957), 567.

12. There is now a very large literature on this. The best recent account is Susan Grayzel, *At Home and Under Fire: Air Raids and Culture in Britain from the Great War to the Blitz* (Cambridge: Cambridge University Press, 2012). See too Ian Patterson, *Guernica and Total War* (London: Profile Books, 2007).

13. On the bombing of Italy, see the excellent new book by Claudia Baldoli and Andrew Knapp, *Forgotten Blitzes: France and Italy Under Allied Air Attack, 1940–1945* (London: Continuum, 2012), 19–22.

14. See Richard Overy, *The Air War, 1939–1945*, 3rd ed. (New York: Potomac, 2007), 39–40.

15. For the argument that it was the Royal Navy that kept Hitler from invasion, see Derek Robinson, *Invasion, 1940: The Truth About the Battle of Britain and What Stopped Hitler* (New York: Carroll & Graf Publishers, 2005), and Anthony J. Cumming, *The Royal Navy and the Battle of Britain* (Annapolis, MD: Naval Institute Press, 2010). Cumming argues that the Royal Navy would not have suffered heavily from German air attack and that the fear of naval intervention persuaded some German commanders that invasion was not possible in 1940.

16. See the account in Richard Overy, *The Battle of Britain*, 2nd ed. (London: Penguin, 2010), 61–68. The best detailed reconstruction of the battle is still John Philip Ray, *The Battle of Britain: Dowding and the First Victory, 1940* (London: Cassell, 2000).

17. The standard history is now Colin Dobinson, *Building Radar: Forging Britain's Early Warning Chain, 1935–1945* (London: Methuen, 2010). See too Alexander Rose, "Radar and Air Defence in the 1930s," *Twentieth Century British History* 9 (1998): 219–45.

18. Adolf Galland, *The First and the Last* (London: Methuen, 1955), 43–44.

19. On the Spitfire and its qualities, see Jonathan Glancy, *Spitfire* (London: Atlantic Books, 2006), and Dilip Sakar, *How the Spitfire Won the Battle of Britain* (Stroud: Amberley, 2010).

20. Sebastian Cox, "A Comparative Analysis of RAF and Luftwaffe Intelligence in the Battle of Britain, 1940," *Intelligence and National Security* 5 (1990): 432–34; F. H. Hinsley et al., *British Intelligence in the Second World War*, vol. 1 (London: Her Majesty's Stationery Office, 1979), 177–82. See too Ralph Bennett, *Behind the Battle: Intelligence in the War with Germany 1939–1945* (London: Sinclair-Stevenson, 1994), 168–202. Bennett concludes that Ultra was "decisive" for Britain's war effort.

21. Almost the only account from the German side is Klaus Maier, "Die Luftschlacht um England," in *Das Deutsche Reich und der Zweite Weltkrieg: Band I* (Stuttgart: DVA, 1979). See too Richard Overy, *The Bombing War: Europe 1939–1945* (London: Allen Lane, 2013), chap. 1.

22. Dobinson, *Building Radar*, 309–12.

23. Overy, *Battle of Britain*, 69–71.

24. The best account of Park's contribution is Vincent Orange, *Park: The Biography of Air Chief Marshal Sir Keith Park* (London: Grub Street, 2001), chaps. 9–11.

25. On the first London raid, the best book is Peter Stansky, *The First Day of the Blitz: September 7, 1940* (New Haven, CT: Yale University Press, 2007). On the German invasion plans, there are only older accounts available, though now published in modern paperback format: Peter

Fleming, *Operation Sea Lion: An Account of the German Preparations and the British Counter-Measures* (London: Pan Books, 2003); Egbert Kieser, *Operation Sea Lion: The German Plan to Invade Britain, 1940* (London: Cassell, 2000). The original documents on Sea Lion, including the army chief of staff documents, are still lodged in the Russian archives at Podolsk and have not been used extensively by historians. These documents show that German preparations were remarkably thorough.

26. Some historians have argued that Hitler never was serious about invading Britain, but was much more interested in planning a campaign against the Soviet Union. This view exaggerates the extent to which Hitler had firmly decided on his Soviet option by September. The Germans made extensive preparations for a cross-Channel invasion, more than were needed for just a bluff. It seems more likely that Hitler was hoping for a quick victory in southern England as long as air supremacy was assured, and was frustrated from achieving it. On the argument that the Soviet turn mattered more, see Jürgen Förster, "Hitler Turns East—German War Policy in 1940 and 1941," in Bernd Wegner, ed., *From Peace to War: Germany, Soviet Russia and the World, 1939–1941* (Oxford: Berghahn, 1997), 117–24; Esmonde Robertson, "Hitler Turns from the West to Russia, May–December 1940," in Robert Boyce, ed., *Paths to War: New Essays on the Origins of the Second World War* (London: Macmillan, 1989), 369–75.

27. Churchill College Archive Centre, CHAR 9/141A/58, notes for a speech to the House of Commons, August 20, 1940: "Never in the field of human conflict was so much owed by so many to so few." A transcript and audio recording can be found online, http://web.archive.org/web/20130116213818/http://fiftiesweb.com/usa/winston-churchill-so-few.htm.

28. Overy, *Battle of Britain*, 32–33, 37–38.

29. On the German statistics, see Williamson Murray, *Luftwaffe* (London: George Allen & Unwin, 1985), 54–58.

30. There is a very good analysis of Dowding's strengths and weaknesses as a commander in Vincent Orange, *Dowding of Fighter Command: Victor of the Battle of Britain* (London: Grub Street, 2008), chaps. 15–16.

31. The best recent account is Grayzel, *At Home and Under Fire*. See too Brett Holman, "The Air Panic of 1935: British Press Opinion Between Disarmament and Rearmament," *Journal of Contemporary History* 46 (2011): 288–307.

32. Barbara Nixon, *Raiders Overhead: A Diary of the London Blitz* (London: Scolar Press, 1980), 26–27.

33. Throughout the campaign, gas bombs were not used, though the British prepared for gas retaliation. Both sides were deterred due to fear of what would happen to their own population. On British preparations, see Overy, *Battle of Britain*, 105–6. More generally on the issue of chemical weapons, see Robert Harris and Jeremy Paxman, *A Higher Form of Killing: The Secret Story of Gas and Germ Warfare* (London: Chatto & Windus, 1982).

34. Richard Overy, *The Bombing War: Europe 1939–1945* (London: Allen Lane, 2013), 92–94.

35. Colin Dobinson, *AA Command: Britain's Anti-Aircraft Defences of World War II* (London: Methuen, 2001), 528–29.

36. RAF Air Historical Branch, German Translations, vol. 5, 7/92, German aircraft losses January–December 1941.

37. Dobinson, *AA Command*, 209–10, 251–58; Dobinson, *Building Radar*, 342–43. For details about night-fighter squadrons, see Basil Collier, *The Defence of the United Kingdom* (London: Her Majesty's Stationery Office, 1957), 269–71, 278–80, and 508–9.

38. The official history is still the best source: Terence H. O'Brien, *Civil Defence* (London: Her Majesty's Stationery Office, 1955).

39. Dietmar Süss, "Wartime Societies and Shelter Politics in National Socialist Germany and Britain," in Claudia Baldoli, Andrew Knapp, and Richard Overy, eds., *Bombing, States and Peoples in Western Europe, 1940–1945* (London: Continuum, 2011), 31–39; Juliet Gardiner, *The Blitz: The British Under Attack* (London: HarperCollins, 2010).

40. Overy, *Air War*, 120.

41. There is much new literature critical of Bomber Command's performance. See Randall Hansen, *Fire and Fury: The Allied Bombing of Germany 1942–1945* (New York: NAL Caliber, 2009), 17–26; Martin van Creveld, *The Age of Airpower* (New York: Public Affairs, 2011), is generally skeptical of the claims made for World War II airpower. On the Butt Report, see Randall Wakelam, *The Science of Bombing: Operational Research in RAF Bomber Command* (Toronto: University Press of Toronto, 2009), 21–23, 34–35. Wakelam puts the report into the wider context of the development of better science-based operational research.

42. A popular critical account is Stuart Hylton, *Their Darkest Hour: The Hidden History of the Home Front, 1939–1945* (Stroud: Sutton Publishing, 2001). See too Todd Gray, *Looting in Wartime Britain* (Exeter: Mint Press, 2009). The best scholarly assessment is Sonya Rose, *Which People's War?: National Identity and Citizenship in Wartime Britain, 1939–1945* (Oxford: Oxford University Press, 2003). On class issues, see Geoffrey Field, *Blood, Sweat, and Toil: Remaking the British Working Class, 1939–1945* (Oxford: Oxford University Press, 2012), chap. 2.

43. The British government also encouraged a propaganda campaign in the United States, playing on Britain's survival under the bombs. See Nicholas Cull, *Selling War: The British Propaganda Campaign Against American "Neutrality" in World War II* (Oxford: Oxford University Press, 1995), chap. 3.

44. Warren Kimball, " 'Beggar My Neighbor': America and the British Interim Finance Crisis, 1940–41," *Journal of Economic History* 29 (1969): 758–72, www.jstor.org/stable/2115709; Richard Overy, "Co-Operation: Trade, Aid and Technology," in David Reynolds, Warren Kimball, and A. O. Chubarian, eds., *Allies at War: The Soviet, American, and British Experience 1939–1945* (New York: St. Martin's Press, 1994), 204–6.

45. Jackson, *British Empire*, 60–63.

46. TNA, AIR 40/288, Air Intelligence report, *The Blitz*, August 14, 1941.

47. On the crisis of merchant shipping, see C. B. Behrens, *Merchant Shipping and the Demands of War* (London: HMSO, 1955), 190–97.

48. See Overy, *Bombing War*, 109–15, for a full analysis of the strategic cost to Britain.

49. The best account in English is Macgregor Knox, *Hitler's Italian Allies: Royal Armed Forces, Fascist Regime, and the War of 1940–1943* (Cambridge: Cambridge University Press, 2000). For the background in Italy, see John Gooch, *Mussolini and His Generals: The Armed Forces and Fascist Foreign Policy, 1922–1940* (Cambridge: Cambridge University Press, 2003). On the navy, see Robert Mallett, *The Italian Navy and Fascist Expansionism, 1935–40* (London: Frank Cass, 1998).

50. On the Italian side, the best account is Giorgio Rochat, *Le Guerre Italiane 1935–1943* (Turin: Einaudi, 2005), chap. 15. The British official history still presents the fullest British Commonwealth account. See I. S. O. Playfair et al., *The Mediterranean and Middle East*, vol. 1, *The Early Successes Against Italy* (London: Her Majesty's Stationery Office, 1954).

51. The best account is Eleanor M. Gates, *End of the Affair: The Collapse of the Anglo-French Alliance 1939–1940* (London: George Allen & Unwin, 1981), 352–64. Operation Catapult, as it was code-named, began on July 3 and ended on July 6, when torpedo bombers destroyed the already damaged *Dunkerque*. A total of 1,297 French sailors were killed and 351 wounded. Vichy France broke off diplomatic relations with Britain as a result. On Churchill's role in the operation, see Richard Hough, *Former Naval Person: Churchill and the Wars at Sea* (London: Weidenfeld and Nicolson, 1985), 165–66.

52. Remarkably little has been written about the naval war in the Mediterranean. Still useful is M. A. Bragadin, *The Italian Navy in World War II* (Annapolis, MD: U.S. Naval Institute, 1957).

53. See Playfair, *Mediterranean and Middle East*, vol. 1. This has recently been reissued by Naval & Military Press (Uckfield, U.K.: 2004). It remains a classic study. On the Italian Navy in the war, see James J. Sadkovich, *La Marina Italiana Nella Seconda Guerra Mondiale* (Gorizia: Editrice Goriziana, 2012).

54. From *Brazen Chariots* by Robert Crisp. Copyright © by Robert Crisp. Used by permission of W. W. Norton & Company, Inc.

55. The Italian forces in the Greek campaign were numerically weaker than the Greek defenders: six Italian divisions of around 12,000 men against four Greek divisions each with 18,000. By mid-November, there were eleven larger Greek divisions against fifteen Italian. Mussolini underestimated Greek resistance and ignored the warnings of his generals that the Italian Army was too poorly equipped for an invasion. The best account is Rochat, *Le Guerre Italiane*, 259–85.

56. Cited in Bernd Stegemann, "The Italo-German Conduct of the War in the Mediterranean and North Africa," in Gerhard Schreiber, Bernd Stegemann, and Detlef Vogel, *Germany and the Second World War*, vol. 3, *The Mediterranean, South-East Europe and North Africa 1939–1941* (Oxford: Oxford University Press, 1995), 654. On the defense of Malta, see Douglas Austin, *Malta and British Strategic Policy, 1925–1943* (London: Frank Cass, 2004), and Michael Budden, "Defending the Indefensible? The Air Defence of Malta, 1936–40," *War in History* 6 (1999).

57. The best recent account is Douglas Porch, *Hitler's Mediterranean Gamble: The North African and the Mediterranean Campaigns in World War II* (London: Weidenfeld & Nicolson, 2004); see too James J. Sadkovich, "Of Myths and Men: Rommel and the Italians in North Africa 1940–1942," *International History Review* 13 (1991).

58. Thomas Jentz, *Tank Combat in North Africa: The Opening Rounds: Operations Sonnenblume, Brevity, Skorpion and Battleaxe, February 1941–June 1941* (Atglen, PA: Schiffer, 1998).

59. Philip Warner, *Auchinleck: The Lonely Soldier* (London: Cassell, 1981), 80–90. On Wavell there are numerous biographies that generally regard him as a soldier unjustly penalized by Churchill. See John Connell, *Wavell: Scholar and Soldier: to June 1941* (London: Collins, 1964); Harold Raugh, *Wavell in the Middle East, 1939–41: A Study in Generalship* (London: Brassey's, 1993).

60. On the Crete campaign, see Callum MacDonald, *The Lost Battle: Crete 1941* (London: Cassell, 1995). On the British reaction to the paratroop threat, see John Campbell, "Facing the German Airborne Threat to the United Kingdom, 1939–1942," *War in History* 4 (1997): 429–33.

61. On the sinking of the *Bismarck*, see the definitive account by Holger Herwig and David Bercuson, *Bismarck* (London: Hutchinson, 2002).

62. The best book is Andrew Thorpe, *Parties at War: Political Organization in Second World War Britain* (Oxford: Oxford University Press, 2009).

63. Bernard Donoughue and G. W. Jones, *Herbert Morrison: Portrait of a Politician* (London: Phoenix Press, 2001), chaps. 20–24. Churchill emphasized this principle in his first speech as prime minister.

64. Stephen Broadberry and Peter Howlett, "The United Kingdom: 'Victory at All Costs,'" in Mark Harrison, ed., *The Economics of World War II: Six Great Powers in International Comparison* (Cambridge: Cambridge University Press, 1998), 59–60.

65. Richard Overy, "Great Britain: Cyclops," in Reynolds, Kimball, Chubarian, eds., *Allies at War*, 120–39.

66. Richard Overy, "Pacifism and the Blitz," *Past & Present* 219 (2013): 201–36.

67. See R. V. Jones, *Most Secret War: British Scientific Intelligence, 1939–1945* (London: Hamish Hamilton, 1978). Jones's account centers heavily on his own participation and achievements, but it remains an indispensable source on the role of science. The best account of Britain's use of its technical and intellectual resources is David Edgerton, *Britain's War Machine: Weapons, Resources, and Experts in the Second World War* (London: Allen Lane, 2011).

68. Ferenc Szasz, *British Scientists and the Manhattan Project* (New York: St. Martin's Press, 1992).

1. Gerhard L. Weinberg, *A World at Arms: A Global History of World War II* (Cambridge and New York: Cambridge University Press, 1994), 264.

2. See G. F. Krivosheev, *Soviet Casualties and Combat Losses in the Twentieth Century*, trans. Lionel Leventhal (London: Greenhill Books, 1997), especially the introduction.

3. For an overview of those repercussions, see Chris Bellamy, *Absolute War: Soviet Russia in the Second World War* (New York: Alfred A. Knopf, 2007), chap. 1.

4. The use of the words *Nazi* and *German* calls for some care. Obviously, not all Germans were Nazis. Some Germans opposed the Nazi Party from the start, actively or passively. Just as obviously, however, the Nazis were Germans, and many Germans who did not see themselves as Nazis nevertheless carried out Nazi policies. This text tries to use *Nazi* when referring to the controlling or ideological elements within the Third Reich, while not shying away from *German* when it seems that a wider sense of responsibility is appropriate.

5. One of the persistent myths to come out of the Nazi-Soviet war was that the Wehrmacht fought honorably, while the SS was responsible for any and all crimes. On the myth itself, see Ronald M. Smelser and Edward J. Davies II, *The Myth of the Eastern Front: The Nazi-Soviet War in American Popular Culture* (Cambridge: Cambridge University Press, 2008). SS stood for *Schutzstaffel*, or "protective echelon." Originally Hitler's personal bodyguard, it grew to be a major paramilitary organization within the Nazi Party, with branches that ran industrial concerns, concentration camps, extermination centers, and the police. There was also an armed contingent, the Waffen-SS, that fought alongside the regular army, but it was by no means separate from the rest of the SS; transfers to and from the other branches were common, as was the Waffen-SS's participation in the crimes. Until late in the war, only dedicated Nazi volunteers could join the SS. It committed some of the Nazi regime's worst offenses. Surprisingly, there are few good works on the organization as a whole, and only one that is recent. See Heinz Hoehne, *The Order of the Death's Head: The Story of Hitler's SS* (New York: Coward McCann, 1970); Robert Koehl, *The Black Corps: The Structure and Power Struggles of the Nazi SS* (Madison: University of Wisconsin Press, 1983); Helmut Krausnick et al., *Anatomy of the SS State* (New York: Walker, 1968); Peter Longerich, *Heinrich Himmler* (New York: Oxford University Press, 2012); and Gerald Reitlinger, *The SS: Alibi of a Nation, 1922–1945*, rev. ed. (New York: Viking, 1968).

6. See David M. Glantz, *Stumbling Colossus: The Red Army on the Eve of World War* (Lawrence: University Press of Kansas, 1998), 26–33.

7. See Weinberg, *World at Arms*, 162–64.

8. David M. Glantz, *When Titans Clashed: How the Red Army Stopped Hitler* (Lawrence: University Press of Kansas, 1995), 23–25.

9. For an overview of the German strategic planning process in 1940, see Geoffrey P. Megargee, *Inside Hitler's High Command* (Lawrence: University Press of Kansas, 2000), 87–92.

10. For a more detailed examination of the economic motives behind Barbarossa, see Adam Tooze, *The Wages of Destruction: The Making and Breaking of the Nazi Economy* (London: Penguin Books, 2006), chaps. 12 and 13. Although the United States was not in the war yet, its antipathy was obvious, and Hitler saw open conflict as inevitable.

11. Some historians indicate that Hitler had made up his mind as early as July 31, 1940, when he told his senior commanders to plan for an invasion the following May. See, for example, Earl F. Ziemke and Magna E. Bauer, *Moscow to Stalingrad: Decision in the East* (New York: Military Heritage Press, 1988), 13; Ernst Klink, "The Military Concept of the War Against the Soviet Union: Land Warfare," in *Germany and the Second World War*, ed. Research Institute for Military History (New York: Oxford University Press, 1996), 4:253–54. Certainly there is evidence that he took the option seriously, but other possibilities were still open to him.

12. The Germans had a long history of favoring short, decisive campaigns and wars. See Robert M. Citino, *The German Way of War: From the Thirty Years' War to the Third Reich* (Lawrence: University Press of Kansas, 2005). Adam Tooze maintains that this was the one and only time that the Germans used a real "Blitzkrieg strategy": a combination of military and economic policy, strategy, and operations designed to win quickly, with the aim of gaining resources for the next phase in the war. See *Wages of Destruction*, chap. 13.

13. On Wehrmacht military planning, see Klink, "Military Concept," 225–325. Also David Stahel, *Operation Barbarossa and Germany's Defeat in the East* (Cambridge: Cambridge University Press, 2009), chaps. 1 and 2; and Megargee, *Inside Hitler's High Command*, chaps. 6 and 7.

14. David Thomas, "Foreign Armies East and German Military Intelligence in Russia, 1941–1945," *Journal of Contemporary History* 22 (1987): 277–78, www.jstor.org/stable/260933; Glantz, *Stumbling Colossus*, 9–11; Glantz, *Titans*, 33. The magnitude of these miscalculations grew out of systemic problems (see below) as well as the difficulty of gathering intelligence in the Soviet Union.

15. Along with the aforementioned sources, see Martin van Creveld, *Supplying War: Logistics from Wallenstein to Patton* (Cambridge: Cambridge University Press, 1977), chap. 7; and Richard L. DiNardo, *Mechanized Juggernaut or Military Anachronism? Horses and the German Army of WWII* (Mechanicsburg, PA: Stackpole, 2008), chap. 3. The figures for German strength come from *Germany and the Second World War*, 4:318.

16. Megargee, *Inside Hitler's High Command*, 124.

17. Ibid., 108–10, 122–23.

18. The most detailed analysis of the attitudes of the German army group and army commanders, unfortunately available only in German, is in Johannes Hürter, *Hitlers Heerführer. Die deutschen Oberbefehlshaber im Krieg gegen die Sowjetunion 1941/42* (Munich: Oldenbourg, 2007). Their part in the meeting is discussed on 9–12. On the March 30, 1941, meeting, see Charles Burdick and Hans Adolf Jacobsen, eds., *The Halder War Diary 1939–1942* (Novato, CA: Presidio Press, 1988), 345–46. This is a severely abridged but still useful version of the German original. For a more complete version, see *War Journal of Franz Halder*, vol. 6, 41–43, available online at http://cgsc.contentdm.oclc.org/cdm/singleitem/collection/p4013coll8/id/3973/rec/1. Readers should be aware that Halder edited his diary heavily after the war.

19. Jürgen Förster, "Operation Barbarossa as a War of Conquest and Annihilation," in *Germany and the Second World War*, 4:485.

20. For more detail on the development of German occupation policy, see Förster, "Operation Barbarossa as a War of Conquest and Annihilation."

21. The literature on these issues is voluminous, but it also tends to be specialized: very few works try to bring together all the threads of German military, economic, and genocidal policies in any great detail. Timothy Snyder, *Bloodlands: Europe Between Hitler and Stalin* (New York: Basic Books, 2010) may be the best general work, and it looks at the Soviet side too. Geoffrey P. Megargee, *War of Annihilation: Combat and Genocide on the Eastern Front, 1941* (Lanham, MD: Rowman & Littlefield, 2006) concentrates on the military aspects. Tooze, in *Wages of Destruction*, goes into more depth on the interaction of economic with military and ideological factors; see chap. 14. Wolfram Wette, *Die Wehrmacht: Feindbilder, Vernichtungskrieg, Legenden* (Frankfurt-am-Main: S. Fischer Verlag, 2002), is also worthy of note; the English edition, *The Wehrmacht: History, Myth, Reality* (Cambridge, MA: Harvard University Press, 2006), is worth consulting, but there are problems with the translation.

22. The best source on these reforms is Glantz's *Stumbling Colossus*, especially chaps. 2 and 5. See also John Erikson, *Stalin's War with Germany* (Boulder, CO: Westview Press, 1984; first published, 1975), chap. 1.

23. For an excellent analysis of the German tank arm and its capabilities vis-à-vis Soviet models, see Stahel, *Operation Barbarossa*, 107–13. No German tank had a gun that could penetrate the armor on a T-34 at over five hundred meters, and only one model could do so reliably at under that distance.

24. Glantz, *Titans*, 24.

25. See Steven J. Zaloga and Leland S. Ness, *Red Army Handbook, 1939–1945* (Thrupp, Stroud, Gloucestershire: Sutton Publishing, 1998), vi–vii.

26. See Glantz, *Stumbling Colossus*, chap. 4.

27. See Glantz, *Titans*, 42–43, and *Stumbling Colossus*, chap. 9; also Geoffrey Roberts, *Stalin's Wars: From World War to Cold War, 1939–1953* (New Haven, CT: Yale University Press, 2006), 61–70.

28. Some actual military developments in the winter and spring of 1941 helped to lull Stalin into a false feeling of security. First, the Germans intervened in North Africa in January, in what looked like a step toward a Mediterranean strategy. Then in April, the Wehrmacht struck into Yugoslavia and Greece. That second move seemed to provide a rationale for part of the German buildup in the East. Historiographically, it became a partial excuse for the failure of Barbarossa, because it supposedly delayed the jump-off date by some weeks, but its effect was actually minimal.

29. The claim has arisen that Stalin actually intended to launch an attack against Germany, but the evidence clearly refutes it. See Glantz, *Stumbling Colossus*, 1–8.

30. For the Soviets, see Glantz, *Stumbling Colossus*, 11–13. A complete German order of battle is available on the website of Dr. Leo Niehorster, http://niehorster.orbat.com/011_germany/41 -oob/_41-oob.html.

31. By the end of June, the Soviets had lost 4,614 aircraft. See Horst Boog, "The Conduct of Operations: The Luftwaffe," in *Germany and the Second World War*, 4:764.

32. On this and what follows regarding the military operations themselves, see Klink, "The Conduct of Operations: The Army and Navy," in *Germany and the Second World War*, 4:525–763; David M. Glantz, *Operation Barbarossa: Hitler's Invasion of Russia, 1941*, 2nd ed. (Stroud: History Press, 2011); Stahel, *Operation Barbarossa*. For the ground-level view from the Soviet side, see Catherine Merridale, *Ivan's War: Life and Death in the Red Army, 1939–1945* (New York: Holt, 2006).

33. Alexander Werth, *Russia at War, 1941–1945* (New York: E. P. Dutton, 1964), 148.

34. These casualty figures are culled from Glantz's works. Readers should be aware that Soviet accounting, especially in this early, chaotic stage of the war, was anything but careful. However, any imprecision does not affect the overall numbers to any meaningful degree. The Battle of Smolensk actually continued for weeks more, as the Soviets launched a major counteroffensive. For an unparalleled analysis, see David M. Glantz, *Barbarossa Derailed: The Battle for Smolensk 10 July–10 September 1941* (2 vols., Solihull: Helion, 2010, 2011).

35. Burdick and Jacobsen, eds., *The Halder Diary*, 446–47; *War Journal* 6, 199.

36. Burdick and Jacobsen, eds., *The Halder Diary*, 493; *War Journal* 7, 13, available online at http:// cgsc.contentdm.oclc.org/cdm/singleitem/collection/p4013coll8/id/3974/rec/16.

37. Glantz, *Stumbling Colossus*, 15. See also David M. Glantz, *Colossus Reborn: The Red Army at War, 1941–1943* (Lawrence: University Press of Kansas, 2005).

38. Burdick and Jacobsen, eds., *The Halder Diary*, 506; *War Journal* 7, p 39.

39. David Stahel, in *Operation Barbarossa*, argues that the Germans had already lost the campaign by this point—in which case, one can ask if they ever had a chance of winning it. Of course, there is always room for contingencies, but the Wehrmacht would certainly have had trouble emerging victorious from the situation by that time.

40. For a more in-depth analysis of the controversy, see Klink, "Military Concept," especially 277–79; and Klink, "Conduct of Operations," 569–93.

41. Some authors, such as R. H. S. Stolfi in *Hitler's Panzers East: World War II Reinterpreted* (Norman: University of Oklahoma Press, 1991), have argued that Germany could have won the war if Hitler had not insisted on these diversions. This counterfactual assertion ignores the state of Army Group Center, which was fighting hard just to hang on to its gains east of Smolensk, and whose logistical support structure was entirely unable to support a buildup for a broad offensive at that point. It also ignores the reality that the Soviets were already preparing to

evacuate Moscow, if need be, and continue the war from farther east. The loss of the capital would have been serious, but not fatal. See Megargee, *War of Annihilation*, 78–82.

42. Glantz, *Operation Barbarossa*, 129. The casualty figures include killed, wounded, and missing for all of the Southwestern Front. Roughly 600,000 became POWs; their fates are discussed below.

43. *Germany and the Second World War*, 4:667–670; Glantz, *Operation Barbarossa*, 136-38.

44. S. Golubkov, *V fashistskom kontslagere, Vospominaniia byvshego voennoplennogo* (Smolensk: Smolenskoe knizhnoe izdatel'stvo, 1958), 103.

45. Snyder, *Bloodlands*, covers all these crimes in some detail.

46. On the ghettos, see Christopher R. Browning, "Introduction," in Martin Dean and Geoffrey P. Megargee, eds., *The United States Holocaust Memorial Museum Encyclopedia of Camps and Ghettos, 1933–1945*, vol. 2, *Ghettos in German-Occupied Eastern Europe* (Bloomington: Indiana University Press, 2012), *xxvii–xxxix*. See also Förster, "Operation Barbarossa as a War of Conquest and Annihilation"; Wette, *The Wehrmacht*.

47. For a closer examination of those orders, see Geoffrey P. Megargee, "Vernichtungskrieg: Strategy, Operations, and Genocide in the German Invasion of the Soviet Union, 1941," in the *Acta* of the International Commission on Military History's Thirty-fourth Annual Congress (Commissione Italiana di Storia Militare, 2009); this includes an English translation of the first order, from General Walter von Reichenau. The original German text of the Reichenau Order is available at www.ns-archiv.de/krieg/untermenschen/reichenau-befehl.php.

48. Geoffrey P. Megargee, "*Vernichtungskrieg*: Strategy, Operations, and Genocide in the German Invasion of the Soviet Union, 1941," in *Acta of the International Commission on Military History's Thirty-Fourth Annual Congress* (Rome: Commissione Italiana di Storia Militare, 2009).

49. The Soviets quickly established their superiority in the art of deception operations: what they called *maskirovka*. Time and time again, right through the end of the war, they were able to fool the Germans as to their capabilities and intentions. This allowed them to build up massively superior forces at the point of attack and strike with operational surprise.

50. On the Soviet counteroffensives, see Glantz, *When Titans Clashed*, 87–94.

51. Debate over Hitler's "stand fast" orders—in 1941 and later—has persisted to the present day. Many former generals, and some historians, have criticized Hitler for his inflexibility and his unwillingness to trust his commanders' judgment. Others have pointed out that, in this first instance, those orders probably salvaged Army Group Center's situation. Later on, Hitler's intrusions into the operation and even tactical spheres would be less helpful—if never quite so absolute nor so counterproductive as his generals claimed after the war.

52. See Megargee, *Inside Hitler's High Command*, 160–61, 172.

53. Glantz, *Operation Barbarossa*, 200; Richard Overy, *Why the Allies Won* (New York: W. W. Norton, 1997), 182–83.

54. By December 31, 1941, the Soviets had established 285 new rifle divisions, 12 re-formed tank divisions, 88 cavalry divisions, 174 rifle brigades, and 93 tank brigades. Glantz, *Stumbling Colossus*, 15.

55. For a detailed examination of Hitler's goals vis-à-vis the United States, see Norman J. W. Goda, *Tomorrow the World: Hitler, Northwest Africa, and the Path Toward America* (College Station: Texas A&M University Press, 1998). See also Tooze, *Wages of Destruction*, 503–505.

CHAPTER 5: JAPAN STRIKES: FROM PEARL HARBOR TO MIDWAY

1. A still useful account of the embargo's effect on Japan's decision for war may be found in Louis Morton, "Japan's Decision for War," in Kent Roberts Greenfield, ed., *Command Decisions* (Washington, D.C.: U.S. Government Printing Office, 1959), 99–124, www.history.army.mil/books/70-7_04.htm. The Japanese side is presented masterfully in Nobutake Ike, *Japan's Decision for War: Records of the 1941 Policy Conferences* (Stanford, CA: Stanford University Press, 1967). See also Herbert Feis, *The Road to Pearl Harbor: The Coming of the War Between*

the United States and Japan (Princeton, NJ: Princeton University Press, 1950), has been up-dated by Jonathan G. Utley, *Going to War with Japan, 1937–1941* (Knoxville: The University of Tennessee Press, 1985), and Michael A. Barnhart, *Japan Prepares for Total War: The Search for Economic Security, 1919–1941* (Ithaca, NY: Cornell University Press, 1987). Edward S. Miller, *Bankrupting the Enemy: The U.S. Financial Siege of Japan Before Pearl Harbor* (Annapolis, MD: Naval Institute Press, 2007), is a thorough treatment of U.S. methods of employing eco-nomic sanctions to curb Japan's aggression on the Asian continent, first in China in the 1930s and later in French Indochina in the early 1940s. Jeffrey Record, *Japan's Decision for War in 1941: Some Enduring Lessons* (Carlisle, PA: Army War College [U.S.] Strategic Studies Insti-tute, 2009), concludes (*v*) that the United States "overestimated the effectiveness of economic sanctions as a deterrent to war, whereas the Japanese underestimated the cohesion and resolve of an aroused American society and overestimated their own martial prowess as a means of defeating U.S. material superiority."

2. H. P. Willmott, *Empires in the Balance: Japanese and Allied Pacific Strategies to April 1942* (Annapolis, MD: Naval Institute Press, 1982), 74; Hayashi Saburo with Alvin Coox, *Kogun: The Japanese Army in the Pacific War* (Westport, CT: Greenwood Press, 1958), 31–33, 42.

3. Willmott, *Empires in the Balance*, 136, 140–41. Fleet Admiral Chester Nimitz later com-mented that the Japanese failure to launch a third strike to complete the job allowed the United States to catch its breath, restore morale, and rebuild its forces. Kimmel endorsed such views and said the destruction of the oil tanks would have been more crippling and forced the withdrawal of the fleet to the West Coast. Gordon W. Prange, *At Dawn We Slept: The Untold Story of Pearl Harbor* (New York: McGraw-Hill Book Company, 1981), 549.

4. Ronald H. Spector, *Eagle Against the Sun: The American War with Japan* (New York: Free Press, 1985), 96; Prange, *At Dawn We Slept*, 30. There was a general disbelief that the Japanese would undertake such a risky venture. Earlier that autumn, for example, Vice Admiral Wil-son Brown, commander of the scouting force with Task Force Three at Pearl Harbor, observed that Japanese pilots were incapable of conducting such a mission "and that if they did, we should certainly be able to follow their planes back to their carriers and destroy the carriers so that it would be a very expensive experiment." Spector, *Eagle Against the Sun*, 96; Prange, *At Dawn We Slept*, 730 and quote 461.

   The first official investigation, commonly known as the *Roberts Report*, concluded that the commanders "failed to make suitable dispositions to meet such an attack. Each failed to evaluate properly the seriousness of the situations. These errors of judgment were the effec-tive causes for the success of the attack." Prange, *At Dawn We Slept*, 600. Both commanding officers protested their relief and blamed Washington for withholding crucial intelligence, which would have caused them to act differently if they'd had it. Washington did withhold information, notably the Magic decryptions of Japanese foreign ministry cables. But the lack of consultation and cooperation between Short and Kimmel on defensive measures in case of war, and their conviction, shared by U.S. Army Chief of Staff General George C. Marshall and President Franklin Roosevelt, that hostilities with Japan were imminent but Pearl Harbor was not threatened, created "a state of preparedness instead of a state of alertness." Short, for example, saw the indigenous Japanese population of Hawaii as the biggest threat and thus parked his aircraft wingtip to wingtip to prevent sabotage and locked up ammunition to pre-vent tampering. Kimmel neglected to patrol the northern approaches to Hawaii because he considered a carrier attack unthinkable. Spector, *Eagle Against the Sun*, 93–94; Prange, *At Dawn We Slept*, 729, quoting remarks by Representative Hamilton Fish.

5. William H. Bartsch, *December 8, 1941: MacArthur's Pearl Harbor* (College Station: Texas A&M University Press, 2003), has an hour-by-hour account of the events told from both sides as well as a judicious analysis of command responsibility for the disaster.

6. Louis Morton, *U.S. Army in World War II: The War in the Pacific: The Fall of the Philippines* (Washington, D.C.: U.S. Government Printing Office, 1953), 90, 96.

7. Willmott, *Empires in the Balance*, 142–43.

8. Greg Kennedy, "Anglo-American Strategic Relations and Intelligence Assessments of Japanese Air Power 1934–1941," *Journal of Military History* 74 (July 2010): 737–73, argues that Western intelligence field reports critical of the Japanese air arm's training system were not based on racist theories that the personnel were inferior but based on the contention that the training was substandard. Likewise, Japanese aircraft were generally inferior to their Western counterparts until the operational appearance of the army's twin-engine Mitsubishi Type 97 (G3M) heavy bomber in 1937 and the navy's A6M, the famous Zero fighter, in 1940.

   To observe that Japan lacked industrial capacity and innovative technologies was to identify shortcomings of equipment, not racist claptrap. Field reports did indicate major improvements in Japanese aircraft, but senior political and military leaders held to their more traditional views of inferior Japanese equipment, formed during the early 1930s. The United States, for instance, had accurate information on the Zero before the outbreak of the Pacific War. Attaché reports from China and Colonel Claire Chennault's observations concerning the Zero's tactical data had reached the War Department by the fall of 1940. In Chennault's case, his reports were dismissed because he was regarded as too much a maverick to be objective. Mark R. Peattie, *Sunburst: The Rise of Japanese Naval Air Power, 1909–1941* (Annapolis, MD: Naval Institute Press, 2001), n51, 330; John Toland, *The Rising Sun: The Decline and Fall of the Japanese Empire 1936–1945* (New York: Random House, 1970), 234. Peattie, *Sunburst*, is a superb account of Japanese naval aviation with appendices on personalities, naval aviation vessels, order of battle, main naval aircraft, and tactics.

9. In December 1941 Brooke-Popham described Japanese infantry that he saw on the Chinese frontier with Hong Kong in December 1940 in those words. Cited in Louis Allen, *Singapore 1941–1942* (London: Frank Cass, 1993), 54.

10. According to a gunner's mate at Pearl Harbor, "There was a deep, powerful thirst for revenge on the part of every enlisted man. I wouldn't have given any Japanese a second of mercy after Pearl Harbor." Cited in Prange, *At Dawn We Slept*, 568.

11. John W. Dower, *War Without Mercy: Race and Power in the Pacific War* (New York: Pantheon Books, 1986), 13. Dower's analysis of racism and warfare is a landmark study. His emphasis on a racist interpretation, however, is monocausal and slights other personal and impersonal factors that combined to make mid-twentieth-century warfare so brutal.

12. Peter Schrijvers, *The GI War Against Japan: American Soldiers in Asia and the Pacific During World War II* (New York: New York University Press, 2005), 220. Schrijvers analyzes multiple factors—terrain, geography, jungle combat, the psychology of mass organizations, human rage, technological and industrial violence—to present a better-rounded appreciation of the nature of combat in Asia.

13. *Papers Relating to the Foreign Relations of the United States. Japan: 1931–1941*, vol. 2 (Washington, D.C.: Government Printing Office, 1943), 794–95.

14. The Imperial Guards drew their conscripts nationwide, as opposed to the numbered divisions, which raised conscripts from their respective regional conscription districts. There was no noticeable difference in training, quality, or battlefield performance.

15. Rikusenshi kenkyū fūkyūkai, ed., *Mare sakusen*, [The Malaya Operation] (Tokyo: Hara shobō, 1971), 18–20, 23–9, 6, 271–75, and appendices 3, 4, 5. This is the Japan Ground Self-Defense Force Staff College, Military History Department's history of the campaign.

16. Kojima Noboru, *Shisetsu Yamashita Tomoyuki* [Historical report; Yamashita Tomoyuki] (Tokyo: Bungei bunkō, 1991), 156, 187–88.

17. Willmott, *Empires in the Balance*, 220; Peter Dennis et al., eds., *The Oxford Companion to Australian Military History*, 2nd ed. (Oxford, Australia, and New Zealand: Oxford University Press, 2008), 341. Training above company echelon was almost nonexistent and combined-arms exercises were not conducted.

18. Brian P. Farrell, *The Defence and Fall of Singapore 1940–1942* (Stroud: Tempus, 2005), provides a recent reassessment of the Malaya campaign. It is the best account of the Singapore

campaign. For a concise but well-informed treatment, see Dennis et al., eds., *Oxford Companion to Australian Military History*.

19. Robert Lyman, *The Generals: From Defeat to Victory, Leadership in Asia, 1941–45* (London: Constable, 2008), 60, 70.

20. Willmott, *Empires in the Balance*, 220; Allen, *Singapore 1941–1942*, 45; Farrell, *The Defence and Fall of Singapore*, 131; Dennis, *Oxford Companion to Australian Military History*, 341. Percival kept four brigades in southern Malaya to counter internal security threats. Allen, *Singapore, 1941–1942*, 94.

21. Lyman, *Generals*, 64 and 73.

22. Ibid., 78.

23. Willmott, *Empires in the Balance*, 127.

24. Lyman, *Generals*, 62–3; Raymond Callahan, *Churchill and His Generals* (Lawrence: University Press of Kansas, 2007), 86–87.

25. Allen, *Singapore 1941–1942*, 54.

26. The British planes sank one transport and heavily damaged two others.

27. Rikusenshi, *Mare sakusen*, 65–73; Allen, *Singapore 1941–1942*, 118–19, 128.

28. Farrell, *Defence and Fall of Singapore 1940–1942*, 146.

29. David Hein, "Vulnerable: HMS *Prince of Wales* in 1941," *Journal of Military History* 77, no. 3 (July 2013): 955–89, offers a fascinating account of the warship's participation in a series of decisive naval and diplomatic events during 1941.

30. Toland, *Rising Sun*, 238–43.

31. Dennis, *Oxford Companion to Australian Military History*, 342.

32. Ibid.

33. Louis Morton, *U.S. Army in World War II: The War in the Pacific: Strategy and Command; The First Two Years* (Washington, D.C.: U.S. Government Printing Office, 1962), 160–80, has a detailed account of ABDACOM.

34. Spector, *Eagle Against the Sun*, 123–25; Lyman, *Generals*, 60; Callahan, *Churchill and His Generals*, 100. Brooke-Popham was relieved on December 23, 1941, but his successor served only a few days because ABDACOM's activation on December 31 eliminated the CinC Far East Headquarters.

35. Rikusenshi, *Mare sakusen*, 149–53; Allen, *Singapore, 1941–1942*, 146–51.

36. Rikusenshi, *Mare sakusen*, 166–68; Lyman, *Generals*, 77.

37. David Horner, *High Command: Australia's Struggle for an Independent War Strategy, 1939–45* (St. Leonards, New South Wales, Australia: Allen & Unwin, 1982), 173–74. A classified British government report not released until 1992 blamed a lack of discipline among Australian troops for contributing directly to the loss of Singapore. While there was poor discipline during the final days of Singapore, it was not a cause of the loss of the so-called Singapore fortress. Dennis, *Oxford Companion to Australian Military History*, 344–45. The Australians, for their part, were extremely critical of British tactics and leadership during and after the Singapore campaign.

38. Allen, *Singapore*, 170–71.

39. Toland, *Rising Sun*, 273.

40. Casualty figures are derived from Allen, *Singapore*, 270.

41. Kojima Noboru, *Taiheiyō sensō (jō)*, (The Pacific war, vol. 1) (Tokyo: Chūkō shinsho, 1965), 161.

42. Willmott, *Empires in the Balance*, 266–67; P. C. Boer, *The Loss of Java: The Final Batles for the Possession of Java Fought by Allied Air, Naval, and Land Forces in the period of 18 February–7 March 1942* (Singapore: NUS Press, 2011), 215 and attachment 3, 598–99; Douglas Gillison, *Royal Australian Air Force, 1939–1942* (Canberra: Australian War Memorial, 1962), 435: "The Conquest of Java Island, March 1942," 1, as of October 14, 2011, available online at www.dutcheastindies.webs.com/java.html.

43. Willmott, *Empires in the Balance*, 292–93. The light cruiser *Marblehead* was so badly damaged that it had to return to New York for repairs; the heavy cruiser *Houston* was able to make repairs locally and remain in service with the fleet.

44. Kojima, *Taiheiyō sensō*, 167–68.

45. Ibid., 168; Boer, *Loss of Java*, 215.

46. Takagi Sōkichi, *Taiheiyō kaisenshi* (A naval history of the Pacific war), rev. ed. (Tokyo: Iwanami shinsho, 1977), 43.

47. Toland, *Rising Sun*, 280–81; Kojima, *Taiheiyō sensō*, 170–71.

48. David C. Evans and Mark R. Peattie, *Kaigun: Strategy, Tactics, and Technology in the Imperial Japanese Navy, 1887–1941* (Annapolis, MD: Naval Institute Press, 1997), 273–81, 499.

49. Kojima, *Taiheiyō sensō*, 172–73.

50. Ibid., 174–75.

51. Boer, *Loss of Java*, 334–43, 491; "The Conquest of Java Island, March 1942," Dutch East Indies, available online at www.dutcheastindies.webs.com/java.html.

52. Kojima, *Taiheiyō sensō*, 175–76. Casualty figures are difficult to ascertain. The Japanese interned 110,000 Dutch men (including military), women, and children, and forced 300 Dutch women to serve in Japanese military brothels. Linda Goetz Holmes, "Dutch Civilian Compensation for Japan and the American Dilemma" (JPRI working paper, no. 84: February 2002), online at www.jpri.org/publications/workingpapers/wp84.html.

53. Louis Allen, *Burma: The Longest War, 1941–45* (New York: St. Martin's Press, 1984), 4–7.

54. General Wavell, for instance, pronounced Burma "a most important but somewhat distracting commitment." Cited in Gillison, *Royal Australian Air Force*, 401.

55. Lyman, *Generals*, 104–5.

56. Field Marshal Viscount William Slim, *Defeat into Victory* (London: Pan Macmillan, 2009), 79–80.

57. Willmott, *Empires in the Balance*, 411; Ian Lyall Grant and Kazuo Tamayama, *Burma 1942: The Japanese Invasion: Both Sides Tell the Story of a Savage Jungle War* (Chichester, West Sussex: Zampi Press, 1999), 54–55.

58. Allen, *Burma*, 29.

59. Lyman, *Generals*, 124.

60. Ibid., 125.

61. Allen, *Burma*, 647; Lyman, *Generals*, 126.

62. Source for accompanying map is Major General S. Woodburn Kirby, *The War Against Japan*, vol. 2, *India's Most Dangerous Hour* (London: Her Majesty's Stationery Office, 1958).

63. Allen, *Burma*, 43–44.

64. Ibid., 48–49.

65. Willmott, *Empires in the Balance*, 196.

66. Spector, *Eagle Against the Sun*, 73–74. The Japanese attackers destroyed twelve of the command's B-17 bombers and thirty-four of its ninety-two P-40 fighters, the only modern U.S. fighter aircraft in the islands. About 77 Americans were killed and 148 wounded. Bartsch, *December 8, 1941*, 410.

67. Spector, *Eagle Against the Sun*, 108–9.

68. Louis Morton, "The Decision to Withdraw to Bataan," in Kent Roberts Greenfield, ed., *Command Decisions* (Washington, D.C.: U.S. Government Printing Office, 1959), 162; Kojima, *Taiheiyō sensō*, 177–78.

69. Morton, *Fall of the Philippines*, 247–48, 272–78; Toland, *Rising Sun*, 262–66.

70. Morton, *Fall of the Philippines*, 467; Michael Norman and Elizabeth M. Norman, *Tears in the Darkness: The Story of the Bataan Death March and Its Aftermath* (New York: Farrar, Straus and Giroux, 2009), is a recent and stirring account of the death march.

71. United States Strategic Bombing Survey (Pacific), Naval Analysis Division, *The Campaigns of the Pacific War* (Washington, D.C.: United States Government Printing Office, 1946), 38–40.

72. The original plan called for the B-25 pilots, whose planes in any case could not land on a carrier, to bomb Japan and then fly to airfields in China. The launch was to occur between

450 and 650 miles from the Japanese coast. Some 775 miles from the coast, however, a picket line of Japanese fishing boats encountered the carrier task force. Stealth compromised, the Americans launched the medium bombers immediately and accepted the risk of encountering an alert enemy or of the bombers running out of fuel before reaching the bases in China. Four B-25s landed at Chinese airfields and one at Vladivostok, Russia. The others ran out of fuel and crash-landed. One crew member was killed in a crash, and Japanese patrols captured eight more. Chinese partisans led the rest to safety through Japanese lines. The Japanese later executed three of these eight prisoners of war for having bombed civilians. Willmott, *Empires in the Balance*, 448–49.

73. Jonathan B. Parshall and Anthony P. Tully, *Shattered Sword: The Untold Story of the Battle of Midway* (Washington, D.C.: Potomac Books, 2005), 33–34.

74. Both operations were independent of the Midway plan. The naval General Staff wanted to extend Japan's northern defensive perimeter to preclude U.S. air attacks from the Aleutians and threaten the U.S.-Soviet maritime line of communication in the North Pacific. The Aleutian operation is usually considered a diversion to draw U.S. forces from the Central Pacific, but there is the argument that the invasion of the Aleutian chain was to begin the same day of the invasion of Midway and thus could hardly serve as a diversion. Parshall and Tully, *Shattered Sword*, 43–47. By extension, the Aleutians appeared to be a feint because American code breakers were aware of the Japanese Navy's fleet dispositions and inferred that the Aleutian force was a diversionary operation to draw the Americans from Midway. The Japanese move into the Southwest Pacific was the first step in interdicting the line of communication between the United States and Australia.

75. Parshall and Tully, *Shattered Sword*, 37.

76. Frederick D. Parker, *A Priceless Advantage: U.S. Navy Communications Intelligence and the Battles of Coral Sea, Midway, and the Aleutians*, United States Cryptologic History, Series 4, World War II, vol. 5 (Fort Meade, MD: Center for Cryptologic History, National Security Agency, 1993), 20. In late May the Imperial Japanese Navy introduced a new cipher, temporarily denying U.S. cryptanalysts access to the contents of their messages.

77. John B. Lundstrom, *The First South Pacific Campaign: Pacific Fleet Strategy December 1941– June 1942* (Annapolis, MD: Naval Institute Press, 1976), x, 85. On December 17, 1941, Kimmel turned over command to Vice Admiral William Pye, commander of Task Force One, his temporary successor. On December 6 Pye had assured subordinates that Japan would not attack the United States. Prange, *At Dawn We Slept*, 469–70, 590.

78. Spector, *Eagle Against the Sun*, 147.

79. Lundstrom, *First South Pacific Campaign*, 106–9.

80. Ibid., 110–13.

81. The planning flaws are analyzed in Parshall and Tully, *Shattered Sword*, 52–59, 408–12. Basically since the Russo-Japanese War (1904–1905), the Imperial Japanese Navy choreographed complicated and highly coordinated operational plans that relied on misdirection and stealth to lure opponents into ambushes. Vice Admiral Nobutake Kondō's Midway Invasion Force was supposed to lure the American fleet into battle. Once the Americans took the bait, Yamamoto's various task forces would simultaneously converge from widely separated points and destroy them. The Battle of Leyte Gulf in October 1944 is also an excellent example of such a planning scenario. Once a plan received approval, the Japanese were reluctant to change it, and tactical commanders were slow to react to new situations, instead repeating standard operations and tactics regardless of enemy responses. Evans and Peattie, *Kaigun*, 500.

82. Parker, *Priceless Advantage*, 57, www.nsa.gov/about/_files/cryptologic_heritage/publications /wwii/priceless_advantage.pdf. There was initial uncertainty over the Japanese objective, which was only identified by the digraph "AF" in radio messages. (The Japanese Navy used digraphs to conceal the identity of locations such as Midway. Thus "AF" alone was meaningless until cryptanalysts associated it with a proper place name.) Relying on a clever deception plan, Midway sent a plain text message reporting that the base was low on water. A few days

later, a deciphered May 20 Japanese message stated that AF had water for only two weeks, thus confirming for the Americans that AF equated to Midway. Parker, *Priceless Advantage*, 42–43, 50–51, 61.

83. Willmott, *Barrier and Javelin*, 343; Parshall and Tully, *Shattered Sword*, 433–34. The aircraft included: from the Army, seventeen B-17 heavy bombers, four B-26 medium bombers fitted for carrying torpedoes; from the Marines, twenty-one old F2A Buffalo fighters, seven F4F fighters, nineteen SBD dive-bombers, and twenty-one old SB2U scout bombers; and from the Navy, six new TBF torpedo planes and a light utility plane. Parshall and Tully, *Shattered Sword*, 96.

84. Parshall and Tully, *Shattered Sword*, chap. 10, 176–204, has the most comprehensive account of this first stage of the battle. Ibid., figure 9-2, 154–55, provides an air operations timeline that illustrates the tempo of air operations for both sides.

85. Ibid., 186, 209–10, 227, 432.

86. The destroyer *Arashi* had been detached from the carrier striking force about an hour earlier to deal with an American submarine, the U.S.S. *Nautilus. Arashi* kept the submarine pinned underwater as carriers moved away. The destroyer was en route to rejoining the main force when sighted by the American flyers.

87. Parshall and Tully, *Shattered Sword*, 186, 209–10, 227, 432; Willmott, *Barrier and the Javelin*, 419–20.

88. Parshall and Tully, *Shattered Sword*, 217.

89. A one-thousand-pound bomb hit *Akagi*'s flight deck directly amidships; as many as five bombs fell on *Kaga*, including a thousand-pounder amidships; and three one-thousand-pound bombs, spaced the length of the carrier deck, turned *Sōryū* into an inferno. Contrary to previous accounts, the Japanese carrier decks were not packed wingtip to wingtip with aircraft, because the Japanese were refueling and rearming below deck. Ibid., 229.

90. Ibid., 249, 251, 253, 327.

91. Ibid., 416–17, 431.

92. Ibid., 58.

93. Richard W. Bates, *The Battle of Midway, Including the Aleutian Phase of June 3 to June 14, 1942: Strategical and Tactical Analysis* (Newport, CT: U.S. Naval War College Press, 1948), 1.

CHAPTER 6: PEOPLE AND ECONOMIES AT WAR

1. Imperial War Museum, London, Speer Collection Box S368, Schmelter interrogation, Appendix 1, "The Call-up of Workers from Industry for the Armed Forces," 7–8.

2. The best account of the performance of American aircrews in combat is Donald Miller, *Eighth Air Force: The American Bomber Crews in Britain* (London: Aurum, 2007). There is also very useful material on loss rates and morale in Mark K. Wells, *Courage and Air Warfare: The Allied Aircrew Experience in the Second World War* (London: Frank Cass, 1995).

3. Bernhard Kroener, "Menschenbewirtschaftung, Bevölkerungsverteilung und personelle Rüstung in der zweiten Kriegshälfte," in Kroener, Rolf-Dieter Müller, and Hans Umbreit, *Das Deutsche Reich und der Zweite Weltkrieg: Band 5/2: Organisation und Mobilisierung des deutschen Machtbereichs* (Stuttgart: Deutsche Verlags-Anstalt, 1999), 853–59.

4. Akira Hara, "Japan: Guns Before Rice," in Harrison, *Economics of World War II*, 253.

5. For Britain, see Great Britain Central Statistic Office, *Statistical Digest of the War* (London: Her Majesty's Stationery Office, 1951), 13.

6. For Germany, see Rüdiger Overmans, *Deutsche militärische Verluste im Zweiten Weltkrieg* (Munich: Oldenbourg Verlag, 2004), 334; for the Soviet Union, G. F. Krivosheev, *Soviet Casualties and Combat Losses in the Twentieth Century* (London: Greenhill Books, 1997), 85.

7. *Statistical Digest of the War*, 1, 11.

8. Krivosheev, *Soviet Casualties and Combat Losses in the Twentieth Century*, 91.

9. Overmans, *Deutsche militärische Verluste im Zweiten Weltkrieg*, 333. Greater Germany included Austria, the areas annexed from Czechoslovakia and Poland, and Alsace-Lorraine, annexed from France.

10. On Britain, *Statistical Digest of the War*, 11. Around 3 million were recruited by 1941, but in 1942 only 547,000; in 1943, 347,000; and in 1944, 254,000. On Germany, see Overmans, *Deutsche militärische Verluste im Zweiten Weltkrieg*, 332–33.

11. Krivosheev, *Soviet Casualties and Combat Losses in the Twentieth Century*, 235–36.

12. Great Britain Air Ministry, *The Rise and Fall of the German Air Force, 1933–1945* (London: Arms & Armour Press, 1983), 283–86. See too Murray, *Luftwaffe*, 229: "the experience and the skill level of German fighter pilots," writes Murray, "spiraled downwards."

13. United States Strategic Bombing Survey, Pacific Theater, Report 1, *Summary Report*, Washington, D.C., July 1, 1946, 10–11, www.anesi.com/ussbs01.htm.

14. Air Force Historical Records Agency, Maxwell AFB, 520.056-188, Statistical Summary Eighth Air Force Operations, 1942–1945; Disc A5835, Eighth Air Force, Growth, Development and Operations, Exhibit 1.

15. Russell F. Weigley, *History of the United States Army* (New York: Macmillan, 1968), 568–69; *Statistical Digest of the War*, 9; Percy Schramm, ed., *OKW Kriegstagebuch*, III (*ii*), 1576, 1597. It is interesting to note that the American Army was larger than either the German Army or the Soviet Army at its peak strength. This reflected, first of all, the emphasis on extensive support services in the U.S. Army, and, secondly, the much lower level of casualties and prisoners of war.

16. *Statistical Digest of the War*, 8. On labor policy in Britain, see Peggy Inman, *Labour in the Munitions Industries* (London: Her Majesty's Stationery Office, 1957).

17. Hugh Rockoff, "The United States: From Ploughshares to Swords," in Harrison, *The Economics of World War II*, 100–101.

18. Rockoff, "United States," in Harrison, *Economics of World War II*, 103–4; Theodore Wilson, "The United States: Leviathan," in Kimball, Reynolds, and Chubarian, *Allies at War*, 182–84. A good case study of this transition is Gerald D. Nash, *World War II and the West: Reshaping the Economy* (Lincoln: Nebraska University Press, 1990), chaps. 3–5.

19. Harrison, *Economics of World War II*, editor's introduction, 21.

20. Ulrich Herbert, *Hitler's Foreign Workers: Enforced Foreign Labor in Germany Under the Third Reich* (Cambridge: Cambridge University Press, 1997), 50–57. In 1938 there were 375,678 registered foreign workers in Germany.

21. Details in Overy, *War and Economy in the Third Reich*, 262–63, 294.

22. The best recent account of German exploitation is Hein Klemann and Sergei Kudryashev, *Occupied Economies: An Economic History of Nazi-Occupied Europe, 1939–1945* (London: Berg, 2012).

23. See, for example, Bernhard Kroener, "Squaring the Circle: Blitzkrieg Strategy and Manpower Shortage," in Wilhelm Deist, ed., *The German Military in the Age of Total War* (Leamington Spa: Berg, 1985), 282–303.

24. The most useful account of Soviet war preparation is Lennart Samuelson, *Plans for Stalin's War Machine: Tukhachevskii and Military-Economic Planning, 1925–1941* (London: Macmillan, 2000).

25. Mark Harrison, "The Soviet Union: The Defeated Victor," in Harrison, *Economics of World War II*, 283–85. See too S. R. Lieberman, "Crisis Management in the U.S.S.R.: The Wartime System of Administration and Control," in Susan J. Linz, ed., *The Impact of World War II on the Soviet Union* (Totowa, NJ: Rowman & Littlefield, 1985), 59–76.

26. Franz Seidler, *Blitzmädchen: Die Geschichte der Helferinnen der deutschen Wehrmacht* (Bonn: Bernhard & Graefe Verlag, 1996), 169.

27. *Statistical Digest of the War*, 9, 11.

28. Overy, *Bombing War*, 132–33.

29. Jeanne Holm, *In Defense of a Nation: Servicewomen in World War II* (Washington, D.C.: Women's Military Press, 1998), 1, 41, 75. On women recruits with the air force, see Craven and Cate, *Army Air Forces*, vol. 6, 102–4, www.ibiblio.org/hyperwar/AAF/VI. Air force efforts

to integrate women from the WAAC into the air-warning program failed, unlike the role of the WAAF in Britain.

30. Holm, *In Defense of a Nation*, 57–59, 48–49.

31. The origins of this ideology are explored in Mark von Hagen, *Soldiers in the Proletarian Dictatorship: The Red Army and the Soviet Socialist State, 1917–1930* (Ithaca, NY: Cornell University Press, 1990).

32. Reina Pennington, *Wings, Women and War: Soviet Airwomen in World War II Combat* (Lawrence: University Press of Kansas, 2001), 1–2; John Erickson, "Soviet Women at War," in John Garrard and Carol Garrard, ed., *World War 2 and the Soviet People* (New York: St. Martin's Press, 1993), 52, 62–69.

33. Alec Nove, "The Peasantry in World War II," in Linz, *The Impact of World War II on the Soviet Union*, 79–84; Lydia Pozdeeva, "The Soviet Union: Phoenix," in Kimball, Reynolds, and Chubarian, *Allies at War*, 157–58.

34. Harrison, "Soviet Union," in Harrison, *Economics of World War II*, 285–86; for an excellent case study of Soviet working conditions, see Lennart Samuelson, *Tankograd: The Formation of a Soviet Company Town: Cheliabinsk, 1900s–1950s* (Basingstoke: Palgrave Macmillan, 2011), 226–36.

35. Hara, "Japan: Guns Before Rice," in Harrison, *Economics of World War II*, 253–55.

36. See Leila J. Rupp, *Mobilizing Women for War: German and American Propaganda, 1939–1945* (Princeton, NJ: Princeton University Press, 1978), 185; Overy, *War and Economy in the Third Reich*, 303–9; Eleanor Hancock, "Employment in Wartime: The Experience of German Women During the Second World War," *War & Society* 12 (1994): 43–68.

37. Rupp, *Mobilizing Women for War*, 171; Rockoff, "United States," in Harrison, *Economics of World War II*, 102–3; Jill Stephenson, *Women in Nazi Society* (London: Croom Helm, 1975), 101; Overy, *War and Economy in the Third Reich*, 305.

38. H. M. Parker, *Manpower: A Study of War-time Policy and Administration* (London: HMSO, 1957), 435–36.

39. Yvonne M. Klein, ed., *Beyond the Home Front: Women's Autobiographical Writing of the Two World Wars* (London: Macmillan, 1997), 146–48.

40. On continued discrimination, see Rose, *Which People's War?*, 107–50; on dilution, see Inman, *Labour in the Munitions Industry*, 57–67.

41. On Germany, see Overy, *War and Economy in the Third Reich*, 307–10; on Britain, see Inman, *Labour in the Munitions Industry*, 122–48, 352–67; Parker, *Manpower*, 441–45; on the United States, see Chester Gregory, *Women in Defense Work During World War II: An Analysis of the Labor Problem and Women's Rights* (New York: Exposition Press, 1974).

42. The best account is David Killingray, *Fighting for Britain: African Soldiers in the Second World War* (Woodbridge: James Currey, 2010).

43. Morris J. MacGregor, *Integration of the Armed Forces, 1940–1965* (Washington, D.C.: Center for Military History, U.S. Army, 1985), 17–24.

44. Sherie Mershon and Steven Schlossman, *Foxholes and Color Lines: Desegregating the U.S. Armed Forces* (Baltimore: Johns Hopkins University Press, 1998), 67, 77–78, 82–83.

45. Ulysses Lee, *The Employment of Negro Troops* (Washington, D.C.: Center of Military History, U.S. Army, 1994), 411–16; MacGregor, *Integration of the Armed Forces, 1940–1965*, 24; Mershon and Schlossman, *Foxholes and Color Lines*, 64–65.

46. Lee, *Employment of Negro Troops*, 286; MacGregor, *Integration of the Armed Forces, 1940–1965*, 28–30. There are numerous books about the Tuskegee Airmen. The best recent account is J. Todd Moye, *Freedom Flyers: The Tuskegee Airmen of World War II* (New York: Oxford University Press, 2010).

47. Robert Asahina, *Just Americans: How Japanese Americans Won a War at Home and Abroad: The Story of the 100th Battalion/442d Regiment Combat Team in World War II* (New York: Gotham Books, 2006), 6–7; Brenda Moore, *Serving Our Country: Japanese American Women in the Military during World War II* (New Brunswick, NJ: Rutgers University Press, 2003), *xi–xii*,

19. The Japanese-American 442nd Regimental Combat Team became the Army's most highly decorated unit.

48. Hara, "Japan: Guns Before Rice," in Harrison, *Economics of World War II*, 254–55.

49. Maggi M. Morehouse, *Fighting in the Jim Crow Army: Black Men and Women Remember World War II* (Lanham, MD: Rowman & Littlefield, 2000), 165–66.

50. The standard history is Herbert, *Hitler's Foreign Workers*.

51. The best account in English is still Wolfgang Sofsky, *The Order of Terror: The Concentration Camp* (Princeton, NJ: Princeton University Press, 1997). See too the recent book of essays edited by Nikolaus Wachsmann and Jane Caplan, *Concentration Camps in Nazi Germany: The New Histories* (London: Taylor & Francis, 2010). For reflections on the irrationality of the system, see Alan Beyerchen, "Rational Means and Irrational Ends: Thoughts on the Technology of Racism in the Third Reich," *Central European History* 30, no. 3 (1997): 386–402.

52. Mark Spoerer, "Recent Findings on Forced Labor Under the Nazi Regime and an Agenda for Future Research," in Gustav Corni, ed., *Forced Laborers and POWs in the German War Economy*, special issue of *Annali dell'Istituto storico italo-germanico in Trento* 27 (2002): 385–86.

53. The best recent account of the exploitation of Jewish labor is Michael Thad Allen, *The Business of Genocide: The SS, Slave Labor, and the Concentration Camps* (Chapel Hill: North Carolina University Press, 2002).

54. On these points, see Mark Harrison, *Soviet Planning in Peace and War, 1938–1945* (Cambridge: Cambridge University Press, 1985), and Robert W. Davies, Mark Harrison, and S. G. Wheatcroft, *The Economic Transformation of the Soviet Union, 1913–1945* (Cambridge: Cambridge University Press, 1994). Full figures in Richard Overy, *The Dictators: Hitler's Germany and Stalin's Russia* (New York: Norton, 2005), 498.

55. Harrison, "Soviet Union," in Harrison, *Economics of World War II*, 282–83.

56. The best accounts of the Soviet home front can be found in William Moskoff, *The Bread of Affliction: The Food Supply in the U.S.S.R. During World War II* (Cambridge: Cambridge University Press, 1990), and John Barber and Mark Harrison, *The Soviet Home Front, 1941–1945* (London: Longman, 1991). There is also good detail in Samuelson, *Tankograd*.

57. See Edwin Bacon, *The Gulag at War: Stalin's Forced Labour System in the Light of the Archives* (Basingstoke: Macmillan, 1994), 139–44. The camp prisoners produced, among other things, 30.2 million mortar shells and 9.2 million antipersonnel mines.

58. Paul Steinberg, *Speak You Also: A Survivor's Reckoning* (London: Allen Lane, 2001), 68–70.

59. Figures in Overy, "Co-operation," in Kimball, Reynolds, and Chubarian, *Allies at War*, 208–10. Useful are Hubert van Tuyll, *Feeding the Bear: American Aid to the Soviet Union, 1941–1945* (New York: Greenwood Press, 1989); Joan Beaumont, *Comrades in Arms: British Aid to Russia 1941–1945* (London: Davis-Poynter, 1980). Lend-Lease transport is covered in Robert W. Coakley and Richard M. Leighton, *Global Logistics and Strategy, 1943–1945* (Washington, D.C.: Office of the Chief of Military History, 1968), 627–55, 845–48.

60. According to his deputy commander Georgy Zhukov; see Richard Overy, *Russia's War: A History of the Soviet Effort, 1941–1945* (London: Penguin, 1998), 194–98. On this subject, compare the rather different views in Pozdeeva, "The Soviet Union," 161, who writes "the blunt fact is that the Lend-Lease Act made no substantial contribution to the victory of the Soviet armed forces at Moscow or Stalingrad."

61. Harold Vatter, "The Material Status of the U.S. Civilian Consumer of World War II: The Question of Guns or Butter," in Geoffrey Mills and Hugh Rockoff, eds., *The Sinews of War: Essays on the Economic History of World War II* (Ames: Iowa State University Press, 1993), 219–42.

62. Rockoff, "United States," in Harrison, *Economics of World War II*, 82–87; Wilson, "United States," in *Allies at War*, ed. Kimball, Reynolds, Chubarian, 176–78. For an early but still useful account of the U.S. war economy, see Frances Walton, *Miracle of World War II: How American Industry Made Victory Possible* (New York: Macmillan, 1956). The standard work remains Harold G. Vatter, *The U.S. Economy in World War II* (New York: Columbia University Press, 1985).

63. For the Ford Company, see Allan Nevins and Frank Ernest Hill, *Ford* (New York: Scribner's, 1963), 226. Ford produced 8,685 bombers to Italy's 7,000 combat aircraft; 371,000 vehicles to Italy's 136,600; and 15,200 tanks and armored vehicles to Italy's 2,800. Italian figures in Istituto centrale di statistica, *Sommario di statistiche storiche Italiane, 1861–1955* (Rome: Istituto Poligrafico dello Stato, 1958).

64. See John M. Haight, *American Aid to France, 1938–1940* (New York: Atheneum, 1970).

65. Warren Kimball, "Beggar My Neighbor: America and the British Interim Finance Crisis," *Journal of Economic History* 29, no. 4 (1969).

66. Richard Overy, "Co-operation: Trade, Aid and Technology," in Kimball, Reynolds, and Chubarian, *Allies at War*, 209–11. A useful account of the program can be found in Alan P. Dobson, *U.S. Wartime Aid to Britain, 1940–1946* (New York: St. Martin's Press, 1986).

67. This was the conclusion reached by Nicholas Kaldor, one of the economists working for the postwar bombing surveys. See Nicholas Kaldor, "The German War Economy," *Review of Economic Statistics* 13, no. 1 (1946): 20. See too Burton H. Klein, *Germany's Economic Preparations for War* (Cambridge, MA: Harvard University Press, 1959), 27.

68. See, for example, Werner Abelshauser, "Guns, Butter and Economic Miracles," in Harrison, *Economics of World War II*, 156–63. By comparison, consumption in the United States *increased* by 13 percent between 1941 and 1945. In earlier historiography, the success of German production despite the impact of bombing was usually attributed to the appointment as minister for armaments and munitions, in February 1942, of Hitler's favorite architect, Albert Speer, who exploited the previously dormant economic potential.

69. See Richard Overy, "Mobilization for Total War in Germany, 1939–1941," *English Historical Review* 103, no. 408 (1988): 613–39; for a general history, see Tooze, *Wages of Destruction*.

70. Adam Tooze, "No Room for Miracles: German Industrial Output in World War II Reassessed," *Geschichte und Gesellschaft* 31 (2005): 439–64.

71. For details on the reaction to bombing, see Overy, *Bombing War*, 450–62; Rolf-Dieter Müller, "Albert Speer und die Rüstungspolitik im totalen Krieg," in Kroener, Müller, Umbreit, *Das Deutsche Reich und der Zweite Weltkrieg: Band 5/2*, 614–39, 659–92.

72. On German society in the last stages of the war, see Ian Kershaw, *The End: The Defiance and Destruction of Hitler's Germany 1944–1945* (London: Allen Lane, 2012).

73. See Vera Zamagni, "Italy: How to Lose the War and Win the Peace," in Harrison, *Economics of World War II*, 177–97.

Conclusion: The War at Midpoint

1. Gordon W. Prange, ed., *Hitler's Words* (Washington, D.C.: American Council on Public Affairs, 1944), 271.

2. Overy, *Why the Allies Won*, 19, for numbers. Earlier in 1941, Hitler is said to have told General Alfred Jodl, chief of operations for the OKW, "We have only to kick in the door, and the whole rotten structure will come crashing down." William L. Shirer, *The Rise and Fall of the Third Reich: A History of Nazi Germany* (New York: Simon & Schuster, 1960), 856.

3. Steven D. Mercatante, *Why Germany Nearly Won: A New History of the Second World War in Europe* (Santa Barbara, CA: Praeger, 2012), 257.

4. Robert Goralski and Russell W. Freeberg, *Oil & War: How the Deadly Struggle for Fuel in WWII Meant Victory or Defeat* (New York: William Morrow, 1987), 336–38, 348. The figures are for 1941 (oil production) and December 1941 (refining capacity).

5. Paul Bairoch, "International Industrialization Levels from 1750 to 1980," *Journal of European Economic History* 11 (1982).

6. Ian Kershaw, *Fateful Choices: Ten Decisions That Changed the World, 1940–1941* (New York: Penguin Press, 2007), 417.

7. *Papers Relating to the Foreign Relations of the United States. Japan: 1931–1941*, vol. 2 (Washington, D.C.: Government Printing Office, 1943), 793.

8. Evan Mawdsley, *December 1941: Twelve Days That Began a World War* (New Haven, CT: Yale University Press, 2011), 176.

9. Churchill, *The Second World War*, vol. 3, *The Grand Alliance*, 606–7. This was, of course, an after-the-fact recollection, but there is independent evidence that his recollection is essentially accurate. At the time—on December 12, 1941—Churchill wrote to his foreign secretary that the "accession of the United States . . . with time and patience will give certain victory." Ibid., 624; see also Overy, *Why the Allies Won*, 32, for an identical opinion from Churchill's chief military advisor, General Hastings Lionel "Pug" Ismay.

10. Churchill, *Grand Alliance*, 620.

11. Kershaw, *Fateful Choices*, chap. 8; Matome Ugaki, *Fading Victory: The Diary of Admiral Matome Ugaki* (Pittsburgh: University of Pittsburgh Press, 1991), 65.

12. I. C. B. Dear and M. R. D. Foot, eds., *The Oxford Companion to World War II*, 1010, for the number.

13. John Ellis, *The Military Book Club's World War II: The Encyclopedia of Facts and Figures* (Military Book Club, 1995), 280, counting aircraft carriers, battleships, cruisers, and destroyers. Overy, looking at a broader range of ships, reckons that in 1943 the United States produced 2,654 "major vessels" to Japan's 122. *Why the Allies Won*, 331.

14. It was later demonstrated that the U.S. Pacific Fleet could sustain a drive across the Central Pacific directly from logistical bases in Hawaii. But that probably would not have been possible had the Japanese not needed to simultaneously devote a large portion of their Pacific-theater resources to fighting MacArthur's Southwest Pacific drive, which was supplied and supported from Australia.

Source attribution does not imply sponsorship, endorsement, or connection with the licensor, creator, or publisher of a work.

All base maps have been made with the following data sources:

Elevation models have been created using data available from the U.S. Geological Survey (USGS). Historic boundaries of Europe are based on the Stanford University Spatial History Project available at GeoCommons, and are published under a Creative Commons license. Hydrological information has been derived from Natural Earth (NE), European Environment Agency's Water Information System for Europe (EEA WISE), or Vector Map Level 0 (VMAP0) data.

CHAPTER 1

1. Copyright Rowan Technology Solutions, 2015.
2. Copyright Rowan Technology Solutions, 2015.
3. Copyright Rowan Technology Solutions, 2015.
   Military layer based on Edward Krasnoborski's map 1, Campaign in Poland 1939, Europe in 1933 and Territorial Changes Resulting from World War I, *West Point Atlas of American Wars*, vol. 2, *1900–1953*, sec. 2 (New York: Praeger, 1959).
4. Main courtyard of the Palais des Nations at Geneva, twentieth century, black-and-white photograph, provided courtesy of L'Illustration (www.lillustration.com).
5. English photographer, *A parade of the walking wounded cases*, 1916, sepia photo, private collection, the Stapleton Collection, Bridgeman Images.
6. E. Schilling, *Germany is crushed by the Treaty of Versailles*, 1931, color lithograph, private collection, Archives Charmet, Bridgeman Images.
7. Achille Beltrame, *Historic beginning of Disarmament Conference in Washington*, November 27, 1921, illustration, De Agostini Picture Library, A. Dagli Orti, Bridgeman Images.
8. *Signal* magazine, number 17, *Il Duce, Benito Mussolini (1883–1945)*, December 1940, lithograph, private collection, Bridgeman Images.
9. Spain: *Nationalist aircraft—Italian Savoia-Marchetti SM-79s—bomb Madrid in late November 1936*, Pictures from History, Bridgeman Images.
10. Japanese photographer, *Japanese Kwatung Army pioneers in Manchuria*, twentieth century, photograph, private collection, Peter Newark Military Pictures, Bridgeman Images.
11. *Tupolev TB-3*, San Diego Air & Space Museum.
12. Vasily Nikolaevich Elkin, *"Long Live the Red Army,"* 1932, color lithograph, Russian State Library, Moscow, Russia, Bridgeman Images.
13. German photographer, *Members of the right-wing Freikorps armed with flamethrower and supported by an armoured car*, 1919, black-and-white photograph, private collection, Peter Newark Military Pictures, Bridgeman Images.
14. Bundesarchiv, Bild 101I-290-1116-07, photo: Zermin.
15. Bundesarchiv, Bild 146-1970-085-36, photo: o.Ang.
16. Pablo Picasso, *Guernica*, 1937, oil on canvas, Museo Nacional Centro de Arte Reina Sofia, Madrid, Spain, Bridgeman Images, Pablo Picasso: copyright 2015 Estate of Pablo Picasso / Artists Rights Society (ARS), New York.
17. Copyright Rowan Technology Solutions, 2015.
    Military layer based on Krasnoborski's map 111, The War with Japan, Territory Seized Prior to July 1937 and Major Japanese Offensive Drives in 1937; and map 112, The War with Japan, Japanese Advances During 1938 and 1939, *West Point Atlas of American Wars*, vol. 2, sec. 2.
18. *Bodies of victims along Qinhuai River out of Nanjing's west gate during Nanjing Massacre*. Moriyasu Murase, Watashino Jyugun Cyugoku-Sensen (My China Front) (Osaka: Nippon Kikanshi Syuppan Center, 1987; revised 2005).
19. Martha Sawyers, "China First to Fight!": United China Relief participating in National War Fund, U.S.A., University of North Texas Libraries, http://digital.library.unt.edu/ark:/67531/metadc367/m1/1/.
20. Copyright Rowan Technology Solutions, 2015.
    Military layer based on Krasnoborski's map 2, Campaign in Poland 1939, German Aggressions, 1936–39, *West Point Atlas of American Wars*, vol. 2, sec. 2.
21. Copyright Rowan Technology Solutions, 2015.
22. Ministry of Information official photographer, *The Munich Agreement, September 1938*, Ministry of Information, Second World War Official Collection, Imperial War Museums, copyright IMW (D 2239).
23. "Remember . . . One More Lollypop, and Then You All Go Home!" Dr. Seuss Went to War Collection, Special Collections & Archives, University of California, San Diego.
24. *Fasces ornament*, brass, twentieth century, private collection, Bridgeman Images.
25. *Japanese battleship* Yamato *under construction at the Kure Naval Base*, Japan, September 20, 1941, photograph, Kure Maritime Museum.

IMAGE

26. Atlas-Guide to the British Commonwealth of Nations and Foreign Countries, Daily Dispatch edition, edited by George Philip. F.R.G.S., Syndicate Publishing, 18 Savoy Street, London, 1924, accessed from Historical Atlas of the British Empire, copyright James Alcock (www.atlasofbritempire.com).

27. *Imperial Japanese Navy aircraft carrier* Akagi *at Kobe, Japan, sometime in 1930*, Kure Maritime Museum, *Japanese Naval Warship Photo Album—Aircraft Carrier[s] and Seaplane Carrier[s]*, edited by Kazushige Todaka (Tokyo: Diamond, 2005).

28. Copyright Rowan Technology Solutions, 2015.
Military layer based on maps from Jean-Bernard Wahl, *Damals und heute-die Maginotlinie: Nordfrankreich-Lothringen-Elsass: Geschichte und Reiseführer* (Hamburg: Mittler, 2000); Jean-Pascal Soudagne, *Comprendre la ligne Maginot* (Rennes: Éd. Ouest-France, 2009).

29. *Abandoned Char B1 tank*, France, 1940, United States National Archives and Records Administration.

30. Lieutenant Davies, War Office official photographer, *The British Army in France, 1940*, Second World War Official Collection, Imperial War Museums, copyright IMW (F 2159).

31. English School, *Cross section view of the Maginot Line*, illustration from the *Illustrated London News*, reprinted in a Hungarian magazine, ca. 1940, color lithograph, private collection, Archives Charmet, Bridgeman Images.

32. English School, *Cross section view of the Maginot Line*, illustration from the *Illustrated London News*, reprinted in a Hungarian magazine, ca. 1940, color lithograph, private collection, Archives Charmet, Bridgeman Images.

33. German photographer, *Maginot Line*, 1939, black-and-white photograph, copyright SZ Photo, Bridgeman Images.

34. *Sir Basil Henry Liddell Hart*, by Bassano, whole-plate glass negative, January 17, 1927, NPG x19203, copyright National Portrait Gallery, London.

35. *Battle of Britain 10 July–31 October 1940: Hawker Hurricanes of Fighter Command, a first line of defence against the incoming German bombers attacking England, flying in formation in the first major battle to be won in the air, World War II*, Universal History Archive/UIG, Bridgeman Images.

36. *Photograph of amphibious tractors on Guadalcanal Island, 08/1942*, General Photographic File of the Department of the Navy, 1943–1958, Record Group 80: General Records of the Department of the Navy, 1804–1983, National Archives and Records Administration.

37. *Soviet-Japanese Conflict of Khalkhyn Gol*, Tass/UIG, Bridgeman Images.

38. Copyright Rowan Technology Solutions, 2015.
U.S. Army rifleman, 1938, Chase Stone, 2015.

39. *Boeing B-17E in flight*, U.S. Air Force, National Museum of the U.S. Air Force.

40. *Mikhail Tukhachevsky*, ca. 1920, photograph, State Museum of the Political History of Russia.

41. Copyright Rowan Technology Solutions, 2015.
Source: Williamson Murray, *The Change in the European Balance of Power, 1938–1939: The Path to Ruin* (Princeton, NJ: Princeton University Press, 1984), 20.

Chapter 2

42. Copyright Rowan Technology Solutions, 2015.

43. Copyright Rowan Technology Solutions, 2015.
Sources: Paul Bairoch, "International Industrialization Levels from 1750 to 1980," *Journal of European Economic History* 11, nos. 1–2 (Fall 1982): 209, 304, 332; John Ellis, *The Military Book Club's World War II: The Encyclopedia of Facts and Figures* (Military Book Club, 1995), 227–28, 273; Mark Harrison, *The Economics of World War II: Six Great Powers in International Comparison* (Cambridge: Cambridge University Press, 1998), 3, 10; and R. J. Overy, *The Air War, 1939–1945* (New York: Stein & Day, 1980), 139.

44. B. von Jacobs, *Portrait of Adolf Hitler*, 1933, oil on canvas, private collection, Bridgeman Images.

45. *Hitler with Generals Keitel and Jodl studying a war map*, published in *Signal* magazine, 1940, photograph, private collection, Peter Newark Military Pictures, Bridgeman Images.

46. Copyright Rowan Technology Solutions, 2015.
Military layer based on Frank Martini's map 4, Poland 1939, Campaign in Poland 1939, Disposition of Opposing Forces on 31 August and the German Plan, USMA History Department.

47. Copyright Rowan Technology Solutions.
Military layer based on Martini's map 5, Central Europe, 1939, Deployment of the Wehrmacht, 1 September 1939, USMA History Department.

48. Copyright Rowan Technology Solutions, 2015.
Sources: Ellis, *Military Book Club's World War II: Encyclopedia of Facts and Figures*, 142–43; Klaus A. Maier et al., *Germany and the Second World War*, vol. 2, *Germany's Initial Conquests in Europe*, trans. Dean S. McMurry and Eward Osers (Oxford: Oxford University Press, 1991), 92, 101; and Charles D. Pettibone, *The Organization and Order of Battle of Militaries in World War II*, vol. 9, *The Overrun & Neutral Nations of Europe and Latin American Allies*, Kindle edition (Bloomington, IN: Trafford Publishing, 2014).

49. Bundesarchiv, Bild 183-L08129, photo: o.Ang.

50. Copyright Rowan Technology Solutions, 2015.
Military layer based on Krasnoborski's map 5, Campaign in Poland, The Breakthrough, Operations, 1–5 September; and map 6, Campaign in Poland 1939, The Exploitation, Operations, 6–14 September, *West Point Atlas of American Wars*, vol. 2, sec. 2.

51. Bundesarchiv, Bild 183-J16050, photo: Karnath.
52. German photographer, *A bombadier in a Heinkel He 111 bomber during the invasion of Poland*, 1939, black-and-white photo, copyright SZ Photo, Bridgeman Images.
53. German photographer, *A German infantry column on the first day of the war, 1st September 1939*, 1939, black-and-white photo, copyright SZ Photo, Bridgeman Images.
54. Copyright Rowan Technology Solutions, 2015.
    Military layer based on Krasnoborski's map 7, Campaign in Poland 1939, The Annihilation, Operations, 15–28 September, *West Point Atlas of American Wars*, vol. 2, sec. 2.
55. Bundesarchiv, Bild 183-S54817, photo: o.Ang.
56. Copyright Rowan Technology Solutions, 2015.
    Military layer based on Krasnoborski's map 11a, Campaign in Norway, 1940, Norwegian Dispositions and Initial German Operations 9 April, *West Point Atlas of American Wars*, vol. 2, sec. 2.
57. Bundesarchiv, Bild 183-H26353, photo: Erich Borchert.
58. Copyright Rowan Technology Solutions, 2015.
59. Copyright Rowan Technology Solutions, 2015.
    Military layer based on Martini's map 9b, Evolution of Plan Yellow, October 1939–January 1940, OKH Plan 29 October 1939, *The West Point Atlas for the Second World War: Europe and the Mediterranean* (Wayne, NJ: Avery Publishing, 1985).
60. Copyright Rowan Technology Solutions, 2015.
    Military layer based on Martini's map 9b, Evolution of Plan Yellow, October 1939–January 1940, OKH Plan 29 October 1939, *West Point Atlas for Second World War: Europe and Mediterranean*.
61. Copyright Rowan Technology Solutions, 2015.
    Military layer based on Martini's map 9c, Evolution of Plan Yellow, October 1939–January 1940, OKH Plan 31 October 1939, *West Point Atlas for Second World War: Europe and Mediterranean* .
62. Copyright Rowan Technology Solutions, 2015.
    Military layer based on L. F. Ellis, *The History of the Second World War: The War in France and Flanders*, United Kingdom Military Series (London: HMSO, 1954), 343.
63. Copyright Rowan Technology Solutions, 2015.
    Sources: I.C.B. Dear and M. R. D. Foot, eds., *The Oxford Companion to World War II* (Oxford: Oxford University Press, 1995), 412; Ellis, *Military Book Club's World War II: Encyclopedia of Facts and Figures*, 146–151; French Army Order of Battle, 10 May 1940, accessed January 15, 2015, http://france1940.free.fr/oob/oob.html; and J. E. Kaufmann and H. W. Kaufmann, *Hitler's Blitzkrieg Campaigns: The Invasion and Defense of Western Europe, 1939–1940* (Conshohocken, PA: Combined Books, 1993), 346–53.
64. Copyright Rowan Technology Solutions, 2015.
    Military layer based on Krasnoborski's map 12, The Campaign in the West, 1940, Fortifications, Disposition of Opposing Forces, and German Plan for the Battle of Flanders, *West Point Atlas of American Wars*, vol. 2, sec. 2; and Martini's map 10, Northwestern Europe, 1940, Campaign in the West, 1940, Disposition of Opposing Forces, and German and Allied Plans for the Battle of Flanders, *West Point Atlas for Second World War: Europe and Mediterranean*.
65. *The German ultimatum ordering the Dutch commander of Rotterdam to cease fire was delivered to him at 10:30h on 14 May 1940. At 13:22h, German bombers set the whole inner city of Rotterdam ablaze, killing 30,000 of its inhabitants*, 1940, Office of Emergency Management, Office of War Information, Overseas Operations Branch, New York Office, News and Features Bureau, National Archives and Records Administration.
66. Bundesarchiv, Bild 101I-569-1579-14A, photo: Dr. Stocker.
67. Bundesarchiv, Bild 121-0412, photo: o.Ang.
68. Copyright Rowan Technology Solutions, 2015.
    Military layer based on Krasnoborski's map 13, The Campaign in the West, 1940, The Battle of Flanders, Operations, 16 May, and Operations Since 10 May, *West Point Atlas of American Wars*, vol. 2, sec.2.
69. Bundesarchiv, Bild 101I-382-0248-33A, photo: Böcker.
70. Bundesarchiv, Bild 146-1971-088-63, photo: Lohmeyer.
71. Copyright Rowan Technology Solutions, 2015.
    Military layer based on Krasnoborski's map 14, The Campaign in the West, 1940, The Battle of Flanders, Situation, 21 May, and Operations Since 16 May, *West Point Atlas of American Wars*, vol. 2, sec. 2.
72. German photographer, *Invasion of Belgium, May 1940*, 1940, color photograph, copyright Galerie Bilderwelt, Bridgeman Images.
73. Bundesarchiv, Bild 101I-139-1112-17, photo: Ludwig Knobloch.
74. Copyright Rowan Technology Solutions, 2015.
    Image: bpk, Berlin/Arthur Grimm/Art Resource, NY. Maps: copyright Rowan Technology Solutions, 2015.
75. Copyright Rowan Technology Solutions, 2015.
    Military layer based on Krasnoborski's map 15, The Campaign in the West, 1940, The Battle of Flanders, Situation, 4 June, and Operations Since 21 May, *West Point Atlas of American Wars*, vol. 2, sec. 2.
76. Charles Ernest Cundall, *The Withdrawal from Dunkirk*, June 1940, Imperial War Museums, copyright IWM (Art.IWM ART LD 305).
77. French photographer, *General Gamelin*, black-and-white photo, private collection, copyright Look and Learn, Elgar Collection, Bridgeman Images.
78. Copyright Rowan Technology Solutions, 2015.

Military layer based on Krasnoborski's map 16, Campaign in the West, 1940, The Battle of France, Situation, 12 June, and Operations since 4 June; and map 17, Campaign in the West, 1940, The Battle of France, The Pursuit, 13–25 June, *West Point Atlas of American Wars*, vol. 2, sec. 2.

79. German photographer, *Adolf Hitler greeting Marshal Pétain in Montoire, France, 1940*, black-and-white photo, copyright SZ Photo, Bridgeman Images.

80. French photographer, *The Germans entering Paris*, from *Signal*, June 14, 1940, 1940, photograph, private collection, Archives Charmet, Bridgeman Images.

81. German photographer, *Adolf Hitler posing in front of the Eiffel Tower after the surrender agreement has been signed in Compiègne, Paris, France, 23rd June 1940*, 1940, photo, private collection, copyright Galerie Bilderwelt, Bridgeman Images.

CHAPTER 3

82. Copyright Rowan Technology Solutions, 2015.

83. *"Together,"* Second World War recruitment poster, twentieth century, color litho, private collection, Prismatic Pictures, Bridgeman Images.

84. Copyright Rowan Technology Solutions, 2015.
Sources: Bairoch, "International Industrialization Levels from 1750 to 1980," 209, 304, 332; and Harrison, *Economics of World War II*, 3, 10.

85. Margery Forbes (fl.1939–40), *Portrait of Winston Churchill*, twentieth century, oil on canvas, private collection, copyright Arthur Ackermann, London, Bridgeman Images.

86. Copyright Rowan Technology Solutions, 2015.
Military layer based on the map The Second World War—A War for Empire (2), The Rational Colonel: History, Politics, Theory, Ancient and Modern, accessed January 15, 2015, http://therationalcolonel.org/2015/02/07/the-second-world-war-a-war-for-empire-2.

87. *Meeting first American food ship to arrive under Lend-Lease to Britain. Right to left: Kathleen Harriman, Lord Woolton, minister of food; Averell Harriman, U.S. Lend-Lease representative; Robert H. Hinkley, U.S. assistant secretary of commerce, watching a consignment of food being lifted from the hold of the ship at a British port*, 1941, Library of Congress Prints and Photographs Division, Washington, D.C.

88. Bundesarchiv, Bild 183-L20414, photo: Stöcker.

89. Copyright Rowan Technology Solutions, 2015.
Military layer based on Dear and Foot, eds., *Oxford Companion to World War II*, 125.

90. *Aircraft spotter on the roof of a building in London. St. Paul's Cathedral is in the background*, Records of the U.S. Information Agency, 1900–2003, Records Group 306, Photographic File of the Paris Bureau of the *New York Times*, ca. 1900–ca. 1950, National Archives and Records Administration.

91. Copyright Rowan Technology Solutions, 2015.
Source: Richard Hough and Denis Richards, *The Battle of Britain: The Greatest Air Battle of World War II* (New York: W. W. Norton, 2005), 372–81.

92. Copyright Rowan Technology Solutions, 2015. Data from Warbirds Resource Group, accessed January 15, 2015, www.warbirdsresourcegroup.org.

93. Bundesarchiv, Bild 101I-342-0603-25, photo: Ketelhohn.

94. Ellis, *Military Book Club's World War II : Encyclopedia of Facts and Figures*, tables 26 and 27, statistical appendix.

95. Ministry of Information official photographer, *The Second World War 1939–1945: Great Britain: Personalities, Air Chief Marshal Sir Hugh Dowding, Commander in Chief of Royal Air Force Fighter Command during the Battle of Britain*, Imperial War Museums, Ministry of Information Second World War Official Collection, copyright IWM (D 1417).

96. Christopher Richard Wynne Nevinson, *Among London searchlights*, private collection, copyright Christie's Images, Bridgeman Images.

97. Royal Air Force official photographer, *Royal Air Force Balloon Command*, 1939–45, Imperial War Museums, Air Ministry Second World War Official Collection, copyright IWM (CH 21007).

98. *Anderson shelter decorated by the house holders*, black-and-white photo, copyright Mirrorpix, Bridgeman Images.

99. Harry Green, *London Underground in the Blitz*, twentieth century, gouache on paper, private collection, copyright Look and Learn, Bridgeman Images.

100. "... and the Wolf chewed up the children and spit out their bones ... but those were *Foreign Children* and it really didn't matter." Dr. Seuss Went to War, Special Collections & Archives, University of California, San Diego.

101. *Women Demonstrating against the Lend-Lease Act of 1941, Pictured with the Congressional Delegates Clare Hoffman and Roy O. Woodruff*, 1941, black-and-white photo, copyright SZ Photo, Bridgeman Images.

102. *"Britain Shall Not Burn,"* 1940, color litho, Peter Newark Historical Pictures, Bridgeman Images.

103. German photographer, *German U-boat docks on the Atlantic Coast, ca. 1939–45*, black-and-white photo, copyright SZ Photo, Bridgeman Images.

104. Royal Observer Corps, *Do a Front Line Job—You Are Urgently Needed in the ROC, Royal Observer Corps*, Imperial War Museums, copyright IWM (Art.IWM PST 0765).

105. Copyright Rowan Technology Solutions, 2015.
   Military layer based on Frank Martini's map 33, The Mediterranean Basin, USMA History Department.
106. John S. Smith, *Fairey Swordfish*, twentieth century, gouache on paper, private collection, copyright Look and Learn, Bridgeman Images.
107. Copyright Rowan Technology Solutions, 2015.
   Sources: Ellis, *Military Book Club's World War II: Encyclopedia of Facts and Figures*, 155; David Hunt, *A Don at War*, rev. ed. (London: Routledge, 1996), 52; and Kenneth Macksey, *Beda Fomm: The Classic Victory*, Ballantine's Illustrated History of the Violent Century, Battle Book Number 22 (New York: Ballantine Books, 1971), 109–21.
108. Copyright Rowan Technology Solutions, 2015.
   Military layer based on Krasnoborski's map 74a, The War in North Africa, Graziani's Advance and Wavell's Offensive (13 September 1940–7 February 1941), *West Point Atlas of American Wars*, vol. 2, sec. 2.
109. Simon Elwes, *Field Marshal Earl Wavell*, 1959, oil on canvas, Bridgeman Images.
110. Bundesarchiv, Bild 146-1977-018-11A, photo: Ernst A. Zwilling.
111. Copyright Rowan Technology Solutions, 2015.
112. Copyright Rowan Technology Solutions, 2015. Military layer based on Krasnoborski's map 74a, "The War in North Africa, Graziani's Advance and Wavell's Offensive (13 September 1940–7 February 1941)," *West Point Atlas of American Wars*, vol. 2, sec. 2.
113. *The second battle of Libya. Before zero hour. The brigadier commanding tank units in Tobruk instructing tank commanders on the operations, using a sand table for demonstration purposes*, Library of Congress.
114. Copyright Rowan Technology Solutions, 2015.
   Sources: R. J. Overy, *Why the Allies Won* (New York: W. W. Norton, 1995), 331; and Ellis, *Military Book Club's World War II: Encyclopedia of Facts and Figures*, 277–78, 280.
115. *An Enigma decryption from Bletchley Park, formed from parts of two messages to the German Army Group Courland (Kurland) on Feb. 14, 1945*, U.S. Air Force, National Museum of the U.S. Air Force.

Chapter 4

116. Copyright Rowan Technology Solutions, 2015.
117. Copyright Rowan Technology Solutions, 2015.
   Sources: Bairoch, "International Industrialization Levels from 1750 to 1980," 209, 304, 332; and Harrison, *Economics of World War II*, 3, 10.
118. Joseph Stalin, *Secretary-General of the Communist Party of Soviet Russia*, ca. 1942, Library of Congress Prints and Photographs Division, Washington, D.C.
119. Kimon Evan Marengo, *Cartoon depicting the uneasy alliance between Hitler and Stalin*, 1939, color litho, private collection, Peter Newark Historical Pictures, Bridgeman Images, images courtesy of Richard and Alexander Marengo.
120. Copyright Rowan Technology Solutions, 2015.
121. Copyright Rowan Technology Solutions, 2015.
   Military layer based on Map I.IV.3, Deployment Directive Barbarossa in Horst Boog, *Germany and the Second World War*, vol. 4, *The Attack on the Soviet Union* (Oxford: Clarendon Press, 1998).
122. Bundesarchiv, Bild 101I-217-0476-20, photo: Scheffler.
123. *German infantry during the invasion of the Soviet Union in 1941*, United States Holocaust Memorial Museum, copyright United States Holocaust Memorial Museum, Washington, D.C.
124. Josef Engelhart, *"Bolshevism Brings War, Unemployment and Famine,"* 1918, color litho, private collection, copyright Galerie Bilderwelt, Bridgeman Images.
125. *Heinrich Luitpold Himmler*, Universal History Archive/UIG, Bridgeman Images.
126. *Soviet prisoners of war*, 1941, black-and-white photo, copyright SZ Photo, Bridgeman Images.
127. Copyright Rowan Technology Solutions, 2015.
128. German photographer, *Portrait of Georgy Zhukov at a parade in Berlin*, 1945, black-and-white photo, copyright SZ Photo, SV-Bilderdienst, Bridgeman Images.
129. *"The Attack into the Unknown," German troops advancing on Stalingrad*, from *Signal* magazine, first edition of January 1942, photo, private collection, Bridgeman Images.
130. Photo provided by author, courtesy of National Archives and Records Administration.
131. Copyright Rowan Technology Solutions, 2015.
   Military layer based on Frank Martini's map 19, Eastern Europe, 1941, German Invasion of Russia, Operations, 22 June–25 August 1941. *West Point Atlas for Second World War: Europe and Mediterranean*; David M. Glantz, *Colossus Reborn: The Red Army at War, 1941–1943* (Lawrence: University Press of Kansas, 2005), 8.
132. Copyright Rowan Technology Solutions, 2015.
   Sources: Boog, *Germany and the Second World War*, vol. 4, *Attack on the Soviet Union*, 222–23; Ellis, *Military Book Club's World War II: Encyclopedia of Facts and Figures*, 166–70; and David M. Glantz, *Companion to Colossus Reborn: Key Documents and Statistics* (Lawrence: University Press of Kansas, 2005), 157–64.
133. Photo provided by author, courtesy of United States Holocaust Memorial Museum.

134.   Photo provided by author, courtesy of National Archives and Records Administration.
135.   Copyright Rowan Technology Solutions, 2015.
       Military layer based on Krasnoborski's map 25a, The War in Eastern Europe, German Summer Offensive of 1941, Operations, 22 June–16 July 1941; map 25b, The War in Eastern Europe, German Summer Offensive of 1941, Operations, 17 July–1 September 1941, *West Point Atlas of American Wars*, vol. 2, sec. 2; and Frank Martini's map 19, Eastern Europe, 1941, German Invasion of Russia, Operations, 22 June–25 August 1941, *West Point Atlas for Second World War: Europe and Mediterranean*; and map 1.1 in Glantz, *Colossus Reborn*, 8.
136.   German photographer, *Operation Barbarossa*, 1941, color photo, copyright Galerie Bilderwelt, Bridgeman Images.
137.   Copyright Rowan Technology Solutions, 2015.
       Military layer based on Frank Martini's map 20, Eastern Europe, 1941, Advance on Moscow, Operations, 26 August–5 December, 1941, *West Point Atlas for Second World War: Europe and Mediterranean*.
138.   *Battle of Moscow*, United States Information Agency, Wikimedia Commons. This image was scanned from Nicholas William Bethell, *Russia Besieged*, World War II (New York: Time-Life Books, 1977).
139.   Bundesarchiv, Bild 146-1970-052-08, photo: o.Ang.
140.   Photo provided by author, courtesy of National Archives and Records Administration.
141.   Bundesarchiv, Bild 183-H26717, photo: o.Ang.
142.   Photo provided by author, courtesy of United States Holocaust Memorial Museum and National Archives and Records Administration.
143.   Bundesarchiv, Bild 101I-138-1083-26, photo: Rudolf Kessler.
144.   *"No Mercy to the Enemy!"* 1942, lithograph, private collection, Peter Newark Military Pictures, Bridgeman Images.
145.   Copyright Rowan Technology Solutions, 2015.
       Military layer based on Frank Martini's map 21, Eastern Europe, 1941, Soviet Winter Offensive, Operations, 6 December 1941–7 May 1942. *West Point Atlas for Second World War: Europe and Mediterranean*.
146.   Copyright Rowan Technology Solutions, 2015.
       Female Soviet sniper, Chase Stone, 2015.
147.   *Soviet Russian poster invoking past Russian heroism*, circa 1942, Universal History Archive/UIG, Bridgeman Images.

CHAPTER 5

148.   Copyright Rowan Technology Solutions, 2015.
149.   Copyright Rowan Technology Solutions, 2015.
       Sources: Bairoch, "International Industrialization Levels from 1750 to 1980": 209, 304, 332; and Harrison, *Economics of World War II*, 3, 10.
150.   Copyright Rowan Technology Solutions, 2015.
       Military layer based on Edward Krasnoborski's map 66, The Far East and the Pacific, 1941, The Imperial Powers, 1 September 1939, *West Point Atlas for Modern Warfare* (Garden City Park, NY: SquareOne Publishers, 2011).
151.   Shori Arai, *Japanese aircraft prepare to take off from carrier*, twentieth century, oil on canvas, private collection, Peter Newark Military Pictures, Bridgeman Images.
152.   Copyright Rowan Technology Solutions, 2015.
       Military layer based on Krasnoborski's map 67, The Far East and the Pacific, 1941, Major Japanese War Objectives and Planned Opening Attacks, *West Point Atlas for Modern Warfare*.
153.   Copyright Rowan Technology Solutions, 2015.
       Sources: Ellis, *Military Book Club's World War II: Encyclopedia of Facts and Figures*, 186; and Leo Niehorster, "7/8 December–Pacific Order of Battle," World War II Armed Forces: Orders of Battle and Organizations, accessed January 15, 2015, http://niehorster.orbat.com.
154.   American photographer, *USS* West Virginia *and USS* Tennessee *on fire during the Japanese attack on Pearl Harbor*, December 7, 1941, photo, private collection, Peter Newark Military Pictures, Bridgeman Images.
155.   Copyright Rowan Technology Solutions, 2015. Data from Warbirds Resource Group, accessed January 15, 2015, www.warbirdsresourcegroup.org.
156.   Frank O. Salisbury, *Franklin Delano Roosevelt*, presidential portrait, thirty-second president of the United States (1933–45), White House Historical Association (White House Collection).
157.   Copyright Rowan Technology Solutions, 2015.
       Okinawa Japanese soldier, Chase Stone, 2015.
158.   Copyright Rowan Technology Solutions, 2015.
       Military layer based on Krasnoborski's map 118, The War with Japan, The Malayan Campaign, Operations, 8 December 1941 to 15 February 1942, *West Point Atlas of American Wars*, vol. 2, sec. 2.
159.   Japanese photographer, *Japanese soldiers during the Battle of Malaya*, 1942, black-and-white photo, copyright SZ Photo, Scherl, Bridgeman Images.
160.   *Loss of HMS* Prince of Wales *and HMS* Repulse, 10 December 1941, U.S. Naval History and Heritage Command.

161. *Australia in the War of 1939–1945*, vol. 4, *The Japanese Thrust* (Canberra, Australia: Australian War Memorial, 1957).

162. Copyright Rowan Technology Solutions, 2015.
Military layer based on Krasnoborski's map 114, The War with Japan, Opening Operations of the Japanese Offensive. *West Point Atlas of American Wars*, vol. 2, sec. 2; and Krasnoborski's map 68, Southeast Asia, 1941, Japanese Centrifugal Offensive, December 1941, Southern Army and Southern Force (Navy) Operations, *West Point Atlas for Modern Warfare*.

163. *Soerabaja, Java. A house in the native quarter wrecked by a Japanese bomb*, 1942, Library of Congress Prints and Photographs Division, Washington, D.C.

164. "*He's Coming South*" poster, 1942, color litho, printed by the Department of Information, Museum of New Zealand Te Papa Tongarewa, gift of Mr. C. H. Andrews, 1967, Bridgeman Images.

165. Copyright Rowan Technology Solutions, 2015.
Military layer based on Charles Robert Anderson, *East Indies: The U.S. Army Campaigns of World War II* (Washington, D.C.: U.S. Army Center of Military History, 2005), 14.

166. Copyright Rowan Technology Solutions, 2015.
Military layer based on S. Woodburn Kirby, *The War Against Japan*, vol. 2, *India's Most Dangerous Hour*, History of the Second World War, United Kingdom Military Series (London: H.M.'s Stationery office, 1958).

167. German photographer, *Japanese infantry in a camp, Burma*, 1942, black-and-white photo, copyright SZ Photo, Scherl, Bridgeman Images.

168. *Pump jacks on a petroleum field in Yenangyaung, Burma*, ca. 1940, black-and-white photo, copyright SZ Photo, Scherl, Bridgeman Images.

169. Thomas E. Stephens, *General Douglas MacArthur*, 1950, oil on canvas, courtesy of the West Point Museum Collection.

170. Copyright Rowan Technology Solutions, 2015.
Military layer based on Krasnoborski's map 119, The War with Japan, Philippine Campaign, American Dispositions, 10 December 1941 and Reactions to Japanese Landings to 23 December; map 120, The War with Japan, Philippine Campaign, Operations in Northern Luzon (22–29 December); and map 121, The War with Japan, Philippine Campaign, Operations in Southern Luzon and the Withdrawal to Bataan, *West Point Atlas of American Wars*, vol. 2, sec. 2.

171. Copyright Rowan Technology Solutions, 2015.

172. Copyright Rowan Technology Solutions, 2015.
Military layer based on Krasnoborski's map 123, The War with Japan, Philippine Campaign, Operations along the Moron-Abucay Line (10–25 January 1942); map 124, The War with Japan, Philippine Campaign, First Japanese Offensive Against the Bagac-Orion Position (26 Jan–23 Feb); and map 125, The War with Japan, Philippine Campaign, The Japanese Breakthrough, 3–9 April, *West Point Atlas of American Wars*, vol. 2, sec. 2.

173. *Bataan about May 1942, the march of death from Bataan to Cabanatuan, the prison camp. Left to right: Samuel Stenzler, Frank Spear, James Mcd. Gallagher*, Omniphoto/UIG, Bridgeman Images.

174. Copyright Rowan Technology Solutions, 2015. Military layer based on Krasnoborski's map 71a, The Far East and the Pacific, 1941, The Battle of the Coral Sea, 6–8 May 1942; and map 71b, The Battle of Midway, 3–6 June 1942, *West Point Atlas for Modern Warfare*.

175. Copyright Rowan Technology Solutions, 2015. Military layer based on Samuel Eliot Morison, *History of United States Naval Operations in World War II*, vol. 4, *Coral Sea, Midway and Submarine Actions, May 1942–August 1942* (Boston: Little, Brown, 1947), 12, 23.

176. Copyright Rowan Technology Solutions, 2015.
Military layer based on Morison, *History of United States Naval Operations in World War II*, vol. 4, 36.

177. Copyright Rowan Technology Solutions, 2015.
Military layer based on Morison, *History of United States Naval Operations in World War II*, vol. 4, 47.

178. Copyright Rowan Technology Solutions, 2015.
U.S. naval aviator, Chase Stone, 2015.

179. Copyright Rowan Technology Solutions, 2015.
Source: Morison, *History of United States Naval Operations in World War II*, vol. 4, 87–93.

180. Copyright Rowan Technology Solutions, 2015.
Military layer based on Morison, *History of United States Naval Operations in World War II*, vol. 4, 94–95.

181. Copyright Rowan Technology Solutions, 2015.
Military layer based on Morison, *History of United States Naval Operations in World War II*, vol. 4, 108–9.

182. Copyright Rowan Technology Solutions, 2015.
Military layer based on Morison, *History of United States Naval Operations in World War II*, vol. 4, 118–19.

183. Copyright Rowan Technology Solutions, 2015.
Sources: Francis E. McMurtrie, ed., *Jane's Fighting Ships 1944–5* (1946; New York: Arco Pub. Co., 1971); and Warbirds Resource Group, accessed January 15, 2015, www.warbirdsresourcegroup.org.

184. *Fleet Admiral Isoroku Yamamoto*, twentieth century, color litho, private collection, Peter Newark Military Pictures, Bridgeman Images.

185. *Admiral Chester W. Nimitz*, twentieth century, black-and-white photo, private collection, Peter Newark Military Pictures, Bridgeman Images.

186. *U.S. Navy Douglas TBD-1 Devastator torpedo plane making an attack against a Japanese aircraft carrier at the Battle of Midway*, June 4, 1942, U.S. Navy National Museum of Naval Aviation.

187. McMurtrie, ed., *Jane's Fighting Ships, 1944–45* (1946; New York: Arco Pub. Co., 1971).

Chapter 6

188. Copyright Rowan Technology Solutions, 2015.
Sources: Bairoch, "International Industrialization Levels from 1750 to 1980," 209, 304, 332; and Harrison, *Economics of World War II*, 3, 10.

189. Copyright Rowan Technology Solutions, 2015.

190. McClelland Barclay, *"This Is Your Firing Line! Don't Slow Up the Ship!"* poster designed by McClelland Barclay, ca. 1939–45, color litho, private collection, DaTo Images, Bridgeman Images.

191. *"More Production,"* 1943, color lithograph, private collection, copyright Galerie Bilderwelt, Bridgeman Images.

192. Copyright Rowan Technology Solutions, 2015.
Sources: Mark Harrison, "Resource Mobilization for World War II: The U.S.A., U.K., U.S.S.R., and Germany, 1938–45," *Economic History Review* 41, no. 2 (1988): 18, table 5, accessed January 15, 2015, http://www2.warwick.ac.uk/fac/soc/economics/staff/mharrison/public/ehr88postprint.pdf; Clarence D. Long, *The Labor Force and War and Transition, Four Countries* (New York: National Bureau of Economic Research, 1952), 16, table 1.

193. Copyright Rowan Technology Solutions, 2015.
Sources: Martin van Creveld, "Through a Glass, Darkly: Some Reflections on the Future of War," *Naval War College Review* 53, no. 4 (2000): 28, citing Russian-language source V. Suvorov, M Day (Moscow: AST, 1994), 476; Ellis, *Military Book Club's World War II: Encyclopedia of Facts and Figures*, 227–28; and Richard M. Leighton and Robert W. Coakley, *Global Logistics and Strategy, 1943–1945* (Washington, D.C.: Office of the Chief of Military History, United States Army, 1968), 14.

194. Copyright Rowan Technology Solutions, 2015.

195. Thomas Hart Benton, *Cut the Line*, 1944, U.S. Navy, Naval Historical Center.

196. Copyright Rowan Technology Solutions, 2015.
Source: Ellis, *Military Book Club's World War II: Encyclopedia of Facts and Figures*, 266–68, 280.

197. Copyright Rowan Technology Solutions, 2015.
Source: R. J. Overy, *War & Economy in the Third Reich* (New York: Oxford University Press, 1994), 312.

198. Copyright Rowan Technology Solutions, 2015.
Images: American School, *The 6,000th B24 Liberator bomber*, twentieth century, litho, private collection, Peter Newark American Pictures, Bridgeman Images; *Riveting a center wing section for a B-24E (Liberator) bomber in the horizontal position at Ford's big Willow Run plant.*, ca. 02/1943, Franklin D. Roosevelt Presidential Library Public Domain Photographs, National Archives and Records Administration, identifier 196387; *Looking up one of the assembly lines at Ford's big Willow Run plant, where B-24E (Liberator) bombers are being made in great numbers.*, ca. 02/1943, Franklin D. Roosevelt Presidential Library Public Domain Photographs, National Archives and Records Administration, identifier 196389; *Installing one of the four engines of a new B-24E (Liberator) bomber on one of the assembly lines of Ford's big Willow Run plant*, ca. 02/1943, Franklin D. Roosevelt Presidential Library Public Domain Photographs, National Archives and Records Administration, identifier 196388; and *"Up and at 'em! Build More B-24's,"* 1941–45, Record Group 44: Records of the Office of Government Reports, 1932–47, local identifier 44-PA-2225, National Archives and Records Administration, identifier 515932. Graph is copyright Rowan Technology Solutions, 2015.

199. Vernon Simeon Plemion Grant, *"Women: There's Work to Be Done,"* 1944, color litho, private collection, copyright Galerie Bilderwelt, Bridgeman Images.

200. Alfred T. Palmer, *Operating a hand drill at Vultee-Nashville, woman is working on a Vengeance Dive-Bomber, Tennessee*, 1943, Library of Congress Prints and Photographs Division, Washington, D.C.

201. Bundesarchiv, Bild 183-J31192, photo: Hoffmann.

202. English photographer, *Women at work, drilling and reaming aircraft wing spar fittings for Blackburn Aircraft, Olympia Works, Leeds*, ca. 1939–45, black-and-white photo, copyright Leeds Library and Information Service, Leeds, U.K., Bridgeman Images.

203. *"This Is Our War . . . Join the WAAC, Women's Army Auxiliary Corps, United States Army,"* University of North Texas Libraries, http://digital.library.unt.edu/ark%3A/67531/metadc172/.

204. *Nurses coming ashore at Normandy*, public domain, American Journal of Nursing Archive, published on *AJN Off the Charts*, Maureen Shawn Kennedy, "As Another June Is Forgotten, Some Notes on Nurses and Normandy," July 3, 2014, copyright *American Journal of Nursing*.

205. Natalia Aleksandrovna Gippius, *The female tractor brigade behind the front in Mordovia in 1942*, ca. 1950s, color litho, Gamborg Collection, Bridgeman Images.

206. *PFC Victor Tampone, an MP on motorcycle stands ready to answer all calls around his area, Columbus, Georgia*, 1942, U.S. National Archives and Records Administration.

207. *"Keep Us Flying! Buy War Bonds,"* 1943, U.S. National Archives and Records Administration, 514823, public domain, NARA.

208. Copyright Rowan Technology Solutions, 2015.
U.S. Army nisei soldier, Chase Stone, 2015.

209. Ben Shahn, *"We French Workers Warn You . . . ,"* 1942, color lithograph, Bridgeman Images, art copyright Estate of Ben Shahn/Licensed by VAGA, New York, NY.
210. *"I Work in Germany . . . ,"* Second World War poster, ca. 1942–43, color litho, Bibliotheque Nationale, Paris, France, Archives Charmet, Bridgeman Images.
211. Bundesarchiv, Bild 183-L04352, photo: o.Ang.
212. Bundesarchiv, Bild 183-H26334, photo: Pips Plenik.
213. Copyright Rowan Technology Solutions, 2015.
214. German photographer, *Female camp internees on the return march to Auschwitz, following forced work in an arms factory outside the camp,* Auschwitz, Poland, 1942, black-and-white photo, copyright SZ Photo, Bridgeman Images.
215. *"Everything for the Front!"* World War II poster, twentieth century, color litho, private collection, RIA Novosti, Bridgeman Images.
216. A. Volochin, *"Under the Flag of Lenin, March to Victory,"* 1941, Soviet propaganda poster, Universal History Archive/UIG, Bridgeman Images.
217. Howard R. Hollem, *Cincinnati, Ohio. Preparing canned pork (Russian: "svinaia tushonka") for Lend-Lease shipment to the USSR at the Kroger Grocery and Baking Company. One pound of pork, lard, onions, and spice go into each can,* 1943, Library of Congress Prints and Photographs Division, Washington, D.C.
218. *Henry J. Kaiser,* U.S. Navy, public domain, Wikimedia Commons.
219. *"When You Ride* Alone *You Ride with Hitler! Join a Car-Sharing Club* Today!" ca. 1941–45, U.S. Office of Emergency Management, Office of War Information, Domestic Operations Branch, Bureau of Special Services, U.S. National Archives and Records Administration.
220. Copyright Rowan Technology Solutions, 2015.
    Sources: H. Duncan Hall, *North American Supply* (London: HMSO, 1955), 430; and Mark Harrison, *Soviet Planning in Peace and War, 1938–1945* (Cambridge: Cambridge University Press, 1985), 258–59.
221. Copyright Rowan Technology Solutions, 2015.
    Sources: Overy, *Air War,* 215; and R. J. Overy, *The Dictators: Hitler's Germany, Stalin's Russia* (New York: W. W. Norton, 2004), 498.
222. Bundesarchiv, Bild 146II-277, photo: Binder.
223. Bundesarchiv, Bild 183-J05235, photo: Ernst Schwahn.
224. Copyright Rowan Technology Solutions, 2015.
    Source: Ellis, *Military Book Club's World War II: Encyclopedia of Facts and Figures,* 278.
225. Copyright Rowan Technology Solutions, 2015.
    Source: Ellis, *Military Book Club's World War II: Encyclopedia of Facts and Figures,* 280.
226. Rowan Technology Solutions, 2015.
    Sources: Peter Chamberlain and Hilary L. Doyle, *Encyclopedia of German Tanks of World War Two* (London: Arms & Armour, 1999), 261–63; Benjamin Coombs, *British Tank Production and the War Economy, 1934–1945* (London: Bloomsbury Academic, 2013), 48; Ellis, *Military Book Club's World War II: Encyclopedia of Facts and Figures,* 277; Michael Green, *American Tanks and AFVs of World War II* (Oxford, UK: Osprey, 2014), 18, 134; Overy, *Why the Allies Won,* 332; and Steve Zaloga and Peter Bull, *Japanese Tanks: 1939–45* (Oxford: Osprey, 2007), 10, 17.
227. Copyright Rowan Technology Solutions, 2015.
    Source: Ellis, *Military Book Club's World War II: Encyclopedia of Facts and Figures,* 278.
228. Henry Koerner, *"United we are strong, united we will win,"* Washington, D.C., University of North Texas Libraries, http://digital.library.unt.edu/ark:/67531/metadc414/.
229. David Wintzer, *Mutterkreuz 3. Stufe,* 1940, public domain, Wikimedia Commons.

Conclusion

230. Political Poster Collection, JA 84, Hoover Institution Archives, courtesy of Hoover Institution Library & Archives, Stanford University.
231. Political Poster Collection, UK 2225, Hoover Institution Archives, courtesy of Hoover Institution Library & Archives, Stanford University.
232. Arthur Szyk, *Japanese attack on Pearl Harbor,* front cover of *Collier's,* no. 12, December 1942, color litho, private collection, Peter Newark Military Pictures, Bridgeman Images. Reproduced with the cooperation of the Arthur Szyk Society, Burlingame, CA, www.szyk.org.
233. *Sieg Heil!,* propaganda pamphlet, Clifford Rogers, private collection.
234. William Henry Vatcher Papers, box 16, folder 1, Hoover Institution Archives, courtesy of Hoover Institution Library & Archives, Stanford University.
235. *England. Cpl. Carroll B. Johnson, Port Arthur, Texas, and Pfc. Carroll Davis, Philadelphia, Pa., at work in their mobile machine shop as part of the 829th Engineers, near Eye, England, (2 Mar 43),* Signal Corps Photo: ETO-HQ-43-1632, U.S. Army Center of Military History.

Page numbers in *italics* refer to picture captions.

Aalborg, 69
Abbeville, 84
Achtung—Panzer! (Guderian), 84
Addis Ababa, 127
Africa, 28, *98*
    British and Italian colonies in, *123*
    East, 126
    Horn of, *123*
    North, *123,* 125, 128, *129,* 132, 281, 289, 303*n*28
    South, 95, *98,* 127, 132
African Americans:
    in military, 254, *255,* 256, *256*
        Tuskegee Airmen, 254, *256*
    women, *246*
    in workforce, *246, 289*
Afrika Korps, 131, 136
agriculture, 239, 242, 259
    in Britain, 124, 135
    in Soviet Union, *251, 252*
aircraft:
    fighter
        barrage balloons and, *114,* 117
        Hawker Hurricane, 110, *111,* 112, 125
        Messerschmitt, *108,* 110
        Mitsubishi Zero, 186, *189,* 224, 306*n*9
        Supermarine Spitfire, *108,* 110, *111,* 112, 114,
            125
        Wildcat, *189*
        see also bombers, bombing
    production of, *276*
aircraft carriers, production of, *276*
Air Raid Precautions Act, 117–18
air raids:
    defense and precautions, 135, 244
    shelters, 118–19
        Anderson, *115,* 118
        in Germany, 259
        London Underground as, *117,* 119
    see also bombers, bombing
Aisne, 88
Akagi, 310*n*89
Albania, 12, 13, 28, 130
Albert Canal, 79
Aleutian Islands, 220, 223, 309*n*74
Alexandria, 127
Algeria, 127
Alsace, 5, 8
Amboina, 200, 201
American-British-Dutch-Australian Command
        (ABDACOM), 198
American Civil War, 254
American Revolution, 254
American Volunteer Group (Flying Tigers), 210,
        211
Amiens, 84
ammunition belt, *258*
Andalsnes, 71
Anschluss, 21–22, 51
Anderson, David, air-raid shelters designed by,
        115, 118
antitank guns, *35*
Aosta, Duke of, 127
Arashi, 310*n*86
Arcadia Conference, 198, *240*
Ardennes Forest, 56, *71,* 77, 78, *79,* 82

armed forces:
    administrative, support, and logistics in,
        238–39
    mobilization for, 233–39, *239*
        age limits and, 233, 235
        in Britain, 235, 275, 278
        casualty rates and, 233–34
        in Germany, 234, 235, 274–75
        for ground combat, 234, 238
        in Japan, 234–35
        in Soviet Union, *175,* 234, 235–38, *239,* 274,
            278
        total recruitment figures, 235–38
        in U.S., 235, 275, 278
    training for, 238, 278
    women in, 235, 242–52
        in Britain, 243–44
        in Germany, 243
        in Soviet Union, *175,* 251–52
        in U.S., 244–51, *249, 250*
    see also specific countries
Armenian Genocide, 21
arms control, 1
    Washington Naval Conference, 10, *10,* 12
Arras, 84
Atlantic Ocean, 132
    Battle of, 124, *243,* 289, 290
atomic bombs:
    Manhattan Project and, 135–36
    Maud Committee and, 135
Attlee, Clement, 133
Auchinleck, Claude, 131, 289
Auschwitz, 256, *263, 264,* 265
Australia, 95, *98,* 220, 289, 290
    MacArthur in, 217
Australian forces, 200, 221
*Australian Official History of the Second World
        War* (Long, ed.), 199
Australian propaganda, *204*
Austria, 6, 254
    Germany and, 21–22, 24, *28,* 51
Austro-Hungarian Empire, 5
    collapse of, *5*
Auxiliary Territorial Service (ATS), 243, 244

B-17 bombers, 42, *45,* 215
B-25 bombers, 220, 308*n*72
Bali, 206–7
Balikpapan, 201
Balkans, 125, 129
balloons, barrage, *114,* 117
Baltic states, 155, 168
Bandung, 209
Bantam Bay, 209
BAR ammunition belt, *258*
Bardia, 129
Barlone, D., 65
barrage balloons, *114,* 117
Bastogne, 238
Bataan, 214, 215–17, *217, 219,* 220
Bataan Death March, 217–19, *219*
Batavia, 209
Battle of Britain, 95, 106–15
    British colonies and, 95
    British prewar preparation and, 106–10

Battle of Britain (*cont.*)
    Churchill and, 106, 114
    fighters and pilots in, *108, 111*
    Galland's account of, 110
    Germany's blockade of Britain in, 102–3, 113
    nuisance raids in, 111
    order of battle for, *106*
    results of, 115
    Royal Air Force bombing in, 95, 100–101
    three stages in, 110
    traditional history of, 114
    weather and, 111, 112
Battle of Britain Day, 113
Battle of Cape Matapan, 128, 132
Battle of France, 74, 75–91, *109,* 112, 128, 141, 148, 281
    Ardennes in, 56, *71,* 77, *77,* 78, *79,* 82
    armistice in, 88–90, *93,* 127
    Belgium in, *70, 71, 74,* 75, 76, 79–82, *83,* 84, 85, 86, 87, 88, 281
    British forces in, 81, *85,* 88, 91
    British losses in, *87*
    Case Red in, 88, *88*
    Case Yellow in, 75–88
    Dunkirk in, 85–87, *85, 87,* 88
    fall of France in, 88, 95, *99,* 127, *183*
    first week of, *78*
    French forces in, *74,* 75, *79,* 80–82, 84–85, *86,* 88
    French operational plan in, 87
    German Panzer advance in, 76–78, *79,* 80–81, *81,* 82, *83,* 84, 85, 86, *91,* 128
    German victory parade in Paris, *91*
    Kesselschlacht in, 84
    in May 10–16, *78*
    in May 16–21, *81*
    in May 21–June 4, *85*
    Mechelen incident in, 76, 91
    Meuse in, 77, 79, 80, *80,* 82, 83, 84
    Netherlands in, 76, 78–82, 87, 281
    Operation Dynamo in, 85–86, *87*
    order of battle for, *72*
    Plan Yellow developed for, *70, 71, 72*
    Rotterdam Blitz in, *75*
    Schwerpunkt in, 78, 82
    Vichy government erected, 90, *90*
Battle of Leyte Gulf, 309*n*81
Battle of the Atlantic, 124, *243,* 289, 290
Battle of the Bulge, 56, 238
battleship, largest, *30*
bayonet, *193*
Beaverbrook, William Maxwell Aitken, Lord, 101
Beck, Ludwig, 165
beheadings, 15
Belgium, 5, 10
    exile government of, 95
    German invasion of, *70, 71, 74,* 75, 76, 79–82, 84, 85, 86, 87, 88, 281
Bennett, Gordon, 199, 200
Berlin, 112, 274
    Nazi rally in, *275*
Big Three, 191
biographies:
    Churchill, Winston, 100
    Dowding, Hugh, 112
    Gamelin, Maurice, 88

Guderian, Heinz, 84
Halder, Franz, 165
Himmler, Heinrich, 147
Hitler, Adolf, 51
Kaiser, Henry J., 270
Liddell Hart, Basil Henry, 40
MacArthur, Douglas, 215
Mussolini, Benito, 12
Nimitz, Chester William, 229
Rommel, Erwin, 128
Roosevelt, Franklin Delano, 191
Rundstedt, Gerd von, 56
Seeckt, Johannes Friedrich Hans von, 21
Speer, Albert, 274
Stalin, Joseph, 141
Tukhachevsky, Mikhail, 45
Wavell, Archibald, 127
Yamamoto, Isoroku, 229
Zhukov, Georgy Konstantinovich, 150
Birmingham, 116
Bismarck Archipelago, 183, 220
Blackburn Aircraft, *249*
Bletchley Park, 134, 136
    see also codes and code-breaking
Blitzkrieg, 19, 21, 43, 47, *60, 63,* 65, *67, 83,* 84, 91, 157, 302*n*12
    against Britain, *see* Great Britain, German Blitz campaign against
    against Poland, *60, 63*
    against Rotterdam, *75*
    against Soviet Union, 157, *158*
    use of word, 292*n*3
blockades, 47, 95, 100, 102–3, 113
Blücher, 69–70, 294*n*26
Bock, Fedor von, 51, 56–58, 76, 77, 161
Bohemia, 24
Bolshevism, 1, 15–16, 18, 43, 45
    German fears of, *146*
    and German invasion of Soviet Union, 142–44, 150
    Reichenau's order and, 172
    in Russian revolution, 1, 15–16, 18, 43, 45, *267*
bombers, bombing, 40, 42, 65
    atomic
        Manhattan Project and, 135–36
        Maud Committee and, 135
    B-17, 42, *45,* 215
    B-25, 220, 308*n*72
    Bristol Blenheim, 117
    British, 95, 100–101
        Germany bombed by, 119–21
        Italy bombed by, 101
    Fairey Swordfish, *124,* 128
    gas, 298*n*32
    German, *58,* 60, *60,* 69, 103, *104,* 108–10, *109*
        Blitzkrieg, *see* Blitzkrieg
        British defenses against, 116–19, 244
    Soviet, *16*
    strategic, 13, 19, 34, 40, 41, *45,* 65
    see also fighter aircraft
bomb shelters, 118–19
    Anderson, *115,* 118
    London Underground as, *117,* 119
Borneo, 183, 200, 201, *201,* 289
Brauchitsch, Walther von, 56–58, 144, 161

Brazen Chariots (Crisp), 130
Brazil, 88
Breda, 81, 87, 88
Brest, *158*
Bretagne, 127
Briand, Aristide, 12
Bristol, 116
Bristol Blenheim bombers, 117
Britain, *see* Great Britain
British Commonwealth, 98, *98,* 136
    in Mediterranean in war with Italy, 124, 125–29
        German intervention and, 129–32
        and importance of Mediterranean to Britain, 132
British Empire, *31, 41,* 47, 95, 98, *99, 102,* 136
British Malaya, 100
    Japan invasion of, 127, 182, 183, *185,* 186, 190–200, *201,* 210, 211, 289
    in December 8, 1941–January 31, 1942, *195*
    Japanese soldiers in, *195*
    Prince of Wales in, 196–98, *196,* 287
    Repulse in, 196, *196,* 287
    Singapore in, 190, 191, 192, *195,* 196, *196,* 198–200, *199, 201,* 217, 289
British Midlands, 116
British Somaliland, 126
British Union of Fascists, 133
Brooke, Alan, 38
Brooke-Popham, Robert, 186, 196
Brown, Wilson, 305*n*4
Browning automatic rifle, *258, 259*
Bryansk, 164
Buchenwald, *263*
Bulgaria, 132, 281
Bulge, Battle of the, 56, 238
Burma, 127, 179, 183, 186, *208,* 210–14, *219,* 289
    Japanese infantry in a camp in, *211*
    oil fields in, *212,* 213
Busch, Ernst, 78
Bushido, 32, *192*
Byelorussia, 168, *170,* 281
Bzura River, 61, 63

camouflage coveralls, *174*
Canada, 95, *98*
    Britain aided by, 123
Cape Matapan, 128, 132
Cape of Good Hope, 132
capitalism, 137
Cardiff, 116
Caroline Islands, 186, 220
Carton de Wiart, Adrian, 72
Case Red, 88, *88*
Case White, *see* Poland, Germany's invasion of
Case Yellow, 75–88
casualties, 274
    in Britain, 235
        civilian, 119
    in Germany, 235
    mobilization and, 233–34
    in Soviet Union, 137, 158, 162, 167, 235–38, 251, 278, 281, 303*n*34
    in U.S., 235
Caucasus, *158,* 176, 289
cavity magnetron, 135

Celebes, 201
Central Europe, 147
Chamberlain, Neville, 22, 23, *27*
Chapayev, Vasily, *176*
Charlemagne, 281
Chelmno, 177
Chennault, Claire, 306*n*9
Cherwell, Frederick Lindemann, Lord, 135
Chiang Kai-shek, 21, 179, 210
childbearing, German medal for, *280*
child care, 252
China, 21
    aid to, 278
    beheadings of prisoners of war in, 15
    Burma and, 210
    Guomindang in, 179
    Japan's invasion of, 21, *23, 24,* 30, 32, 179,
        182, *185,* 186, 192, 278
    Mukden Incident and, 15
    Nanking Massacre in, 21, *24*
    U.S. as ally of, *245*
    Washington Naval Treaties and, 10
Churchill, Winston, 95, 112, 115, 124, 127,
        136, 289, 290
    Battle of Britain and, 106, 114
    in Big Three talks, 191
    biography of, 100
    bombing and, 101, 121
    code breaking and, 134
    Dunkirk and, 86, 101
    House of Commons address of, 101
    Japanese military and, 287
    Java and, 207–8
    Norway and, 67
    Pearl Harbor and, 287
    political solidarity and, 133
    political warfare campaign and, 99
    Roosevelt's meetings with, 198
    science and, 135
    U.S. and, 98, 100
    U.S. resources and, *283*
    Wavell and, 127, 211
civil defense:
    in Britain, 117–19, 124, 135, 244
    in Germany, 243
Civilian Conservation Corps (CCC), 35,
        292*n*17
Civil War, 254
Clausewitz, Carl von, 86
coal, 144, 263
coats, *44*
codes and code-breaking, 134
    Enigma, 110, 134, 136, 290
    Italian codes, 127, 128
    Japanese codes, 220, 223, *227,* 290,
        305*n*4
    Magic, 290, 305*n*4
    Ultra, 100, 110, 132, 134, 136, 220, 223,
        229, 230
Cold War, 141
Communism, 1, 16, *18,* 21, 27, 100
    in Britain, 133
    fall of, 265
    German ideology and, *146,* 148
    and Germany's invasion of Soviet Union,
        133, 150, 151, 169
    in Soviet propaganda, *176*

    in Soviet Union, 133, 141
    women's roles and, 251
Compiègne, 88
concentration camps, 147, 256, 261, *264*
    Auschwitz, 256, *263, 264,* 265
    map of, *263*
conscientious objectors, 135
Copenhagen, 69
Coral Sea, Battle of, 220–22, *221,* 223, 229,
        230
    conclusion of, May 8, *224*
    Japanese plan in, *222*
    in May 6–7, *223*
Corregidor, 215, 217, 220
Coventry, 116, 117, 119–20
coveralls, camouflage, *174*
Crécy-sur-Serre, 85
Crete, 127, 132, 281
Crisp, Bob, 130
Cunningham, Alan, 127
Cyrenaica, 129
Czechoslovakia, 5, 6
    exile government of, 95
    Germany and, 22, 23, 24, *26,* 38, *152*
    partitioning of, *26*
    tanks of, *152*

Daily Worker, 133
Daladier, Edouard, 22
Dalton, Hugh, 99–100, 133
Danzig, 6
Darwin, 206
Davis, Benjamin O., Jr., *256*
Dawes Plan, 14
Deep Operations, 38, 43, 45, 292*n*18
De Gaulle, Charles, 39, 101–2
    in Battle of France, 85
Denmark, 67, *67,* 69, 90–91, 281
Depression, Great, 12, 14, 20, 42, *43,* 51, 191,
        239
Dickinson, Goldsworthy Lowes, 5
Dietl, Eduard, 72–74
Dinant, 84
Directed Battle doctrine, 39
disarmament, 1
    Washington Naval Conference, 10, *10,* 12
Dnieper River, 155, 162
Donets Basin, 155
Dönitz, Karl, 282
Don River, 166, 289
Doolittle, James H., 220
Doolittle Raid, 220
Doorman, Karel, 208, 209
Dornier Do 17, *109,* 110
Douglas, Sholto, 112
Douhet, Giulio, 13
Dowding, Hugh, 108–9, 115
    biography of, 112
Dr. Seuss, *28, 118*
Dunkirk, 85–87, *85, 87,* 88, 101
Dutch East Indies, *see* Netherlands East
        Indies
Dvina River, 155, 157
Dyle River, 81, 87, 88, 295*n*48

Eagle Day, 111
East Africa, 126

Eastern Europe, 170
    Germany and, 147
    Soviet Union and, 141
East Indies, *see* Netherlands East Indies
East Prussia, 38, 51, 56
Eben Emael, *76,* 79
economies, 31, 263–74, 278
    Depression and, 12, 14, 20, 42, *43,* 51, 191, 239
    of Germany, 264, 269–74
    of Great Britain, 123, 135, 136, 275
    guns-or-butter trade-off and, 263–64, 265,
        267, 269
    mobilization and, *244*
        see also mobilization
    of Soviet Union, 241–42, 263–65, 272–74
    total war and, 233, *244*
    of U.S., 265–69
    war production and, *see* war production
Egypt, 126, 127, 128, *129,* 131, 132, 281
Eiffel Tower, *93*
El Agheila, 129
English Channel, *72,* 76, 77, *85,* 91
Enigma, 110, 134, 136, 290
Enterprise, 224, 227
equipment, field, *44*
Eretan Wetan, 209
Eritrea, 126–27
Estonia, 5, 157
Ethiopia, 12, 13, 28, 41, 126, 127
ethnic nationalism, 5, 22
Europe:
    Allied invasion of, 56
    Central, 147
    Eastern, 170
        Germany and, 147
        Soviet Union and, 141
    outbreak of World War II in, 35, 51, *61,*
        179, 191
    Versailles Treaty and, *5,* 6–7
Exercise Weser (*Weserübung*), 67, 69–75

factories:
    American, 270, *272, 283*
    British, 253, 287
    German, *261, 272*
    I. G. Farben, 265
    Soviet, 252, 264, 270
Fairey Swordfish, *124,* 128
Far East, 103, 125
Fascism, 95
    in Britain, 133
    in Italy, 12, 13, 15, *27–28, 28,* 191
Fedyuninsky, Ivan, 157
field equipment, *44*
fighter aircraft:
    barrage balloons and, *114,* 117
    Hawker Hurricane, 110, *111,* 112, 125
    Messerschmitt, *108,* 110
    Mitsubishi Zero, 186, *189,* 224, 306*n*9
    Supermarine Spitfire, *108,* 110, *111,* 112,
        114, 125
    Wildcat, *189*
    see also bombers, bombing
Final Solution and Holocaust, 51, 137, 147,
        169, *170,* 176–77, 261
Finland, 281
    Soviet war with, 140, 141

Finnish snipers, *175*
fire service, 135
Flanders, 84, 88
flight helmet, *225*
flying suit, *225*
Flying Tigers, 210, 211
food, 144, 150, 151, 170, 252
    agriculture, 239, 242, 259
        in Britain, 124, 135
        in Soviet Union, *251, 252*
    Lend-Lease, for Soviet Union, *268*
footwear, *193*
forced labor:
    in France, for Germans, *259, 261*
    in Germany, 147, 255–61, *262*
    in Japan, 255
    Soviet gulags, 153, 168, 264
Ford Motor Company, 268, 270
Fornebu, 70
Fourteen Points, 5, 22
fragmentation grenade, *193*
France, 5, 7–8, 27, 28, 58, 65, 101, 102, 103
    Alsace-Lorraine, 5, 8
    Battle of, 74, 75–91, *109,* 112, 128, 141,
        148, 281
        Ardennes in, 56, *71,* 77, 78, *79,* 82
        armistice in, 88–90, *93*
        Belgium in, *70, 71, 74,* 75, 76, 79–82, *83,*
          84, 85, 86, 87, 88, 281
        British forces in, 81, *85,* 88, 91
        British losses in, *87*
        Case Red in, 88, *88*
        Case Yellow in, 75–88
        Dunkirk in, 85–87, *85, 87,* 88, 101
        fall of France in, 88, 95, *99,* 127, *183*
        first week of, *78*
        French forces in, *74,* 75, *79,* 80–82,
          84–85, 86, 88
        French operational plan in, 87
        German Panzer advance in, 76–78, *79,*
          80–81, *81,* 82, 83, 84, 85, 86, *91,* 128
        German victory parade in Paris, *91*
        Kesselschlacht in, 84
        in May 10–16, *78*
        in May 16–21, *81*
        in May 21–June 4, *85*
        Mechelen incident in, 76, 91
        Meuse in, 77, 79, 80, *80,* 82, 83, 84
        Netherlands in, 76, 78–82, 87, 281
        Operation Dynamo in, 85–86, *87*
        order of battle for, *72*
        Plan Yellow developed for, *70, 71, 72*
        Rotterdam Blitz in, *75*
        Schwerpunkt in, 78, 82
        Vichy government erected, 90, *90*
    Czechoslovakia and, *26*
    declaration of war against Germany, *61*
    empire of, 47
    forced labor in, *259, 261*
    and German invasion of Norway, *69,* 71
    German reparations to, 14
    Maginot Line of, 31, *32, 37,* 38, 39, *74,* 88
    military of, 39
        antitank guns of, *35*
        Directed Battle doctrine in, 39
        preparations for World War II, 26
        tanks of, *77,* 81

    Poland and, 51
    strategy planned for World War II, 30–31,
        35
    strength of, *51*
    Treaty of Versailles and, 1, 8
    United States and, *51*
    U.S. aid to, 269
    Vichy regime in, 90, *90, 259, 261*
    Washington Naval Treaties and, 10
    in World War I, 39, 82
Franco, Francisco, 12, 20
French Indochina, 179, *183,* 192, 196, 211,
    289, 290
Freyberg, Bernard, 132
friction, 86
Fuller, J. F. C., 40, 41

Galland, Adolf, 110
Gallipoli, 100
Gamelin, Maurice, 87–88
    biography of, 88
gas bombs, 298n32
gas masks, *44*
Geisel, Theodor, *28,* 118
Gembloux, 80–81
Generals and Generalship (Wavell), 127
General Treaty for Renunciation of War as an
    Instrument of National Policy, 12
Geneva Naval Conference, 10, 12
George VI, King, 134
German Army Group Center, 150
German Empire, 6
Germany, 6, 18
    aggression of, 5, 7
    Freikorps in, *18*
    reparations and, 1, 14
    Russia and, 1, 21
    Jewish community in, 27, 51
    lands surrendered by, 5
    League of Nations and, 7, 20
    Schlieffen Plan of, *70*
    Treaty of Versailles and, 1, 6, 8, *8,* 14, 18,
        19, 20
    U.S. loan to, 14
    Weimar, 21
    in World War I, 19, 27, 30, 51, 82, 88, 141,
        144, 168
Germany, Nazi, 20, 31, 179, 191
    aggression and expansion of, *26, 27, 28,*
        30, 38
    air raid shelters in, 259
    Allied naval blockade of, 47, 95
    Allied propaganda leaflets dropped on, *285*
    Austria and, 21–22, 24, *28,* 51
    in Battle of Britain, 95, 106–15
        British colonies and, 95
        British prewar preparation and, 106–10
        Churchill and, 106, 114
        fighters and pilots in, *108, 111*
        Galland's account of, 110
        Germany's blockade of Britain in,
          102–3, 113
        nuisance raids in, 111
        order of battle for, *106*
        results of, 115
        Royal Air Force bombing in, 95,
          100–101

        three stages in, 110
        traditional history of, 114
        weather and, 111, 112
    in Battle of the Bulge, 56
    Blitz campaign against Britain, 100,
        115–21, 132, 136, 281
        assessment of, 122–25
        "Britain Shall Not Burn" poster, *120*
        civilian casualties from, 119
        and civilians' moves to countryside,
          119
        defenses against night bombing, 116–17
        German cities bombed by Royal Air
          Force in, 119–21
        impact on British strategy, 122
        in London, 112, *113,* 116, *118*
        material effects of, 123–24
        myth of, 122
        Nixon's account of raid in, 116
    Britain as target of, 76, 91–93, *93*
    casualties of, 235
    central position of, *54*
    civil defense in, 243
    concentration camps of, 147, 256, 261, *264*
        Auschwitz, 256, *263, 264,* 265
        map of, *263*
    Czechoslovakia and, 22, 23, 24, *26,* 38, *152*
    declarations of war against, *61*
    Economic Staff East of, 150
    economy of, 264, 269–74
    Enigma code of, 110, 134, 136, 290
    factories in, *261, 272*
        I. G. Farben, 265
    Food Ministry of, 150, 151
    forced labor in, 147, 255–61, *262*
    France invasion (Battle of France), 74,
        75–91, *109,* 112, 128, 141, 148, 281
        Ardennes in, 56, *71,* 77, 78, *79,* 82
        armistice in, 88–90, *93,* 127
        Belgium in, *70, 71, 74,* 75, 76, 79–82, *83,*
          84, 85, 86, 87, 88, 281
        British forces in, 81, *85,* 88, 91
        British losses in, *87*
        Case Red in, 88, *88*
        Dunkirk in, 85–87, *85, 87,* 88
        fall of France in, 88, 95, *99,* 127, *183*
        first week of, *78*
        French forces in, *74,* 75, *79,* 80–82,
          84–85, 86, 88
        French operational plan in, 87
        German Panzer advance in, 76–78, *79,*
          80–81, *81,* 82, 83, 84, 85, 86, *91,* 128
        German victory parade in Paris, *91*
        Kesselschlacht in, 84
        in May 10–16, *78*
        in May 16–21, *81*
        in May 21–June 4, *85*
        Mechelen incident in, 76, 91
        Meuse in, 77, 79, 80, *80,* 82, 83, 84
        Netherlands in, 76, 78–82, 87, 281
        Operation Dynamo in, 85–86, *87*
        order of battle for, *72*
        Plan Yellow developed for, *70, 71, 72*
        Rotterdam Blitz in, *75*
        Schwerpunkt in, 78, 82
        Vichy government erected, 90, *90*
    French workers and, *259, 261*

Gestapo in, 56, 147
GNP (gross national product) of, 240
ideology of, 137, 150–51, 169
intelligence in, 147, 149
Italy as ally of, 12, 27
London bombed by, 112, *113,* 116, *118*
long-term outlook for, 144
in Mediterranean, 129–32
military (Wehrmacht) of, 19, 20, 21, 27,
    40, 47, 67–69, 84, 85, 90, 91, 239,
    278, 281
    Armed Forces High Command
        (Oberkommando der Wehrmacht;
        OKW), 150, 286
    Army High Command
        (Oberkommando des Heeres; OKH),
        56, 160
    Blitzkrieg strategy of, *see* Blitzkrieg
    bombers of, *58,* 60, *60,* 69, 103, *104,*
        108–10, *109*
    concentric operations method of, 51
    deployment and organization of, *54*
    glider troops, *76*
    goals and values of, 150
    horses in, 47, *63, 144,* 147, 158
    infantry, 47, *83, 91,* 145
    Kesselschlacht strategy of, *52,* 64, 84
    Luftwaffe (air force), *see* Luftwaffe
    mobilization for, 234, 235, 274–75
    mobility of, 147
    Panzer forces, *see* Panzer forces
    preparations for World War II, 26
    reserve divisions, 64
    size of, 239
    submarines (U-boats) of, 34, *121,* 124,
        133, 134, 136, 282–83, 287, 289
    tanks of, 60, 83, *83, 261, 272; see also*
        Panzer forces
    Waffen-SS, 147, 301*n*5
    women in, 243
mobilization for workforce in, 233, *238,*
    274–75
Poland and, 23–24, 38–40, 42, 51
Poland invasion (Case White), 51–65, 75,
    90, *109,* 140, 153, 281, 293*n*9
    Blitzkrieg in, *60, 63*
    German bomber in, *60*
    German plans for, *52*
    German troops marching, *61*
    Kesselschlacht in, *52,* 64
    Luck's account of, 59
    order of battle for, *54*
    Poland's defeat in, 64, 65
    in September 1–14, *57*
    in September 15–22, *62*
    Soviet forces in, *62,* 63
    Warsaw in, *52,* 54, 56, *57,* 59, 60–61,
        63, 64
racial war of, 149–51
reparations and, 20
Rhineland and, 20, 24, *26,* 51
rise of, 18–24, 30
Scandinavia invasion, 65–75
    Allied forces and, *69,* 71–74, 75
    burning Norwegian village, *67*
    Denmark, 67, *67,* 69, 90–91, 281
    Exercise Weser (*Weserübung*), *67,* 69–75

Norway, 67, *67,* 69–72, *69,* 71–75, 90–91,
    281, 294*n*19
Sweden, 67
Schutzstaffel (SS) in, 147, 150, 151, 169,
    301*n*5
    Einsatzgruppen, 147, 151, 169
Soviet Union and, 27, 38, 45
Soviet Union invasion (Operation
    Barbarossa), 56, 117, 130, 133, 136,
    137–77, 281, 289
    Allies in, *140*
    in August 26–December 5, *162*
    Blitzkrieg in, 157, *158*
    Bolsheviks and, 142–44, 150
    casualties in, 137, 158, 162, 167, 235–38,
        251, 278, 281
    civilians and villages in, 169–70
    Communists and, 133, 150, 151, 169
    in December 5–May 7, *172*
    ferocity and ruthlessness in, *158,* 168,
        171
    German defeat in, 177, 303*nn*28, 39
    German infantry in, *145*
    German motor convoy in, *159*
    German photographs of, *151*
    and German views of Soviet Union,
        145–46, 148
    as Great Patriotic War, 137
    Hitler and, 136, 137, *140,* 141, 142–45,
        150, 153, 161, 162, *162,* 165, 175, 281,
        298*n*26, 303*n*41, 304*n*51
    Hitler's ordering of, 145, 301*n*11
    importance of, 137
    initial operations in, 155–61
    Japan and, 179
    Jews and, 142–44, 150, 151, 169, 172
    on June 22, *155*
    in June 22–August 25, *161*
    Kiev in, 56, 84, 155, 157, 161, *162*
    Leningrad in, 150, 155, 157, 158, 161,
        162, *162,* 166, 281
    Lithuania in, *152,* 281
    mass shootings in, *169*
    miscalculations in, 155
    moral elements in, 137, 301*n*5
    Moscow in, 150, 155, 158, 161, 162,
        164–67, *164, 166,* 172, *172,* 281
    Nazi ideology and, 167, 169, 170
    Operation Typhoon in, 162, *162*
    order of battle for, *157*
    Panzers in, *149, 152, 158, 162*
    as racial war, 149–51
    and Russian territories as living space
        for Germans, 142–44, 150, 281
    scale of fighting in, 137
    Smolensk in, 155, 157–58, 303*nn*34, 41
    Soviet citizens starved in, 151
    Soviet counterattack in, 127–75
    Soviet mobilization and reorganization
        in, *159*
    Soviet plans and preparations in,
        152–55
    Soviet prisoners of war in, *148,* 151,
        168, 169
    Soviets' blocking of Germans' one-
        campaign effort in, 175
    Soviet scorched-earth program in, 170

Soviet soldier's account of first day of,
    157
Soviet women in combat roles in, *175,*
    251–52
Stalin and, 137, 140, 141, 145, 148, 152,
    153–55, 157, 162, 166–67
Stalingrad in, 150, 176, 289
strategies in, 137–45
struggle behind the lines in, 167–70
tanks in, *149*
three German forces in, *142,* 155–57,
    161–67
three turning points in, 175–77
as total war, 137
Ukraine in, 56, 158, 161, *162, 167,* 168,
    265, 281
U.S. and, 176
weather and, *164,* 165, *175,* 281
Wehrmacht's attitudes and practices
    and, 149
Wehrmacht's logistical and personnel
    challenges in, 146–48
Wehrmacht's operation plans for,
    145–49
Soviet Union's non-aggression pact with,
    40, 43, 47, 133, 141, *142,* 168, 179
strength of, *51*
Sudetenland invaded by, 22, 24, *28*
in Tripartite Pact, 179
victory years of, 47–93
war against U.S. declared by, 176
war-fighting advantages and
    disadvantages of, 47
war production in, 239, 240–41, *244,*
    269–74
women in workforce in, 252
see also Hitler, Adolf; Nazi Party
Gestapo, 56, 147
Gilbert Islands, 183, 186, 289
Göring, Hermann, 111, 116, 269
Gosplan, 264
Graziani, Rodolfo, 126, *126,* 128
Great Britain, 5, 7–8, 27, 28, 58, 65, 95–136,
    179
    African empire as source of laborers and
        soldiers for, 253–54
    agriculture in, 124, 135
    air-defense system of, *104*
    Air Raid Precautions Act in, 117–18
    air raid shelters in, 118–19
        Anderson, *115,* 118
        London Underground as, *117,* 119
    in Battle of Britain, 95, 106–15
        British colonies and, 95
        British prewar preparation and,
            106–10
        Churchill and, 106, 114
        fighters and pilots in, *108, 111*
        Galland's account of, 110
        Germany's blockade of Britain in,
            102–3, *113*
        nuisance raids in, 111
        order of battle for, *106*
        results of, 115
        Royal Air Force bombing in, 95,
            100–101
        three stages in, 110

Great Britain; in Battle of Britain (*cont.*)
     traditional history of, 114
     weather and, 111, 112
  in Battle of France, 81, *85, 87,* 88, 91
  Burma and, 127, 179, 183, 186, *208,* 210–14,
     219, 289
     Japanese infantry in a camp in, *211*
     oil fields in, *212,* 213
  Canadian aid to, 123
  casualties of, 235
     civilian, 119
  civil defense in, 117–19, 124, 135, 244
  commercial shipping of, *121,* 124, 134, *243*
  Commonwealth forces in war with Italy,
     124, 125–29
     German intervention and, 129–32
     and importance of Mediterranean to
        Britain, 132
  Commonwealth of, 98, *98,* 136
  Communism in, 133
  Conservative Party in, 133
  Czechoslovakia and, *26*
  declaration of war against Germany, *61*
  economy of, 123, 135, 136, 275
  Empire of, *31,*41, 47, 95, 98, *99, 102,* 136
  exile governments hosted by, 64, 95
  factories in, 253, 287
  factors behind survival of, 133–36
  German Blitz campaign against, 100,
     115–21, 132, 136, 281
     assessment of, 122–25
     "Britain Shall Not Burn" poster, *120*
     civilian casualties from, 119
     and civilians' moves to countryside,
        119
     defenses against night bombing,
        116–17
     German cities bombed by Royal Air
        Force in, 119–21
     impact on British strategy, 122
     in London, 112, *113,* 116, *118*
     material effects of, 123–24
     myth of, 122
     Nixon's account of raid in, 116
  and German invasion of Belgium, *74*
  German reparations to, 14
  German underwater campaign against,
     121
  German war plans against, 76, 91–93, *93*
  GNP (gross national product) of, 240
  industry converted to war production in,
     135
  intelligence in, 100, 101, 103, 110
  Italy's war with
     bombing in, 101
     colonies and, *123*
     in Mediterranean, 124, 125–29
     Operation Compass in, *125, 126,* 128,
        129
  Japan and, 28–30
  Labour Party in, 133
  London
     Germany's bombing of (Blitz), 112, *113,*
        116, *118*
     night defense in, *113*
     Royal Observer Corps in, *106*
     Underground in, *117,* 119

Malaya and, *see* British Malaya
Mediterranean operations of, 124, 125–29
     Rommel's first offensive and, *129*
  military of, 40, 41
     advantages and limitations of, 132, 136
     mobilization for, 235, 275, 278
     preparations for World War II, 26, *27,*
        41, 106–10
     rearmament, 23, *27*
     Royal Air Force, *see* Royal Air Force
     Royal Navy, *see* Royal Navy
     tanks of, 100
     women in, 243–44
  National Service Act in, 135
  Norway and, 67, 69, 71–74
  observer corps in, *106,* 109–10
  Pearl Harbor attack and, 287
  Poland and, 51, 64
  political solidarity in, 133–34, 136
  political warfare and propaganda of,
     99–100, 119
  racist attitudes toward Japanese in, 186
  science in, 135
  Soviet Union and, 136, 144
  strategies of, 30–34, *35,* 98–106, 124, 136
  strength of, *51*
  Treaty of Versailles and, 1, 8
  U.S. and, *51,* 136
  U.S. supplies to
     armaments, 95, 98–99, 296*n*5
     Lend-Lease, *103,* 119, 122–23, 191, 269,
        272
  war production in, 239, *244, 249*
     weapons, *133*
  Washington Naval Treaties and, 10
  workforce in, 239
  in World War I, *7,* 34, 135
Great Crash, 14, 18–20
Great Depression, 12, 14, 20, 42, 43, 51, 191,
     239
Greece, 28, 125, 127, 303*n*28
  Italy's war with, 129–32, 300*n*54
     German forces and, 132, 281
grenade, *193*
Grumman Wildcat fighters, *189*
Guam, 183, 186, 190
Guderian, Heinz, 19, 59, 64, *162*
  biography of, 84
  in Case Yellow, 78, *79,* 82, 83, 85
  Hitler and, 84
Guernica (Picasso), *22*
gulags, 153, 168, 264
guns-or-butter trade-off, 263–64, *265, 267,* 269

Hague, 79
Halder, Franz, 77, 144, 158, 159, 161, 165–66
  biography of, 165
  Hitler and, 161, 165
Harding, Warren G., 10
Hastings, Battle of, 289
Hawaii, 305*n*4
  Pearl Harbor, 42, 223, 305*n*4
     defense of, 185
     Japanese attack on, *see* Pearl Harbor
        attack
Hawker Hurricane, 110, *111,* 112, 125
Heinkel bomber, 110

helmets:
  American
     army, *44*
     M1, *258*
     naval aviator, *225*
  Japanese, *193*
Heydrich, Reinhard, 177
Hill, Diana Murray, 253
Himmler, Heinrich, biography of, 147
Hinnöy, 72
Hiryū, 229–30
Historical Liaison Group, 165
Hitler, Adolf, *8,* 45, 47, *54,* 59, 65, 116, 289,
     290
  actions and strategies considered by,
     141–42
  appeasement of, 23, *27, 28,* 51, 153
  Austria and, 21–22
  biography of, 51
  Britain invasion postponed by, 112–13
  Case Yellow and, 76, 85, 86, 91
  chancellorship gained by, 18, 20, 41, 51
  coup attempted by, 18
  Dunkirk and, 86
  expansionism of, *26*
  Final Solution and Holocaust perpetrated
     by, 51, 137
  German reparations and, 20
  Gold Cross medal created by, *280*
  Guderian and, 84
  Halder and, 161, 165
  Himmler and, 147
  ideology of, 27
  London bombing and, 112
  Mediterranean and, 130–31
  Munich Agreement and, 23
  Mussolini and, 12, 125–26
  Nazi-Soviet Non-Aggression Pact and, *142*
  Norway invasion and, 72
  in Paris, *93*
  Pearl Harbor attack and, 283–87
  Plan Yellow and, *72*
  plot against, 56, 84
  rise of, 18–24
  Reichenau's order and, 172
  Rommel and, 128
  Rundstedt and, 56
  Schutzstaffel (SS) and, 147, 301*n*5
  Seeckt and, 21
  Soviet invasion (Operation Barbarossa)
     and, 136, 137, *140,* 141, 142–45, 150,
     153, 161, 162, *162,* 165, 175, 281,
     298*n*26, 303*n*41, 304*n*51
  Soviet invasion ordered by, 145
  Soviet military and, *16*
  Speer and, 274
  U.S. and, 176, 282, 283–86
  U.S. resources and, *283*
  Versailles treaty and, 20
  as war leader and strategist, 51, *52*
  war production and, 272
  in World War I, 51
Hoepner, Erich, 80
Holland, 75
Holocaust and Final Solution, 51, 137, 147,
     169, *170,* 176–77, 261
Homma, Masaharu, 215, 217

Hong Kong, 190, 210, 217
Hoover Dam, 270
Horn of Africa, *123*
Hornet, 220, 224
horses, in German military, 47, *63, 144,* 147, 158
Hoth, Hermann, 84
Houston, U.S.S., 209
Hull (city), 116
Hull, Cordell, 287
Hungary, 5, *26,* 281
Hurricanes, 110, *111,* 112, 125
Hutton, Thomas, 210, 211, 213–14

I. G. Farben, 265
Iida, Shōjirō, 210
Illustrious, 128
Imamura, Hitoshi, 200, 207, 209–10
India, 95, *98, 123,* 125, 127, 132, 210, 211, 289, 290
Indochina, 179, *183,* 192, 196, 211, 289, 290
Indomitable, 196
Infantry Attacks (Rommel), 128
Inside the Third Reich (Speer), 274
intelligence:
　British, 100, 101, 103, 110
　codes and code-breaking, 134
　　Enigma, 110, 134, 136, 290
　　Italian codes, 127, 128
　　Japanese codes, 220, 223, *227,* 290, 305*n*4
　　Magic, 290, 305*n*4
　　Ultra, 100, 110, 132, 134, 136, 220, 223, 229, 230
　German, 147, 149
Iran, 126, 265
Iraq, 126, 127
Ireland, 95
iron, 67, 291*n*4
isolationism, 1, 8, 20, 30
　of U.S., 30, 31, 34, 42, 95, *118,* 283
Israel, 40
Istanbul, 100
Italy, 15, 27, 30, 38, *240,* 281, 286
　black soldiers in, 254
　Britain's war with
　　bombing in, 101
　　colonies and, *123*
　　in Mediterranean, 124, 125–29
　　Operation Compass in, *125, 126,* 128, *129*
　codes used by, 127, 128
　enters World War II, 13, 101
　Ethiopia invaded by, 12, 13, 28, 41
　Fascism in, 12, 13, 15, 27–28, *28,* 191
　Germany as ally of, 12, 27
　Greece's war with, 129–32, 300*n*54
　　German forces and, 132, 281
　League of Nations and, 7
　military of, 13, 27–28
　　navy, 127–28
　　preparations for World War II, 26
　strength of, *51*
　Treaty of Versailles and, 1, 8
　in Tripartite Pact, 179
　Washington Naval Treaties and, 10

Jablunka Pass, 59
Jahore Province, 199
Japan, 28–30, 38, 125, 179–231, *183,* 290
　in American propaganda, *285*
　in Australian propaganda, *204*
　B-25 bomber attacks on, 220, 308*n*72
　Burma attacked by, 127, 179, 183, 186, *208,* 210–14, *219,* 289
　　Japanese infantry in a camp, *211*
　　oil fields and, *212,* 213
　Bushido ethos in, 32, *192*
　centrifugal offensive of, 183
　China invaded by, 21, *23, 24,* 30, 32, 179, 182, *185,* 186, 192, 278
　Chinese prisoners of war beheaded by, 15
　codes used by, 220, 223, *227,* 290, 305*n*4
　in Coral Sea battle, 220–22, *221,* 223, 229, 230
　　conclusion of, May 8, *224*
　　Japanese plan in, *222*
　　in May 6–7, *223*
　economic sanctions and embargoes on, 179–82
　forced labor in, 255
　French Indochina and, 179, *183,* 192, 196, 211, 289, 290
　and German invasion of Soviet Union, 179
　in Khalkhin Gol battle with Soviet Union, 150, 179
　Kwantung Army of, *14*
　League of Nations and, 7, 15
　as liberator of Asian countries, *286*
　MacArthur in, 215
　Malaya invaded by, 127, 182, 183, *185,* 186, 190–200, *201,* 210, 211, 289
　　in December 8, 1941–January 31, 1942, *195*
　　Japanese soldiers in, *195*
　　Prince of Wales in, 196–98, *196,* 287
　　Repulse in, 196, *196,* 287
　　Singapore in, 190, 191, 192, *195, 196, 196,* 198–200, *199, 201,* 217, 289
　Manchukuo puppet state of, *14,* 32, 179
　Manchuria invaded by, *14,* 15, 32, 41, 179
　in Midway battle, 183, 190, 220–30, *221, 227,* 309*n*74
　　Japanese plan for, *227*
　　order of battle for, *227*
　　torpedo bomber at, *230*
　　Yamamoto in, 222, 309*n*81
　militarism in, *23,* 32, 191, *192*
　military of, 15, 30, 32
　　aircraft, 306*n*9
　　battleships, *30*
　　carrier planes, *184*
　　Churchill's view of, 287
　　mobilization for, 234–35
　　preparations for World War II, 26
　　soldier with gear, *192*
　mobilization in, 234–35, 252
　Mukden Incident and, 15
　Nanking Massacre and, 21, *24*
　nationalism in, 32
　Netherlands East Indies and, 179, 182, 183, *183, 185,* 186, 190, 290
　oil and, 32, 179–82, 190, 200, 201, 206, *212,* 213

Pearl Harbor attack by, 35, 100, 182, 184–89, *189,* 190, 198, 210, 220, 229, 290
　American propaganda following, *285*
　Big Three talks and, 191
　British reaction to, 287
　and German invasion of Soviet Union, 176
　Hitler and, 283–87
　internment of Japanese Americans following, 255, *259*
　investigation of, 305*n*4
　opening attacks in, *185*
　"Remember Pearl Harbor," 186
　Roosevelt and, 190, 191, 305*n*4
　Tennessee and *West Virginia* in, *189*
　Yamamoto in, 229
　Philippines attacked by, 183, *185,* 186, 190, 200, *201,* 210, 214–20, 289
　　Bataan in, 214, 215–17, *217, 219,* 220
　　Bataan Death March in, 217–19, *219*
　　Luzon in, 214, 217, *217*
　　MacArthur and, 214–15, 217, *217*
　propaganda map of, *282*
　racist attitudes toward Japanese, 186, 196, *285,* 306*n*9
　Soviet Union and, 28–30, 179
　Soviet Union's neutrality pact with, 179
　Treaty of Versailles and, 8
　in Tripartite Pact, 179
　U.S. and, 28–30, 179, *182,* 190
　Washington Naval Treaties and, 10
　women in workforce in, 252
　in World War I, 32
Japanese Americans:
　in internment camps, 255, *259*
　second-generation, *259*
　in war effort, 255, *259*
Java, 190, 198, 200–210, 289
　Battle of the Java Sea, 209
　initial Japanese operations in, *201*
　Japanese seizure of, *206*
　war damage in, *204*
Jews:
　anti-Semitism and, *146*
　forced labor and, *170*
　and German invasion of Soviet Union, 142–44, 150, 151, 169, 172
　in Germany, 27, 51
　Germany's murder of, 51, 137, 147, 169, *170,* 176–77, 261
　Nazi ideology and, *146,* 169
　Reichenau's order and, 172
Jodl, Alfred, *52,* 161
Joffre, Joseph, 88
Jomard Passage, 221
Jones, Reginald Victor, 135
Jungenfeld, Ernst von, 80–81
Junkers, 110
Jupiter, 209
Jutland, 69, 209

Kaiser, Henry J., biography of, 270
Kaiser Shipyard, 270
Kaga, 310*n*89
Kalidjati, 209
Karlsruhe, 69

Kazakhstan, 168
Keitel, Wilhelm, *52*
Kellogg, Frank B., 12
Kellogg-Briand Pact, 12
Kenya, 100, 126, 127
Khalkhin Gol, 150, 179
Khrushchev, Nikita, 150
Kiev, 56, 84, 155, 157, 161, *162*
Kimmel, Husband, 184–85, 305*n*4
Kirponos, Mikhail, 157
Kiruna, 67
Kleist, Ewald von, 78
Kluge, Günther von, 78, 86
Kondō, Nobutake, 309*n*81
Korean War, 215
Kota Baharu, 186, 191, 196
Kristiansand, 69
Kroger, *268*
Küchler, Georg von, 77
Kursk, 84, 150
Kwantung Army, *14*

Ladies May Now Leave Their Machines (Hill),
    253
Lamon Bay, 215
Langley, Jimmy, 86
Latvia, 5, 281
League of Nations, 5, 7, 12, 20
    Germany and, 7, 20
    headquarters of, *6*
    Japan and, 7, 15
    United States and, 7–8
leggings, *44, 193*
Lemnos, 132
Lend-Lease, 265, 269
    aid to Britain, *103, 119,* 122–23, 191, 269,
        272
    aid to Soviet Union, *268, 272*
    opposition to, *119*
Lenin, Vladimir, 16, 141, *267*
Leningrad (Saint Petersburg), 150, 155, 157,
    158, 161, *162,* 166, 281
Lexington, 220, 221
Leyte Gulf, Battle of, 309*n*81
Libya, 126, *126,* 127, 129, 131, 281
Liddell Hart, Basil Henry, 41
    biography of, 40
life preserver, *225*
Lindemann, Frederick, 135
Lingayen Gulf, 215
List, Wilhelm von, 78
Lithuania, 5, *6*
    German advance into, *152,* 281
Liverpool, 116
Lombok Strait, 207
London:
    Germany's bombing of, 112, *113,* 116, *118*
    night defense in, *113*
    Royal Observer Corps in, *106*
    Underground in, *117,* 119
London Naval Conference, 10
Lorraine, 5, 8
Lost Generation, *7,* 8
Low Countries, 103
    see also Belgium; Netherlands
LSTs (Landing Ships, Tank), *242*
Luck, Hans von, 59

Luftwaffe, 47, 269, 281
    black soldiers and, 254
    Britain attacked by, 103, 106, 108–17, 119
    in Battle of France, 78, 79
    communications in, 64
    Fliegerkorps, 74–75
    Guernica raid of, *22*
    navigation aids of, 135
    in Norway, 69, 70, 72, 74–75
    in Poland, 54, 61, 63, 64
    Rotterdam attacked by, *75*
    Soviet women pilots' bombing of,
        251–52
    training for, 238
Lutz, Oswald, 84
Luzon, 214, 217, *217*

Maastricht appendage, 80
Mabatang, 217
MacArthur, Douglas, 229
    in Australia, 217
    biography of, 215
    Pearl Harbor attack and, 185
    in Philippines, 214–15, 217, *217*
    Truman and, 215
Macon, U.S.S., *225*
Magic, 290, 305*n*4
Maginot Line, 31, *32, 37,* 38, 39, *74,* 88
Makassar Strait, 206
Malaya, 100
    Japan invasion of, 127, 182, 183, *185,* 186,
        190–200, *201,* 210, 211, 289
        in December 8, 1941–January 31, 1942,
            195
        Japanese soldiers in, *195*
        Prince of Wales in, 196–98, *196,* 287
        Repulse in, 196, *196,* 287
        Singapore in, 190, 191, 192, *195,* 196,
            196, 198–200, *199, 201,* 217, 289
Malta, 130–31, 132
Manchukuo, *14, 32,* 179
Manchuria, *14,* 15, 32, 41, 179
Manhattan Project, 135–36
Manila, 214, 215, 217
Manstein, Erich von, 19
    in Case Yellow, *71, 72,* 76–77
Marne, 87
Marshall, George C., 217, *259,* 305*n*4
Marxism, *267*
    see also Bolshevism
Massawa, 126–27
Mastelarz, Kazimierz, 293*n*9
Matilda tanks, 128
Mauban, 217
Maud (Military Application of Uranium
    Detonation) Committee, 135
McCorquodale, Angus, 86
Mechelen incident, 76, 91
Mediterranean, 95, 103, 281, 289
    black soldiers in, 254
    British Commonwealth's war with Italy in,
        124, 125–29
        Operation Compass in, *125, 126,* 128,
            129
    colonies in, *123*
    German intervention in, 129–32
    Hitler and, 130–31

    importance to Britain, 132
    Operation Battleaxe in, *129,* 131
    Operation Brevity in, *129,* 131
    Operation Crusader in, 130, *131*
Mein Kampf (Hitler), 18
Menado, 201, 210
merchant shipping, *121,* 124, 134, *243*
Mers-el-Kébir, 127
Messerschmitt aircraft, *108,* 110
Meuse, 77, 79, 80, *80,* 82, 83, 84
Middle East, 126, 132
    Wavell in, 127, 128
Midway, Battle of, 183, 190, 220–30, *221, 227,*
    309*n*74
    Japanese plan for, *227*
    order of battle for, *227*
    torpedo bomber at, *230*
    Yamamoto in, 222, 309*n*81
Milch, Erhard, 272
Minsk, 155, 157
Missouri, U.S.S., 215
Mitsubishi Zero fighters, 186, *189,* 224,
    306*n*9
mobile machine shop, *289*
mobilization, 31, 135, 233–42, 274–78
    for armed forces, 233–39, *239*
        age limits and, 233, 235
        in Britain, 235, 275, 278
        casualty rates and, 233–34
        in Germany, 234, 235, 274–75
        for ground combat, 234, 238
        in Japan, 234–35
        in Soviet Union, *175,* 234, 235–38, *239,*
            274, 278
        total recruitment figures, 235–38
        in U.S., 235, 275, 278
        women in, *175,* 235, 242–52
    guns-or-butter trade-off and, 263–64, 265,
        269, *267*
    of minorities, 253–61
    total war and, 233, 242, *244*
    for workforce, 233, *238*
        African Americans and, 239–40,
            289
        forced labor and, 255
        in Germany, 233, *238,* 274–75
        in Japan, 252
        juveniles in, 233, 239–40, 252, *262*
        prisoners in, 233, 242
        women in, 233, 239–40, 242–53
Modlin, 64–65
Mogilev, *170*
Moldova, 281
Molotov, Vyacheslav, 40
Molotov-Ribbentrop Pact (Nazi-Soviet Non-
    Aggression Pact), 40, 43, 47, 133, 141,
    142, 168, 179
Mönchengladbach, 101
Mongols, 148
Montcornet, 85
Mont Kemmel, 84
Monthermé, 81, 84
morale, 100, 101, 115, 119, 122, 150, 275
Moravia, 24
Mordovia, *251*
Moore, Spencer, 256
Morrison, Herbert, 133

Moscow, 150, 155, 158, 161, 162, 164–67, 172, *172*, 281
    tank traps around, *164*
    winter near, *166*
Mosley, Oswald, 133
Moulmein, 212
Mount Natib, 217
Muar River, 199
Mukden Incident, 15
Munich Agreement, 23
Murmansk, 265
Mussolini, Benito, 15, 22, 41, 287
    biography of, 12
    Hitler and, 12, 125–26
    and Italy's war with Britain, 125–26
    military and, 13, 27–38
    and war with Greece, 129, 300*n*54

Nagumo, Chuichi, 184
Namsos, 71, 72
Nanking, 21
    Rape of, 21, *24*
Napoléon I, Emperor, 64, 142, 144, 147, 281
Narvik, 67, *69,* 74, 294*n*34
Nautilus, U.S.S., 310*n*86
Naval War College, 230
Nazi, use of word, 301*n*4
Nazi Party (National Socialist German
        Workers' Party; NSDAP), 8, 18, *18,*
        20, 51, 167, 172, 191
    Allied propaganda leaflets and, *285*
    Berlin rally of, *275*
    Einsatzgruppen, 147, 151, 169
    Himmler in, 147
    ideology of, 137, *146,* 147, 169
        women and, 243
    and invasion of Soviet Union, 167, 169, 170
    Reichenau's order and, 172
    rise to power, 18, 51, 141
    Schutzstaffel (SS), 147, 150, 151, 169
    social promises of, 20
    Speer in, 274
    Waffen-SS, 147, 301*n*5
    see also Germany, Nazi
Nelson, Donald, 268
Netherlands, 10
    exile government of, 95
    in Case Yellow, 76, 78–82, 87, 281
Netherlands East Indies (Dutch East Indies),
        179, 182, 183, *183, 185,* 186, 190, 290
    oil in, 32, 190, 200, 201, 206
Nevsky, Alexander, *176*
New Britain, 220
New Deal, 35, 191
    Civilian Conservation Corps, 35,
        292*n*17
New Guinea, *219,* 220, 289
New Zealand, 95, *98*
Nimitz, Chester W., 220, 223, 305*n*3
    biography of, 229
Nixon, Barbara, 116
NKVD, 165, 168
North Africa, *123,* 125, 128, *129,* 132, 281,
        289, 303*n*28
North Korea, 215
Norway, 103
    exile government of, 95

German invasion of, 67, *67,* 69–72, *69,*
        71–74, 75, 90–91, 281, 294*n*19
    burning Norwegian village, *67*
Novy Targ, 59

Ockenburg, 79
O'Connor, Richard, 128–29, 131
Ohio River, *242*
oil, 132, 289
    Britain and, 123, 126, 132
    in Burma, *212,* 213
    Germany and, 101, 123, 144
    Japan and, 32, 179–82, 190, 200, 201, 206,
        212, 213
    in Netherlands East Indies, 32, 190, 200,
        201, 206
    in U.S., 283
Operation Bagration, 150
Operation Barbarossa, *see* Soviet Union,
        Germany's invasion of
Operation Battleaxe, *129, 131*
Operation Brevity, *129, 131*
Operation Compass, *125, 126,* 128, *129*
Operation Crusader, 130, *131*
Operation Dynamo, 85–86, *87*
Operation Mars, 150
Operation Sea Lion, 111
Operation Typhoon, 162, *162*
Operation Uranus, 150
Oslo, 69, *69,* 70, 75
Ottoman Empire, 21

Pa-an, 213
Pacific, 183
Pacific War, 287–89, 290
    American army in, 239
    beginning of, *182*
    Burma, 127, 179, 183, 186, *208,* 210–14,
        219, 289
        Japanese infantry in a camp in, *211*
        oil fields in, *212,* 213
    Coral Sea, 220–22, *221, 223,* 229, 230
        conclusion of, May 8, *224*
        Japanese plan in, *222*
        in May 6–7, *223*
    Doolittle Raid in, 220
    Germany-first strategy and, 198, *240*
    Java, 190, 198, 200–10, 289
        Battle of the Java Sea, 209
        initial Japanese operations in, *201*
        Japanese seizure of, *206*
        war damage in, *204*
    major vessels sunk in, *230*
    Malaya, 127, 182, 183, *185,* 186, 190–200,
        201, 210, 211, 289
        in December 8, 1941–January 31, 1942,
        195
        Japanese soldiers in, *195*
        Prince of Wales in, 196–98, *196,*
        287
        Repulse in, 196, *196,* 287
        Singapore in, 190, 191, 192, *195,* 196,
        196, 198–200, *199, 201,* 217, 289
    Midway, 183, 190, 220–30, *221, 227,*
        309*n*74
        Japanese plan for, *227*
        order of battle for, *227*

        torpedo bomber at, *230*
        Yamamoto in, 222, 309*n*81
    order of battle for, *186*
    Pearl Harbor attack, 35, 100, 182, 184–89,
        189, 190, 198, 210, 220, 229, 290
        American propaganda following,
        285
        Big Three talks and, 191
        British reaction to, 287
        and German invasion of Soviet Union,
        176
        Hitler and, 283–87
        internment of Japanese Americans
        following, 255, *259*
        investigation of, 305*n*4
        opening attacks in, *185*
        "Remember Pearl Harbor," 186
        Roosevelt and, 190, 191, 305*n*4
        Tennessee and *West Virginia* in, *189*
        Yamamoto in, 229
    Philippines, 183, *185,* 186, 190, 200, *201,*
        210, 214–20, 289
        Bataan in, 214, 215–17, *217, 219,* 220
        Bataan Death March in, 217–19, *219*
        Luzon in, 214, 217, *217*
        MacArthur and, 214–15, 217, *217*
    turning point of, 220
    as war without mercy, 186
Palembang, 206
Panama Canal, 42
Panay, U.S.S., 21
Panzer forces, 19, *34,* 47, 51, 56, 58–59, 61,
        63, 64
    in Battle of France, 76–78, *79,* 80–81, *81,*
        82, 83, 84, 85, 86, *91,* 128
    in Operation Barbarossa, *149, 152, 158,*
        162
    and tank traps around Moscow, *164*
    Tiger tanks in, *149*
Papua New Guinea, 220
parachute, *225*
Paris:
    German victory parade in, *91*
    Hitler in, *93*
Park, Keith, 111, 115
Patton, George S., Jr., 44
Pearl Harbor, 42, 223, 305*n*4
    defense of, 185
Pearl Harbor attack, 35, 100, 182, 184–89, *189,*
        190, 198, 210, 220, 229, 290
    American propaganda following, *285*
    Big Three talks and, 191
    British reaction to, 287
    and German invasion of Soviet Union,
        176
    Hitler and, 283–87
    internment of Japanese Americans
        following, 255, *259*
    investigation of, 305*n*4
    opening attacks in, *185*
    "Remember Pearl Harbor," 186
    Roosevelt and, 190, 191, 305*n*4
    Tennessee and *West Virginia* in, *189*
    Yamamoto in, 229
Percival, Arthur, 191, 192, 196, 199–200, *199,*
    210
Persia, 265

Perth, 209
Pétain, Philippe, *90*
Philippines, 183, *185,* 186, 190, 200, *201,* 210,
    214–20, 289
    Bataan in, 214, 215–17, *217, 219,* 220
    Bataan Death March in, 217–19, *219*
    Luzon in, 214, 217, *217*
    MacArthur and, 214–15, 217, *217*
Philosophical Study of the Art of War, A
    (Gamelin), 88
phone communications, *122*
phony war, 65–67
Picasso, Pablo, *22*
pistol, *258*
Pittsburgh, PA, *242*
Plymouth, 116
Poland, 5, 6–7, *26,* 40, 88, 166, 168
    exile government of, 64, 95
    Britain and, 51, 64
    Germany and, 23–24, 38–40, 42, 51
    Germany's invasion of (Case White),
        51–65, 75, 90, *109,* 140, 153, 281,
        293*n*9
        Blitzkrieg in, *60, 63*
        German bomber in, *60*
        German plans for, *52*
        German troops marching, *61*
        Kesselschlacht in, *52,* 64
        Luck's account of, 59
        order of battle for, *54*
        Poland's defeat in, 64, 65
        in September 1–14, *57*
        in September 15–22, *62*
        Soviet invasion of, *62,* 63, 168
        Warsaw in, *52,* 54, 56, *57,* 59, 60–61,
        63, 64
    Russia's war with, 15–16, 24
Polish Corridor, 6, 56, 58
Pomerania, 51, 56
Port Moresby, 220, 222
Portsmouth, 116
Portugal, 10
Poznań, 54
Prince of Wales, H.M.S., 196–98, *196,*
    287
Prioux, René, 80–81
Pripet Marshes, 153
prison camps, *see* concentration camps
prisoners of war:
    Chinese, beheading of, 151
    Soviet, *148,* 151, 168, 169
propaganda, 274, 275
    Allied leaflet, *285*
    American, Japanese demonized in,
        285
    Australian, *204*
    British, 99–100, 119
    for home-front workers, *237*
    Japanese map, *282*
    Soviet, *176, 267,* 275
Prosna River, 59
prostitution, 255
proximity fuse, 135

Rabaul, 220
radar, *104,* 109, 110, 111, 117, 120
Raeder, Erich, 67

railways:
    British, 123
    Russian, 147
Rangoon, 198, *208*
Rape of Nanking, 21, *24*
rasputitsa, 165, 175
Red Army, 140–41, 146, 148, 150, 152–53
Reichenau, Walter von, 77
Reinhardt, Georg-Hans, 78, 84
Repulse, H.M.S., 196, *196,* 287
Resistance movements, 99
Rhineland, 20, 24, *26,* 51
Ribbentrop, Joachim von, 40
Ribbentrop-Molotov Pact (Nazi-Soviet Non-
    Aggression Pact), 40, 43, 47, 133, 141,
    142, 168, 179
rifles:
    Browning automatic, *258, 259*
    Japanese infantryman, *193*
    Soviet sniper, *174*
    U.S. Army, *43, 44*
Robert E. Peary, 270
Roberts Report, 305*n*4
Rogers Bill, 250
Romania, 63, 64, 281
Rommel, Erwin, 56, 59, 127, 131, *131,* 136,
    281, 289
    biography of, 128
    first offensive in Mediterranean campaign,
        129
    Hitler and, 128
    Meuse crossing of, 82
Roosevelt, Franklin Delano, 95, 98,
    289
    in Big Three talks, 191
    biography of, 191
    black soldiers and, 254, 256
    Churchill's meetings with, 198
    Japanese Americans and, *259*
    Lend-Lease program of, 265, 269
        aid to Britain, *103, 119,* 122–23, 191,
        269, *272*
        aid to Soviet Union, *268, 272*
        opposition to, *119*
    New Deal of, 35, 191
        Civilian Conservation Corps, 35,
        292*n*17
    Pearl Harbor attack and, 190, 191,
        305*n*4
    Soviet aid and, 265
    war production and, 268
Rostov, 56, 166
Rotterdam, 79
    German bombing of, *75*
Royal Air Force (RAF), 95, 100–101, 103,
    108–15, 119–21, 136, 281
    Bomber Command, 106, 136, 281
    Fighter Command, 108–12, 114,
        122
    Germany bombed by, 119–21
    Italy bombed by, 101
Royal Navy, 10, 41, 95, 100, 102, 103, 127,
    136, 287
    Prince of Wales, 196–98, *196,* 287
    Repulse, 196, *196,* 287
Royal Observer Corps, *106,* 109–10
Ruhr, 101

Rundstedt, Gerd von, 51, 84
    biography of, 56
    Case Yellow and, *72,* 76–77, 86
    Hitler and, 56
    in Poland invasion, 58–59
    in Soviet invasion, 56
Russia, 7, 27, 43
    Bolsheviks in, 1, 15–16, 18, 43, 45, *267*
        see also Bolshevism
    civil war in, 1, 15–16, 43, *176*
    Germany and, 1, 21
    October Revolution in, 141
    Poland's war with, 15–16, 24
    Treaty of Versailles and, 1
Russian Empire, collapse of, 5, *5,* 15
Russo-Polish War, 15–16, 24
Rydz-Smigly, Eduard, 52–54

Saigon, 196
Saint Petersburg, *see* Leningrad
Salween River, 211, 212, 213
Sambre River, 80
Sauckel, Fritz, 255–56
Scandinavia, German invasion of, 65–75
    Allied forces and, *69,* 71–74, 75
    burning Norwegian village, *67*
    Denmark, 67, *67,* 69, 90–91, 281
    Exercise Weser (*Weserübung*), *67,* 69–75
    Norway, 67, *67,* 69–72, *69,* 71–74, 75, 90–91,
        281, 294*n*19
    Sweden, 67
Schlieffen Plan, *70*
Schuschnigg, Kurt, 21–22
Schutzstaffel (SS), 147, 150, 151, 169, 301*n*5
    Einsatzgruppen, 147, 151, 169
science, 135
Scotland, 103
Scott, Bruce, 213
Sears Roebuck, 268
Second Sino-Japanese War, 23
Sedan, 82, 83, 84, 87
Seeckt, Johannes Friedrich Hans von, 19
    biography of, 21
Seuss, Dr., *28,* 118
Shanghai, 15, 21
shipbuilding, 252
shipping, *121,* 124, 134, *243*
shipyards, *242, 243*
    Kaiser, 270
Shōhō, 221
Shōkaku, 221
Short, Walter, 185, 305*n*4
Shōzō, Tominaga, 15
Siberia, 168
Sicily, 130
Signal, 151
Silesia, 51
Singapore, 190, 191, 192, *195,* 196, *196,*
    198–200, *201,* 217, 289
    defense of, *199*
Sino-Japanese War, Second, 23
Sittang, 212, 213–14
Slavs, 5, 142, 169
Slim, William, 213
Slim River Bridge, 198
Slovakia, 5, 24, 51
Smolensk, 155, 157–58, 303*nn*34, 41

sniper rifle, *174*
snipers, *175*
sniper scope, *174*
Socialism, 16
soldiers with gear:
    Japanese soldier, *192*
    Soviet sniper, *175*
    U.S. army rifleman, *43*
    U.S. infantryman with Browning
        automatic rifle, *259*
    U.S. naval aviator, *224*
Sollum, 131
Solomon Islands, 220, 229, 289
Somalia, 126
Somaliland, 127
Somme, 88
Sōryū, 310*n*89
South Africa, 95, *98,* 127, 132
Southampton, 116
South Korea, 215
Soviet Union, 5, 16, 43, 100, 290
    agriculture in, *251,* 252
    Britain and, 136, 144
    casualties of, 137, 158, 162, 167, 235–38,
        251, 278, 281, 303*n*34
    class struggle and, 137
    Cold War and, 141
    Communism in, 133, 141
    Eastern Europe and, 141
    economy of, 241–42, 263–65, 272–74
    factories in, 252, 264, 270
    Finland's war with, 140, 141
    Five-Year Plans of, 241
    Germany and, 27, 38, 45
    Germany's invasion of (Operation
        Barbarossa), 56, 117, 130, 133, 136,
        137–77, 281, 289
        Allies in, *140*
        in August 26–December 5, *162*
        Blitzkrieg in, 157, *158*
        Bolsheviks and, 142–44, 150
        casualties in, 137, 158, 162, 167, 235–38,
            251, 278
        civilians and villages in, 169–70
        Communists and, 133, 150, 151, 169
        in December 5–May 7, *172*
        ferocity and ruthlessness in, *158,* 168,
            171
        German defeat in, 177, 303*nn*28, 39
        German infantry in, *145*
        German motor convoy in, *159*
        German photographs of, *151*
        and German views of Soviet Union,
            145–46, 148
        as Great Patriotic War, 137
        Hitler and, 136, 137, *140,* 141, 142–45,
            150, 153, 161, 162, *162,* 165, 175, 281,
            298*n*26, 303*n*41, 304*n*51
        Hitler's ordering of, 145, 301*n*11
        importance of, 137
        initial operations in, 155–61
        Jews and, 142–44, 150, 151, 169, 172
        on June 22, 155
        in June 22–August 25, *161*
        Kiev in, 56, 84, 155, 157, 161, *162*
        Leningrad in, 150, 155, 157, 158, 161,
            162, *162,* 166, 281

    Lithuania in, *152,* 281
    mass shootings in, *169*
    miscalculations in, 155
    moral elements in, 137, 301*n*5
    Moscow in, 150, 155, 158, 161, 162,
        164–67, *164, 166,* 172, *172,* 281
    Nazi ideology and, 167, 169, 170
    Operation Typhoon in, 162, *162*
    order of battle for, *157*
    Panzers in, *149, 152, 158, 162*
    as racial war, 149–51
    and Russian territories as living space
        for Germans, 142–44, 150, 281
    scale of fighting in, 137
    Smolensk in, 155, 157–58, 303*nn*34, 41
    Soviet citizens starved in, 151
    Soviet counterattack in, 127–75
    Soviet mobilization and reorganization
        in, 159
    Soviet plans and preparations in,
        152–55
    Soviet prisoners of war in, *148,* 151,
        168, 169
    Soviets' blocking of Germans' one-
        campaign effort in, 175
    Soviet scorched-earth program in, 170
    Soviet soldier's account of first day of,
        157
    Soviet women in combat roles in, *175,*
        251–52
    Stalin and, 137, 140, 141, 145, 148, 152,
        153–55, 157, 162, 166–67
    Stalingrad in, 150, 176, 289
    strategies in, 137–45
    struggle behind the lines in, 167–70
    tanks in, *149*
    three German forces in, *142,* 155–57,
        161–67
    three turning points in, 175–77
    as total war, 137
    Ukraine in, 56, 158, 161, *162, 167,* 168,
        265, 281
    U.S. and, 176
    weather and, *164,* 165, 175, 281
    Wehrmacht's attitudes and practices
        and, 149
    Wehrmacht's logistical and personnel
        challenges in, 146–48
    Wehrmacht's operation plans for,
        145–49
Germany's non-aggression pact with, 40,
    43, 47, 133, 141, *142,* 168, 179
Gosplan in, 264
Great Terror in, 168
GNP (gross national product) of, 241, 242
gulag camp system in, 153, 168, 264
industrialization of, 16, 43, 241, 253
Japan and, 28–30, 179
Japan's neutrality pact with, 179
in Khalkhin Gol battle with Japan, 150,
    179
League of Nations and, 7
military of, *16,* 38, 432, 278
    air force, 152–53
    bombers of, *16*
    Deep Operations doctrine of, 38, 43,
        45, 292*n*18

    mobilization for, *175,* 234, 235–38, *239,*
        274, 278
    preparations for World War II, 38, 40
    Red Army, 140–41, 146, 148, 150, 152–53
    size of, 239
    sniper, *175*
    tanks of, *149,* 152
Nazism and, 141
NKVD in, 165, 168
Poland invaded by, *62, 63,* 168
propaganda in, *176, 267,* 275
purges in, 38, 43, 140–41, 168
tractor brigades in, *251*
Treaty of Versailles and, 8
U.S. aid to, 265
    food, *268*
war production in, 239, 240, 241–42,
    263–65, *267,* 272
Spain, 281
    civil war in, 12, 13, 20
    Guernica bombing in, *22*
Special Operations Executive (SOE), 99–100
Speer, Albert, 272
    biography of, 274
Spitfires, *108,* 110, *111,* 112, 114, 125
spotters, *122*
Spruance, Raymond, 224
Stalin, Joseph, 16, *16,* 43, 290, 303*n*28
    in Big Three talks, 191
    biography of, 141
    brutality and oppression of, 137, 141, 168
    Five-Year Plans of, 241
    and German invasion of Soviet Union, 137,
        140, 141, 145, 148, 152, 153–55, 157,
        162, 166–67
    name of, 141
    Nazi-Soviet Non-Aggression Pact and,
        142, 179
    purges of, 38, 43, 140–41, 168
    in Soviet propaganda, *176*
    Tukhachevky and, 43, 45
    Western aid and, 265
    Zhukov and, 150
Stalingrad, 150, 176, 289
Stalinism, 167
steel, 263, 291*n*4
Steinberg, Paul, 265
Steinkjer, 72
stock market crash, 14, 18–20
Student, Kurt, 132
submarines, 41
    German (U-boats), 34, 41, *121,* 124, *133,*
        134, 136, 282–83, 287, 289
subversion, 100
Sudan, 126
Sudetenland, 6, 22, 24, *28*
Suez Canal, 95, *123,* 126, 281, 289
Sumatra, 200, 206, 289
Sunda Strait, 209
Sun Li-jen, 213
Supermarine Spitfire, *108,* 110, *111,* 112, 114,
    125
Surabaya, 208
Suvorov, Aleksandr, *176*
Sweden, 67, 147, 281
sword bayonet, *193*
Syria, 88, 127

Taiwan, 185
tanks, 19, *34*
    antitank guns, *35*
    British, 100
        Matilda, 128
    Czech, *152*
    French, *77, 81*
    German, *261, 272*
        see also Panzer forces
    production of, *261, 272, 277*
    Soviet, *149,* 152
Tarakan, 201, 210
Taranto, *124,* 128, 132
telephone communications, *122*
Tenasserim, 212
Tennessee, U.S.S., *189*
Ten-Year Rule, 12
Thailand, 191, 192, *208,* 211, 213
Tiger tanks, *149*
Timor, 200, 206
Timoshenko, Semyon, 152
Tobruk, 127, 129, 131, *131*
Todt, Fritz, 274
Tōjō, Hideki, *192,* 289–90
Tooze, Adam, 272, 302n12
torpedoes, 30, 103, 208, 224, *230,* 282
    German bomber, *104*
total war, 31
    German-Soviet conflict as, 137
    mobilization for, 233, 242, *244*
        see also mobilization
    Nazi rally and, *275*
    World War II as, 233
tractor brigades, *251*
Treaty of Versailles, 1–5, 7–8, 21, 22, *26,*
    56
    Europe after, *5, 6–7*
    Germany and, 1, 6, 8, *8,* 14, 18, 19,
        20
    second- and third-order effects of,
        6
trekking, 119
Triandafillov, Vladimir, 292n18
Tripartite Pact, 179
Trondheim, 71–72, 74, 75
trousers, *44*
trucks, military, production of, *277*
Truk, 186, 220
Truman, Harry S., 191, 215
    MacArthur and, 215
Tuchman, Barbara, 155
Tukhachevsky, Mikhail, 38, 43, 292n18
    biography of, 45
Tunisia, 128
Turkey, 21
Tuskegee Airmen, 254, *256*
Twomey, Laurence, 38

U-boats, 34, 41, *121,* 124, *133,* 134, 136,
    282–83, 287, 289
Ukraine, 242
    German invasion and, 56, 158, 161, *162,*
        167, 168, 265, 281
Ultra, 100, 110, 132, 134, 136, 220, 223, 229,
    230, 290
United Kingdom, see Great Britain
United Nations, 215

United States, 27
    African Americans in
        in military, 254, *255,* 256, *256*
        in workforce, *246, 289*
    arms supplied to Britain by, 95, 98–99,
        296n5
    Britain and, *51,* 136
    casualties of, 235
    China as ally of, *24*
    Churchill and, 98, 100
    Civil War in, 254
    economy of, 265–69
    factories in, 270, *272,* 283
    France and, *51*
    Germany-first strategy of, 198, *240*
    Germany's declaration of war against,
        176
    and Germany's invasion of Soviet Union,
        176
    GNP (gross national product) of, 240,
        268–69
    Hitler and, 176, 282, 283–86
    isolationism of, 30, 31, 34, 42, 95, *118,* 283
    Japan and, 28–30, 179, *182,* 190
    Japanese Americans
        in internment camps, 255, *259*
        second-generation, *259*
        in war effort, 255, *259*
    League of Nations and, 7–8
    Lend-Lease program of, 265, 269
        aid to Britain, 103, *119,* 122–23, 191,
            269, *272*
        aid to Soviet Union, *268,* 272
        opposition to, *119*
    loan to Germany, 14
    Manhattan Project in, 135–36
    military of, 34–35, 42
        army rifleman, *43*
        blacks in, 254, *255,* 256, *256*
        deployment of army (including air
            forces), *240*
        Eighth Air Force, 239
        infantryman, *259*
        Japanese Americans in, 255
        mobilization for, 235, 275, 278
        naval aviator, *224*
        naval power, 10, 34, 42
        preparations for World War II, 42
        shipped to Britain and Soviet Union,
            243
        size of, 239
        women in, 244–51, *249*
    neutrality of, 20, 95, 191
    oil in, 283
    in Pacific War, 239
        see also Pacific War
    Pearl Harbor attack, 35, 100, *182,* 184–89,
        189, 190, 198, 210, 220, 229, 290
        American propaganda following, *285*
        Big Three talks and, 191
        British reaction to, 287
        and German invasion of Soviet Union,
            176
        Hitler and, 283–87
        internment of Japanese Americans
            following, 255, *259*
        investigation of, 305n4

    opening attacks in, *185*
    "Remember Pearl Harbor," 186
    Roosevelt and, 190, 191, 305n4
    Tennessee and *West Virginia* in, *189*
    Yamamoto in, 229
    racist attitudes toward Japanese in, 186,
        285, 306n9
    resources of, 283, *283*
    Revolutionary War of, 254
    strength of, 7
    Soviet Union aid from, 265
        food, *268*
    as trade leader, 14
    Treaty of Versailles and, 1
    war production in, *237, 239,* 265–69
    War Production Board in, 268
    Washington Naval Treaties and, 10
    workforce in, 239–40
United States Strategic Bombing Survey, 269,
    270
U.S. Army Historical Division, 165
U.S.S.R., see Soviet Union

Valkenburg, 79
Verdun, *90*
Versailles Treaty, see Treaty of Versailles
Victor Emmanuel III, King, 12
Victoria Point, *208,* 211
Vittorio Veneto, 128
Vladivostok, 265, 309n72
Volga River, 289
Voroshilov, Kliment E., 43
Voznesensky, Nikolai, 264
Vyazma, 164

Waffen-SS, 147, 301n5
Wainwright, Jonathan, 217
Wake Island, 183, 186, 190
war production, 239–40, 274
    of aircraft, *276*
    of aircraft carriers, *276*
    in Britain, 239, *244,* 249
        weapons, *133*
    in Germany, 239, 240–41, *244,* 269–74
    GNP (gross national product) and, 240
    lack of collaboration among Axis powers
        in, 278
    of military trucks, *277*
    patriotism and, *270*
    posters for, *237*
    resources of principal belligerents, *234*
    shipyards in, *242*
    in Soviet Union, 239, 240, 241–42, 263–65,
        267, 272
    of tanks and self-propelled guns, *277*
    in U.S., *237, 239,* 265–69
    women in, *249*
Warsaw, *52,* 54, 56, *57,* 59, 60–61, 63, 64
Warthe River, 59
Washington Naval Conference, 10, *10,* 12
Washington Naval Treaties, 10
Wavell, Archibald, 128, 131, 198–99, 200,
    207–8, 210–14
    biography of, 127
Wehrmacht, see Germany, Nazi, military of
Weimar Republic, 14
welder, German, *246*

Weser River, 69
Weserübung (Exercise Weser), *67,* 69–75
West Virginia, U.S.S., *189*
W Force, 132
Wietersheim, Gustav von, 78
Wildcat fighters, *189*
Wilson, Woodrow, 10
    Fourteen Points of, 5, 22
Winter War (Soviet Union–Finland conflict),
    140, 141
Witzig, Rudolf, 79–80
women:
    African-American, *246*
    in armed forces, 235, 242–52
        in Britain, 243–44
        in Germany, 243
        in Soviet Union, *175,* 251–52
        in U.S., 244–51, *249, 250*
    child care for, 252
    gender discrimination and, 250, 252
    German, childbearing medal for, *280*
    prostitution and, 255
    in workforce, *244*
        in Britain, 250–51, 252–53
        in Germany, *246,* 252
        in Soviet Union, *251,* 252, 253
        in U.S., *246,* 250–51
Women Accepted for Volunteer Emergency
    Service (WAVES), 244, 250
Women Airforce Service Pilots (WASPs),
    250
Women's Army Auxiliary Corps (WAAC),
    244, *249,* 250
Women's Army Corps (WAC), 244, *249, 250*

Women's Auxiliary Air Force (WAAF),
    243–44
Women's Royal Naval Volunteer Reserve, 243
workforce:
    forced labor
        in France, for Germans, *259, 261*
        in Germany, 147, 255–61, *262*
        in Japan, 255
        Soviet gulags, 153, 168, 264
    mobilization for, 233, *238*
        African Americans and, 239–40, *289*
        forced labor and, 255
        in Germany, 233, *238,* 274–75
        in Japan, 252
        juveniles in, 233, 239–40, 252, *262*
        prisoners in, 233, 242
        women in, 233, 239–40, 242–53
    minorities in, 253–54
World War I, 27, 30–31, 88, 278
    armistice in, 88
    black soldiers in, 254
    Britain in, *7,* 34, 135
    collapse of Austro-Hungarian and Russian
        Empires at end of, 5, *5,* 15
    cost of, 1, *7,* 20
    end of, 1, 8, 10
    France in, 39, 82
    Germany in, 19, 27, 30, 51, 82, 88, 141,
        144, 168
    Halder in, 165
    Hitler in, 51
    Japan in, 32
    lessons drawn from, 26, 31, 35, 42, 233
    naval powers in, 10

    outbreak of, 5
    peace following, 10–12
    phony war period of, 65–67
    Treaty of Versailles following, *see* Treaty of
        Versailles
    Verdun, *90*
World War II:
    Allied success in, *279*
    Axis conquests in, 281
    midpoint of, 281–90
    military expenditures in years leading
        to, *45*
    outbreak of war in Europe, 35, 51, *61,* 179,
        191, 282
    preparations for, 26–42, *46*
    road to, 1–46
    as total war, 233

Yamamoto, Isoroku:
    biography of, 229
    at Midway, 222, 309*n*81
    in Pearl Harbor attack, 229
Yamashita, Tomoyuki, 191, 199–200
Yamato, 30
Yenangyaung, 213
Yorktown, 220, 221, 223, 224, 227, 229
Young Turks, 21
Ypenburg, 79
Yugoslavia, 28, 132, 281, 303*n*28

Zero fighters, 186, *189,* 224, 306*n*9
Zhukov, Georgy Konstantinovich, 179
    biography of, 150
Zuikaku, 221

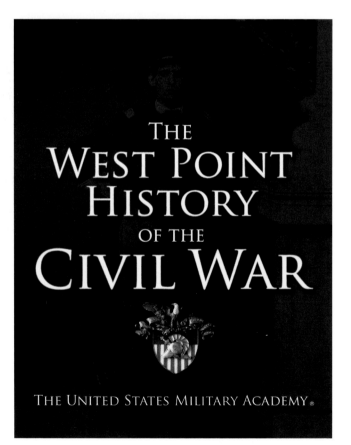